Violentologies

OXFORD STUDIES IN AMERICAN LITERARY HISTORY

Gordon Hutner, Series Editor

Violentologies

VIOLENCE, IDENTITY, AND IDEOLOGY
IN LATINA/O LITERATURE

B. V. Olguín
University of California, Santa Barbara

OXFORD
UNIVERSITY PRESS

OXFORD

UNIVERSITY PRESS

Great Clarendon Street, Oxford, OX2 6DP,
United Kingdom

Oxford University Press is a department of the University of Oxford.
It furthers the University's objective of excellence in research, scholarship,
and education by publishing worldwide. Oxford is a registered trade mark of
Oxford University Press in the UK and in certain other countries

First Edition published in 2021

Impression: 1

Published in the United States of America by Oxford University Press
198 Madison Avenue, New York, NY 10016, United States of America

British Library Cataloguing in Publication Data

Data available

Library of Congress Control Number: 2020947981

ISBN 978-0-19-886309-0

DOI: 10.1093/oso/9780198863090.001.0001

Printed and bound by
CPI Group (UK) Ltd, Croydon, CR0 4YY

For my father, Ben Montez Olguin, and mother, Antonia Valdez Olguin …and in honor of our family Soldados Razos:

Natividad Ojeda Loredo, Soldado, Caballería, División del Norte, Revolución Mexicana

Miguel Saucedo Valdez, Soldado, Caballería, Ejército Federal, Revolución Mexicana

Juan Montez, private, US Army, Wounded-in-Action, France, WWI

Secundino Silva, private, US Army, Philippines, WWII

Victor Manuel Ledesma, private, US Army, Killed-in-Action, Normandy, WWII

Adán Valdes, corporal, US Army, Africa, WWII

Frank Lopez, sergeant, US Marine Corps, Wounded-in-Action, US war in Vietnam

Debra Valdez, sergeant, US Army, Germany

Jorge Valdez, gunnery sergeant, US Marine Corps, Afghanistan

John Brian Silva, specialist, US Army, Germany

No one concerned with history and politics can remain unaware of the enormous role violence has always played in human affairs; and it is at first glance rather surprising that violence has so seldom been singled out for special consideration.
—HANNAH ARENDT, *Violence* (1970)

A massive uprooting of dualistic thinking in the individual and collective consciousness is the beginning of a long struggle, but one that could, in our best hopes, bring us to the end of rape, of violence, of war.
—GLORIA ANZALDÚA, *Borderlands/La Frontera: The New Mestiza* (1987)

{ CONTENTS }

{ PHOTOGRAPHS }

{ ACKNOWLEDGMENTS }

My *compañera*, wife and colleague, Bernadette, and best friend and
son, Ross Anthony, have provided the love, support, confidence,
and conversation that buoyed this two-decade-long book project,
and broader set of inquiries of which it is part. My parents, Antonia
Valdez Olguin and Ben Montez Olguin, have guided me to this vocation and lifelong mission as a barrio intellectual by their resilience as
members of the proletariat. My brothers Anthony and Adrian
remind me to stay grounded in the awareness of our obligations to
each other and humanity in the wake of all the harm capitalism has
wrought in our lives and the lives of others. My *primo* (cousin) Alfred
"Freddy" Porras, the family historian and barrio educator, has helped
recover extended family journeys that inform this book. He also
provided the inspiration and challenges to remember the next
generations in all we think and do. My *prima* Lydia Hernandez also
recovered the US Army photograph of our second cousin Victor
Manuel Ledesma, whose death on June 14, 1944, from combat
wounds suffered in the WWII Allied D-Day invasion of Normandy,
anchors this study in family tragedy. My departed uncles Nicanor
"Nick" Valdez, Enrique "Quique" Valdez, and Juan "Johnny" Valdez
have taught equally valuable martial lessons of survival in our barrio
Magnolia, which I carry as both a badge and a burden that this book
in part tries to explicate and atone.

I owe an unpayable debt to Aldo Garza, my homeboy de Corpus,
who was forced to drop out of the University of Houston after losing
financial aid, which led him to join the Air Force as another economic recruit. He reminds me that many Raza in the US military are
aware of the real enemy despite their day jobs.

I am also grateful for the many people who generously shared
insights and constructive critiques in dialogues about this book, and
the much larger struggle of which it is part. They include Louis
Mendoza, Omar Santiago Valerio-Jimenez, Maria Eugenia Cotera,
Sheila Contreras, Sonia Saldívar-Hull, Norma Alarcón, José David
Saldívar, Emilio Zamora, Ramón Saldívar, John Phillip Santos, Ray

Santisteban, Jimmy Mendiola, Marco Cervantes, Gregg Barrios, Javier Rodriguez, Rosaura Sánchez, Beatrice Pita, and Maggie Rivas Rodriguez. Fellow traveler George Mariscal, a combat veteran from the US war in Vietnam and distinguished scholar, continues to inspire by his generous and compassionate intellectual activism, and his bravery in helping us confront the ideological interrogations necessary for any liberatory praxis. Graduate students Robert Moreira, Susana Ramírez, Sonia Valencia, Derek Delgado, Roberto Macías, Magda Garcia, Marina Chavez, Alejandro Prado, Jordan Hallbauer, Unita Ahdifard, Clinton Terrel, Kevin Whitesides, Yunuen Gomez-Ocampo, Erick Rodriguez, and Jéssica Malinalli Coyotecatl Contreras worked as research assistants and were part of the circle of interlocutors without which this book never would have come to fruition.

The National Endowment for the Humanities (NEH) awarded me a Faculty Research Award in 2005 to develop this project. This book also was informed by my NEH fellowship to attend the 2005 Summer Seminar, "Human Rights in the Era of Globalization," facilitated by Andrew Nathan at the Center for Human Rights at Columbia University, and the 2010 Summer Institute, "From Metacom to Tecumseh: Alliances, Conflicts, and Resistance in Early America," facilitated by Scott Stevens at the D'Arcy McNickle Center for American Indian and Indigenous Studies at the Newberry Library in Chicago. I also received two related Grants-in-Aid from Arte Público Press' Recovering the US Hispanic Literary Heritage Project.

Of the many senior scholars and theorists who helped prepare me to undertake this project and my vocation two deserve special mention: Nicolás Kanellos and Tomás Ybarra-Frausto. Both gave me important opportunities and never gave up on my ability to rise to their expectations. Lorenzo Cano and Tatcho Mindiola opened the door for me to meet their challenges, as well as new ones, that led toward dialectical trajectories. This intellectual and political journey was facilitated by fellow travelers at Stanford University—Mary Louis Pratt, Ramón Saldívar, Yvonne Yarbro-Bejarano, David Palumbo-Liu, Robert Warrior, Michael Predmore, Lauro Flores, María Herrera-Sobek, and Don Luís Leal. Jesús Rosales and family, Gabriella Gutierrez y Muhs, Rosalva Aída Hernández Castillo, and Benjamin Ortiz became family during this oftentimes difficult time of discovery.

Former colleagues and collaborators at Cornell University remain friends and interlocutors who continue to model how one can remain true to the humanist vocation within otherwise privileged institutions. They include Satya Mohanty, Ken McClane, Helena Maria Viramontes, Eloy Rodriguez, Hortense Spillers, Biodun Jeyifo, Paula Moya, and Michael Hames-García, among many more.

The University of California, Santa Barbara, English Department and Division of Humanities and Fine Arts provided a welcoming environment, as well as material support to complete this project. There are too many colleagues and fellow travelers to thoroughly list. But I offer a special thanks to comrades in the Center for Modernism, Materialism, and Aesthetics, particularly the numerous graduate and undergraduate affiliates, as well as faculty affiliates Enda Duffy, Maurizia Boscagli, Glyn Salton-Cox, Candace Waid, Jennifer Wicke, Bishnupriya Ghosh, and Bernadette Andrea.

I am especially grateful to John and Jody Arnhold, and the Regents of the University of California, for their support in creating the Robert and Liisa Erickson Presidential Chair in English, which has enabled me to begin charting new global horizons for Latina/o and broader American Studies through the Global Latinidades Project, of which this book is part. Robert "Bob" Erickson for whom the endowed chair is named is a fellow wheelman and has become a friend and interlocutor who continues teaching across generations through his inquiry and visual art. As a lifelong learner, Bob has become an inspiration to me, as he has been to generations of interlocutors.

The greatest challenges for me as a researcher and writer have come from Gordon Hutner, general editor of *American Literary History* and editor of the *Oxford Studies in American Literary History*. He published the exploratory article in *American Literary History* in 2002 that became the basis of this book. The review and editing process for this book has been the most rigorous and grueling I have ever encountered, and I am grateful as it has pushed me to produce the best I can, though I know from experience there is always much more that could have been added, cut, or explicated.

There are many more scholars, activists, and fellow travelers whose insights, actions, and examples underscore that this book, or any book, is never enough to transform our objective and subjective realities. These include our departed comrades John "Juancho" Stanford, Fred Ho, Ernesto Bustillos, *y por supuesto*, Raúl Salinas. *¡Todos Presentes! ¡Hasta la Victoria, siempre!*

c/s

{ EPIGRAPH ACKNOWLEDGMENTS }

Hannah Arendt epigraph is from *On Violence* (New York: Houghton Mifflin Harcourt, 1970), p. 8. Copyright 1970, 1969, by Hannah Arendt. Reprinted by permission of Houghton Mifflin Harcourt Publishing Company.

Gloria Anzaldúa epigraph is from *Borderlands/La Frontera: The New Mestiza* (San Francisco: Aunt Lute, 2007), p. 102. Copyright 1987, 1999, 2007, 2012 by Gloria Anzaldúa. Reprinted by permission of Aunt Lute Books.

William Shakespeare epigraph is from *Shakespeare Adaptations: The Tempest, The Mock Tempest, and King Lear* (London: J. Cape, 1922), p. 22. Cited material is in the Public Domain and is reprinted courtesy of the Division of Rare and Manuscript Collections, Cornell University Library.

Jacques Derrida epigraph is from "Différance," *Margins of Philosophy*, Translator Alan Bass (Chicago: University of Chicago Press, 1982), p. 16. Copyright 1982 by University of Chicago Press. Reprinted by permission of the University of Chicago Press.

Alurista epigraph is from "El Plan Espiritual de Aztlán," *Aztlán: Chicano Journal of the Social Sciences and the Arts* 1.1 (Spring, 1970): p. iv. Copyright 1970 by Regents of the University of California. Reprinted by permission of the Regents of the University of California.

Juan Bernal epigraph is from *Memoria*, Unpublished Manuscript No. D-43, Translator Earl R. Hewitt (Bancroft Collection of Western and Latin Americana, University of California, Berkeley, 1877). Cited material is in the Public Domain and is reprinted courtesy of the Bancroft Collection of Western and Latin Americana, University of California, Berkeley.

{ PREFACE }

From Fort Knox, Kentucky, to Havana, Cuba

TESTIMONIAL REFLECTIONS ON RACE, WAR, AND REVOLUTION

> You taught me language; and my profit on't
> Is, I know how to curse. The red plague rid you
> For learning me your language!
> —Caliban in *The Tempest* (1611),
> by William Shakespeare

This book began long before that steamy July afternoon in 1985 when I was lost, again, deep in a sticky briar patch in the piney hills of Fort Knox, Kentucky. I had been searching all day for a gray metal disk so small I could have missed it had I been standing on top. Like other US Army Reserve Officer Training Corps (ROTC) cadets in my platoon, I had become disoriented during a land navigation exercise designed to repeatedly throw us off course. "Just like Drill Sergeant Baumeister," I thought, "to hide the mark in a thicket of thorns so he could ride us all day for missing the rally point on time." But I was wrong. It was me. I either had inverted the coordinates or used the sextant upside down. And who knows how good my vectors were. If you are off by just a degree on a few ten-meter stretches, the cumulative effect of the deviation could add up to kilometers. Worse, the surrounding terrain features looked like the same spurs, ridges, and valleys I had just humped with a sixty-pound rucksack. I stopped in a small opening in a valley by a stream to get my bearings and catch a breath. As I took a knee, careful to keep the load balanced even though all I wanted to do was just throw it off, the air immediately thickened with individual bird chirps that soon became a series of lilting sharp whistles, then songs, a whole orchestra of different colored miniature musicians unleashed and ecstatic.

Had it been there all along?

I was brought back to my predicament by a rattle and snapping branches deep in a thicket. "Cadet! Do you know where we are?"

I shouted, only to be confronted by a six-foot-tall white-tailed buck that bolted at me with its full rack aimed like a bayonet charge. At the last moment, it leaped over me as if it were a helicopter and disappeared into the sky before I had a chance to react. Had this been a war, I would have been dead since I dropped my M-16 as I fell backward. I laid silent, weighted down by the metal-framed rucksack, staring up at the bough of pine needles, aware but immune to thorns tearing through the olive drab into my skin, the reassuring sound of birds all around. I could not help but laugh. "Beautiful," I remember thinking about the forest that was so different from the crumbled streets and concrete sidewalk of Magnolia, my barrio in Houston, Texas. "Yea, this would be beautiful if not for all this shit." I did not have the language to verbalize the dissonance that had already starting to seep into my thoughts about what I was doing. But deep down I knew something was wrong.

I was preparing to join the US Army as an airborne infantry officer to fight the "evil communists" who had turned our "backyard" in Latin America into a battleground. The hyperbole of the Cold War had reached me just like it had virtually everyone in the United States, and I had bought it all. My presence at Cadet Basic Camp at the US Army Base in Fort Knox, Kentucky, was the culmination of my socialization into a model of manhood in an extended family that included boxers, soldiers, and street-fighting convicts, with several murderers, too. I was so determined to follow in the footsteps of my grandfathers, uncles, and cousins that I enlisted in the US Army while still in high school. A lingering ear injury from my amateur boxing career, however, resulted in a medical discharge on the day I was picked up by the Army recruiter for transport to Fort Jackson, South Carolina, where I had been scheduled for Basic Training to be followed by Airborne Jump School, and then Ranger School.

Yet, even this fortuitous injury did not deter me: I joined the US Army ROTC detachment at the University of Houston a year later after my ear had been treated and healed. I underwent two years of field training exercises that included amphibious and helicopter air assault training, in addition to small weapons and small unit tactics. This was followed by training at Fort Knox. It was a Mexican American boy's dream: rifles and explosives for toys, a uniform that brought pride to my parents and awe to my younger brothers, a sense of belonging, a mission for the country I believed was my own. I was one of the top cadets in my company: I excelled at every task and

FIGURE P.1. *The author (front) on a night field training exercise, US Army Base at Fort Knox, Kentucky, 1985. Courtesy of B. V. Olguín.*

challenge and had the highest scores on aptitude tests. Despite the obvious lack of diversity—I was just one of three Latina/o cadets in a company of 250 at Fort Knox—I was falling in love with the Army. It would have been my career, my life...if not for Pancho Villa!

During one of several required ROTC seminars on US Military Affairs that taught cadets the official US Army Cold War doctrine, the instructor—US Army Colonel Bowers—gloated about how the continental United States had never been invaded by a foreign power. Despite his historical error in discounting the War of 1812, which included a British invasion, and the US-Mexico War of 1846–1848, which included battles on both sides of the future border, all the cadets joined in celebration, including me. Amid the jubilation another cadet raised his voice to say, "except Pancho Villa, but we kicked that Mexican's ass all the way back across the border."

The colonel smiled. Other cadets continued to gloat. I stopped. I was the only Mexican American in a classroom of ten uniformed cadets. No one met my eyes, but everyone felt my rage as I eyeballed

FIGURE P.2. *The author (center) on honor guard artillery battery, US Army Base at Fort Knox, Kentucky, 1985. Courtesy of B. V. Olguín.*

the cadet sitting across, my flushed dark-brown face furrowed with scenarios involving his equipment failure on the rappelling tower, a slip from the rubber dingy during amphibious assault training at Lake Conroe outside Houston, a fall from the Chinook helicopter that ferried us back and forth from the Gulf Coast, an accidental discharge of my M-16 at the firing range....

Since my childhood visits to my mother's hometown of Palaú, in the northern Mexican province of Coahuila, I had been taught about our *Villista* heritage. As an infant, I even met my maternal great grandfather, Natividad Ojeda Loredo, who had served as a cavalry-man in Villa's famed *La División del Norte*. This was the same division that had been raiding US properties and businesses in retalia-tion for the US recognition of Villa's rival, Venustiano Carranza, an ally of the elite landowners who had declared himself president of Mexico even before the war was over. On March 9, 1916, Villa's forces invaded and briefly occupied Columbus, New Mexico, leaving sev-eral US civilians and soldiers dead, which prompted a US expedition into Mexico. The US Army never succeeded at capturing the wily Villa, and General John Pershing, who had been sent to hunt him down, was reduced to negotiating with "that Mexican" before the American unit was diverted to Europe for WWI. (Ironically, a paternal uncle—Juan Montez—would be wounded in that war fighting in the US Army against German troops.)

We knew the story well—the one where Villa kicked the Americans' asses, sending them back across the border—and everyone in my maternal family knew which side we were on. Even though one half of the family had long established itself in the United States as American citizens, we were Villistas and proud of it. With few exceptions, the family's other half across the border in Mexico continued to work as poor subsistence farmers, with some still living on the small family plot assigned to my maternal great grandfather in exchange for ten years of combat service with Villa's famed División del Norte. It continued to be a working cornfield for three generations after the war. During our visits to Mexico, we stayed in this small adobe and dark-brown dirt-floor house that reminded us of our Villista legacy. Family members still live in this house, and as late as my teenage years, they continued to use a communal barnyard and grazing field that was part of the *ejido* collective farm system institutionalized after the revolution. One of my fondest memories is milking cows with my uncle and cousins on this large parcel of land near the river that no one owned and everyone was free to use. I remember passing the bucket of fresh warm frothy milk in a communal ritual that went back longer than anyone could remember.

Even though I had not realized it then, everything changed for me on that day when my efforts to fit into the US Army as just another soldier in green were inadvertently rejected because my color was brown and my family legacy included the anarchist black and communist red of the Mexican Revolution. The other cadets reminded me of something I had somehow forgotten (or tried to forget): I was a Villista. This made all the difference in my family's past and in my own future.

The personal and political changes I subsequently underwent were slow and circuitous, unpredictable and even wild, but steadily involved a recognition that I had drifted to the wrong side of my family history by pursuing a career in the US military. While in London, England, on a study abroad semester following my training at Fort Knox—and my classroom encounter with lingering US Army racism and imperialism—I found myself in an apartment building composed of white American liberals who were incessant in their attacks on the right-wing politics I espoused at the time.[1] Before I knew it, I found myself listening to my housemates' arguments despite their unacknowledged racism, partying with British anarchist punk rockers, stumbling into what was then the largest antinuclear weapons demonstration in history, and sharing frequent cups of tea at a local bookstore with one of my British professors, a representative of Amnesty International. A professor of European history, she eventually introduced me to several fellow travelers from across Europe, including, to my surprise, the Soviet Union—the evil empire I had been training to fight. In London I dated an Irish Republican woman whose uncle confided that they also were Irish Republicans and internationalists. My political education continued over many pints of Guinness that began with a toast to the San Patricios, Irish conscripts who defected from the US military during the US-Mexico War of 1846–1848 to join their Catholic compatriots from Mexico in the fight against bigotry and imperialism. This encounter with Chicana/o history by way of Irish rebels and fugitive fighters against colonialism and imperialism had a delayed yet lasting impact.

Upon my return to the United States some of my new European friends kept in touch, and I began taking courses in Mexican American Studies at the urging of a friend, Aldo Garza, who later was forced to join the Air Force after losing his financial aid in his second year in college. Aldo never returned to his studies, becoming another economic recruit in the US military. At the same time, the secretary of the ROTC program was an active member of CISPES—Citizens in Support of the People of El Salvador—and had been plastering the bulletin boards outside the ROTC building with CISPES event fliers until she was finally transferred out of the Department of Military Science. This made my decision not to return to the ROTC unit much easier, especially after a university friend, Noe Peña, who had just formed a Chicana/o student organization called *Hijos del Sol* ("Sons of the Sun"), came right out and said: "Carnal [Blood Brother], what the fuck are you doing?! You are about to join the wrong Army!" I refused to sign the contract that would have committed me to six years of service as an officer in the US Army. I wore my uniform one last time to the funeral of my paternal grandfather—mi 'Buelito Silva—who had served as an airplane mechanic in a forward operating base in the Philippines during WWII. Then I burned it.

Twenty years after being lost in a thorny thicket in Kentucky, I found myself lost again, this time in Cuba. I was riding in a small white Soviet Lada sedan along an unlit crumbling country road on my way to join a group of Americans who had arrived a day before at Ciudad Escolar Camilo Cienfuegos. I had traveled to Cuba through Mexico in defiance of the US embargo, without the US government license required of US citizens. Our rendezvous point was a small town in the northern part of the island that was dedicated to teacher education in honor of a grade school student who had been killed by an American bomb during one of the many acts of sabotage perpetrated by US-backed counterrevolutionaries following the Cuban revolutionary victory in 1959. As we passed late night strollers, including a group of *jineteras* ("jockeys," or sex workers) and hustlers who had been driven to desperation by the decades-long US economic blockade, the driver Luís shared an allegory about his rickety radio and the small house fan he had rigged to work as the car air conditioner. "Ésta es de nosotros," he told me. He emphasized that he did not care what anyone thought about his contraption because it was theirs, and he would do anything necessary to make it work, punctuating his message with "coño," the Cuban exclamation mark. I had come to Cuba as a member of the 37th contingent of the Venceremos Brigade, an organization formed by American internationalists that had been traveling to Cuba since 1969 for volunteer labor, educational exchanges, and people-to-people diplomacy in solidarity with the Cuban revolution.[2] In the early years, *brigadistas*, as we are called, met with North Vietnamese and other international revolutionaries. More recently, we joined internationalists from dozens of countries to build and refurbish schools and housing complexes; plant, harvest, and weed agricultural fields; and incessantly dialogue into the dawn about what it meant to be a revolutionary and, more importantly, what we were willing to do to help build a socialist society and, ultimately, communist revolution worldwide. The many questions we asked and challenges we posed to each other have taken me toward prisoner-solidarity work, community-literacy projects, and paramedic school and volunteer work as an Emergency Medical Technician, in addition to ongoing dialogues and initiatives with comrades throughout the United States, Europe, Canada, and Latin America.

The personal and political transformations that transpired between Kentucky and Cuba continue to this day. The changes are complicated and nonlinear. But I have found my voice as a member of José David Saldívar's "School of Caliban":

FIGURE P.3. *The author with Generoso, veteran of the Cuban Revolution, 37th Contingent of the Venceremos Brigade, Granma Province, Cuba, 2006. Courtesy of B. V. Olguín.*

FIGURE P.4. *The author at the Havana book market, 2006. Courtesy of B. V. Olguín.*

a group of engaged writers, scholars, and professors of literature who work under a common political influence, a group whose different (imagined) national communities and symbologies are linked by their derivation from a common and explosive reading of Shakespeare's last (pastoral and tragicomic) play, *The Tempest*. The phrase also emblematizes not just the group's shared subaltern subject positions, but the "schooling" that their enrollment in such an institution provides. (1991, 123)

Like Caliban, I dare to speak back to colonial and imperial oppressors in the oppressor's own language with the full knowledge that I also am part of the empire. And I have found my bearings as a Chicano communist, an ironic almost antithetical pairing that nonetheless involves a long and inspiring legacy: Emma Tenayuca, Carlos Córtez, Ricardo Sánchez, and my personal friend and former *brigadista* Raúl Salinas, among many more fellow travelers. My Villista great grandfather Natividad Loredo was one, too.

Nonetheless, I am still burdened by many questions about Chicana/o and Latina/o identity, and our complex status as colonized subjects, yet relatively comfortable Americans, who benefit from capitalism and US imperialism. Even more difficult issues surround the relationship between masculinity and soldiering, racial identity and ideological transformation, internationalism and the lingering national question, as well as the nature of revolution and what constitutes revolutionary praxis. These inquiries, I have learned over the years, must come from the difficult and oftentimes painful work of *autocrítica*, the revolutionary practice of assessing and addressing one's own faults and relationships to power. *Concientización*—the epiphanic understanding of the subjective and objective conditions shaping one's own life vis-à-vis the lives of others—is predicated upon *autocrítica* as a daily activity. For this process to become truly revolutionary, of course, it must be part of organized collective action.

This book is offered as part of a community *autocrítica* and larger meditation on the many transformations of Latina and Latino soldiers and civilians in different eras up to the present who have repeatedly been forced to confront—or try to ignore—the question of what side Latina/os should be on, or if there is anything so clear and defined as "sides." This inquiry oftentimes takes a lifetime, and always involves deaths, traumas, and loss that should never have occurred.

This book recounts many of these tragedies, including the fact that so many Latina/os, especially Latina/o enlisted soldiers, never had the chances and privileges that my fortuitous boxing injury presented: a university education that gave me space and time to meditate and grow ideologically. This study is dedicated to them; and it is my extended *desculpa* and attempt to make sense of it all. However, neither this book, nor I, can ever make up for the opportunities and choices that were stolen from friends such as Aldo Garza or the long list of family Soldados Razos who had few options but to join one military or another. In some cases they did not join but were drafted. Among these are my maternal great grandfather, a subsistence farmer, who was taken away from the family for ten years to fight with Pancho Villa's División del Norte during the Mexican Revolution; paternal great grandfather Miguel Saucedo Valdez, a soldier in the Mexican Federal Army whose shameful legacy as a merciless executioner of Villistas forced my grandparents to elope to San Antonio, Texas; great uncle Juan Montez, a private in the US Army who was wounded in the trenches of WWI that left him with a metal plate in his head, giving him a lifelong aversion to anything cold; paternal grandfather Secundino Silva, who shared with me the Japanese bayonet and sword he brought home from his service in the Philippines in WWII, after which he remained among the lumpenproletariat of Austin, Texas, until his death; second cousin Victor Manuel Ledesma, a teenaged US Army private wounded in the invasion of Normandy who died from his combat wounds and whose body was repatriated to the United States ten years later with a military honor guard posted at the Chalmers Courts Housing Projects, where my extended family would continue to live in poverty for three more generations; maternal uncle, tío Adán Valdes, who recounted baffling stories to me and my cousins about killing Nazis in Africa and always carried his US Army discharge papers to prove his military service to skeptical relatives and racist police and immigration officers; uncle Frank Lopez, who served two tours in the US war in Vietnam as a US Marine and suffered Post-Traumatic Stress Disorder (PTSD) for the remainder of his life; cousin Debra Valdez who escaped an abusive relationship by joining the US Army to serve in Cold War Germany, where she was posted to a missile silo; and, among several more cousins and other relatives, my primo Jorge Valdez, who joined the Marines to escape the police dragnet searching for his father and elder brother for murder, only to be deployed to hunt other people's fathers and brothers in Afghanistan during the US War on Terror. The legacy of the US military's impact on my family extends to my *primas* Sonia and Esmeralda, and *sobrina* ("niece") Priscilla, who worked in Kuwait and Iraq as defense contractors during this boundless war and came home forever changed in a multiplicity of economic, personal, cultural, and spiritual ways. The cycle continues with Esmeralda's son John Brian joining the US Army during the War on Terror for lack of any better job options despite his college education.

There are no easy answers for understanding this legacy of war and violence on my extended family. But my *compañera*—comrade, life partner, and wife—Bernadette has called my attention to another complexly situated colonial subject, Edward Said, whose citation of Italian communist Antonio Gramsci's prescription for individual and mass *concientización* is especially apt for this meditation on my ongoing process of *autocrítica* vis-à-vis this family legacy, and broader Chicana/o and Latina/o community histories:

> The starting-point of critical elaboration is the consciousness of what one really is, and is 'knowing thyself' as a product of the historical processes to date, which has deposited in you an infinity of traces, without leaving an inventory.... Therefore, it is imperative at the outset to compile such an inventory.   (qtd. in Said 1979, 25)

Thus, all I can do is recover the inventory and offer my *grito* as one of many Latina/o internationalist scholars and activists collectively seeking to offer an alternative method for understanding the subjective and objective conditions that have determined and overdetermined our role as cannon fodder and petty functionaries for one government or another. Above all else, this book is one small effort to articulate a new synthesis that must, necessarily, involve the defeat of capitalism and imperialism. It will be a long process, but it has already begun, and must continue, by any means necessary. *¡Hasta la Victoria, siempre!*

Violentologies

VIOLENCE, IDEOLOGY, AND
SUPRA-LATINA/O ONTOLOGIES

*The subject as consciousness has never manifested itself except as
self-presence. The privilege granted to consciousness therefore signifies
the privilege granted to the present; and even if one describes the
transcendental temporality of consciousness…, one grants to the
"living present" the power of synthesizing traces, and of incessantly
reassembling them.*

—JACQUES DERRIDA, *Margins of Philosophy* (1982)

Mexican American French Foreign Legion volunteer Jaime Salazar
opens and closes his 2005 memoir, *Legion of the Lost: The True
Experience of an American in the French Foreign Legion*, with a dramatic twilight escape from military police transporting him to the
Legionnaire unit from which he had deserted several weeks earlier.
Salazar—whose Legionnaire *nom de guerre* is Juan Sanchez—knows
fellow Legionnaires "will beat me to a pulp" (2005, 215). In the "best-
case scenario" (2005, 226), the corporals will rape him for violating
the pledge of *honneur et fidélité* to this brotherhood of arms he joined
a year earlier in 1999. Like many Legionnaire *engagé volontaire*, or
enlisted volunteers, who tire of the incessant brutality, forced labor,
and banal regimen of garrison life, Salazar/Sanchez deserted before
completing the five-year enlistment that would have bestowed
French citizenship promised to everyone who joins this renowned
military unit of international volunteers. Entry into the French
Foreign Legion as prospective French citizens, however, requires
recruits to surrender their passports, thereby renouncing their

Violentologies: Violence, Identity, and Ideology in Latina/o Literature. B.V. Olguín, Oxford University Press (2021).
© B.V. Olguín.
DOI: 10.1093/oso/9780198863090.001.0001

previous allegiances and identities. Salazar/Sanchez recalls this fateful moment:

> I slid that precious document with its small-print warning that join-
> ing a foreign army is grounds for loss of citizenship through the grille
> and wondered whether I would ever see it again.   (2005, 13)

One year after surrendering his US passport, the twenty-six-year-old Salazar/Sanchez finds himself on the run throughout France from Legionnaire *Police Militaire* and the federal *Gendarmerie*. To elude them he poses as a skinhead teenage skateboarder, hitchhiking victim of Arab pickpockets, and engineer traveling to a new job (2005, 220). In exchange for a ride, he even has sex with a "bearlike" female truck driver he initially mistook for a man, extending his new chameleon-like identity across a range of gendered and sexualized possibilities (2005, 221). Detained at the US Embassy gate because he had no documents to prove his American citizenship, Salazar/Sanchez eventually succeeds at convincing officials that he is an absent-minded tourist who overstayed his visa. With his reissued US passport, Salazar/Sanchez evades an international warrant for his arrest, finally escaping to his family home in Lafayette, Indiana.

But he soon realizes that Lafayette and the United States are no longer his home. After confiding to his mother, "I'm just not comfortable in America" (2005, 236), he promptly leaves for Europe again, pursuing a series of meandering adventures, odd jobs, and whimsical plans that take him back and forth across the Atlantic.

In this neopicaresque narrative—the *ne plus ultra* for an investigation into the intersections of violence, identity, and ideology—Salazar/Sanchez presents a radical expansion of the geopolitical and ideological contours of the centuries-long legacy of US Latina/o soldiering and militarized models of citizenship. His provisional membership in the quintessentially colonialist French Foreign Legion disrupts persistent teleological mappings of Latina/o ontologies (theories of being) and attendant epistemologies (theories of knowing) as inherently antithetical to US hegemony and Western imperialism. As elaborated throughout this book, this legendary French military unit is but one of many local and global performative spaces where soldiers, combatants, and wartime noncombatants from various Latina/o communities—Mexican American, Chicana/o, Puerto Rican,

Cuban American, Dominican American, Salvadoran American, Honduran American, Guatemalan American, and mixed-heritage genealogies—instantiate a wide range of militarized subjectivities. This book's fundamental argument is that such spaces and subjectivities challenge prevailing theories and paradigms in Latina/o Studies: resistance, transnationalism, mestizaje, interstitiality, and third-space agency, as well as various models of cultural and political citizenship. Rather than emerging as an anomaly, Salazar/Sanchez can be seen as a paradigmatic *supra*-Latina/o subject who articulates his militarized persona, transnational gnosis, and inchoate negotiations of ideology—his real and imagined relationships to power—through, and beyond, his Latina/o heritage and contemporary theories of *Latinidad*, or Latina/o identity broadly defined. He thus invites further interrogation of the role of soldiering, whether in state-sponsored militaries or nonstate paramilitary units, in shaping Latina/o modalities. This interrogation also requires attention to the full spectrum of "violences" intersecting with, and extending beyond, soldiering and wartime contexts that involve equally diverse and complex gender, sexuality, class, ethnic, and racial formations.

Salazar/Sanchez's multiple migrations through citizenship, genealogy, and ideology offer important touchstones for interrogating extant and emerging Latinidades. The self-identified *enfant terrible* "son of underpaid Mexican immigrants" and Purdue University alumnus, as blazoned on the back cover of his book, Salazar/Sanchez had been captivated by the highly romanticized French Foreign Legion since childhood. This fascination intensified during a period of postgraduate anomie and new job as a mechanical engineer at the Chicago office of the German conglomerate Siemens, replete with an expense account and a fast-track executive training program, during which he surreptitiously read Legionnaire literature. In 1999 he quit his job, stored his Mercedes, and fled to Paris, the site of earlier college sojourns. Motivated by a nostalgic masculinist reading of Henry David Thoreau, he tells a fellow recruit, "I'm going to learn how to live off the land, sleep rough, and reconnect with my animal origins" (2005, 26). Salazar/Sanchez soon finds himself among South African bigots, Russian brawlers, German skinheads, Polish Nazis, and American racists. Once ensconced within prison-like Legionnaire bases and subjected to brutal training regimens and predatory peers, Salazar/Sanchez regrets his decision to join this band of miscreants.

FIGURE I.1. *French Foreign Legionnaire "Juan Sanchez" on a training exercise with Legionnaires in 1999. Courtesy of Jaime Salazar.*

"I was in the Legion," he somberly reflects, "being transformed into a mindless brute" (2005, 91) (Figure I.1).

Salazar/Sanchez represents a new type of Latina/o hybrid subject that has yet to be investigated in Latina/o Studies: the global supra-Latina/o whose ontological and epistemological formation extends through—and far outside—the geopolitical parameters of the continental United States and its sphere of influence, and even farther outside conventional Ethnic Studies frameworks. Like all Legionnaire recruits, Salazar/Sanchez was given a new identity and a number to go with his *nom de guerre* Juan Sanchez: "Legionnaire 191224." His fellow recruits subsequently hail him as "Johnny from Kentucky" (2005, 61), "Aryan brother" (2005, 149), and "my KKK comrade" (2005, 197) because they misidentified him as "Spanish" and read his pale skin as European. These monikers are uttered by recruits who have abandoned their nations but still retain their xenophobia: they frequently use terms such as "Kaffir" and "Nigger," along with other anti-Arab, anti-Muslim, and even anti-Mexican epithets. For instance, when an Afrikaner Legionnaire complains that "kaffir...savages have taken over my country," a white American Legionnaire and former US Army soldier from Tulsa, Oklahoma, commiserates by responding, "Same thing in America…we're invaded by browns from Mexico" (2005, 104–5).

This racist, colonialist, and imperialist legacy is related to the roots of the French Foreign Legion. King Louis-Philippe formed the unit in 1831 to free France's bourgeoisie from the dirty work of military service. The Legion helped absorb the lumpenproletariat and acculturate immigrants, who were promptly sent to occupy military garrisons in French colonies throughout the world. The Legion gained its greatest fame—and enduring infamy—for its ventures in Africa, and particularly French-occupied Algeria, in the nineteenth and twentieth centuries. Early in his memoir, Salazar/Sanchez acknowledges the French Foreign Legion's racist legacy: "with traditions inherited from former Nazis, the treatment of people of other races or creeds has often been appalling" (2005, 45). Ironically, Salazar/Sanchez is interpellated as Legionnaire Juan Sanchez through racialized, and outright racist, barracks bonding as a member of the *mafia Anglaise*. Within the ranks of the French Foreign Legion, affinity groups called "mafias" are formed around linguistic heritage. Sanchez's English-speaking Legionnaire mafia consists of Afrikaner veterans of the South African apartheid regime, but also is expanded outside the linguistic affinity group to include a German Skinhead, a Dutch ex-Hell's Angel, and a Finnish army veteran, in addition to a racist white American who sports a Germanic-font tattoo that reads "POLAR BEARS RULE."

In a further irony, and in contradistinction to the nostalgic "roots" narrative that animates much of Latina/o life writing, Jaime Salazar's interpellation into Legionnaire Juan Sanchez occurs through his encounters with Legionnaire history in Mexico, his parents' birthplace. Before his enlistment, he had visited the Legionnaire Museum in Aubagne, France, outside the port city of Marseille. While there, he wandered into the sacrosanct *Crypte*, which contains relics of past Legionnaire campaigns in France's colonial wars. Among the relics is the wooden hand of *Capitaine* Danjou, one of the few Legionnaire survivors of the April 29, 1863, Battle of Camerone, outside of Veracruz, Mexico. "The place reeks of heroic death" (2005, 8), Salazar writes. After enduring and surviving the grueling selection process, he participated in a ritual commemorating Legionnaire consummation of their signature oath of death-before-surrender in the annual Camerone Day ceremony

(2005, 32). This Legionnaire martyrdom—he later records using Orientalist rhetoric—is reinforced through rituals and singing:

> Les chants [the songs] are given special importance in the Legion. They tell of death, hardship, suffering, and leaving a homeland hoping to return after five years. Some are old Wehrmacht songs like "Oh, du schöner Westerwald." Many are for sweethearts left behind—"Eugénie," "Monica," "Veronica," and "Adieu! Ma Charmante Blonde." The subliminal message is that a glorious death is a passport to eternal life and happiness, not unlike the seventy-two virgins waiting in paradise for the fundamentalist Muslims who die in jihad.   (2005, 43)

This event, commemorated every April 30 in all Legionnaire bases throughout the world, involves reenactments of the battle between sixty-five Legionnaires against two thousand Mexican troops under the command of President Benito Juárez. The Mexican soldiers were fighting to expel forty thousand French troops buttressing "emperor" Maximilian Hapsburg, who had been installed by French dictator Napoleon III. Salazar/Sanchez, proud of his link to this heroic Legionnaire legacy, claims:

> Today, whenever Mexican soldiers pass the memorial, they are ordered to present arms. The story of Camerone encapsulates the Legion tradition of no surrender, even in the face of certain annihilation.   (2005, 33)

Contrary to this representation, Mexican nationalist sentiment precludes any deference to invading foreign troops, even though the Legion's exploits in Mexico certainly are romanticized in popular French ballads, such as Eugénie.[1] Concurrently, Mexican and Mexican Americans commemorate the French defeat in Cinco de Mayo (May 5) celebrations that Salazar/Sanchez does not mention.

By the time he participates in the Camerone Day ceremony, which fetishizes the wooden hand relic from the battle, Jaime Salazar had already been transformed into Legionnaire Juan Sanchez. He recalls that, "as the hand passed in front of me, I felt ready to die for the Legion" (2005, 34). For Salazar-cum-Sanchez, the term foreign now refers to his estrangement from the United States. At the Legionnaire graduation ceremony, for instance, he recalls how every recruit's past nationality is recognized on the nameplate alongside their *nom de guerre*, and further decentered by their new allegiance:

> When the time came for the oath of loyalty, we stood *au garde-à-vous* holding our *képis blancs* down the side of our right legs by the peak. "*Nous promettons de servir la patrie, la France, avec honneur et fidélité*" [We pledge to serve the fatherland, France, with honor and loyalty], we roared in one voice. The company captain gave the order: "Don *képis!*" Our hands swept up together to our heads and snapped back down to our sides. (2005, 69)

After this pledge of allegiance to France, he recalls, "For me, this was the finest hour in my life" (2005, 70). But his new identity is not necessarily based upon nationality:

> The Legion's motto, *Legio Patria Nostra*, "The Legion is Our Fatherland," was more meaningful to us than laying down our lives for a country that most of us knew little about. (2005, 45)

In a subsequent telephone conversation with his father, who is upset that his son left a promising career as an engineer to "join the army," Salazar/Sanchez tries to convince him that the French Foreign Legion is "not just an army, it's like a family." He adds: "We've got a few bad apples in the mix, but these are my brothers. I'd give my life for them. For the first time, I feel like I belong" (2005, 81–2) (Figure I.2).

This type of unit bonding is a fundamental part of basic military training, but for Salazar/Sanchez, it layers, rather than completely replaces, national identity or premilitary subjectivities. Having undergone the graduation ceremony and attendant rituals, Juan Sanchez is a French Foreign Legionnaire. Although he is not yet a French citizen (and because of his desertion he never will become one), he is no longer fully or unambiguously American. Even his Mexican American and broader Latino subjectivity as Jaime Salazar is destabilized through the palimpsestic cipher "Legionnaire 191224." Yet, traces of all his subjectivities remain. As a result of his transnational soldiering performed in the service of French nationalism, colonialism, and imperialism, Salazar/Sanchez's Mexican and American genealogy is rendered *sous rature*: under erasure but

FIGURE I.2. *Mexican American French Foreign Legionnaire "Juan Sanchez" in Paris in 2000. Courtesy of Jaime Salazar.*

traceable; liminal and radically inchoate. Already having effaced a crucial marker of his Mexican heritage—Cinco de Mayo—he even forgot the US national anthem when asked to sing it by a curious Legionnaire veteran from Spain (2005, 63). He similarly did not care about seeing a US flag disrespectfully placed upside down in a bar, which provoked his fellow Oklahoma Legionnaire to start a fight (2005, 150). Salazar/Sanchez earlier had expressed shock the first time he stood at attention as France's tricolor flag was raised because he realized he "was now serving in a foreign army" (2005, 31). Yet, he later describes visiting US military observers he encountered during maneuvers with the regular French Army as being "from a foreign army as far as I was concerned" (2005, 140).

Salazar/Sanchez's aversion to the US military is decidedly different from Chicana/o cultural nationalist, Latin American regionalist, and Marxist internationalist rejections of the US military's role in colonialism and imperialism. Rather, his interpellation as a transnational, postnational, and even transracial soldier—the post-Latino "Aryan brother" who surrendered his US citizenship and eschews the Mexican nationalism encoded in Cinco de Mayo celebrations—involves his adoption of the French Foreign Legion's racialized colonialist logic. For instance, he describes Algerian National Liberation

Army (ALN) guerrillas who wrested their country's independence from France in 1962 as "a terrorist group" (2005, 21); retells an Orientalist story about ALN guerrillas eating an "oven-baked infant" (2005, 17); and recounts Legion stories about indigenous Algerian Berber women's violence against occupying Christians from France, which purportedly included skinning alive captured Legionnaires (2005, 20). The ALN eventually deteriorated into an authoritarian organization and brutal government, yet he is noticeably silent about the widely documented French use of torture in this extended colonial occupation by France.

In a *coup de grace* conversion scene characteristic of the masculinist signifying practices of heterosexual male soldiers, Salazar/Sanchez further disarticulates his new French Foreign Legionnaire identity from his American citizenship and his Mexican American heritage through an Eiffel Tower fling with a "liberal" white American exchange student. "Ellen" masturbates him in public while recounting her sexual fantasies as he also masturbates her. In the process, she pays him a "compliment" by saying, "you don't act like a Mexican. I mean, you speak perfect English and are well-educated and stuff" (2005, 159). He adds to her casual racism with a palimpsest of neoimperialist Legionnaire signifying in response to a passing young man he calls an "Arab," who had shouted, "I wouldn't sacrifice my blood for a foreign land" (2005, 160). Adding to the carnivalesque absurdity of the scene, which includes mothers passing with baby carriages, he grunts, "Why do these North Africans always want to fuck with me at the least convenient times?" (2005, 160). In her *in flagrante* retort, Ellen counters, "From what I heard, it seems you guys did a lot of bad stuff in their country." He shoots back:

> That's a load of crap! Wherever Legion boots touched North African sand, water flowed and wheat fields grew. It was thanks to us that decent people there could live happy and sleep sound. (2005, 160)

In a rehearsal of this hypermasculinist and hyperbolic colonialist discourse, the cover of the first edition of his book includes a photographic insert of Salazar/Sanchez on parade wearing the distinctive Legionnaire white *képis* (or round caps), superimposed atop sand dunes flowing into the horizon (Figure I.3). Although there is no flowing water or any wheat fields, the image nonetheless connotes the French Foreign Legion's boundless, timeless reign. Juan Sanchez is a metonym for this mythos, and more.

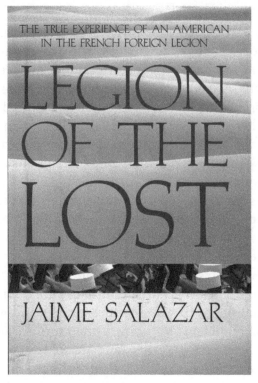

FIGURE I.3. *Book Cover with Jaime Salazar, center, as French Foreign Legionnaire*
"Juan Sanchez." Courtesy of Jaime Salazar.

Situating the Discrepant Latina/o Archive

It would be a gross understatement to say that Jaime Salazar's performances of his Legionnaire subjectivity as Juan Sanchez are beyond
the geopolitical and multicultural scope of Latina/o Studies, in which
even transnational paradigms continue to privilege the US-Mexico
borderlands, Caribbean locales, and parts of Central and South
America as the *axis mundi* and loci of enunciation for Latina/o subjects. Contrary to various articulations of Latina/o soldiering as US
political, cultural, or transnational citizenship, Salazar/Sanchez's
performance is transcultural, postcitizen, and anything but a claim
to inclusion in the United States. It is neither a recuperation of a
heritage country and culture, nor a fixation on his disenfranchisement
as an American citizen from a minority and historically marginalized
community. Moreover, Salazar/Sanchez's agency as an interstitial
subject and his geocultural expansion of transnational mestiza/o

sensibilities cannot be presumed to be inherently oppositional to US imperialism, as most accounts of Mexican American, Chicana/o, and Latina/o mestizaje propose. Rather, he introduces the complex transracial and postcitizen supra-Latina/o subject who is simultaneously transnational, postnational, and supranational, even as this figure embodies French protonationalist and Western imperialist power. Salazar/Sanchez ultimately consolidates his new identity as a supra-American, provisionally post-Latino, and immanently French imperialist soldier through global geographic navigations and performances of actual and symbolic violences. Yet, he is more than merely a mystified subaltern subject; on the contrary, he is fully actualized, empowered, and literally armed in the service of French nationalism and imperialism.

In a seeming paradox, Salazar/Sanchez's mobility and malleability resonate with and extend Chicana feminist theorist Chela Sandoval's lucid paradigm of differential consciousness as a multinodal negotiation. In *Methodology of the Oppressed*, which has profoundly and productively shaped Latina/o Studies, Sandoval articulates four modalities of subaltern "oppositional consciousness" (2000, 1)—equal rights, revolutionary, supremacist, and separatist—along with a corresponding fifth flexible tactic that enables subaltern subjects, particularly marginalized women of color, to negotiate power through various types of oppositional agency. As disturbing as it may be for the field, which has thrived on an oppositional posture predicated upon theories of counterpower such as differential consciousness, Salazar/Sanchez reminds us that such strategies may also be claimed by colonialists and imperialists. Significantly, Sandoval acknowledges the susceptibility of reactionary appropriations of the tactics of differential consciousness:

> The differential mode of social movement and consciousness *depends on* the practitioner's ability to read the current situation of power and *self-consciously choosing* and adopting the ideological stand best suited to *push against* its configurations, a survival skill well known to oppressed peoples. (2000, 59, emphasis added)

Salazar/Sanchez reveals how seemingly inchoate subaltern agency could involve tactical calculations that comprise a negotiated *hegemonic*, rather than oppositional, subject position. Moreover, what if other similarly marginalized subjects decide through rational analysis of subjective and objective conditions that their immediate individual and broader community interests are served by supporting, rather than "pushing against," the hegemonic configuration? Might their tactics also involve the performance of a strategic *hegemonic third-space agency*? Could there be a hegemonic third-space soldiering, a militarized mestizaje, as it were, that occurs outside conventional theories that presume Latina/o culture, subjectivity, and agency as immanently or even inherently opposed to racism, colonialism, capitalism, and imperialism?

Jaime Salazar's French Foreign Legion alter ego Juan Sanchez suggests affirmative answers to these inquiries and invites expanded interrogations of the wide range of relationships between Latina/o militarized subjectivities and ideology, in addition to broader discussions of the salience of violence in Latina/o theories of being and knowing. Moreover, Salazar/Sanchez's hybrid subjectivity illuminates how US Latina/o soldiering and citizenship not only are intertwined but also frequently disarticulated in complex ways. He is a very different type of Latina/o than those generally privileged in Chicana/o, Latina/o, and Ethnic Studies more generally: he is the mystified subject of colonialism and the resistant subject of history, and simultaneously neither. His enlistment as a soldier in the French Foreign Legion thus provokes a radical expansion of *différance*, as defined by Jacques Derrida in the epigraph above. Derived from the French verb *différer*, which means "to defer" and "to differ," this doubling enables deconstructivist—and later, postmodernist, neo-Marxist, and decolonialist—claims that words, signs, and extant paradigms are inherently inadequate: they must continually refer to what they are not, to approach a definition of what they are, without ever fully accomplishing the task.

In his groundbreaking study, *Chicano Narrative: The Dialectics of Difference* (1990), Ramón Saldívar productively redeploys Derrida, in dialogue with Marxist and materialist theories, to argue that Chicana/o difference is performed through a tense antithetical relationship with American capitalism, beginning in the nineteenth century and extending into the twentieth. Specifically, by building upon Américo Paredes's influential recentering of the epic heroic corrido as the *Ür*-narrative of Mexican American Pyrrhic resistance in *With His Pistol in His Hand: A Border Ballad and Its Hero* (1958), Saldívar consolidates the paradigmatic Chicana/o resistant subject through a reading of Chicana/o narrative as dialectical rather than simply oppositional. Subsequent Latina/o Literary and Cultural Studies scholars have theorized Chicana/o and Latina/o difference in a multiplicity of ways that continue to intersect with, but also diverge from, Saldívar's provocative synthesis. For instance, in Rodrigo Lazo and Jesse Alemán's edited anthology, *The Latino Nineteenth Century* (2016), contributors productively complicate a Chicano-centered dialectics of difference by proposing "Latino" as a trope rather than an unambiguously coherent category, as in Kirsten Silva Gruesz's "errant Latina/o"; Robert Irwin McKee's "Almost Latino"; and Alemán's repurposed "trans-American." These terms grapple with multidirectional migrations in which nineteenth-century subjects from Latin America acculturated into US society. Some of these migrants identified with their new host's domestic US Latina/o populations even after they returned (or were forcibly returned) to their previous "home" countries. Gruesz, McKee, and Alemán remind us that there are no adequate signifiers for the inchoate liminal and highly mobile spatial ontologies that in the nineteenth century were anything but anomalous. Frances Aparicio (2019) adds "Intralatina/o" to the mix to account for contemporary subjects of dual or multiple Latina/o heritages born of pan-Latina/o intermarriage, who engage in complex cultural and political negotiations as part of their increasingly common hybrid Latinidades. She thus further pressures the centrality of Chicana/os, and especially the stability of "Latina/o" as a category, in theories of Latinidad. Marissa López takes us even further by provisionally disarticulating "Latinidad" from race to emphasize the experiential. Drawing on Michael Hames-García's attention to the Latina/o body's "agential reality with its own causal role in making meaning" (Hames-García 2008, 327), López proposes to "see race both as noun and verb but understand it to be *in* rather than *on* the body" (2019, 5– 6). Latinidad, she productively suggests, is shaped by so many experiences we have failed to adequately measure *in tandem*. Salazar/Sanchez demonstrates that such discrepant "Latina/o" subjects extend beyond the nineteenth century, the United States, and conventional theories of race, and in far more directions than anyone has yet to anticipate.

This book likewise takes as its point of departure the inherent inadequacy of signifiers such as "Chicana/o" and "Latina/o," "Chican@" and "Latin@," and more recent gender and sexuality inclusive "Chicanx" and "Latinx," as well as "Latine" and other variants, with the aim of more fully accessing their referents: distinctly racialized, sexualized, and gendered human subjects with intersecting and diverging histories from the nineteenth century to the present and immanent future.[2] The aforementioned scholars provide strategic tools for reassessing the violent dislocations and relocations (including and extending beyond formal warfare), and the ongoing disarticulations and rearticulations of a wide array of Latina/o modalities, or Latinidades. This is not a rehearsal of the stereotypical nihilist tendencies of deconstruction, or postmodern relativism, as McKee's "Almost Latino" category suggests.[3] On the contrary, the prism of violence pressures static understandings of Latinidades by illuminating the proliferation of specific permutations of "Latina/o" performative theories of being and knowing. This book's strategic use of supra-Latina/o—with the "supra" prefix referring to multiple pre-, anti-, and even post-Latina/o formations overdetermined by violence—further is in dialogue with the interlocutors that Jennifer Harford-Vargas has placed in conversation to discuss the "homogenizing effect" of the term Latina/o (2017, 24).[4] Using the rubric of "Pan-Latina/o" and "Trans-Latina/o," she explicates "the Latina/o counter-dictatorial imaginary" in Latin American and Latina/o literature as being opposed to authoritarianism, and particularly the legacies of Latin American dictatorships, and to a lesser degree, authorial dictatorship. However, Harford-Vargas ultimately places political violence, and violence in general, outside of Latinidades except as a pathological trace, and thus is antithetical to this study on the centrality of violence in Latina/o ontologies and epistemologies.

Throughout modernity, warfare has paradoxically extended a nationalist paradigm alongside the threat of national transformation and even annihilation through soldier and civilian encounters with their antithetical counterparts on and off the battlefield. Concomitantly, wartime encounters produce new syntheses and subject formations within and across nationalities and cultures. Indeed, in war (whether it involves nation-states or nonstate actors), as well as in interpersonal violence (starting with the domestic space), human beings are killed, wounded, and traumatized, with survivors and bystanders alike transformed in myriad ways. Their new subjectivities and attendant agency are dialectically related to these transformative violences. Thus, violent articulations of Latinidades—such as Salazar/Sanchez's discrepant supra-Latina/o instantiation—may be distinct in terms of their personal coordinates, but they are far from anomalous in their violence-based performance of extraterritorial, transracial, and supranational modalities that are directly related to their historico-political milieu. Ultimately, this book's excavation of diverse and often discrepant Latina/o subjectivities rejects the idea that warfare, atrocities, and other forms of violence, along with their perpetrators, are outside of Latinidad. Rather, violence is central to the proliferation of Latinidades, which are inherently plural.

Recentering Violence in Latina/o Studies

As a point of departure in recentering violence in excavations of new Latinidades, and in reinterpretations of familiar ones, the World Health Organization (WHO) 2002 *World Report on Violence and Health* offers a useful definition:

> Violence is the intentional use of physical force or power, threatened or actual, against oneself, another person, or against a group or community, which either results in or has a high likelihood of resulting in injury, death, psychological harm, maldevelopment, or deprivation.
>
> (Krug et al. 2002, 4)

In contradistinction to the WHO's proposed interventions to eradicate violence, which the organization defines as a social aberration, myriad anthropologists, psychologists, political scientists, and cultural theorists continue to debate the nature of violence in human contexts. Some argue that individual and large-scale violence is as old as the species. Others posit that violence is a relatively recent phenomenon, emerging 10,000 years ago with rising population densities after the First Agricultural Revolution that brought increased social contact and competition for resources.

Pursuing the latter trajectory, Nelson Maldonado-Torres argues that modernity from the fifteenth century onward is subtended by the naturalization of hierarchies through warfare that, along with accidental mineral discoveries and technological developments, enabled Europe to become globally dominant. Invoking the coterminous projects of the Spanish Reconquista on the Iberian Peninsula and Spanish conquest and colonization of the Americas, he proposes 1492 as:

a crucial point for understanding the constitution of the episteme
and social order that I define here as a paradigm of war...a way of
conceiving humanity, knowledge, and social relations that privileges
conflict or *polemos*. (2008, 3)

Elaborating on Edmundo O'Gorman's (1998) and Walter Mignolo's
(2005) meditations on the "invention" of the Americas, along with
what Anival Quijano (1992) calls the "coloniality of power,"
Maldonado-Torres asserts that the transculturated populations in
the Americas were born of violence and, as the ancient Greek term
polemos signifies, embody it. Following these scholars, José David
Saldívar (2011)—along with many more Chicana/o and Latina/o,
feminist, postcolonial, and decolonial theorists—anticipates and extends this argument to emphasize counterhegemonic self-fashioning
in the Americas that, purportedly, is articulated against violence,
since for such theorists, violence is analogous to coloniality. Arturo
Aldama's prescient anthology, *Violence and the Body: Race, Gender,
and the State* (2003), productively examines "the materiality of physical and representational violence on the 'otherized' body" across a
wide global expanse of case studies to show the prevalence of violence as political praxis and human culture (2003, 5). However, the
constitutive essays still present discursive and physical violences,
and their horrific embodied effects, as the antithesis to a fully actualized subjectivity.[5]

Yet, most historical materialists reject the idea that violence is
antithetical to subject formation. Franz Fanon's emphasis on the
constitutive power of violence is a bridge between the Old Left, New
Left, and contemporary neo-Marxists. He recognizes that "the colonized man [sic] finds his freedom in and through violence" (Fanon
2004, 44). However, he also recognizes the violence-as-power dialectic as a lingering paradox that degenerates into pathologies, which
inevitably undermine the newly decolonized nation and subject.
Fanon's materialist psychoanalytic dialectic revolves around the
brutal irony that posits violent reconstruction and destruction as a
persistent, and perhaps perpetual, cycle. Elaine Scarry qualifies
Fanon's recentering of violence as a constitutive force, noting that
certain types of violence, such as torture, involve the destruction of
agency, identity, and the very notion of "the real" for victims (Scarry
1987, 27). Importantly, Scarry reminds us that even as torturers
monopolize violence to claim omniscience and omnipotence for

their own self-fashioning, their model of reality, though palpable, remains a highly tenuous narratological act dependent upon the perpetuation of their violent acts. She thus reveals that violence, as Fanon posited, is the mediator, medium, and more: an *Ür*-narrative. Neo-Fanonian scholars of the Afro-Pessimism school more overtly propose epic violences such as trans-Atlantic slavery as the preexisting script for contemporary Black subjectivity that can never be fully transcended. Frank Wilderson (2008, 2020), for instance, argues that the multiple violences constituting this horror have forever transformed the structural and subjective conditions of the African diaspora such that all aspects of Black life are imprinted with its elements. Achille Mbembe (2019) extends this Afro-Pessimist trajectory by explicating contemporary "necropolitics" in genocidal slavery, settler colonial, and ultranationalist xenophobic contexts throughout the Americas (antebellum US South), Middle East (contemporary Palestine), southeastern Europe (1990's Balkans warfare), and parts of Central Africa (Rwanda Tutsi genocide). He argues that violent death has become the ultimate means of subjugation, as well as the principle means of resistance, that is, a counterhegemonic self-actualization through the ultimate self-negation.

A range of other poststructuralist and neo-Marxist theorists explicate the instrumentality of violence, with dissenting views over its epistemic value and constitutive power that nonetheless reiterate the centrality of violence in human society. In the passage that serves as the first epigraph to this book, Hannah Arendt asserts that violence is everywhere, and everywhere ignored to our detriment. Seeking to privilege human agency, she adds that "violence is by its nature instrumental" and has no "essence" (1970, 51). Yet, oddly, in discussing the status of violence in modern revolutions, Arendt deemphasizes its power to transform society:

> Only after the disintegration of the government in power has permitted the rebels to arm themselves can one speak of an 'armed uprising,' which often does not take place at all or occurs when it is no longer necessary. (1970, 48–9)

Theories of war and revolution by Carl von Clauwsitz, Leon Trotsky, Mao Tse-tung, Emma Goldman, Che Guevara, and others—actualized in some cases by successful revolutions in contexts preceding military superiority or even strategic equilibrium—rebut Arendt's reservations about the role of overt violence and armed insurrection in revolutionary movements. Arendt's coverage of the 1945–1946 Nuremburg trials nonetheless underscores her awareness about the danger of ignoring violence's everyday iterations and perpetrators, from military commanders and political leaders to petty bureaucrats and everyday civilians. Michel Foucault's elaborations on panopticism's interiorization of violence (1995), as well as Michael Hardt and Antonio Negri's explications of the layers of violence embedded in labor exploitation and geopolitics in the late capitalist world-system they call "Empire" (2001), productively synthesize Arendt's ambivalence about the power of ever-present violence by reminding us that utilitarian violences have meaning and make meaning. This point is the basis of some of the most productive elements of Afro-Pessimism noted above, as well as some Critical Race Studies scholarship focused on structural racism, which together bring these concerns to the fore in contemporary contexts.

Slavoj Žižek (2008) productively intervenes in the ongoing debate about the nature of violence and its relationship to power (and counterpower), and especially subject formation, by distinguishing between "subjective" and "objective" violences. The former refers to one's experience of violence at the physical and psychological levels, and the latter manifest as symbolic (e.g., epithets) and systemic (i.e., political economy). In Žižek's neo-Frankfurt School adaptation of the base-superstructure model, the subject is negotiated in the interplay between the subjective and objective iterations of multiple forms of violence. Here, Žižek's subject-in-formation, who is interpellated through negotiations of subjective and objective violences, offers an expansive and flexible model for this enterprise. He adds a productive gloss of Adorno's (1990) "negative dialectic" with an insistence on a subject's historicity and materiality as being continually shaped and reshaped by contingent events. Žižek thus informs this book's attention to the foundational role of violence in the sedimentation of an array of Latina/o, and especially supra-Latina/o formations, which are always in process, but still whole at each junction.

Žižek's useful typology notwithstanding, his insistence that detached "sideways glances" offer distance and freedom from emotion required for analytical precision, is ultimately dangerous (2008, 3). Alicia Gaspar de Alba and Georgina Guzmán (2010), Rosalinda Fregoso and Cynthia Bejarano (2010), and many more scholars of the femicides in US-Mexico border regions insist it is negligent to efface the palpable existence and perspectives of victims, which in this case involves primarily young working-class Mexican women. These scholars demonstrate how empathy and the intense emotional dimension of this work, along with their unabashed partisanship, are fundamental and necessary dimensions, particularly in violent misogynist contexts. As Sandoval (2000) underscores, empathy and various forms of "love" are profoundly powerful acts in their own right.[6] Any study of violence—and especially violence as ontological—must not lose sight of the empathetic exigencies demanded by this work, both on the ground and theoretical. Indeed, if we are ever able to approximate the new society Gloria Anzaldúa envisions in her resonant 1987 magnum opus, *Borderlands/La Frontera: The New Mestiza*—the utopia defined by the "end of rape, of violence, of war" cited as the second epigraph to this book (2007, 80)—we will need to explicate candidly and clearly the salience of violence in our lives and in our world, and violence *as* our lives and our world.

Clearly, the prevalence of global warfare, interpersonal violences, and trauma has preoccupied political, social, and cultural theorists for millennia, and certainly for the last century. This ranges from post-WWI existentialist disillusionment with modernist euphoria over the machine (particularly war machines); post-WWII and post-Holocaust Frankfurt School recognition of the important role of culture and human agency in shaping subjectivity in a violent capitalist and imperialist world order; and postmodernist anomie in the late capitalist era that manifested as the "death of the subject," demise of master narratives, and end to teleological order in general. On the latter, Fredric Jameson warns that:

> this whole global, yet American, postmodern culture is the internal and superstructural expression of a whole new wave of American military and economic domination throughout the world: in this sense, as throughout class history, the underside of culture is blood, torture, death, and terror.   (1992, 5)

These distinct epistemic traditions, and especially Jameson's attention to the still-enduring American military hegemony in the twenty-first century, remind us that the constitutive destructiveness of warfare and related violences functions as a prism through which we can explicate, and continually reinterpret, culture and the diverse range of new subjectivities that proliferate over time and place.[7] This charge is particularly pertinent regarding Latina/o subjectivities, which have yet to be assessed as functions of violence per se, though there certainly is a cottage industry of psychoanalytic and cultural nationalist scholarship, testimonials, and practicums about Latina/o healing from various forms of violence that indirectly point us in this direction.[8] Furthermore, and in contradistinction to prevailing theories in Latina/o Studies, Latina/o subjects of violence demonstrate how Latina/o agency can be as hegemonic as it is oppositional. *It may even be more hegemonic than oppositional.*

Drawing upon the array of political, cultural, and literary theorists cited in this introduction, as well as many more who are engaged in the chapters that follow, this book proposes violence as fundamental to, and indeed the engine of subjectivity, whether hegemonic or subordinate, and as we saw with Salazar/Sanchez, between and beyond these coordinates. My aim is to offer materialist assessments of a capacious range of Latina/o ontological and related epistemological formations, with violence being the principle prism. In this book, *ontology* refers to the larger issue of the nature of being, but it is also circumscribed to refer to particular "Latina/o ontologies," or modalities of Latina/o beingness, that are recovered and explicated as distinct geopolitical, historical, and cultural phenomenon. Similarly, *epistemology* refers both to the scientific study of knowledge formations over time and place, and to specific modes of knowing in proliferating "Latina/o epistemologies." Both categories—Latina/o ontologies and Latina/o epistemologies—are fundamentally plural. This book engages texts and histories that cover the overt violence of warfare, and the often effaced violences of rape, torture, beatings, murder, mass killing, enslavement, cultural chauvinisms, and other harmful practices that constitute the ways real and metaphorical wars and battles have impacted Latina/o life. Extending Louis Mendoza's (2001) dialogue with Hayden White in his exploration of Chicana/o narrative as counter-historiography, my explications of Latina/o subjectivities across literary and performative genres thus reveal *Latina/o history as violence.*

Supra-Latina/o Violentologies

This book's use of "violentologies" as an operative neologism for discussing Latina/o ontology and epistemology, as well as agency and ideology, is in dialogue with Colombian sociologists who identify as *violentólogos*, or "violentologists": scholars of violence who study the century-old Colombian civil war and intersecting narco-violences. Initially convened by anthropologist Jaime Arocha Rodríguez, historian Gonzálo Sánchez Gómez, and colleagues at the Institute for Political Studies and International Relations at the National University of Colombia in the late 1970s, these *violentólogos* published multiple volumes of interdisciplinary cultural studies and policy analysis reports, most notably, *Colombia: Violencia y Democracia* (Arocha Rodríguez and Sánchez Gómez 1987).[9] These scholar-activists sought to identify the causes and address the material roots of multiple types of violence that, they argue, have come to permeate all aspects of Colombian culture and society. In his 2012 retrospective, *Violentología: una aproximación pura a la violencia*, Franco Caviglia reiterates that violence permeates human culture, and may even be its essence (37). For Caviglia and most *violentólogos*, violence is the basis of their Colombian epistemology, and more: it is ontological.

My adaptation of this term intersects with but also diverges in significant ways from Colombian violentólogos, as well as newer variants. To start, I reject the mass media commodification of an exoticized, and ideologically suspect, version of violentology as exemplified by photojournalist Stephen Ferry in his 2012 photographic folio, *Violentology: A Manual of the Colombian Conflict*. While well-intentioned photojournalism, this set of oversized prints exoticizes Colombian victims of violence and effaces the historical and material foundations of the horrors depicted, to the point where the book becomes scopophilic rather than analytic. My use of *violentology* also is quite different from recent criminological recodifications of the term as a quantitative extension of criminology and policing, which is becoming pronounced in new Russian criminology. In contrast to these commodifying and criminalizing gestures, I extend the Colombian sociological subfield across multiple borders, including various discursive and disciplinary boundaries. In this book, *violentologies* is a verb: a hermeneutic informed by the Colombian *violentólogo* practice of explicating the materiality and historicity of violence in modern Colombian culture and identity. I also use *violentology* as a noun that refers to a distinct theory of being (a violence-based ontology), and a distinct way of knowing (or violence-based epistemology). Both are undergirded by different types of violence experienced by US-born or -raised Latina/os, or recently immigrated Latin Americans in the United States. This inventory of violence includes warfare, but also extends into the cultural and political dimensions of lived experiences in a highly militarized, capitalist, imperialist, and heteropatriarchal society such as the United States and its dominions, but also beyond. The overarching category of supra-Latina/o violentology removes the pathological resonance from its Colombian precursor in order to restore the term's vitality for illuminating how culture and subjectivity, as well as power and counterpower, are shaped by and articulated through various types of violence, from the interpersonal to the international. The category of a supra-Latina/o violentology, as used in this book, does not celebrate violence, nor does it callously represent violence as somehow "good" for determining new Latinidades. Instead, I recognize violence for its omnipresence and constitutive force, especially for US-born, -raised, or recently immigrated Latina/os, whose divergent roots intersect through US colonial and imperial violences.

Violentologies, then, signals violence as constitutive of being and knowing in a range of Latina/o modalities that exist within international, transnational, supranational, and global constellations. The term *violentologies* refers to culturally specific subjects defined by violence, such as Latina/o warrior archetypes and, to be sure, diametrically opposed antiwar pacifist modalities, plus many more. It also signifies the epistemologies of violence: the political and philosophical logic and goals of certain types of violence such as torture, military force, and other forms of harm. Significantly, a violentology is an identity overdetermined by violence but which still involves a subject's agency and relative empowerment. A Latina/o violentology is thus a performative theory of being and a theory of knowledge, in addition to a form of agency. As noted in this introduction, these Latina/o violentologies are plural, or rather, there are many iterations of a Latina/o violentology. As Salazar/Sanchez reveals, these formations are ideologically diverse and extend far beyond terrains that have been mapped in Latina/o Studies.

Violentologies is also a methodology. As a hermeneutic, the violentological method illuminates the radically diverse and problematically empowering ways that Latina/os have negotiated power— through violence, antiviolence, or both—over a wide expanse of time and place, and from often conflicting ideological positions in their ongoing personal and political self-fashioning. This complicated negotiation of power covers well-known historical figures such as Tejano General Ignacio Saragoza Seguin, who led Mexican troops against the French Foreign Legion in the Battle of Puebla on May 5, 1862, that freed Mexico from French colonial rule. It also includes figures at the other end of the ideological spectrum, such as Mexican American Jaime Salazar, who joined the French Foreign Legion over one hundred and thirty years later. Violentologies, which focuses on violence-based, rather than identitarian, models of subjectivity, is capacious and incisive enough to account for everyone between and beyond these ideological poles, something that dominant resistance, third space, mestizaje, cultural citizenship, transnationalism, and related paradigms are incapable of doing primarily because of their latent solipsistic, nostalgic, and celebratory trajectories.

Violentologies underscores how Latina/o ontologies and attendant epistemologies are chronotopal in the Bakhtinian sense—a function of time and space, or "time-space"—and fundamentally defined by multifarious forms of violence. By recognizing the centrality of violence, we free ourselves to follow the evidence of the ever-expanding—and increasingly discrepant—Latina/o archive into uncertain and even dangerous zones and unfamiliar territories across diverse borders, oceans, and continents. Violentologies is especially useful for explicating Latina/o ideologies in the Althusserian sense of "the imaginary relationship of individuals to their real conditions of existence" (Althusser 1971, 109). As a hermeneutic, violentologies also enables us to identify the troubling ways that pathological and even imperialistic violences are just as integral to the theoretical subjects animating Latina/o Studies as are the purportedly revolutionary forms of violence that inform the field's genesis and growth. In other words, violentologies enables us to account for the myriad and ever-evolving Latina/o real and imagined relationships to power that have been underexamined, undertheorized, ignored, and excluded from the field. The ultimate goal of this book is to thicken explications of the complexities and contradictions inherent to Latinidades, which is essential for any effective theory of liberatory praxis.

In this enterprise, there is a danger, of course, that violence can rise to the level of a meta-narrative. After all, this book privileges violence in proliferating local and globalized contexts that continually synthesize new Latinidades, which inevitably are in dialogue with intersecting and diverging variations. Yet, as the above theorists of violence (and antiviolence) indicate, violence in its multiple iterations is an ever-present variable in what we have come to understand as spatial ontologies, including within Chicana/o and Latina/o contexts. Indeed, the idea of *violence as history* and *history as violence* forms the basis of the most provocative Latina/o Spatial Studies work, even though the constitutive nature of violence is not always acknowledged as central to specific Latina/o spatial poetics and place-based identities. Important exceptions include Anzaldúa, who in *Borderlands/La Frontera* and elsewhere underscores how violence remains fundamentally inscribed in familiar home spaces and cultural geographies, as well as in their proposed pacifist antitheses. Anzaldúa models the intelligent, creative, and courageous efforts required to recognize and reimagine preexisting and ongoing harm as a method for refashioning liberatory paradigms of knowledge and self. Raúl Homero Villa (2000) and Mary Pat Brady (2002), as well as subsequent Latina/o Spatial Studies scholars such as Roberto D. Hernández (2018), remind us that interpersonal and inter-group violences intersect with other systemic violences in the geographies of urban and rural developments, border walls, and other built environments that shape Latinidades throughout the United States and its territories. These include urban renewal projects predicated upon the forced removal of local populations, a fate that has affected numerous Latina/o communities. It further involves segregation practices and policies that circumscribe the locations and quality of places where the majority of Latina/os, people of color, and poor people live.

The violence of geography is also a function of the geographies of violence, which also shape the types of agency and identities that emerge in particular places. Mary Pardo (1998) underscores this relation in her study of grassroots Mexican American women's organizing against a state prison and a toxic waste incinerator in the already highly militarized and impoverished carceral barrio of East Los Angeles. Materialist Latina/o criminology and penology studies by Juanita Diaz-Cotto (2006), Dylan Rodríguez (2006), Ruth Gilmore (2007), Joy James (2003), Mike Davis (2006), and my earlier work in *La Pinta: Chicano/a History, Culture, and Politics* (2010), has long identified violence—from the carceral society to prisoner subcultures and internecine barrio warfare—as inextricable from the hierarchical and fetishistic episteme of capitalism. The legacies of imperialist warfare, ongoing racialized gendered class stratifications, and racist, sexist policing and penality have distinguished much of

Latina/o history by shaping the land and the people on it. As an important addition, Nicole Guidotti-Hernández's recovery of Mexican American complicity in warfare against the Yaqui recognizes violence as a productive force in history, and particularly Latina/o history, by identifying the destruction of individuals, peoples, and nations as a function of Chicana/o performances of upward mobility (2011, 6). This legacy of interpellation includes active Latina/o participation—and even leadership—in genocidal wars against Native Americans and indigenous peoples throughout the world from the nineteenth century to the present, as I have shown elsewhere (2018).

As detailed in the chapters that comprise this book, violentologies signals violence-based ontologies and violence-based epistemologies—and, indeed, *violence as being* and *violence as knowing*—but it also seeks to explicate the variable ideologies of Latina/o *violence as agency*. Scarry's aforementioned discussion of violence as a mechanism for knowing and marking one's claim to being, or lack thereof, thus is a recurring touchstone for considering how the violences extending through and beyond uniformed combatants ultimately expose the limits of what we thought we knew about Latinidades. The fifty case studies of supra-Latina/o violentologies elaborated in this book, and more than fifty additional intersecting frames of reference, underscore the many possible trajectories arising from this loss of certainty over the "real" nature of Latinidades. These formations extend beyond conventional understandings of the category, hence the *supra-* prefix. Moreover, these supra-Latina/o—and in some cases post-Latina/o—formations do not always go in expected or desired directions. At times the dissolution of familiar models of Latina/o identity into a multiplicity of new violentological categories—from xenophobic settler colonialists, international communists, and imperialists that include a Mexican American member of the French Foreign Legion—can be disturbing, inspiring, and quite bizarre, sometimes all at once. But these complex and often contradictory supra-Latina/o violentologies are very real and far more prevalent than scholars have been willing to recognize. Ultimately, this shift in perspective requires an exercise in *autocrítica*—a self-critical gaze—if Latina/o Studies is to align more accurately with the objective and subjective realities of the communities it purports to represent. Salazar/Sanchez, who is one of a long line of *Soldados Razos* whose fighting and writing have recentered violences as constitutive of discrepant supra-Latina/o subjects, propels the critical gaze essential for accurately assessing various Latinidades in all their complexity.

The *Soldado Razo* as Floating Signifier

Strikingly, in an episode following his desertion from the French Foreign Legion, Salazar/Sanchez identifies with an Algerian teenager he sees on the Paris metro, telling him, "I'm from an immigrant family myself" (2005, 230). He refers both to his biological Mexican-immigrant parents, who are indirectly colonial subjects in the United States, and his French Foreign Legion family of immigrant soldiers, who were directly involved in the colonization of Algeria and several more countries and regions. With this gesture, Salazar/Sanchez further layers his violence-based identity, constituted by various constellations of ethnicity and race, place and social space, and legal and cultural citizenship. In particular, his supra-Latina/o violentology consists of the partially erased yet still visible Mexican heritage and provisionally forfeited but later reclaimed American citizenship that coexist just beneath the palimpsestic cipher of French Foreign Legionnaire 191224. He thus signals the still insufficiently theorized *Soldado Razo*, a Mexican American soldier archetype that roughly translates as "buck private," the military moniker for the lowest rank of soldier. The Soldado Razo originally was figured as Mexican American and male but now includes a broader array of Pan-Latina/o soldiers who also are female, as well as queer. Mexican matinée idol Pedro Infante's 1943 version of the popular song, "Soldado Razo" (also spelled phonetically as "Soldado Raso"), added to the figure's fame. Composed by songwriter Felipe Valdez Leal, the song's most famous stanzas are pathos-laden and vainglorious laments:

> Me voy de soldado raso
> voy 'ingresar a las filas
> con los valientes muchachos
> que dejan madres queridas
> que dejan novias llorando
> llorando su despedida.
> [...]
> Mi linda guadalupana
> protéjela a mi bandera
> y cuando me haga en campaña
> muy lejos ya de mi tierra
> les probaré que mi raza
> sabe morir donde quiera.

[I'm going to be a soldier
I'm going to enter the ranks
with all of those brave and young boys
who leave their beloved mothers
who leave their dear girlfriends crying
crying and crying their good byes.
[...]
My dear Virgin Guadalupe
please protect this flag of mine
and when I am on a campaign
very far from this land of mine
I will prove that we Mexicans
are willing to die wherever.][10]

As the lyrics indicate, this Latina/o soldier anthem espouses masculinist conceits interwoven with a transnational fatalism that proclaims the whole world as a stage for the performance of Mexican cultural nationalism that is actualized through combat death. This globalized ritual of necro-nationalism does not necessarily involve an imperialist impulse, as colonial New Spain and modern Mexico were formed by colonialism in the sixteenth century and experienced a series of colonialist invasions in later centuries. While Mexico certainly is a settler colonial society, it also has been subject to so many foreign invasions it dedicated a museum to this legacy, *El Museo Nacional de las Intervenciones*! Furthermore, even as modern Mexican troops continue to wage war against insurgent indigenous communities, particularly the Zapatistas, they rarely venture abroad except as members of the US military, or as part of multinational forces led by the United States.[11] In this song, the Soldado Razo conscript, also referred to as a *soldado peón*, or "peasant soldier," proclaims a defiant though Pyrrhic reclamation of their agency as a member of "la Raza," which translates as "my people," but also preserves racial connotations, as in "my race."[12] Despite the Soldado Razo's implicit awareness of their subordination by warmongers, an implicit imagined necro-community resonates alongside the realization that they likely will never see their country again (e.g., "I will prove that we Mexicans / are willing to die wherever.") Their agency is simultaneously fatalist and morbid, but also salient political critique. Unfortunately, this figure's complexities continue to be elided through simplistic binaries that alternately posit the Soldado Razo as the paradigmatic Mexican American US citizen who demonstrates their civic legitimacy through military service, or as the quintessential resistant subject who fights a litany of injustices arising from US capitalism and imperialism.

The Soldado Razo archetype, however, has always involved dissonant meanings. The figure appears as a picaresque buffoon known as *el pelado* (the "peeled" and exposed one) made famous by Mexican actor Manuel Moreno's signature character Cantinflas. The Soldado Razo also appears as a signifying subaltern soldier who indirectly critiques US militarism through satire and humor, particularly in early 1940s *Carpas*, or traveling tent show extravaganzas.[13] Significantly, the underclass *pelado* permutation of the Soldado Razo has migrated upward to include Latina/o officers in the US military, transforming this otherwise subaltern figure into a floating signifier that can account for increased Latina/o upward class mobility. This resonance is associated with WWII veterans, who are renowned as the "Mexican American Generation" for their successful legal challenges to segregation in the postwar United States that led to increased Latina/o integration and economic and political empowerment.[14] The Soldado Razo is best known as an immanently oppositional subject in the cultural production and attendant scholarship about Chicana/os during the US war in Vietnam. Luis Valdez's *Teatro Campesino*, or "Farmworker Theater," for instance, staged the Vietnam War Soldado Razo as a tragic mestizo. Ironically, this permutation recycled European colonialist narratives that efface indigenous and mixed-heritage agency, even as it sought to displace such stereotypes.[15] Recent adaptations in literary and cinematic genres diversify gendered permutations of this archetype as an oppositional figure through hybrid fusions with other figures such as the celebrated Mexican Revolution *Soldadera* and the *Pachuca/o*, that is, underclass 1940s Zoot Suit-wearing hipsters.[16] Adding to the carnivalesque disruptions of the Soldado Razo as an oppositional figure, the popular Tejano band Little Joe y La Familia's version of *Soldado Razo* originally released during the 1990–1991 Persian Gulf War in Kuwait and Iraq opens with a quote from US President George Bush: "This aggression will not stand!" Alluding to former Iraqi President Saddam Hussein's 1990 invasion of neighboring Kuwait, these words are overlain with an accordion Polka prelude of the US national anthem, followed by the song. This version of *Soldado Razo* even grafts a new chorus from "America the Beautiful" to close the recording: "America! America! / God shed his grace on thee, / and crown thy good with brotherhood / from sea to shining sea!"—with an additional imperialist refrain of "From sea to shining sea!" (2010).[17]

Jaime Salazar's memoir about his experiences as Mexican American French Foreign Legionnaire Juan Sanchez was published at the crest of the US War on Terror that interpellated—and still interpellates—Latina/os in a wide array of old and new Soldado Razo roles. His book thus exposes and pressures intersecting and diverging ideological trajectories in Latina/o soldiering and attendant performances of transnational and supranational subjectivities. These modalities extend through, and far beyond, imperialist stereotypes of the enemy Mexican soldier, or untrustworthy Mexican American ally in the US-Mexico War from 1846 to 1848, which resulted in Mexico ceding half of its territory to the United States. The Treaty of Guadalupe-Hidalgo, signed on February 2, 1848, offered the people from this US-occupied territory a prisoner's dilemma: retain Mexican citizenship and leave their homes, or remain in the US and become US citizens. Following this war, the United States wrested control of Spain's island colonies by co-opting their independence movements, with Puerto Rico joining the US Virgin Islands, Guam, Northern Mariana Islands, and Palau as US Territories or Commonwealths. Salazar/Sanchez's French Foreign Legionnaire permutation of the Soldado Razo is not concerned with this legacy or with the broader formation of the Latina/o antithetical citizens incorporated into the US empire after the Spanish-American War of 1898. His unconventional variation on the Soldado Razo archetype challenges reductive representations of the assimilationist WWI and WWII Soldado Razo; strategically subversive soldiers and activists of the 1960s and 1970s; internationalist Marxist partisans in Central American and Caribbean revolutions of the 1980s and 1990s; and ultrapatriotic soldiers of the Persian Gulf War. He is none of the above. During the US War on Terror, the Soldado Razo also took other forms that added to the ideologically inchoate nature of this floating signifier: suspected Al Qaeda operatives, Special Forces neofascists, conscientious objectors, high-ranking generals, and CIA torturers. Ultimately, Salazar/Sanchez's French Foreign Legionnaire Soldado Razo reminds us that this signifier can be attached to multifarious "signifieds" across time, place, and ideology. Violence is the Soldado Razo's only constant feature.

The turbulent history of Mexican American soldier encounters with wartime France alone challenges the prevailing Soldado Razo master narratives that posit Latina/o soldiering as either an unambiguously empowering heroic performance of national (or transnational) citizenship, or the site of purportedly anticolonial and antiimperialist interventions. At one end of the ideological spectrum, former school teacher and US Army infantryman Private José Luz Saenz's 1933 WWI combat diary, *Los méxico-americanos en la Gran Guerra y su contingente en pro de la democracia, la humanidad, y la justicia*, represents the author's US combat experience abroad in the "Great War" as a strategic step in reasserting Latina/o claims to their presumed rights as US citizens (Figures I.4, I.5, and I.6). Pursuant to this end, Saenz promotes a chauvinistic claim of Mexican American superiority over Europeans, particularly Germans and German-descent Americans. After surviving gruesome trench warfare against German troops in France, which included poison gas attacks, Saenz joined other Mexican American military veterans and civilian activists in 1929 to cofound the conservative and ultrapatriotic League of United Latin American Citizens (or LULAC). This organization's nomenclature deliberately attempted to recenter a model of Mexican American

FIGURE I.4. *José Luz Saenz as a schoolteacher, 1908. Courtesy of the Benson Latin American Collection, University of Texas at Austin.*

FIGURE I.5. *US Army Private José Luz Saenz, circa 1918. Courtesy of the Benson Latin American Collection, University of Texas at Austin.*

whiteness: its members claimed "Latin American" heritage to avoid the negative racial connotations of "Mexican." This nomenclature was part of strategic maneuvers to claim full enfranchisement for Mexican American and Latina/o US citizens, which included successful efforts to have Mexican Americans legally classified as "White."[18]

Recounting the train ride through Texas that eventually led him to France, Saenz discusses the broader significance of his soldiering: he introduces a martial and ethical claim to superiority over racist European-descent, or white, Americans in addition to the Germans he would fight in France:

As the sun was setting we passed by Dittlinger [Texas], a community where many Mexicans worked and where I taught their children for one year. For me, that farming area is another battleground. I fought battles there until I convinced county officials to pay the teacher for the schooling of our children...

Now that I wear the uniform of a warrior I have the hope of winning other battles that will bring justice for our people...It was exactly

here, in this farming community, where it occurred to me to pick up
a rifle. I was driven by the mistreatment that our people face in these
parts, where the Teutonic and German races predominate. They are
ungrateful, they deny us equality as a people, and they forget the
thousand and one guarantees given their ancestors when they came
to colonize these lands... And I think that those of us who have offered our services to fight the unjust and prideful Germans across the
ocean could begin by making an example of the Izcariots, the bad
citizens that we often encounter.   (Zamora 2010, 73)[19]

Most WWI soldiers—such as my paternal great uncle Juan Montez,
a US Army draftee from the lumpenproletariat who was wounded in
France—were content merely to have survived the horrors of modern
warfare.[20] Saenz wanted much more. Ironically, in contrast to Saenz's
determination to return to the United States from France to reclaim
a more robust allotment of his American citizenship rights, Jaime

FIGURE I.6. Los Mexico-Americanos en la Gran Guerra *(Artes Gráficas, San
Antonio, 1933), by José Luz Saenz. Courtesy of the Benson Latin American
Collection, University of Texas at Austin.*

Salazar flees the United States for France in a fit of anomie arising from the privileges of middle-class US citizenship that Saenz helped secure for Latina/os.

Jaime Salazar's relocation and rearticulation of his Mexican American subjectivity as provisionally French is also substantially different from the legions of Allied soldiers who participated in the WWII D-Day invasion of Normandy that freed France from Nazi occupation. Exactly 2,499 US soldiers in this effort—including my second cousin Victor Manuel Ledesma of the US Army's 90th Infantry Division—were killed in combat (Figure I.7.) In gratitude, France ceded part of Normandy to serve as a cemetery in perpetuity for US military personnel killed in action.[21] These dead US soldiers became part of France, physically and forever, even though none of them were fighting for France. While different from Salazar/Sanchez's military service in France as a Legionnaire, these WWII soldiers pose the obvious but still undertheorized issue of how transnational soldiering—living, fighting, and especially dying abroad—both enables and undermines Latina/o efforts to embody and enjoy *any* citizenship. Indeed, in spite of US Army Private Victor Manuel Ledesma's military service and sacrifice as a draftee, his extended family continued to reside in the Chalmers Courts Public Housing

FIGURE I.7. *US Army Private Victor Manuel Ledesma, Serial Number 18031047, circa 1944. Photo in personal possession of the Author. Courtesy of B. V. Olguín.*

Complex in East Austin, Texas, for several generations after his death. To this day, many family members remain part of the perennially disenfranchised lumpenproletariat and working classes from which the overwhelming majority of enlisted soldiers are drawn.

It is often said that soldiers fight and die for each other, with broader geopolitical matters remaining outside their immediate battlefield concerns. This is as true for the dead and wounded Mexican American soldiers in WWI and WWII France, as it is for Jaime Salazar's alter ego Juan Sanchez, who pledges his allegiance to fellow denaturalized, postcitizen, provisionally French, and always already foreign Legionnaires. Yet, Salazar/Sanchez offers a supranational and ideologically complicated model of the Soldado Razo abroad whose significance extends beyond the martial clique: his chaotic, messy, and diverse performance of Latinidad pressures celebratory accounts of Latina/o transnational soldiering and subjectivity in other wartime contexts. These extend into the eighteenth- and nineteenth-century US Indian Wars, in which proto-Latina/o subjects fought against indigenous peoples on behalf of Spanish, Mexican, Texan, and even US governments, while sometimes also fighting against these very governments.

Salazar/Sanchez also complicates supranational, and variously internationalist, ideologies that have inspired Latina/os to hit the road, pick up the pen, and in some instances take up arms in support of causes in direct opposition to US geopolitical and military objectives. This includes combat against US troops, many of whom, of course, are Latina/os. These permutations of the Soldado Razo involve Pan-Americanist solidarity, related regionalisms, revolutionary nationalisms, as well as numerous iterations of anarchist antinationalism and communist internationalism. Driven by these ideologies, Latina/os joined insurgencies and revolutionary movements in Mexico, El Salvador, Nicaragua, and Argentina from the 1970s to the early 1990s. They are part of the ongoing Zapatista uprising from the 1990s to the present. And Latina/os are active in supporting the *independentista* struggle in Puerto Rico, particularly the socialist trajectory, as well as defiantly socialist Cuba. This legacy of Latina/o supranational and internationalist soldiering and solidarity also extends to several countries in Europe and around the globe, from the Spanish Civil War to partisan activities in the Soviet Union, Maoist China, and even Libya as special guests of the late Muammar

Gaddafi, who was renowned for his support of anticolonial and antiimperialist struggles, including those occurring within the United States and its colonies.

Salazar/Sanchez anticipates the evolving racialization and spatialization of the Soldado Razo archetype in other directions as well. In the more recent military campaigns of the US War on Terror, the Soldado Razo reprises its perennial role as untrustworthy ally and outright US enemy. They are the always suspect ethnic minority soldier who, increasingly, includes Latina/o Muslims suspected of allegiance to Al Qaeda or the Islamic State in Iraq and Syria (or ISIS) simply because they are Muslims.[22] Latina/os continue to occupy their predominant role in front line combat units for a variety of reasons, including the constructions of Latino males as a martial caste, as George Mariscal (2003, 2010) and Carlos Vélez-Ibañez (1996) have explicated. But Latina/os also have assumed new roles in top command posts as generals, senior CIA officers, and even government-sanctioned torturers! The civilian Latina/o members of xenophobic militias patrolling the US-Mexico border further compound the vexing ideological performances of the Soldado Razo's militarized models of US citizenship. Ever-present Latina/o antiwar activists add to this carnivalesque cacophony. If we include utopian and dystopian science fiction literature and film genres that feature Latina/o soldiers who sometimes are not just post-Latina/os, but cyborgs and posthuman subjects, this complex legacy extends into the imagined transspecies and intergalactic futures far outside standard Latina/o Studies paradigms that still largely presume human embodiment as necessary for Latina/o subjectivity.[23]

Yet, to date there has been no account of the Soldado Razo's vast spatial range, ontological and epistemological complexity, and expansive ideological variations. Neither has there been a reckoning of Latina/o soldiering, postnational citizenship, and postcitizen subjectivities, all of which are shaped by violence. More precisely, scholars have not accounted for the way different types of violence impact the role of place, time, and space in shaping Latinidades. Many studies on Latina/o soldiering suffer from their virtues: they are too myopic in celebratory profiles of Latina/o soldiers as paradigmatic citizens, or too conveniently critical of Latina/o soldier failure to comprehend the global geopolitical dimensions of the external and internal wars they fight as straight, gay, or lesbian soldiers. Latina/o Spatial Studies explications of transnational borderlands mestizaje and mulattaje, interstitial and third-space agency, as well as various citizenship models are only partially successful at illuminating hyperlocalized yet always globally resonant Latina/o spatial ontologies. But they cannot account for figures such as Salazar/Sanchez, who demonstrates that these "glocal" Latina/o subjects may be as hegemonic as they are oppositional, or even alternatively hegemonic in their opposition to the United States! The otherwise productive Latina/o Spatial Studies scholarship does not account for how Latina/o transnational subjectivities can be postnational and postcitizen, outernational and extraterritorial, and even immanently post-Latina/o, while remaining supra-Latina/o palimpsests. Jaime Salazar's transformation into the Mexican American French Foreign Legion Soldado Razo Juan Sanchez, who is rendered *sous rature* many times over, features this range of possibilities and simultaneities par excellence.

While Latina/o Literary and Cultural Studies scholars have identified ideological ruptures enacted through oppositional poetics, performances, and politics, they have not accounted for the radically discrepant, yet coherent, palimpsestic violentology modeled by Salazar/Sanchez and the many subjects like him. He may be unique, but he is not alone in modeling a supra-Latinidad that extends beyond the reified category of "Latina/o." Moreover, Salazar/ Sanchez's militarism and imperialist apologia may actually be more consistent with the views of the majority of Latina/o soldiers and civilians over time and place! The open secret in Latina/o Studies is that the great majority of Latina/os are *not* the celebrated resistant subjects who populate the reading lists of undergraduate courses in the academy. Rather, Latina/os are just as mystified as the great majority of Americans. Yet, they are not *just* mystified subjects because their investment in US capitalism and imperialism affords palpable class and social mobility, as well as first world privileges, however relative and circumscribed they may be because of lingering racialized, gendered, and sexualized class segmentations.[24] Rational choice is a component in Latina/o interpellation within capitalism that, as Foucauldian theories of power and Gramscian models of (counter) hegemony illustrate, could also accommodate the illusion of resistance through critiques of discrimination that strategically avoid attention to the structures that maintain these inequalities.

The field's general neglect of populist literary forms and cultural sensibilities that fall outside petty bourgeois tastes—and especially assimilationist progress narratives or resistance discourses—further exacerbates the Latina/o Studies lacuna regarding Latina/o ideological diversity. These include the ever-growing corpus of Latina/o combat memoir; Latina/o science fiction literature and film; Latina/o spy memoir; Latina/o police procedurals; real-time and reality war television programs featuring Latina/o contestants; low-brow, drug-themed scatological comedy films; and sports spectacles infused with violent ultrapatriotic signifying. These popular genres and spectacles, in addition to more conventional cultural production, reveal that evolving Latina/o relationships with—and growing proximity to—the hegemonic exercise of power is far more complicated than the field has acknowledged. Jaime Salazar's perplexing yet provocative narrative, which is part of a long legacy of Latina/o wartime writing and multimedia cultural production from the nineteenth century to the present, invites new theorizing about soldiering, warfare, and the status of violence in Latina/o life, culture, and history. Phrased otherwise, the Soldado Razo offers new opportunities for theorizing the postcitizen Latina/o and the proliferation of supra-Latina/o violentologies that extend through and very far beyond the overbearing and contradictory Latinidad-as-resistance and resistance-as-citizenship dyad. Violentologies facilitates these difficult explications by refusing to accept convenient fallacies and teleologies. It instead offers materialist mappings of supra-Latinidades within the chronotopal coordinates of the local and the global.

This book thus engages ongoing and emerging questions and challenges confronting Latina/o Studies and intersecting fields. First, are we willing to allow ongoing Latina/o ontological and epistemological syntheses to extend as far as they appear inclined to go, even if some of these supranational relocations evacuate the reified category of Latinidad of its presumed a priori counterhegemonic status? If so, what happens to Latina/o Studies as currently configured? Even more importantly, how do supra-Latina/o subjectivities and agency relate to revolutionary movements (and not just efforts to reform and integrate capitalism) over time and place, and especially into the future? Also, if violence is the constitutive element in all Latina/o chronotopes, can supra-Latina/o violentologies supersede what Fanon has called the problem of violence: the ever-present specter of internecine killings and more banal daily violences that cumulatively threaten the success of the revolution facilitated by armed insurrection? Finally, how might related extratextual performances enable or

impede—or enable *and* impede—the continued evolution of new
Latinidades toward ever-more-nuanced ends? These and other questions animate the following chapters, which are offered in the spirit
of *autocrítica* pursuant to a paradigm shift in the field that propelled
me, as I shared in the preface, from the potentially lethal Soldado
Razo archetype of Mexicano-Chicano-Tejano masculinity toward an
ongoing multivalent *lucha revolucionaria*, or "revolutionary struggle," that remains grounded in these roots.

Chapter Summaries

This book is divided in two parts, each focusing on different aspects
of the military and related violences subtending an expansive range
of Latina/o ontologies, epistemologies, and ideologies, or as codified
in this study's operative compound neologism, supra-Latina/o violentologies. Part I—"Warfare and Latina/o Archetypes"—consists of
two chapters that explicate the conceits, contradictions, and complexities of extant and new variations of foundational Latina/o
Studies archetypes. The first chapter examines Latina/o encounters
with and reclamations of indigeneity from the eighteenth century to
the present. Deploying violentologies as a heuristic device and hermeneutic prism, it focuses on established and emergent Latina/o autobiographical literary genres, cinematic texts, performative popular
culture spectacles, as well as recently recovered archival materials
and unique oral histories. These cumulatively reveal the wide spectrum of Latina/o antipathies toward, and affiliations with, Native
nations and indigenous peoples in the United States and abroad. This
chapter thus foregrounds the ideological diversity of supra-Latina/o
violentologies by examining the myriad Latina/o involvements in
the US Indian Wars vis-à-vis ambidextrous, albeit ambivalent,
Latina/o neoindigenous, as well as problematic indigenist performances of XicanIndia/o and LatIndia/o modalities. These include
mixed-heritage, lesbian, gay, bisexual, transgender, queer, intersex,
and nonbinary (LGBTQI+), as well as Two-Spirit warrior paradigms
in Indian Country and elsewhere.

Chapter 2 is devoted to the WWII-Soldado Razo archetype that
anchors Latina/o civic and cultural citizenship models, transnational
mestizaje and hybridity paradigms, and also hypermasculinist warrior hero discourses. Through a reassessment of familiar, as well as

neglected and undertheorized literary and performative texts, the chapter examines the conservative—specifically heteronormative, capitalist, and protoimperialist—nature of prevailing triumphalist historiographies of the WWII Soldado Razo as a member of the pro- verbial "Greatest Generation." Both familiar and new permutations of WWII-Soldado Razo archetypes, as well as related civilian figures, reveal this subject's varied negotiations of ideology. In the process they complicate our understanding of the racialized, gendered, and sexualized texture of this epochal milieu and its Latina/o protago- nists. Indeed, this chapter's case studies reveal that the Soldado Razo actually anchors WWII-era supra-Latina/o violentologies ranging from hyperlocal cultural nationalisms, protofascist imperialisms, frequently ignored WWII-era Marxist internationalisms, and proto- queer warrior heroes intertwined with homosocial and simultane- ously homoerotic Pachucos!

Part II—"Violence and the Global Latinidades"—consists of three chapters devoted to mapping the theoretical subjects of Latina/o Studies across a global terrain. Chapter 3 commences this recovery of an expansive plurality of globalized Latinidades by exploring Latina/o-Asian wartime encounters in life-writing genres, wartime cinema, and performative popular culture such as spoken word and Hip Hop from WWII to the War on Terror. In addition to reassessing established and canonized texts about Latina/o wartime encounters with specific Asian nations, peoples, and cultures from WWII, the Korean War, and the US war in Vietnam, the chapter also recovers the neglected legacy of Latina/o exoticist and neo-Orientalist travel- ogues in Cold War China and, more recently, in Iraq, Afghanistan, and Turkey. The wide range of these Latina/o encounters with the broader transcontinental space of Eurasia, the colonialist chronotope of the "Orient," and equally complicated notion of the *Ummah*, or global community of Muslims, involves a multiplicity of transversal LatinAsian violentologies. These pressure for radical expansions of Latina/o mestizajes beyond conventional frameworks predicated upon Judeo-Christian and Mesoamerican legacies, and also challenge the lingering resistance paradigm.

The fourth chapter disentangles the distinct ideologies often conflated under the expansive and notoriously vague rubric of Latina/o "transnationalism." It first interrogates the limits of Radical Regionalism Studies by explicating the specter of nationalism in Emma Pérez's ostensibly contestatory Tejana lesbian feminist regionalist historical fiction. The chapter further deconstructs the Latina/o Studies fixation on hyperlocalities and faux transnational-isms by interrogating the various aestheticizations of violence in Latina/o literatures about Central American civil wars, femicides in the US-Mexico border, and revolutionary insurgencies throughout North, Central, and South America, in addition to the Caribbean. It closes by underscoring Pan-Latina/o political diversity through the recovery of testimonial prose and poetry from Latina/o internation-alist partisans and combatants vis-à-vis the antitestimonial mem-oirs, novels, and poetry by and about right-wing Latina/o soldiers and CIA officers.

The fifth and final chapter focuses on how the War on Terror's permutations of Latina/o war literature, theater, television, film, and popular music present methodological and political challenges to conventional understandings of Latina/o relationships to power as inherently oppositional to US imperialism. These relatively new genres include Latina/o War on Terror combat action memoir and related oral histories; wounded warrior narratives; protofascist Special Forces *Über*-warrior memoir and biographical profiles; conscientious objector *testimonio*, ideologically ambivalent wartime theater, and pacifist performance art; military command memoirs by junior and senior officers; as well as Latina/o spy memoir, biography, and historical fiction. Despite the authors' profound differences in cultural heritage, experiences, and aesthetic capacities, their cultural productions cohere around intersecting, and diverging, violence-based theories of knowledge and being. They also demonstrate the stark right-wing turn in a large segment of contemporary Latina/o life writing, which accentuates the wide range of ideological trajectories identified in earlier chapters.

The book concludes with an assessment of the 2015 Broadway hit *Hamilton: An American Musical* by mixed-heritage (Puerto Rican, Mexican, black, and white) Lin-Manuel Miranda, which emerges as the quintessential violentological text and supra-Latina/o chrono-tope. This *sui generis* phenomenon models all the conceits and con-tradictions explicated throughout this book, while also consolidating the vexed and vexing Latina/o move from the margins to the center. My assessment of this spectacle as part of the ever-more discrepant Latina/o archive, which consists of widely diverging supra-Latina/o and even post-Latina/o violentologies, underscores the need for a paradigm shift in our understanding of the ontological and episte-mological pasts, presents, and futures of Latina/o Studies.

PART I

Warfare and Latina/o Archetypes

Caballeros and Indians

LAND, WAR, AND THE INDIAN QUESTION IN LATINA/O AUTOBIOGRAPHY, HISTORICAL FICTION, AND POPULAR CULTURE

In the spirit of a new people that is conscious not only of its proud historical heritage but also of the brutal gringo invasion of our territories, we, the Chicano inhabitants and civilizers of the northern land of Aztlán from whence came our forefathers, reclaiming the land of their birth and consecrating the determination of our people of the sun, declare that the call of our blood is our power, our responsibility, and our inevitable destiny.

—ALURISTA, Preface, *El Plan Espiritual de Aztlán*
([1969] 1970)

I tackled one of the enemy close at hand and, after escaping the arrows which he let go at me, I succeeded in putting a bullet through his body at the hips. The Indian fell flat on his face. Seeing this, Cornelio Hernández, who was near me, ran toward the Indian, shouting, "Now, I'll get his duster" ("Ahora le quito el zorro"), but, when he had come near him, the Indian raised himself suddenly and drove an arrow through his neck, just below his Adam's apple, where the arrow remained. The Indian, who must have used the last of his strength in this attack, fell backward dead. Hernández, badly wounded as he was, dragged himself to the body, took out a service knife he had and tried to drive it into the Indian's sides, but it broke. With the piece that was left, however, he succeeded in opening a great wound and, as he drove the stub of a knife to the Indian's heart, as though the dead body could hear him, he said, "I pardon thee, my brother; I pardon thee, my brother."

—JUAN BERNAL, *Memoria* (1877)

Violentologies: Violence, Identity, and Ideology in Latina/o Literature. B.V. Olguín, Oxford University Press (2021).
© B.V. Olguín.
DOI: 10.1093/oso/9780198863090.001.0002

The evening a diminutive twenty-two-year-old dark-brown man with curly black hair and goatee read his verse preface to "El Plan Espiritual de Aztlán" at the National Chicano Liberation Youth Conference in Denver on March 30, 1969 (excerpted as the first epigraph above), Chicana/o indigeneity became a central trope in Chicana/o literature, historiography, and related social movements. The reader, Alberto Baltazar Urista Heredia—who took the pen-name Alurista—would become renowned for his Nahuatl glosses, white cotton frock, and calf-length pants characteristic of indigenous dress in southern Mexico. Such neoindigenous performances were common in the 1960s and 1970s cultural nationalist spectacles that punctuated the political mobilizations and violent confrontations collectively known as the Chicano Movement. Following Alurista's performance and the subsequent reification of Chicana/o indigeneity through a multiplicity of neoindigenous paradigms and essentialist indigenist discourses, a new accounting of ideology in Chicana/o and Latina/o encounters with Native Americans and indigenous people is in order. We need to reassess the variable and undertheorized performances of race and indigeneity in wartime, as well as militarized civilian "peacetime" contexts throughout the world, that subtend the oftentimes violent encounters between Latina/os and indigenous peoples and nations from the nineteenth century to the present. Accordingly, this study on the ideological vicissitudes of violence-based supra-Latina/o ontologies, epistemologies, and agency necessarily traverses through foundational Latina/o Studies discourses on indigeneity.

Chicana/o and Puerto Rican cultural nationalisms of the 1960s and 1970s have been thoroughly critiqued for their masculinism. However, their indigenist conceits persist, especially claims to the cultural capital of indigeneity models assumed to be inherently subaltern and antiimperialist. Curtis Marez critiques the Chicana/o cultural nationalist fetish on indigenous heritage and the discursive recuperation of the ancient Aztec homeland of Aztlán as a nostalgic "*indigenismo* of the antique" (2001, 267). Regardless of such critiques, feminist and queer Aztláns, as well as environmental and transnational Aztlánesque discourses, continue to emerge.[1] The resilience of Aztlán is enabled by the flexible root metaphor, *mestizaje*, or racial and cultural hybridity involving indigenous and European heritages. Alurista's bronze, an amalgamated dark-brown metal, has since been supplanted by an ever-expanding gallery of borderlands paradigms and interstitial and third-space modalities performed through an infinite number of intersections and negotiations. Puerto Rican, or *Boricua*, cultural nationalists take similar license in their metaphor, *Borinquen*, a permutation of the indigenous Taíno term *Borikén* that roughly translates as "land of the valiant lord," and which refers to the contemporary island nation of Puerto Rico.[2] In these Latina/o cultural nationalist paradigms, a nostalgic indigenismo remains as the unacknowledged specter.

Latina/o mestizajes and related *mulattajes* (or Amerindian, African, and European fusions) have always been vexed concepts, complex historical realities, and contradictory forms of agency among Latina/os. As revealed in this chapter, these are overdetermined by multiple violences.[3] Mestizajes and mulattajes embody local and global traumas, as well as performances of power and counterpower, which are never unidirectional. María Josefina Saldaña-Portillo (2001, 2016) argues, for instance, that Mexican and Chicana/o deployments of mestizaje-as-citizenship enact a transborder erasure of specific indigenous people. Antonia Castañeda (2001) and Tomás Almaguer (2008) remind us that mestizaje is inaugurated by mass rape of indigenous women. Albert L. Hurtado (1999) and Lisbeth Haas (1996) recover the gendered, racial, cultural, and economic stratifications in the colonial southwest actualized through biological, political, and religious mestizajes. In the late-seventeenth to early-nineteenth centuries, Haas notes, Mexican and Mexican American mestiza/os—provisionally incorporated into the Spanish mission system as Christianized "gente de razón" ("people of reason")—were not recognized as European, yet were still identified as more "civilized" than non-Christian "Indios" (1996, 31). Sheila Marie Contreras (2008) adds that nineteenth-century Mexican nationalist and late-twentieth-century Chicana/o cultural nationalist literary reclamations of indigeneity ironically rely on modernist, colonialist, and corresponding primitivist discourses by British and American colonizers, settlers, anthropologists, and museum curators. Taunya Lovell Banks extends such contrapuntal archaeologies by arguing that Mexican and Chicana/o models of mestizaje reinforce "the denial of anti-black bias," while also "reinforcing conscious and unconscious notions of white superiority" (2006, 204). Juan Flores (1993) explains how this Eurocentric bias permeates throughout competing Latin American, Caribbean, and Puerto Rican ontologies. These include José Enrique Rodó's 1900 treatise *Ariel*, which proposed the European patriarch Prospero from Shakespeare's *The Tempest* (1611) as a paradigmatic figure for Latin America in contradistinction to Roberto Fernández Retamar's ([1971] 1989) privileging of Caliban. Similarly, racial stratifications persist in Boricua cultural nationalism despite longstanding attempts to theorize, and variously reclaim, Puerto Rican mulattaje, beginning with Antonio Salvador Pedreira's 1934 treatise on Puerto Rican syncretism, *Insularismo*; José Luís González's 1980 historical topography of Puerto Rican racial genealogies; and subsequent case studies in Miriam Jiménez Román and Juan Flores's 2009 *The Afro-Latin@ Reader: History and Culture in the United States.*

In addition to the racial ambivalences inscribed in competing accounts of mestizaje and mulattaje, Ramón Gutiérrez (1998), Antonia Castañeda (2001), Ned Blackhawk (2008), James Brooks (2001), and David Weber (2006) have uncovered colonial and postcolonial Mexican and Mexican American violence against Indians throughout North America. Yet no studies have undertaken a metacritical examination of Mexican American, Puerto Rican, or broader Latina/o antipathies toward Native Americans and indigenous people throughout the world. This hostility from the early colonial period to the present is legible, if often *sous rature*, in Mexican American, Chicana/o, Puerto Rican, and mixed-heritage Latina/o autobiographical narratives and historical fiction. The majority of these texts deploy models of mestizaje and mulattaje that inadvertently—but unmistakably—are figured as "not-Indian," that is, "white." From the 1835 War of Texas Independence to the War on Terror occupations of Afghanistan and Iraq, Latina/o encounters with indigenous people and nations have involved settler colonial violence and coordinated warfare as constitutive of Latinidad. Nonetheless, as illustrated in Juan Bernal's *testimonio*, excerpted as the second epigraph to this chapter, mid-nineteenth-century encounters between Californios and Native Americans were intensely violent even as they involved ambivalent recognitions of filiation.[4] Bernal, for instance, recalls his fellow Californio Cornelio Hernández calling an Indian warrior "my brother." Hernández even goes so far as to "pardon" this Indian for causing his own mortal wound while Hernández stabs the corpse to ensure his enemy "brother" is dead. In the introduction, I venture that various forms of interpersonal and historical violences overdetermine these and other messy Chicanidades and Latinidades, which do not fit easily into extant theoretical and critical frameworks. These violence-mediated modalities of being and knowing—their violentologies—entail ide-ologies that vary widely over time, place, and politicized social space. The violent scene Bernal recounts, for instance, reveals how supra-Latina/o violentologies—that is, paradigms extending through and beyond conventional models of Latinidad—interpellate ambivalent relationships to indigeneity at foundational moments in Chicana/o and Latina/o history. These fraught claims demand a reassessment of the Latina/o indigenous and indigenist paradigms, which I explicate as part of a broad and inchoate spectrum of *LatIndia/o* violentologies.

The balance of this chapter offers a range of violent (mis)recognition scenes in select Mexican American, Chicana/o, Puerto Rican, and mixed-heritage Latina/o life writing, including biography, auto-biography, memoir, and historical fiction, in addition to real-time war television serials, popular music, and political spectacles. These genres, many of which present protonational subjects, illustrate how the era invoked by Latina/o cultural nationalists as an indigenous, mestiza/o, and mulatta/o "paradise lost," involved far more inchoate negotiations of race, place, and power than have been allowed in the reified simulacra of Latina/o—and especially Chicana/o and Boricua—cultural nationalist discourses. The grotesque and bloody hand-to-hand combat Bernal recalls, for instance, stands in stark contrast to the battles Alurista and his heirs imagine, so much so that the performance of Mexican American and Chicana/o indigeneity has been rendered into an unstable palimpsest. Even though Aztlán and Borinquen present different genealogies and constituent ele-ments, Taína/o indigeneity occupies a similarly ambiguous status in contemporary Puerto Rican cultural nationalist autobiographical lit-erature and performance. Indeed, Boricua indigeneity discourses are equally complex and contradictory for their embedded nostalgia and (mis)recognitions.

As this chapter returns to the violent colonial triangulation of Europe, the Americas, and Africa in the making and remaking of foundational Latina/o Studies metaphors and archetypes, several questions emerge. Can contemporary Latina/o claims to indigeneity survive a replay of the battles imagined and recounted by Alurista and Bernal, or Rodó, Pedreira, and Fernández Retamar, in addition to subsequent generations of Chicana/o, Puerto Rican, and other Latina/o authors? Can, and should, broader Latina/o indigenist claims to subaltern abjection-as-counterhegemonic agency persist in the wake of continued discoveries of violent settler-colonialist texts by nineteenth- and early twentieth-century Mexican Americans, in addition to analogous contemporary Puerto Rican and mixed-heritage Latina/o war narratives that similarly traffic in neocolonialist discourses? What happens to resistance paradigms in Latina/o Literary and Cultural Studies after we recover antiindigenist recognition scenes in recently canonized proto-Chicana/o, Boricua, and Pan-Latina/o fiction, nonfiction, and performance? How do models of mestizaje recover African heritage beyond a fetish on race, or rejection of it, and how do theories of mulattaje-as-autochthonous avoid reifying indigenous genocide in the recuperation and performance of Afro-Latinidad? And how might the conflicted but sometimes collaborative encounters between Latina/os and specific Indian nations in the eighteenth, nineteenth, and early twentieth centuries inform the twentieth and twenty-first century subjectivities of Latina/os who have embarked on the "Red Road": that is, Latina/os who live as mestiza/os and mulatta/os, and as retribalized Native Americans or still detribalized XicanIndia/os, Boricuas, LatIndia/os, and AfroLatIndia/os?[5] Finally, how do broader mixed-heritage XicanIndia/o and neoindigenous Boricua LGBTQI+ warrior subjectivities offer new avenues for productively destabilizing indigenist replications of heteropatriarchal models of Latinidades and indigenous warrior traditions?

The violentological hermeneutic is ideal for addressing these inquiries. Indeed, by placing Alurista's and Bernal's writings in a transhistorical dialogue with nineteenth-century Tejano settler colonist and soldier Juan Seguin's 1858 memoir, and Mexican American mountain man Andrew Garcia's neopicaresque autobiography *Tough Trip through Paradise, 1878-1879*, we can transcend the solipsistic limits of identity politics by attending to their intersecting but vastly different ideologies of violence. Similarly, the antiindigenous rhetoric in foundational proto-Chicana/o historical fiction such as Américo Paredes's historical tragedy, *George Washington Gómez: A Mexicotexan Novel* (1936–1940), and Eve Raleigh and Jovita González's jointly authored historical romance, *Caballero: A Historical Novel* (c. 1930s), inevitably undermine lingering celebratory renderings of nineteenth- and early twentieth-century proto-Chicana/o figures. These proto-Chicana/o settler-colonialist texts anticipate subsequent Latina/o and indigenous encounters and syntheses. Accordingly, this chapter assesses poetry, prose, and performance by XicanIndio Raúl Salinas, also known by his adopted

Suquamish Nation name Autumn Sun; Antonio "Poke" Espera, a mixed-heritage Latino, Euro-American, and Native American US Marine featured in Evan Wright's 2004 journalistic reportage and related 2008 HBO serial, *Generation Kill*; and Felipe Rose, a gay male, mixed-heritage black, Puerto Rican Taíno, and Lakota Sioux performer in the disco band, The Village People, who also is known by his indigenous name Swift Arrow.

Juan Seguin and the Eurocentric Order of Nineteenth-Century Tejano Settler Colonialism

Any archaeology of Latinidades is a fraught enterprise. Most Latina/o Studies historiographies situate the Texas independence war from 1835 to 1836 as the transition from colonial Latin American history to US Latina/o history. This process extends into the US-Mexico War from 1846 to 1848, when the United States invaded, occupied, and annexed half of Mexico's territory. The Spanish American War in 1898 is another nodal point: it resulted in the US imperialist occupation of the Philippines and the Pacific and Caribbean island nations of Guam, Palau, Cuba, Puerto Rico, and part of the Virgin Islands archipelago. Most surviving nineteenth- and early twentieth-century archival and autobiographical evidence about this layered colonial milieu comes from the *criollo* elite—or nonmestiza/o and nonmulatto European-descent people born in the Americas. In Texas, these criollos were the beneficiaries of mestiza/o and mulatta/o Texas Mexican, or Tejana/o, as well as Native American and African American peonage in a social and politico-economic order that involved fluid but still recognizable racial and racist hierarchies. Tejana/o life writing narratives, along with other documentary evidence such as muster rolls of Tejano Confederate soldiers that Jerry Don Thompson (2000) has recovered, destabilize Chicana/o cultural nationalist invocations of the mid-nineteenth century as the genesis of proto-Chicana/o resistance to the "gringo" invasion of which Alurista writes in his 1969 "Preface" to *El Plan de Aztlán*. Adding to the dissonance, Thompson (2000), Rosalie Schwartz (1974), Raúl A. Ramos (1998), and Arnoldo De León (1983, 1997) even identify Tejana/o slaveholders and slave hunters!

Juan Seguin, the grandson of French-descent settlers who later invited white Protestant colonists to the Mexican province of Coahuila y Tejas, adds to the ignoble list of nineteenth-century

Latina/o elites. Seguin has been reclaimed as a hero of the Texas independence war from 1835 to 1836 (also known in Mexico as a war of secession called *La Traición*, or "The Betrayal"). In 1939, the Texas town of Walnut Springs was renamed in Seguin's honor. The dissensus about Juan Seguin's legacy makes his discrepant biography impossible to assimilate within extant resistance discourses or celebratory mestizaje, third-space, and transnational-citizenship paradigms frequently used to theorize the era. Why? Seguin's 1858 memoir and correspondence indisputably construct his Tejano identity as white and anti-Indian, with racialized violence at the nexus.[6] Seguin thus represents one of the earliest, and ugliest, iterations of a supra-Latina/o violentology: this subject is fundamentally racist and settler colonialist, even as Seguin reflects on his own racialized abjection as a colonized Tejano toward the end of his life.

Juan Seguin is infamous for fighting against Mexico in the Texas war of secession from Mexico, then against his former Texan and Tejana/o allies in the US-Mexico War ten years later, from 1846 to 1848. He is less scrutinized, however, for his role as an "Indian hunter," the murderous honorific used to legitimate appropriative white settler-colonialist claims to Native status in the nineteenth-century American West. For Seguin and other nineteenth-century Tejana/os, Indians are antithetical figures—antisubjects, as it were—whose subjugation and elimination enables the inauguration of an enduring violence-based Tejana/o claim to the region. In a letter to the Texas Comptroller in 1874, Seguin expresses the colonialist nature of his Tejano consciousness that led him to join in the fight to make Texas an independent proslavery nation after Mexico had outlawed slavery six years earlier. He recalls, for instance, how "many previous to our being surrounded at the Alamo had received furloughs from Bowie and Travis in order to look after their families who were exposed to the same dangers," which he specifies as "the attacks of Indians" (1991, 190). In addition to his de facto proslavery agenda, his binary location of Indians as Others factors into the 1836 Alamo battle, an infamous symbol for competing—and collaborating—white Texan as well as criollo, or white, and even mestiza/o Tejana/o claims to Indian land. This thirteen-day battle between approximately 200 proslavery Texas independence advocates and 1,500 mostly indigenous and mestizo Mexican conscripts occurred at an abandoned mission in San Antonio de Bexar. The secessionist defeat, and subsequent execution of surviving proslavery rebels, became a rallying cry propelling the province's independence from Mexico. Texas promptly joined the alliance of Confederate States of America, which it supported in the US Civil War.

Significantly, at the start of the Alamo battle, Seguin had been given the mission of securing reinforcements from secessionist Texan General Sam Houston. However, as Seguin recalls in his memoir, his unit of Tejano volunteers was diverted to guard Tejana/o and white Texan settler ranches along the San Antonio River against what he frequently calls "depredations of the Indians" (80, 107). The diversion of Seguin's small force to fight Indians may not have made a difference in the Alamo battle, except for saving him from death at the hands of Mexican General Antonio López de Santa Anna, who regarded Tejano insurrectionists as traitors. Nonetheless, Seguin's role in the War of Texas Independence/La Traición triangulates a relationship that continues to be inaccurately represented as an exclusively Mexican-versus-Texan affair. Indians were seen as obstacles to both settler-colonialist claims, and thus were targeted for extinction by white (largely Protestant) Texans, as well as Spanish-descended Catholic Tejana/os. There is a substantial body of scholarship about Mexican and US military campaigns against Indians; the effacement of Tejana/o complicity—and even leadership—in this genocide demands a reassessment of the celebratory invocations of indigeneity and mestizaje as operative terms in Chicana/o and Latina/o Studies.

The reassessment of Latina/o indigeneity paradigms and related archetypes inevitably must confront the history of Tejana/o settler colonialism, in which Seguin served a foundational role. Jesús Frank de la Teja's introduction to his translation of Seguin's memoirs and related documents references correspondence from Seguin's mission in 1834 to negotiate with "Comanche leader Casimiro to discuss mutual problems with Tonkawa" (1991, 20). These documents also reveal that in 1836, John A. Wharton, Secretary of War for the Republic of Texas, subsequently ordered Seguin *not* to fight the Comanche as the US government was trying to make peace with them (1991, 144). Sam Houston sent a similar letter in 1837 (1991, 152). However, Seguin's fanatical bigotry persisted and continued to propel his colonialist designs. In a report to Sam Houston in 1837, Seguin recounts the presence of several tribes that are "hostile to our cause"

(1991, 158). In another 1837 letter to his commanding officer General Albert Sidney Johnston, Seguin reports killing several Indians that his company of Tejano volunteers encountered:

> From appearances I have good reason to believe that they had been in among the American settlements and have no doubt committed depredations there as they had American horses with them, no arrows left in the quivers, and from other certain signs on those whom we killed I drew this conclusion.   (1991, 167)

These "other certain signs" are never specified. But Seguin's frequent references to all Indians as "savages" (1991, 168)—especially his frequent pairing of "Indian" with "depredation"—distinguish Tejano identity from Indians at the moment cultural nationalists such as Alurista invoke to propose Chicana/o identity as inherently indigenous and oppositional to white American settler colonialism.[7] For many Indians, eighteenth- and nineteenth-century Tejana/os were also white, or allied with them, and thus not easily distinguishable from the "gringos" of whom Alurista writes.

Seguin hated Indians as much as he loved their land, and these sentiments were powerful enough to have him form mutual alliances with former and future enemies on both sides of the evolving border region. Despite his quarrel with Mexican centralism and encroaching white American settler colonialism that would challenge his own criollo settler colonial hegemony, Indians were Seguin's principal villains. He thus repeatedly formed alliances and provisional truces with his Mexican and white American foes to fight them. Indians claimed Native status to the land, which challenged—and unified— otherwise competing Tejana/o and white Texan colonial projects. Indeed, even between the 1835-1836 Texas secession from Mexico and the 1846–1848 US-Mexico War, during which Seguin became a victim of the white Texan racist pogroms against Tejana/os that eventually led him into exile in Mexico, Seguin continued to collaborate with the Texan government in fighting Indians. In 1840, he even joined forces with Mexican General Mariano Arista—against whose troops he previously fought in the Texas war of secession—to hunt Indians (primarily Comanche) who had been conducting raids on both sides of the newly redrawn border (1991, 41). In recalling his intercession between Texas and Mexico (his former enemy and subsequent ally in the US-Mexico War), Seguin recalls the goal was to reach an "understanding with the executive of Texas regarding pursuit of the Indians who committed depredations on both frontiers" (1991, 91).[8] These shifting binational allegiances were perfectly consistent with Seguin's violent border gnosis, which was decidedly less iconoclastic than Walter Mignolo suggests in his otherwise provocative model in *Local Histories, Global Designs* (2000), and far less empowering than Postcolonial and Ethnic Studies' explications of subversive mimicry propose. Similarly, third-space and transnational frameworks are grossly inadequate for explicating Seguin's violent nineteenth-century settler-colonialist ideology, which is consummately Eurocentric, anti-Indian, and genocidal.

Despite his service to General Sam Houston's settler-colonialist Texan forces, Seguin eventually found himself in a position similar to the Indians he hated, hunted, and killed. He wrote his 1858 *Memorias* as a form of political spin-doctoring to dispel Texan charges of treason for having fought against his former Texas allies in the US-Mexico War. His immediate goal was to obtain a military pension from Texas for having fought against Mexico in the Texas war of secession. Ironically, he decries "the straggling American adventurers, who were already beginning to work their dark intrigues against the Native families, whose only crime was that they owned large tracts of land and desirable property" (1991, 89). Seguin foregrounds subsequent creative Chicana/o uses of tribal affiliations when he identifies as a "Coahuiltexan" (qtd. in De la Teja 1991, 130), his criollo appropriation of Coahuiltecan, one of the tribes subsumed into the Euro-American category of "Texas Mission Indians," and, paradoxically, "Texan." This self-reference culminates Seguin's Tejano project, which is predicated upon the eradication of specific Indian nations and peoples in conjunction with the appropriation of their land. Significantly, the coloniality of this early iteration of a violence-based model of being ultimately rejects discourses on Latinidad that privilege indigeneity. Indeed, physical descriptions of Seguin underscore his whiteness. For instance, Seguin was profiled in an 1870s *Laredo Times* article that described him as an eighty-year-old whose "complexion is fair" and who is "of pure Castilian descent, his ancestors being of the first colony that come from the Canaries" (qtd. in De la Teja 1991, 191). This genealogically inaccurate and Eurocentric rhetoric appropriates the noun *Native* by turning it into an adjective, *native*, as in "a native of this land," which Seguin claims. Yet, he rejects indigeneity and the abjection it signifies, something Seguin is loath to incorporate into his peculiar Tejano regionalist paradigm. He was not alone in these sentiments, and inaugurated generations of equally retrograde settler-colonialist Tejana/o, Chicana/o, and Latina/o ontologies and epistemologies.

George Washington Gómez, Nuevo Santander, and Américo Paredes's Settler-Colonialist Proto-Chicano Conceits

Américo Paredes, often celebrated as a precursor to Chicana/o cultural nationalism, situates his claims of Tejano-as-Native, and Tejano resistance to white Protestant settler colonialism as counterhegemonic, during and immediately after the battles Seguin fought. Paredes (*Pistol*, 1958) is renowned for recuperating the early twentieth-century vernacular octosyllabic acoustic martial ballad form known as the epic heroic *corrido*, or "running verse," as a performative master narrative for Mexican American antiimperialist resistance. Ramón Saldívar (*Chicano Narrative*, 1990; *The Borderlands*, 2006), José E. Limón (1992), and Teresa McKenna (1991) have extrapolated from Paredes's thesis to propose Chicana/o literature as a modern analogue to the corrido's oppositional interventions. Saldívar has argued that Chicana/o identity constitutes the antithesis to white American imperialism, with Chicana/o narrative being "not so much the expression of this ideology of difference as it is a production of that ideology" (*Chicano Narrative*, 1990, 8). For the past quarter century, the field of Chicana/o Literary and Cultural Studies has thrived under this provocative and productive claim. Nonetheless, there still is no full accounting of the racialized gendered complexities and ideological contradictions arising from the violent subtext that animates the theory of Chicana/o difference as inherently counterhegemonic.

A violentological hermeneutic reveals how the dialectics of difference undergirding Paredes's poetry, fiction, and overall discourse, complicate depictions of Mexican American and Chicana/o resistance to US imperialism as continuous and unambiguously counterhegemonic. As I have argued elsewhere ("Reassessing," 2005), Paredes's textualized model of Pocho consciousness is a Chicana/o analogue to W. E. B. DuBois's African American "double consciousness," in addition to being a precursor to Gloria Anzaldúa's "mestiza consciousness." Paredes's Mexican American "mimic man," however, continually reiterates, and simultaneously undermines, his colonial status and purportedly decolonial designs. The Pocho's ambivalence centers on racialized masculinist violence and outright warfare. Paredes's 1934 poem, "Bolívar's Dream" (*Cantos*, [1937] 2007), for instance, introduces the Pocho's conflicted positionality and agency through a racially fluid invocation of the Aztec Mexica war deity Mexitli, alongside criollo independence leader Simón Bolívar, to whom he turns as alternatives to his predicament as a US colonial subject. This simultaneous invocation of Mesoamerican figures alongside settler-colonialist criollo "independence" warrior heroes demonstrates the strategic obfuscatory memory about the past that Lorenzo Veracini (2010) describes as a fundamental feature of settler-colonialist claims to Native status.

Having vacillated between depictions of his own Pocho identity as both a curse and a badge of honor as I previously argued ("Reassessing," 2005), Paredes's contemporaneous 1930s bildungsroman, *George Washington Gómez: A Mexicotexan Novel* (1990), compounds the contradictory racial geographies of his Pocho alter ego's anticolonial yearnings. This novel presents the Pocho as a racially ambiguous regionalist formation trapped within a Fanonian colonial psychosis that unravels into a multivalent yet consummately settler-colonialist violentology. Significantly, the protagonist, George Washington Gómez, is the son of a Tejano murdered by the racist Texas Rangers, a law enforcement unit that also served as a paramilitary death squad to quell lingering Mexican-cum-Mexican American dissent following the US-Mexico War. Paredes's borderlands character receives his dissonant name after a family debate that ends with his mother's wish for him "to have a great man's name," she proclaims, "because he is going to be a great man among the Gringos" (1990, 16). His father chooses the name of "the great North American, he who was a general and fought the soldiers of the king" (1990, 16). The subsequent borderlands pidgin Spanish slippage of the family's pronunciations of "Washington" devolves into "Guálinto," the name he is called throughout the novel. This palimpsestic moniker becomes a borderlands legacy the protagonist, who was born with light skin, will negotiate his entire life through real and figural violences.

After Guálinto's father is murdered shortly after this naming ceremony, the young boy is raised by an uncle. This man had promised his dying brother never to reveal the atrocity so Guálinto could grow free of the racialized antiimperialist rage that animated the family's male relatives. Guálinto subsequently becomes the paradigmatic Mexico-Texan mimic man whose identity is performed as a masculine tragicomic Pocho: he is a more or less assimilated Mexican American uncomfortable and out of place both among his Mexican American community and also the broader white American populace. This figure is not the empowered and self-validating male analogue to Anzaldúa's new mestiza, as scholars of Paredes's writing suggest. On the contrary, while at times the adolescent Guálinto appears headed toward becoming a Mexican American avenger, he becomes a spy for the US Army. Worse, on the eve of World War II, he is sent to the borderlands to conduct surveillance on his own community. This plot feature resonates with the WWI German government's appeal to Mexico to join its cause against the Allies in exchange for assistance in regaining territory it lost to the United States.[9] To further complicate matters akin to a classical Greek tragedy, Guálinto is married to a blond white American woman whose father, the author alludes, is the Texas Ranger who killed Guálinto's father!

Throughout the novel Paredes depicts Pocho signifying and Mexican American anomie as a colonial condition. However, his rendering of Guálinto within the old colonialist trope of the tragic mestizo, along with the profound discursive slippage in his racialized poetics, ultimately situate the narrative—and the author's regionalist and always already nationalist imaginary—within hegemonic ideology than many Paredes scholars appear willing to acknowledge. At one level, Paredes marks how Guálinto's father-in-law complains to his daughter of her husband's "nigger name" (1990, 284), presumably referring to the preponderance of prominent black men named George Washington in the post-Reconstruction African American community. This passage clearly enables a critique of white bigotry. But Paredes's contradictory racial politics emerge in other scenes that limit this potential. For instance, the novel introduces a character called "El Negro" (1990, 17–23), a Tejano insurgent with an African genealogy who is depicted in positive terms. Yet, El Negro never evolves beyond a stock figure. He disappears immediately after being introduced. This vanishing black male figure reveals

Paredes's inability to incorporate a coherent model of blackness into his fictional archaeology of a purportedly antiimperialist Tejano identity, a problem replicated throughout Chicana/o literature until relatively recently.[10]

Paredes's novel includes even more troubling ambivalence in scenes where Guálinto imagines a Tejano utopian project requiring violent—and genocidal—Tejano warfare against Indians. Earlier described as light-skinned, Guálinto foregrounds his masculinist racialized desire through his marriage to a blond white wife. Guálinto both loves and hates his whiteness and harbors the same ambiguous feelings toward the new white American order. In early childhood scenes he even imagines battles against the Texas Rangers, for whom a banana tree serves as the surrogate for his dagger thrusts (1990, 67–8). But even in this scene, Guálinto's ambivalent whiteness is decidedly *not* Indian. Toward the end of the novel, for instance, the omniscient narrator recalls the imaginative battles of this failed Pocho warrior hero, which include a symbolically significant fantasy scene in which he reconquers his Tejano homeland:

> He would imagine he was living in his great-grandfather's time, when the Americans first began to encroach on the northern provinces of the new Republic of Mexico. Reacting against the central government's inefficiency and corruption, he would organize rancheros into a fighting militia *and train them by using them to exterminate the Comanches.* Then, with the aid of generals like Urrea, he would extend his influence to the Mexican Army. He would discover the revolver before Samuel Colt, as well as the hand grenade and a modern style of portable mortar. In his daydreams he built a modern arms factory in Laredo, doing it all in great detail, until he had an enormous, well-trained army that included Irishmen and escaped American Negro slaves. Finally, he would defeat not only the army of the United States but its navy as well. He would reconquer all the territory west of the Mississippi River and recover Florida as well.
>
> (1990, 282, emphasis added)

This settler colonial dream sequence occurs as Guálinto is sleeping next to his pregnant white wife while on the aforementioned secret US Army assignment to spy on the Mexican American community.

In a rehearsal of Seguin's Tejano xenophobic settler-colonialist violentology, Paredes gives us a tragic hero caught in imaginative battles against and for various layers of Spanish, criollo, and white

US settler colonialism and global imperialism. His alternative is not much different than the system he decries. In the above scene, for instance, the author uses a banal matter-of-fact descriptive tone in his reference to the extermination of Comanches as a prelude to a competing-imperialist, multiracial war against nineteenth-century white filibusterers who colonized half of Mexico—itself a settler colonial society—beginning with the province of Coahuila y Tejas. This tone, paired with Paredes's recurring references to this region by its Spanish settlement name of Nuevo Santander, reveals a Tejano settler-colonialist nostalgia.[11] In this imagined Tejano utopia, the old patriarchal pastoral order is romanticized with complete disregard for the genocidal violence and forced servitude that enabled its existence. This includes the attempted extermination of the Comanches, indentured servitude of indigenous and mestizo peasants through the *encomienda* system, and black chattel slavery on both sides of the border.[12]

These contradictory signifying practices pressure José David Saldívar's description of Paredes as a "'decolonialist' intellectual" (*Border Matters*, 1997, 52). In Paredes's articulation of the cultural nationalist ideal—the recovery of lands his Spanish Mexican ancestors violently occupied that have since been occupied by white American invaders—he reveals that Native Americans are excluded, and necessarily executed. The scene might be recognized as decolonial Pocho signifying if Paredes had not decried, to his death, the loss of *Nuevo Santander*, the colonialist term he preferred over *Texas, Tejas, the borderlands*, or even *Aztlán*.[13] It was the criollo settlement supplanted upon Indian lands, primarily Comanche territory, for which he yearned. For him, the subsequent battle to reclaim this ancestral land was among masculinist, patriarchal Tejano *caballeros* and white cowboys, and this fight necessarily involved battle against Indians.

"This Indian-Infested Wilderness": Chicana Feminist Orientalism in Eve Raleigh and Jovita González's *Caballero*

The Tejano settler-colonialist violentology animating *George Washington Gómez* may be less anomalous in pre-1960s Tejana/o prose than Chicana/o Studies scholarship suggests. The celebrated novel *Caballero: A Historical Novel* by Eve Raleigh (the pseudonym for Margaret Eimer, a white Missouri transplant to Texas) and Jovita González, for instance, further complicates the ideological resonance of Mexican American negotiations of mestizaje and indigeneity in the nineteenth and early twentieth century. Written in the 1930s and 1940s (but not published until 1996), the novel is set in South Texas between the Texas war of independence, and the US-Mexico War. Both a historical novel and a romance narrative, it focuses on the waning Mexican colonial semifeudal order in the region. The novel dramatizes the decline of Don Santiago Mendoza y Soría, the scion of a Tejana/o ranching family that traces its roots to Spanish nobility, and the rising independence and empowerment of his daughters and a cryptically gay son. All siblings engage in taboo relationships, in-cluding marriage, with white American males who arrive as part of the ascendant US capitalist order. María Cotera jointly recovered the novel with José E. Limón, and duly critiques the elite context of the narrative. Yet, despite its ambiguous depictions of the US settler-colonialist project, which is as patriarchal as the Mexican order it is replacing, *Caballero* nonetheless is lauded as a precursor to Chicana and Latina feminist critiques of masculinist paradigms of Mexican American, Chicana/o, and Latina/o subjectivity. In the epilogue to the novel Cotera cites Angie Chabram Dernersesian to situate *Caballero* as the protofeminist antithesis of Paredes's *With His Pistol in His Hand*, and the phallocentric shadow it casts over Chicana/o Studies: "[*Caballero*'s] multiplicity of voices provides a literary coun-terpoint to the emergent myth of the singular Chicano 'warrior hero' who battles the forces of outside oppression 'with his pistol in his hand,' while maintaining a patriarchal code of oppression within the home" (Cotera 1996, 340).

Vincent Pérez (2006), however, qualifies readings of *Caballero* as protofeminist. He argues that the novel's genealogical location between the *hacienda* nostalgia of nineteenth- and early twentieth-century Latin America, and American southern plantation epics such as Margaret Mitchell's 1936 *Gone with the Wind*, trap *Caballero* within the hierarchical racialized teleologies of these traditions. After all, one of the most important pairings in *Caballero* involves Don Santiago's youngest daughter, Susanita, who is described as hav-ing "smooth, creamy skin" (Raleigh and González 1996, 50), and is named after a grandmother who was "golden haired and green eyed" (1996, 20). She marries US Army Lieutenant Robert Warrener, a Virginia plantation owner and slaveholder. This pair will close the

narrative by cradling their mixed-heritage but consummately white
child. In a symbolically significant scene, Lieutenant Warrener will
be the person who discovers Don Santiago's dead body, with the
Don's crumpled fist full of earth from the hacienda that Warrener
will now legally own under the patriarchal land tenure policies of the
new Anglo-American common law, which deprived married women
of inheritance rights. This new US juridical order supplanted
Mexican-Spanish Roman law, under which Susanita would have
retained a claim to her father's estate. Of this vexed Euromestizaje,
Pérez adds:

> In *Caballero* (hacienda) pastoralism symbolically serves the "south-
> ern cause" of marking Yankee (capitalist) difference, a not unexpected
> consequence of interethnic romantic unions that symbolically unite
> the two seigneurial "Souths" as much as they do Americans and
> Mexicans. Mirror-image pastoral descriptions of the plantation and
> hacienda consummate the regional "marriage." (2006, 103)

Pérez extends debates in Postcolonial and Decolonial Studies that
question the presumed subaltern status of third world cosmopoli-
tans—including elite US-born or raised Latina/os—who claim the
relative cultural capital of being labeled as Other without confronting their racial or class privilege. Pérez's reading of *Caballero's*
seigneurial milieu demonstrates the contingent nature of the subaltern designation in Chicana/o Studies. Moreover, in this novel,
war and romance, and wartime romance, disrupt the overextended
resistance paradigm.

Raleigh and González's Eurocentric racialized signifying practices
have remained largely unacknowledged. This is surprising given that
the novel features cross-ethnic marriages among white Tejanas and
white Americans, with no cross-racial and cross-class unions
between elite Mexican or American whites with darker-skinned
mestiza/o peons or Indians. The novel thus relies on neocolonial
logic and language that create a troubling geometry of signification:
the marginal mestiza/o subjects of *Caballero* frame a racialized narrative order in which the effaced (and erased) indigenous Other
enables the empowerment of white Mexican subjects at the center of
the narrative. These white Mexican-cum-Mexican American figures
are indirect beneficiaries—as well as outright perpetrators—of violence against Indians and mestiza/o peons. Jacques Derrida reminds

us, however, that ignored utterances and supplemental signs simultaneously undergird and undermine a text's meaning.[14] In *Caballero*, "native" light-skinned criollo Mexican privileges inevitably are threatened as this population increasingly becomes hyphenated—and figurally darkened—as "Mexican-American," and subsequently displaced through a new layer of imperial violence by other European-descent settler colonialists and imperialists from the expansionist United States. Ironically, *Caballero's* purportedly feminist retort thus segues with Paredes's settler-colonialist nostalgia.

Ultimately, this celebrated novel relies upon Indians and mestizos as its substrate: it figures them as little more than geohistorical props *sous rature* who frame, as negative reference points, the otherwise visionary constructions of the empowered transethnic—but unmistakably white—Mexican American feminist and gay male subjects of history. As a case in point, early in the novel mestizaje is troped as marginal, literally and figurally blackened, and thus fundamentally abject:

> A few vaqueros from the range camps, burnt almost black by the daily sun and eternal winds, walked stiffly on bowed legs and stood, shy as strangers, just inside the gate, circling worn large hats in nervous fingers. (1996, 5)

Feeling uneasy as they enter their criollo overlord's compound, these *vaqueros*, or Mexican cowboys, whose legs have become deformed by the mounted ranch work into which they were born in the neofeudal encomienda system, are uncomfortably aware of their intrusion into the narrative gate. They dare not venture further. Nor do they speak. The authors would never allow it. Arguably, in a chronicle about residual criollo settler colonialism at the moment of its absorption into an expansionist white American settler colonialism, they simply could not allow it. *Caballero* is about someone else. Thus, even as the novel recuperates and recenters Tejana, as well as Tejano gay male subjects, it reifies the silence, subordination, and violent elimination of the underclass, racialized indigenous and mestiza/o Others whose exclusion is constitutive of this depiction of nineteenth-century Tejana feminist and Tejano gay male empowerment.

The authors reiterate and compound this rhetorical landscape a few sentences later. In a scene that reads as a critique of taboo desire embedded in traditional patriarchy, Susanita's upperclass Mexican whiteness again claims its central space in the narrative plot. Echoing José Enrique Rodó's Eurocentric paradigm for the Americas, Raleigh and González write:

> He [Don Santiago] still insisted that the gorgeous hair [of his daughter Susanita] be allowed to hang in braids like a child's, as if that would keep her a child a little longer. As she stopped to squeeze his hand and return his tender smile, he twisted the end of a braid round his finger, marveling anew at the spun-gold fineness and sheen of this heritage from his Asturian ancestors—already so rare among his people that it seemed a gift from heaven. Lovely was the cream skin, delicate the molding of the red lips. And her eyes were like limpid green water upon which a vagrant cloud had left a remembrance of gray. (1996, 5)

As is the case with the Mexican American female characters in María Amparo Ruiz de Burton's 1885 historical romance *The Squatter and the Don*, another celebrated Mexican American novel set among an elite family of white Spanish-descent Californios in the same period, Raleigh and González's protagonist Susanita is never given the opportunity to disavow the privilege of her whiteness, which is fetishized by her father and other *caballeros*, or gentlemen ranchers. While this passage can be read as the authors' illumination of the many ironies in this racially polarized context, Susanita's whiteness is never troped outside the discursive confines of the neo-Petrarchan model of "fair" beauty. In contrast, the authors depict peons, as a class, as barely human in their half nakedness and public scatological performances:

> Servants came out of the rooms opposite, their flat huaraches making flapping sounds on the portico floor. Peons came on silent bare feet through the small gate from their quarters outside the wall; dozens of them, from naked infants suckling noisily at bare young breasts down to bent, old people. (1996, 4)

Despite the profound ruptures the novel proposes, its critique of patriarchy manifestly relies on tired racial and class—and specifically racialized class—binaries that are enforced by physical, epistemic, and figural violences.

Native Americans fare worse in the Eurocentric cultural logic of *Caballero*. Labeled "Indians" and lumped together in a nondifferentiated mass of people with no tribal affiliations, they are consistently associated with savagery through direct pairings of the term "Indians" with bestial references such as "infested" (1996, 282) and "marauding" (1996, 56, 262). This racist language is never overtly or even implicitly challenged by any character. Conversely, the elite Mexican and Mexican American characters who refer to white Americans as "Gringos" (1996, 48, 51, 78) and "barbarians" (1996, 52, 230, 253) are invariably unreliable or overzealous caricatures. For instance, Don Santiago's first-born son Alvaro, the protégé of the hacienda don and warrior hero, conveniently dies in battle against the Americans to clear the way for his sister's white American husband to take over his father's estate. The Don's gay son and daughters ventriloquize the epithets directed at "Gringos" for the express purpose of debunking these characterizations, enabling the consummation of cross-cultural white bonding in a series of interethnic pairings and marriages between white Mexican and white American characters. There is only one racialized critique that some white American settlers cannot overcome. Don Gabriel, another Tejano aristocrat, verbalizes it as he somberly reflects on the fait accompli of US domination of their land: this process began, he recalls, with the Texas war of independence and Mexican General Santa Anna's surrender to "that infidel, squaw-loving Samuel Houston" (1996, 9). This inflammatory distancing of Tejana/o characters from Native Americans and other indigenous people is never challenged. Significantly, and disturbingly, of all the caballeros introduced in the novel, anti-Indian Don Gabriel is the only one represented as pensive, rational, and sound. In *Caballero*, Euromestizajes are acceptable; white-Indian pairings are not. B. J. Manríquez has proposed that *Caballero* presents, but then undermines, "Don Santiago's arrogance and racism" against white Americans (2000, 174). In truth, however, Raleigh and González's antiindigenous signifying practices actually reinforce racist depictions of mestiza/os and Indians in the guise of challenging the neofeudal socioeconomic order that gave rise to these depictions. *Caballero* certainly is a feminist novel, but it is a racist one, too.

T. Jackie Cuevas (2018) has recovered *Caballero* as a protoqueer narrative, but even this provocative reclamation does not disrupt the novel's resonance as an antimestizaje narrative of the border. Ironically, in addition to failing as a counterpoint to Paredes's recentering of the masculinist borderlands Pocho, *Caballero* also is an unwitting antithesis to Anzaldúa's decidedly lesbian, indigenous-centered, dark-skinned model of Chicana feminist subjectivity and agency she called the new mestiza. Raleigh and González instead locate their narrative of Mexican American women's empowerment on "this Indian-infested wilderness" (1996, 282). Their repeated references to such tropes of savagery fix the narrative space at the margins of civilization. This rhetoric renders the novel as a violently discursive site for colonialist self-actualization and, at the other end, mestizaje damnation. This discursive feature is reminiscent of Jean Rhys, Joseph Conrad, Rudyard Kipling, J. Frank Dobie, and legions of other white European and white American cultural imperialist authors.

The gendered racial poetics of *Caballero* invite an adaptation of Joyce Zonana's critique of Charlotte Bronte's exoticist cultural imperialist symbology in her 1847 novel *Jane Eyre*, which Zonana dubs "Feminist Orientalism" (1993, 592).[15] Following Edward Said's 1979 critique of Western imperialist signifying in *Orientalism*, and Walter Mignolo's similar excavations in his 1995 *The Darker Side of the Renaissance: Literacy, Territoriality, and Colonization*, a host of Latin American literature scholars have noted how Spanish colonialists overlaid their preceding racist imperialist encounters with Moors onto the dark-brown-skinned indigenous population they encountered in the Americas. The related term *moreno*, which survives in the contemporary Mexican and Chicana/o lexicon as "brown," is so powerful a racial signifier it has replaced *pardo*, the standard Castilian term for the color. This imbedded memory of racial conquest appears in a multiplicity of forms in *Caballero*, such as Don Santiago's name, which comes to the New World from the Spanish epic hero "Santiago Matamorros" or "Saint James the Moor Killer." This archetype is part of a fictionalized gallery of figures who buttress an allegorical superstructure pitting the Christian West against the Muslim East. Some accounts locate St. James's appearance in key battles in the Christian effort to reclaim the Iberian Peninsula after 700 years of Muslim Moroccan rule. Revealingly, in *Caballero* the Mexican border town of Matamoros located across the river from Fort Brown, where the first battle in the US-Mexico War occurred, is a retreat and refuge for the Mendoza y Soría family and other hacienda criollo families. Rather than offering a critique of empire through this geographic irony, the imaginative language of *Caballero* is consequently structured as an imperialist palimpsest. Yet, the authors rely on situational irony in the scene in which the caballero patriarch dies with a handful of earth that the new white American patriarch will inherit. Even in this scene, the authors seem oblivious to another irony: the resultant loss of Mexican women's inheritance rights in the new US juridical order that in many respects is the antithesis of feminism.

This discursive legacy inevitably undermines the novel's oppositional pretentions. Its traffic in the tropology of Spanish imperialism that has migrated to the US-Mexico borderlands reveals a violently racialized imperialist symbolic system in an otherwise visionary narrative of nineteenth-century feminist and queer agency. González and Raleigh unfortunately situate their chronicle of proto-Chicana feminist and proto-Chicano gay empowerment within an elite criollo framework: Native and mestiza/o inhabitants are depicted as childlike, dark figures standing just a few steps within the gate, hat in hand, head down, trembling, and barely daring to cast their own gaze into the narrative space. The distinct nineteenth-century Tejana Feminist-Orientalist, settler-colonialist violentology featured in the novel did not recognize Indians and mestiza/os as speaking subjects of history, even as the narrative relied upon them to frame a new episteme.

"A Leopard in a Cage": Andrew Garcia's Ethnic and Racial Shape-Shifting in the American West

As noted, the aforementioned Mexican American and coauthored white American and Tejana narratives about nineteenth-century wartime encounters between Latina/os and Indians fail to introduce well-rounded black, mestiza/o, or indigenous characters. Yet, they also refuse to peddle patronizing simplistic portraits of white characters who purportedly "go native" only to return home more "ennobled" after their time among "noble savages," a trope that has animated a persistent trajectory of American literature from the eighteenth century to the present. Andrew Garcia's controversial *Tough Trip through Paradise,* a record of his "frontier" life in Montana from 1878 to 1879, lies between violently Eurocentric poetics, and the appropriative invocations of indigeneity by cultural nationalists such as Alurista. Garcia's abridged memoir, composed in the late nineteenth century and posthumously published in 1967, narrativizes his life of ethnic and racial shape-shifting among several Native American tribes and an assortment of picaresque miners, outlaws,

FIGURE 1.1. *Mexican American mountain man Andrew Garcia in Montana, circa 1890. Courtesy of Montana Historical Society Photograph Archives, Helena, Montana.*

and Montana mountain men in the intensely violent nineteenth-century American West[16] (Figure 1.1). Garcia's narrative enacts a radical ambiguity that neither effaces nor reifies ethnic or racial boundaries in the broader performances of Tejana/o and proto-Chicana/o identity formation, particularly those revolving around Mexican American indigeneity. Rather, Garcia consolidates a hybrid subjectivity in the interstices between the warring peoples and races that collide in events leading up to the 1877 Nez Perce War.[17] Unlike the anti-Indian Tejana/o violentologies discussed above, Garcia synthesizes a hybrid proto-*LatIndio* alternative that he repeatedly places under erasure in responsible and productive ways. Ironically, he preserves the viability of indigenous-based Latinidades by circumscribing, and even denying, Latina/o claims to indigeneity.

Garcia's narrative involves a more complicated martial and antiromantic negotiation of Mexican American whiteness and indigeneity than the proto-Chicana/o historical figures and writers discussed throughout Chapter 1, even as it intersects with the lethal ambivalence inscribed in Juan Bernal's 1887 memoir. Garcia opens by rehearsing the legacy of *castas*, the racialized hierarchies, or castes, from colonial Mexico. For instance, he peppers *Tough Trip through Paradise* with epithets such as "bad Injun" (1967, 25, 385, 421), "good Injun" (1967, 150), "copper colored" (1967, 22, 317), and "nigger" (1967, 63). Some of these terms, disturbing as they are, nonetheless operate as floating signifiers that enable subtle but significant reclamations and critical revisions of the conventional racial logic of the nineteenth century, placing Garcia in tense dialogue with the Latina/o literary canon. One example involves his etymology and subsequent use of the term *squaw*, an Algonquian term that literally refers to a woman, but which also carries more derogatory racist meanings in colonial contexts. Some lay etymologies also define the term as a vernacular form of *vagina*, which accentuates its racist and sexist virulence. Furthermore, it has heterosexist and homophobic connotations when used to denigrate a white male who marries an Indian woman, and a male who is seen as "effeminate" for doing "women's work." Dubbed the "Squaw Kid" (1967, 136, 446) by fellow mountain men in Montana for his marriage to a Nez Perce woman and his relative assimilation into the Nez Perce community, Garcia never contests the term's gendered sexualized assaults on women or his own masculinity, nor does he resist denigrating allusions to miscegenation.

However, even as he is interpellated into the racist sexist logic of his milieu, Garcia partially deconstructs the exoticist indigenist stereotype of the passive and submissive Indian-woman-as-lover. According to Diane Smith, Garcia was motivated in part by a desire to "present a positive portrait of Indian women" (2008, 14). After uncovering evidence that photos of the three Indian women Garcia claimed were his wives may actually have been widely circulated professional photos, with one possibly being a popular studio photo of a Navajo male, Smith adds:

> the portraits, with their individualized dignity, may not have pictured his actual wives, but they apparently represented the way in which Garcia wanted his wives to be remembered. More significantly, they appear to be the lens through which he wanted the "Squaw Kid" to be viewed. (2008, 18)

The photo of a possible Two-Spirit (or a person who embodies an interstitial third gender) "wife," as well as Garcia's "Squaw Kid" moniker, invite provocative queerings of Garcia's fluid navigations of gender and sexuality in the hypermasculinist world of Montana mountain men. From this liminal space, Garcia pursues his dual goal of honoring his Native wives and contextualizing his acculturations and limited assimilations in Indian Country. He does so by introducing a counterpoint to the prevailing paternalistic romanticism of the era. Smith notes that Garcia's memoir was initially imagined as a three-volume biography of his Nez Perce wife In-Who-Lise. This motive also involves a profound intervention: in one episode where he and In-Who-Lise are captured and face certain death among white Montana settlers determined to avenge Nez Perce killings of their comrades a few days earlier, Garcia reiterates how his Indian wife demands her own role as a speaking subject of history. Garcia, who is negotiating for their lives, initially advises her not to reveal her English-speaking skills to their assailants, who slander her with epithets as if she were not present. But she shoots back:

> Yes, call me Injun, call me a squaw, that's all right; I am that. Evil white dog that you are, who can only fight a squaw, just call me an Injun bitch again, and I'll kill you this time where you stand.   (1967, 434)

This encounter can be collapsed into the tropology of the American West, where Indian and mestiza women are depicted as hot-blooded and ill-tempered spinsters. But the frequency with which In-Who-Lise occupies speaking roles in this dialogic narrative creates a unique space in a nineteenth-century Mexican American text for a well-rounded Native American woman's subjectivity and resistant agency. Notably, similar references to indigenous women are completely absent from any of the previously discussed texts in Chapter 1, including *Caballero*, where they are even more effaced than the novel's indigenous and mestizo male peons who appear in the novel.

This is not to say that Garcia is less of a settler-colonialist than Seguin, Paredes, or Raleigh and González. After all, *Tough Trip through Paradise* involves pseudo-anthropological taxonomies of the virtues and pathologies of various Native and mixed-heritage subjects, including "Mexican half-breed" (1967, 19), and particularly "half-breed American greaser" (1967, 114), who are sometimes his allies but mostly villains. Yet, and quite significantly, Garcia reserves his most incisive critiques for white men, including whites of

"Spanish" descent, a category of the era used for Mexican Americans such as Juan Seguin and the criollo protagonists of *Caballero*. Garcia's designation of Mexican Americans as "white," distanced these historical figures and fictional characters from the more overtly racialized mestiza/os or, to use Garcia's term, "half breeds," which he shortens as "Breed" (1967, 38, 400, 423). Using his own subject position as a point of departure, Garcia proffers a theory of whiteness that does not efface Spanish American (also read as Mexican American) whiteness; rather, he acknowledges and historicizes it as colonialist and fundamentally violent, if not outright evil. Garcia writes:

> the English and French were not any good either.... Bad as they were, however, they were angels compared to the people I came from.
>
> (1967, 79)

Having previously described himself as a "woolly Texan from Spanish America" (1967, 6), he adds, "I was born on the Rio Grande in southwest Texas and near the New Mexico line being of Spanish-American extraction" (1967, 360). That is, he is marking his own violent whiteness as a Mexican American. He concludes his eugenicist self-reflection by noting, "I was not raised for nothing in that glorious country down on the Rio Grande, where they could cut a throat twice for a dollar" (1967, 63).

Despite his self-deprecating candor, Garcia's hyperbolic neo-Western narrative—a genre distinguished by nominal cultural exchanges and frequent episodes of graphic violence against Native Americans—is significant for its refusal to offer a reductively linear portrayal of going native, or even a standard American unilateral tale of a subject who goes native to later return home as an ennobled indigenized white man. Garcia instead begins by recognizing his own bigotries and colonialist legacy as a white Mexican American:

> The Spaniards, in brutality, cruelty and treachery outshone them all, and were known, hated and feared more than all others by the Indian. Having this deadly hatred born in me and having seen the cruelty and deviltry of the Indians, it could not be expected that I would have had any love for the Indian. Before, I had always helped those who were hunting them down.   (1967, 79)

A few lines later, he adds, "the Indian was only fighting for his life and liberty and a square deal, which he knew, from past experience, that he could not get from a white man" (1967, 79). This humanist identification comes after a nine-year period when Garcia lived as a member of the Nez Perce and Pend d'Orielle communities as the husband of his Nez Perce Indian wife, In-Who-Lise, and later, two Pend d'Oreille Indian wives, Squis-squis, followed by Mal-lit-tay-lay. Garcia's experience—which was mined for the 1970 Hollywood film *Little Big Man* starring Dustin Hoffman—includes the obligatory misrecognition scenes characteristic of captivity narratives, in which Garcia's whiteness is not immediately recognized by other whites, who almost kill him after confusing Garcia for an Indian (1967, 385).

Garcia's metacritical meditations about his violent navigations of race, gender, and sexuality make him a quintessential violentological subject. Indeed, the violence of Garcia's milieu includes genocidal wars by whites against Indians, intertribal conflict resulting in the killing of his wife In-Who-Lise by a Blackfoot warrior, and gratuitous beatings, robberies, and murders by the mixed lot of miscreants lumped together in the romantic moniker "mountain men."[18] Garcia—the Squaw Kid—is weaned and defined by these and other violences. Furthermore, his mountain man subjectivity inevitably becomes a supra-Latina/o violentology in the neo-Hobbesian dystopic context where no one can escape the *bellum omnium contra omnes* (the war of all against all) because there is no omnipotent central government in the region to act as an arbitrator. There is no fixed nation-state that controls the space, so neither citizenship claims nor liminal sensibilities are sufficient to keep one alive. Instead, Garcia survives because of his virtuosity as a horseman, hunter, marksman, distrust of everyone, hand-to-hand combatant skills, willingness to kill, actual killing of diverse people, and versatile cross-cultural shape-shifting.

Garcia also recognizes the inherent limit of his shape-shifting and the old colonialist trope of going native, a discourse inscribed with multiple rhetorical and kinetic violences, primarily against indigenous people. He instead marks the liminal status he occupies after realizing he never really went Native even as he appears to have done so. In the masculinist logic of his narrative, he emphasizes that his last wife, Barbara Voll, was white. Later in life Garcia was ensconced with Voll deep in the Montana mountains, except for forays among whites in town as he pursued various occupations; his main activity was telling stories about his life as a Montana mountain man. His great epiphany comes from realizing that after marrying four women—three Indian and one white—and living almost a decade among and as a provisionally adopted member of at least two Indian tribes, in addition to another decade of life among diverse trappers, horse thieves, murderers, and miners in Montana, Garcia never succeeded at becoming a "white man" again.

Resisting the progress narrative trajectory of Raleigh and González's *Caballero,* or the tragic mestizo and criollo narrative frameworks of Paredes's *George Washington Gómez* and Seguín's *Memorias,* Garcia's *Tough Trip through Paradise* begins and ends with reflections on Mexican American whiteness and his own ambivalent indigeneity. "It is forty-three years today since I left them and tried again to be a white man," he writes. Garcia concludes, "Though I now follow the white man's ways and have a good home, and many will tell you I ought to have no kick coming, still I am a leopard in a cage" (1967, 6). Garcia's choice of metaphors is significant because a leopard is wild, not native to the Americas, and it has dark spots interspersed among its dark gold fur. More importantly, in contrast to contemporary constructions of Mexican American and Chicana/o difference (whether it be indigenous or mestiza/o) as inherently subaltern and opposed to US settler colonialism and imperialism, Garcia painstakingly recovers and recognizes his Spanish-descent whiteness to chart his difference as a "white Indian," then as an incompletely reassimilated white Mexican American—in Montana of all places! In so doing, he places Mexican American indigeneity under erasure yet again, but in radically different ways than in the Latina/o life writing genres explicated in Chapter 1. Garcia thereby anticipates contemporary rearticulations of XicanIndia/o and LatIndia/o paradigms, replete with racialized gendered slippages, contradictory negotiations of power, and occasional revolutionary potential.

"Ah Thot Yew Wuz a Real Injun": The Red Road and XicanIndia/o Internationalism

Andrew Garcia's liminal white Mexican American indigeneity provides a candid meditation on the possibilities and limits of the trope of going native, which subsequent generations of Latina/os have performed through ever more complicated, diverse, and ideologically distinct neoindigenous XicanIndia/o and LatIndia/o paradigms.

For instance, Inés Hernández-Ávila (formerly Hernández-Tovar), of Nez Perce and Chicana heritage, is renowned for her multilingual fusions of indigenous and mestiza/o chants and popular Chicana/o conjunto songs. Patrisia Gonzales, of Kickapoo, Comanche, and Macehual descent, is a journalist, research scholar, and community educator who recuperates pre-Columbian medicinal, dietary, and ritual practices as part of a XicanIndia/o decolonial politic. Margo Tamez, of Chicana and Lipan Apache heritage, is a scholar and activist engaged in a multifaceted feminist Pan-Indian rejuvenation of ritual practice, as well as a battle to reclaim ancestral and family lands the US government has expropriated to extend the US-Mexico border wall. Many more Chicana/o and Boricua authors claim indigenous heritage and tribal affiliations through birth, adoption, marriage, and other avenues specific to individual tribal nations, including Luis J. Rodriguez (Chicano and Apache), Jimmy Santiago Baca (Chicano and Apache), and Lorna Dee Cervantes (Chicana and Chumash).

Raúl R. Salinas, whose pen name is raúlrsalinas, offers another permutation in the long and convoluted genealogy of XicanIndia/o identities whose array of ideological trajectories can be fully understood by attention to their distinct violent subtexts. He is renowned for antilyric explications of his Pachuco and Pinto subjectivity in the seminal 1970 Chicana/o poem, "A Trip Through the Mind Jail," and 1980 book, *Un Trip Through the Mind Jail Y Otras Excursions*. Salinas also presents an archive that chronicles his path from Chicana/o detribalization to indigenous reclamation, anticipating foundational mestiza neoindigenous reclamation projects such as Anzaldúa's epochal 1987 *Borderlands/La Frontera*. Salinas's decades-long solidarity work with various Native American and global indigenous organizations and communities includes his marriage to a woman from the Suquamish Nation and the birth of their child. He also produced a collection of poems, *Indio Trails: A Xicano Odyssey through Indian Country*, written from the 1970s to the 1980s, and published in 2006 under his adopted Suquamish name, Autumn Sun. This book, along with related writings and activities on behalf of the American Indian Treaty Council, Leonard Peltier Defense Committee, and Ejército Zapatista para la Liberación Nacional (Zapatista National Liberation Army known by the Spanish acronym EZLN), punctuates Salinas's XicanIndia/o violentology: it is an *insider's* XicanIndio account of Native American and global indigenous history during the violent era of the Red Power Movement and contemporaneous indigenous decolonial struggles that included armed insurrection throughout Indian Country in North, Central, and South America from the 1960s to his death in 2008.

Raised in Austin, Texas, by his Chicana mother and a white WWII Navy veteran stepfather, Salinas spent twelve years in prison for drug possession and distribution convictions. While in prison, his independent and group study in Chicana/o and broader Latina/o history and culture led him to poetry. His poetic progressively evolved from expressions of existentialist angst to a cultural nationalist sensibility. Salinas's interactions with Puerto Rican independentista and black and white revolutionary prisoners eventually led to his development of a communist internationalist vision.[19] Upon his release from prison in 1972, conditions of his parole prevented Salinas from returning to Texas, so he moved to Seattle, Washington, where he had support from activist professors at the University of Washington. He eventually gravitated toward a network of Chicana/o and Indian activists. Amid his activities with various organizations that intersected at El Centro de la Raza, he was adopted into the Suquamish Nation, which bestowed upon him the name, Autumn Sun. Significantly, Salinas's autobiographical poetry introduces a further complication to Chicana/o indigeneity because, like most Chicana/os, Salinas was detribalized but also retribalized and, according to him, always already indigenous. While his indigenous heritage is marked upon his dark-brown skin—which he underscored through his frequent use of the XicanIndia/o term-of-endearment "Skinz"—it is difficult to trace exact ancestral tribal affiliations after several centuries and layers of mestizajes, all of which are inscribed by multiple violences.

Salinas alludes to the lingering legacy and multiple layers of this trauma in the poem, "Conversation in a Greyhound Bus Depot Coffee Shop." It opens his aptly titled 2000 debut recording, *Los Many Mundos of Raúl Salinas: Un Poetic Jazz Viaje con Friends*, and his aforementioned 2006 collection, *Indio Trails*, the last book published during his lifetime. The dramatic dialogue reads in its entirety:

> "Say buddy are yew a injun?"
> Well hell yea, man.
> "Whut kind?"
> What kind!? Mexican!

"Oh. ah thot yew wuz a real injun."
As he proceeded to tell me
(quite boringly)
about his 1/64th blood quantum
and his Cherokee PRINCESS grandmother;
my prison-like coffee was getting cold,
my bus was pulling out…
and
it
was
time
to go! (3)

In this poem, Salinas's picaresque poetic persona has little patience for the familiar white American appropriations of stereotypical models of indigeneity, even as he is aware of the troubling role eugenics has played in classifications of indigenous peoples through blood quantum laws. In an illustration of his dialogic poetics, Salinas provides the voice for both speakers in a performance of the poem for the 2000 documentary video, *Voices from Texas* by Ray Santisteban, replete with Texas country twang and urban Chicano convict attitude (Figure 1.2). Salinas thereby enacts a XicanIndio paradigm that racializes, without essentializing, the detribalized, though still indisputably indigenous nature, of his own Chicanismo, or Chicano subjectivity. His *ars poetica* thus is both a phenomenological and an ontological intervention. It also is an *ars politica*. In the introduction to *Indio Trails*, Louis Mendoza aptly notes:

> Readers familiar with Salinas' poetry and political work already know that his life's journey has been one of constant exploration and transformation, a journey that, among other moments of *conscientizaçao*, included a new awareness that as a Chicano his history and destiny are intertwined with that of American Indians. For him, however, this was never a moment for solipsistic self-indulgence, but a call to action, an obligation that required him to integrate two identities he had been taught to think of as distinct from one another. The result was a Xicanindio perspective that charted a path for his politics and his poetry. (2006, xi)

Violence is the unifying thread in Salinas's multiple journeys of transformation in underdeveloped barrios, jail and prison battlegrounds;

FIGURE 1.2. *Raúl Salinas in "Conversation at a Greyhound Bus Station,"* Voices from Texas *(2007), by Ray Santisteban. Courtesy of Ray Santisteban.*

insurgent movements in Mexico, Puerto Rico, and the United States; as well as international solidarity activities in support of decolonial wars of national liberation and mature revolutions.

The journey motif Salinas adopted as his signature poetic traverses a range of subjectivities and activities whose ideologies were all shaped by multiple violences that he redirected into proactive political praxis. Among his many persona, Raúl Salinas identified as a Zapatista, an anarcho-communitarian indigenous paradigm that continues to animate his followers who gravitate around the fourth incarnation of Resistencia Bookstore, which he founded in Austin, Texas, in the 1980s. The name of the bookstore came to resonate as a Zapatista "sitio de resistencia," or an autonomous liberated zone outside government control, which also implies contestatory identities outside the polis. Before his Zapatista phase, Salinas identified as a Marxist-Leninist, and in an earlier period of postprison life, he was an avowed Maoist.[20] Throughout his life, Salinas was a dialectical thinker, and continually sought to synthesize binaries. This included his pairing of the Indian Red Road with the international communist struggle for which red—as a symbol for the blood of revolutionary violence—likewise serves as a central metaphor in his *oeuvre*. Salinas's model of Chicana/o indigeneity accordingly involves a hybrid and transspatial identity that encompasses all of Indian Country (the Americas), in addition to other subordinated parts of the world, from farms to factories, and the farthest reaches of the world's mountains, jungles, plains, and deserts. Salinas's never-ending negative dialectical performance of his self as many selves continually being synthesized also includes a corresponding communist internationalist logic that includes armed struggle as a necessary part of liberatory praxis required to transform a capitalist imperialist world.

Salinas forged a revolutionary internationalist XicanIndio vision out of a long history of collaborations that bear out his transracial, international, and supranational politics. For instance, in addition to being a member of the Venceremos Brigade, an organization founded by Americans dedicated to supporting Cuba's socialist revolution, Salinas was trained and prepared to join the final offensive of the Sandinista Revolution in 1979 alongside his San Francisco, California, compatriots Chicano Alejandro Murguía and Nicaraguan American Roberto Vargas, among others.[21] Shortly before Salinas's planned departure to Nicaragua, however, the Leonard Peltier Defense Committee dispatched him to assist Peltier—who had escaped from a US prison—infiltrate into Canada to seek political asylum. Significantly, Salinas's solidarity with the Marxist-influenced Sandinista Revolution coexisted with his critique of Sandinista abuses of indigenous people, specifically the English-speaking, mixed-heritage Afromestiza/o Meskito Indians, many of whom joined the anti-Sandinista counterrevolutionary insurgents out of frustration with Sandinista rejections of their claims for cultural and territorial autonomy[22] (Figures 1.3 and 1.4). In fact, Salinas's lifelong engagement with social movements in support of various oppressed populations in struggle continued to navigate both poles of the Red-as-Indian and red-as-communist dyad, so that he was never doctrinaire or static in his XicanIndio paradigm.

Salinas's Marxist XicanIndio politics also were in dialogue with indigenous socialist interlocutors far outside the Americas. He was part of a delegation of Chicana/os who traveled to Libya in 1981 by invitation of then-leader Muammar Gaddafi, an indigenous Bedouin who had adapted an anticolonial, African-centric, indigenous, and Islamic socialist movement that sought to bridge the ancient with

FIGURE 1.3. *Legion of the Lost: The True Experience of an American in the French Foreign Legion (Berkley Caliber, 2005), by Jaime Salazar*

FIGURE 1.4. *Raúl Salinas with Sandinista Soldiers, Nicaragua, circa 1980. Courtesy of Lawrence Salinas and the Raúl Salinas Estate.*

the modern. Gaddafi codified this philosophy of praxis he called the *Jamahiriya* ("state of the masses") in his 1975 *Green Book*.[23] Salinas also worked with Zapatistas and traveled to the Lacandon jungle in Chiapas to participate in an EZLN congress. This relationship with indigenous communities in Southern Mexico who took up arms in the early 1990s to challenge their extreme economic, social, and political oppression, began much earlier: the inside jacket to Salinas's 2000 audio recording, *Los Many Mundos de raúlrsalinas*, includes a collage with a photo of Salinas holding an M-2 carbine rifle during insurgent training in the 1970s (Figure 1.5). During this time, Chicana/os had been engaging in cross-border dialogues and col- laborations with segments of the Mexican left, which had been engaging in mass mobilizations, including armed insurrection, fol- lowing the Mexican government's massacre of students in 1968 as part of its dirty war against leftists.

Salinas's recuperation of indigeneity, and his global inflection of a complex revolutionary XicanIndio epistemology and ontology, all

FIGURE 1.5. *Raúl Salinas, insurgent training in unknown location, circa 1970s. Courtesy of Lawrence Salinas and the Raúl Salinas Estate.*

traverse through the hyper local barrio of his youth. Salinas became renowned as a Pinto (or Chicano prisoner) poet for his 1970 poem, "A Trip Through the Mind Jail," which is celebrated as one of the four foundational poems in modern Chicana/o literature.[24] However, his poetic is not solely grounded in his Pinto, and Pachuco (barrio hipster) subjectivities. Rather, his philosophy of art was articulated as part of his *compromiso y deber*—commitment and obligation—as a XicanIndio who was recognized in multiple communities as an elder, or a wise and ethical teacher and arbitrator. It is important to note that one does not claim the mantel of an elder; rather, this accolade is ascribed to one by community members. In his poem "About Invasion and Conquest," first published in his 1995 poetry collection, *East of the Freeway*, and republished in *Indio Trails* (2006, 90-1), Salinas demonstrates his XicanIndio raison d'être. A dramatic dialogue, the poem opens with a catalogue of postconquest atrocities before presenting a youthful speaker who asks: "Who will live to tell / of what happened to us, Grandmother?" She responds that "among the survivors / there will be poets" (lines 34-5, 37-8). Salinas closes the poem with his figurally transgendered poetic persona joining the conversation:

> And today, when 500 winters have passed,
> among the survivors
> are poets
> sitting in circle
> telling the story
> of peoples in struggle
> in total
> > Resistencia!
> and with plena
> > Dignidad. (lines 47-56)[25]

Before the completion of this poem, Salinas was a delegate on an International Indian Treaty Council trip to an international human rights symposium in Geneva, Switzerland, in 1981 (Figure 1.6). He journeyed there not just to speak on behalf of Indians, but *as* an Indian, with his XicanIndio identity serving as a de facto tribe similar to the Métis in Canada and the Meskito in Nicaragua, in addition to many more contexts outside the United States.

As with Garcia, no extant paradigm in Latina/o Studies can fully account for Salinas's navigations of detribalization and retribalization,

FIGURE 1.6. *Raúl Salinas/Autumn Sun (fourth from left) with fellow members of the American Indian Treaty Council, circa 1970s. Courtesy of Lawrence Salinas and the Raúl Salinas Estate, and Stanford University Green Library Special Collections.*

localized national and internationalist filiations, as well as vernacular barrio and global communist sensibilities. These journeys entailed multiple transformations and, importantly, can never be disarticulated from various violences: the predatory barrio boy of Salinas's gangster days is intertwined with his prison survival tactics and ultimate transformation into a revolutionary; similarly, his postprison retribalization as an indigenous activist segues with kinetic theories of revolutionary violence he deployed in solidarity with oppressed peoples throughout the world.

Indian Countries: LatIndia/os and the Problem of US Citizenship

The category of supra-Latina/o violentologies is precise yet flexible enough to accommodate a wide range of LatIndia/o paradigms that variously replay the dissonant legacy of Latina/o ambivalence and antipathy towards, and multiple violences against, Native Americans and indigenous people throughout the world, which coexists with instances of mutual identification and solidarity. Within this spectrum lie contradictory performances of LatIndia/o subjectivity that purport to be oppositional to, yet ultimately are constitutive of US imperialism. The flamboyant indigenous-identified character in *Rolling Stone* journalist Evan Wright's (2004) real-time war reportage and David Simon and colleagues' related 2008 HBO series, *Generation Kill*, dramatically illustrates this paradox. The book and television series focus on a platoon of soldiers from the First Marine Reconnaissance Battalion involved in the 2003 US invasion of Iraq, which US troops euphemistically called "Indian Country" in an allusion to the nineteenth-century Indian Wars in which US troops were conscious that natives saw them as invaders. The television series is a simulacrum many times over. In addition to invoking this antiindigenous refrain, which Stephen Silliman identifies as "a narrative of US colonialism, triumphalism, and Othering" (2008, 237), the series uses US troops as actors who play themselves in the war the series depicts. This blurring of fact and fiction is compounded by cartoon characters, of all things, which adds an additional layer of absurdity that is impossible to unpack without attending to the violences inscribed within the ideologically flexible LatIndia/o paradigm. In one scene, for instance, a multiracial group of US Marines spends a break in their overland trek through the Iraqi desert meditating on the mechanics of masturbation. In the ensuing homosocial discussion that distinguishes their identities as postmodern picaresque male warrior heroes, one Marine reports witnessing another masturbate to the 1995 animated film *Pocahontas*, which features the eponymous Indian "princess" as a dark-skinned and voluptuous adolescent. When a white soldier, Sergeant Brad Colbert, adds to the absurd carnivalesque scene by admitting he likes the film, Sergeant Antonio "Poke" Espera, whose character is based on a real soldier who self-identifies as a mixed-heritage Latino (of unspecified group), German American, and Native American, breaks in:

> Naw, naw, naw, naw, Brad. You cannot say you like *Pocahontas*. The genocide of my people is turned into a cartoon musical with a singing raccoon? I mean, think about it, dawg, the real story of Pocahontas is about a bunch of white boys who come to my land, bribe the corrupt Indian chief, kill off all the warriors and fuck the Indian princess silly. Would the white man make a story about Auschwitz where the inmate falls in love with the guard and they go off singing love songs with dancing swastikas?   (Simon et al. 2008, n.p.)

Sergeant Colbert shoots back: "Poke, what the fuck are you anyway? Your wife is half white, you talk like you're black, most of your friends are fucking white, and every once in a while, when you feel like it, you throw in with the Indians. Is it just that you're whatever race happens to be cool at the moment?" (2008, n.p.). Sergeant Espera concedes, adding a self-deprecating stereotype to his genealogy: "You got a point, dawg. I don't hang out with Mexicans.... Every time I go into a liquor store with one, I'm afraid we're gonna rob the place. Mexicans are scary motherfuckers" (2008, n.p.)

The next scene involves combat maneuvers against Iraqis, followed by periodic atrocities against civilians. These serve as a mere backdrop in a drama about a war whose chief strategy revolves around the US military's feeble attempts to co-opt Iraqi tribes and religious groups to serve as US proxies. Roberto J. González (2008) aptly proposes the US invasion of Iraq as analogous to the US Indian Wars since much of Iraq is organized under tribal, clan, and extended family kinship networks similar to Indian Country. In this global indigenous context, Sergeant Espera is burdened by his US citizenship, and Marine Corps identity, which render his racially fluid LatIndio identity into an ideologically inchoate formation. He reminds us of the many nuances that oftentimes are effaced by classifications of mestizaje-as-indigeneity and indigeneity-as-resistance to empire. In fact, Sergeant Espera emerges as the antithesis to Raúl Salinas's XicanIndio Marxist internationalism. For instance, in the book version of *Generation Kill*, Espera's frustrations over the suspension of the bloody US Marine siege of Falluja in 2004 reveal his confused ideological navigations of race, violence, and empire:

> What happened to the old-school White Man who so viciously destroyed my people and enslaved our culture? I didn't join the White Man's side for this. Negotiating with the enemy... No, the White Man don't negotiate. Unconditional fucking surrender. It ain't over in Falluja until a bunch a Marines are standing on top of a pile of rubble looking down at any survivors, telling them, "You shut the fuck up and do what I say. If you behave, maybe in a hundred years, we'll give you a casino." (2004, 364)

As explored in Chapter 5, the growing number of Latina/o accounts of their participation in the US War on Terror occupations of Iraq and Afghanistan confirm that Sergeant Espera's intertwining of awkward self-effacing "anti-racist" critique with imperialist and proto-fascist desire is anything but anomalous.

There are, of course, a large number of alternative performative LatIndia/o paradigms that diverge from Espera's paradoxically anticolonialist and simultaneously US imperialist Marine Corps LatIndio/o violentology. This growing and increasingly discrepant archive steadily complicates the "Indian Question," as it were, almost raising violence and antiviolence to the level of a meta-narrative in Latina/o life writing. That is, these narratives of violence almost exist to meditate on their own existence, since they are continually synthesizing Latinidades. But something more real is at stake. Contemporaneous to Sergeant Espera's signifying as the contemporary permutation of the nineteenth-century Indian scout and mercenary whose survival is intertwined with settler colonial success, new antiimperialist Chicana/o-Indian coalitions challenge antiimmigrant legislation and attendant racist pogroms that figure Latina/o immigrants as illegal, alien, and nonnative to the Southwestern United States. These collaborations include the occupation of a Border Patrol station in Tucson, Arizona, on May 21, 2010, by a multiracial group of twelve people of various ages and demographic backgrounds. Two of the six student occupiers who chained themselves to structural beams in the facility were enrolled members of the O'odham Nation. Bureau of Indian Affairs identification cards confirming their tribal affiliation provided a layer of relative protection against the police brutality that has accompanied such protests in the past because their presence required relative nation-to-nation diplomacy.

The O'odham Solidarity Across Borders Collective's press release tropes the LatIndia/o paradigm yet again. It proclaims:

> On this day people who are Indigenous to Arizona join with migrants who are Indigenous to other parts of the Western Hemisphere in demanding a return to traditional Indigenous value of freedom of movement for all people. (2010, n.p.)

This dramatic real-life episode of Chicana/o-India/o solidarity involves a rehearsal of the complicated mestizaje identification scenes Curtis Marez has analyzed in the cultural and political economy of Comanche captivity trade in eighteenth-, nineteenth-, and early twentieth-century New Mexico. In negotiating Comanche captivity, Mexicans and Mexican Americans engaged in strategic essentialist deployments of mestizaje to claim Indian and non-Indian identities depending upon the circumstances. Throughout their navigations, these Mexican Americans were recognized as indigenous by their Comanche captors, who sometimes became lifelong family (Marez

2001, 268–9). There are, of course, profound differences between the Comanche legacy of Mexican and Mexican American captivity and the 2010 occupation of a border patrol station. Yet, this occupation of the quintessential symbol of binaries—a government installation where the borders of nation and identity are enforced—nonetheless involved enrolled members of an Indian nation that embraced (rather than captured), Latin American immigrant and Chicana/os as native to the region (and Native) precisely because of their mestizaje. Together—as Pan-Indian people—they confronted US hegemony with direct action.

Reclaiming Genocide: Disidentificatory Dance and AfroLatIndia/o Two-Spirit Warrior Heroes

In a reiteration of the complicated yet enduring potential of mestizaje that united members of the O'odham Nation with Amerindian migrants and detribalized-cum-supratribal Chicana/os, Felipe Rose (Ortiz)—a mixed-heritage black, Puerto Rican, Taíno, and Lakota Sioux member of the 1970s multiracial gay male disco group the Village People—introduces a Gay AfroLatIndia/o subjectivity that further expands the gamut of LatIndia/o paradigms. Rose is re-nowned—and also infamous—for the plains Indian eagle feather headdress (also known as a war bonnet) he would don as the Indian "character" alongside bandmembers who performed as stock figures from the 1970s Greenwich Village gay scene: buffed white construction worker in a hard hat; white leather-clad biker with handlebar mustache; black motorcycle cop; white cowboy in a ten-gallon hat; and black sailor in a white Navy uniform (Figures 1.7 and 1.8). Rose continued to perform as a founding member of the group until its formal dissolution in 2018, and sings solo under his Lakota name, Swift Arrow. Gabriel S. Estrada (2012) has reclaimed Felipe Rose/ Swift Arrow as a gay Latino icon, though Estrada refers to his indigenous name only once, in quotation marks, suggesting a circumscribed recognition of this part of his identity. A violentological herme-neutic, however, reveals how Felipe Rose/Swift Arrow transforms the otherwise ambivalent LatIndia/o archetype into a relatively em-powered figure: it recognizes the multiple violences inscribed in his layered identity and, moreover, maps how his reclamations and redeployments of harm, however imperfect and ideologically

FIGURE 1.7. *Original members of the Village People, with Felipe Rose/Swift Arrow (center), 1978, by Can't Stop Productions. Courtesy of Felipe Rose Enterprises.*

FIGURE 1.8. *Felipe Rose/Swift Arrow, circa 1978 by Can't Stop Productions. Courtesy of Felipe Rose Enterprises.*

inchoate they may be, ultimately animate a complex queering of indigenous Latinidades.

Felipe Rose/Swift Arrow foregrounds this intervention in the website historiography of his long and diverse career: it depicts him as a ballet dancer with El Ballet de Puerto Rico at the Lincoln Center in New York, dancer in Tito Puente's famous Afro-Latin Jazz Combo, backup singer for various musical groups, and performer in community theater productions. This genealogy segues with his identification as a "Shadow Walker," a term that has different tribal resonances, but which Felipe Rose/Swift Arrow describes as "a native name for one who walks in two worlds" (Rose 2019, n.p.). He further extends this intercultural identity by claiming another Pan-Indian formation—the Two-Spirit subject—which refers to a nonbinary third gender, with contemporary usage also referring to the broader community of LGBTQI+ people.[26] These gender, sexuality, cultural, and racial mestizajes set the stage for a dramatic reclamation of the violences that have shaped his life and multiple communities.

Indeed, Felipe Rose/Swift Arrow tropes his indigeneity—and indigeneity in general—as multiple mestizajes. Contrary to being ahistorical, as critics alleged because of his flamboyant and, to some, irreverent campy performance of gay indigeneity on stage with the Village People, Felipe Rose/Swift Arrow insists he was never *not* Indian. In a statement on an earlier version of his website, he uses the authoritative third-person voice of a biographer to insist:

> Felipe is a native New Yorker with roots in Brooklyn. His Puerto Rican mother and Native American father are reflected in the cloth-ing and accessories that he dons to perform which depict his blood lines and which he has been wearing long before the birth of the mega group, VILLAGE PEOPLE.
>
> This is not just a costume. It is also his public statement of where he comes from and his long association with Native American groups across the country.   (Rose 2016, n.p.)

His theatrical adaptation of Pan-Indian personae—and even Hollywoodesque Indian accoutrements—never involved "playing Indian," as Estrada suggests in his invocation of Phillip Deloria's (1998) incisive critique of the way Native Americans and non-Native Americans performed commodified kitschy models of faux-indigeneity for various audiences (Estrada 2012, 344). He had been reclaiming and performing his indigeneity since he was a teenager, in which he used Pan-Indian accoutrements, including a Pawnee hair style, various buckskin styles, and emblems from his own Lakota Sioux community (Figure 1.9). Moreover, Felipe Rose/Swift Arrow's provocative recuperation of his pan-indigeneity (e.g., the use of war paint and war bonnet apparently "out of context") is a

FIGURE 1.9. *Felipe Rose/Swift Arrow in New York City, aged seventeen years, 1977. Courtesy of Felipe Rose Enterprises.*

disidentificatory rehearsal of genocide or, rather, the multiple genocides of black, Puerto Rican, Lakota, Taíno, and LGBTQI+ people. José Esteban Muñoz (1999) has proposed that Queers of Color negotiate ideology through an appropriative hybrid aes-thetic—disidentification—in which denigrating and stereotypical portraits are reclaimed and restaged as over-the-top-campy spectacles as defiant acts of empowerment. Felipe Rose/Swift Arrow's disidentificatory reclamations could not help but be performed through the multiply layered mestizajes of all his genealogical strands, including the stereotypes. This diverse gamut of subjectivities inevitably will involve apparent dissonances even as the disidentifi-catory performance accomplishes its contrapuntal ends. Ion Davies calls this inchoate assemblage "post culture," in which a new habitus is adapted from the "fragments" that remain following horrific episodes of genocide and historical erasures (1990, 204).

Felipe Rose/Swift Arrow's postmodern and carnivalesque pastiche also intersects with various theories of "survivance," Gerald Vizenor's

(1998) term proposing survival and continued existence as de facto resistance to genocide. This praxis emphasizes the recovery, rejuvenation, renovation, and at times reinvention of culture as more than just a survival strategy: it also is an ontological and epistemological act infused with an oppositional, though sometimes ideologically inchoate, resonance. For instance, Felipe Rose/Swift Arrow performs a somber though still celebratory ritualized disidentificatory reconstruction of a supra-Latina/o, pan-indigenous, violence-infused identity in a performance of his song, "Trail of Tears." At the Fifth Annual Native American Music Awards in Milwaukee, Wisconsin, on September 7, 2002, Felipe Rose/Swift Arrow exchanged his signature war bonnet for a modified horsehair forelock that complemented waist-long hair, which are fashion accoutrements from various tribes (including his paternal Lakota Sioux) (Figure 1.10). His attendant choreography of this tragic operatic multimedia spectacle blended his training and experience in ballet, disco, and Native American dance. The resulting performance features modern and traditional buckskin dance fusions replete with flamboyant disco twirls and an innovative synchronic hand routine of twirling bright yellow flags. Throughout the performance, Felipe Rose/Swift Arrow

FIGURE 1.10. *Felipe Rose/Swift Arrow Performance at the Fifth Annual Native American Music Awards in Milwaukee, Wisconsin, September 7, 2002. Courtesy of Felipe Rose Enterprises.*

dances in unison with an assortment of Native American dancers performing fancy dancing, grass dancing, and northern traditional dancing. This Pan-Indian montage functions as a figural (though not literal) Ghost Dance that facilitates communal reunion with ancestors, purging of pain, and healing from the trauma of warfare and ongoing genocide. The *YouTube* video of this performance also features Felipe Rose/Swift Arrow leading the tribe out of a teepee to begin the group dance. A founding member of the Village People, for which he served as one of several accompanying singers and dancers, here he emerges onstage as the primary vocalist. Yet, Felipe Rose/Swift Arrow is not the "leader," per se, nor solely a "performer." Rather, he emerges as a spokesperson, and perhaps an elder: he is a repository and disseminator of pan-tribal knowledge and philosophy. Felipe Rose/Swift Arrow's community is not solely the Lakota Sioux or AfroTaíno people of his father and mother, respectively, but the tribes that were subjected to the violent Indian Removal Act of 1830: Chickasaw, Choctaw, Muscogee Creek, Seminole, and members of several more tribes. His constituency is Pan-Indian, and this necessarily includes mixed-heritage subjects like him, who embody the pastiche of US American genocidal designs on Native peoples, blacks, Latina/os, LGBTQI+, and additional abjected communities.

Felipe Rose/Swift Arrow's lyrics recount and reclaim these violences as the basis of a syncretic model of disidentificatory pan-indigeneity. Recounting the forced march of various Indian peoples from the southeastern parts of what became the US toward present day Oklahoma, the dozen-strong youth chorus of dancers on stage begins the performance by referencing the starvation of these Native men, women, and children:

> One tribe.
> One home.
> One trail.
> One road.
> One heart.
> One seed.
> Proud people.
> With not enough to eat.   (Rose 2002, n.p.)

The song continues with a succinct paean to Indian survivance that takes the ritual performance toward its crescendo and resolution:

> Not knowing,
> but not afraid,
> they held
> their head up high.
> On the trail of tears
> they weren't afraid to die.   (2002, n.p.)

This rendering of Native American survivance (e.g., "They held / Their head up high") becomes the axis around which Felipe Rose/ Swift Arrow reclaims and recasts the tragedy in the ensuing lyrics and in the overall performance: the genocide is followed by the victory of their persistent existence. This disidentificatory performance thus is also a ceremonial healing, however incomplete and unsatiating it may be due to the enormity of the trauma and its enduring legacy.

As a self-identified Shadow Walker, Felipe Rose/Swift Arrow performs his most dramatic move by transforming this multitribal catastrophe, which did not include his Lakota Sioux ancestors (though they suffered their own genocidal traumas), into a Pan-Indian experience and survivance epistemology. This is the experience of "one tribe," as the chorus and his solo singing repeatedly reiterates. The refrain "one tribe / one home / walking down the trail of tears," also functions as a second chorus that introduces a new collective, transhistorical, and mobile spatial ontology forged in the walking and remembering together. The cathartic crescendo follows:

> What is gone
> was there before.
> What we know now
> won't hurt us anymore.

This ritual purging of pain does not occur by reenacting it through dance, but by collectively performing a pan-indigenous circle of remembrance as a survivance through a nonhierarchical movement of individual dancers from different tribes all going in the same direction in the same circle.

This provocative intervention notwithstanding, Felipe Rose/Swift Arrow's transformation of the warrior hero into a visionary Two-Spirit elder and healer is not without its contradictions. Given the diversity of warrior paradigms, identities, and societies across Indian Country, it is difficult for his poetic persona to avoid intersections with contemporary Native American soldiering in the US military. The 2016 version of his website included a photo of the flag-draped coffin of a Native American US Marine killed in the War on Terror as it was transported by a horse-drawn carriage to a burial site on one of the many Indian reservations created by the US government as part of its genocidal settler colonialism. The accompanying text reads:

> I would like to honor all our brothers sisters who have fought the battles in this Country...Please join me in silent prayer for all our fallen Warriors.

The conflation of "brothers sisters" is profound for its resistance to a forced gender and sexuality binary. Furthermore, Felipe Rose/Swift Arrow's choice of the preposition "in" (e.g., "the battles *in* this country") instead of "for" (as in "for this country") also is revealing even if it may have been unintentional. Coupled with the visual image of the horse-drawn casket on an Indian reservation gravesite, this homage inevitably links foreign US wars against tribal peoples and nations in Iraq and Afghanistan to domestic US wars against tribal peoples and nations, including his own. The two "Indian Country" referents discussed throughout Chapter 1, thus merge in this visual and verbal montage.

Felipe Rose/Swift Arrow also recognizes that Native American military service is complex. Stephen Silliman documents how Native American soldiers oftentimes identify their US military service as a defense of, and service to, their own tribe despite the inevitable cooptation of their warrior identities by the same US military ("Words," 2012, n.p.). Native American and Vietnam War veteran and scholar Tom Holm adds that since WWII, the high Native American military enlistment rate—the highest per capita than any other ethnic group—is motivated by two "probable reasons": economic hardship and "loyalty" (1996, 30–1). However, Holm's subsequent explanation reveals this last motive to be more of a dependence than a "loyalty" because of federal control over all jobs and services that Indians receive on reservations. In this enduring colonial configuration, Felipe Rose/ Swift Arrow's reference to "the battles in this Country" seems both ambiguous and prescient for its inclusion of the many types of warriors, battles, and battlegrounds he recovers through his own violentological hermeneutic and performative identity.

In a populist twist on Felipe Rose/Swift Arrow's expansive relocation of the warrior hero archetype onto a broader horizon—the entire earth—his 2016 version of the website closes with an announcement of a planned comic book, "The Adventures of Swift Arrow, aka

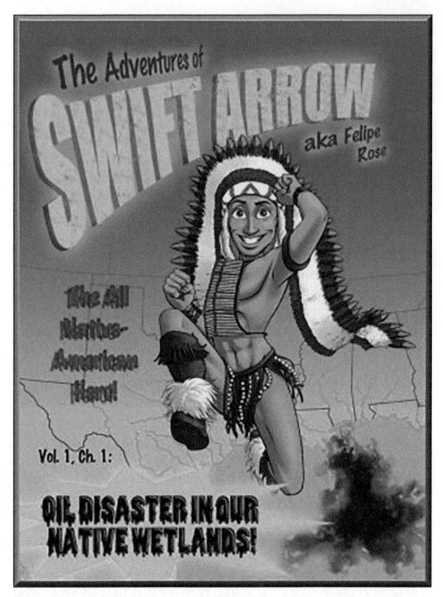

FIGURE 1.11. *Planned first issue of* The Adventures of Swift Arrow *comic book (2010), by Felipe Rose/Swift Arrow and illustrator Morgan Lawson. Courtesy of Felipe Rose Enterprises.*

Felipe Rose," which bears the tagline: "The All Native-American Hero" (Figure 1.11). His use of a muscular alter ego in a war bonnet might again ruffle feathers, as it were, for appearing to reproduce stereotypes. However, the cover of the inaugural issue reiterates the particularity, and proliferation, of different types of battles he is waging as a new type of disidentificatory Two-Spirit, Shadow Walker, warrior hero, and elder. These include Native American environmentalism, which is featured as a cover story on the British Petroleum oil spill in 2010 titled, "Oil Disaster in Our Native Wetlands!" Rather than being another cartoon legitimation of European colonization of Native lands, such as the Pocahontas film that Espera and his fellow Marines evoke in the 2008 HBO serial *Generation Kill, The Adventures of Swift Arrow* offers a materialist anticolonial queer camp AfroLatIndia/o subject who engages in activist interventions across a wide range of issues. Many of the violences he knows, embodies, and challenges are a threat to all people and the earth's very existence, such that his gay LatIndia/o warrior hero ultimately becomes an archetypical champion for particular affinity groups and for everyone.

Macho Man

HOMOSOCIAL SOLDIERING AND IDEOLOGICAL DISSENSUS IN MEXICAN AMERICAN WWII MEMOIR, THEATER, AND FILM

Filmmaker Ken Burns's exclusion of Latina/o soldiers from his 2007 documentary film, *The War*, touched a raw nerve for Latina/os who still gaze upon *retablos*, or three-dimensional photographic shrines, to uniformed family members who served in WWII, and in subsequent US wars. As noted in the introduction, this effacement extends to my second cousin, US Army Private Victor Manuel Ledesma, who died at the age of eighteen, several days after being wounded in combat against the Nazis in the 1944 WWII Allied D-Day invasion of Normandy. Ironically, he was fighting an enemy who had adapted many of its eugenicist ideas and apartheid practices from US academics and policy makers.[1] These include forced sterilization programs targeting racial minorities and the poor, in addition to the creation of racially segregated enclaves such as Indian reservations and concentrated housing projects like the Chalmers Courts public housing complex in east Austin, Texas, where family members lived for several generations after Victor's death. Ken Burns duly included an African American soldier among his four profiles. But the de facto effacement of Latina/o contributions to the US WWII effort extended Tom Brokaw's overtly Eurocentric 1998 anthology about WWII veterans, *The Greatest Generation*. A March 13, 2007, resolution by the American G.I. Forum—the largest Latina/o veteran's organization in the country—added to the thousands of emails, letters, and rallies expressing outrage over these exclusions. This organization, founded in 1948 by Mexican American WWII veterans, sought to block the airing of Burns's film on Public Broadcasting

Violentologies: Violence, Identity, and Ideology in Latina/o Literature. B.V. Olguín, Oxford University Press (2021).
© B.V. Olguín.
DOI: 10.1093/oso/9780198863090.001.0003

Service (PBS) channels. Adding insult to injury, PBS had scheduled the film to premier one week after the Mexican Independence Day, *el Dieciseis de Septiembre*, a widely celebrated holiday in Mexican American communities. The American G.I. Forum insisted that Burns's taxpayer-funded project recognize—and, indeed, celebrate—Latino WWII soldiers. Its resolution emphasized:

> Hispanic/Latino individuals during World War II were the most decorated minority group to receive this Country's highest award, "The Congressional Medal of Honor." (2002, n.p.)

This familiar assertion invokes a military citation that oftentimes is awarded posthumously. It also intersects with the neoeugenicist Latino "martial caste" stereotype that George Mariscal (1999, 2003, 2010) has critiqued as operative in military recruitment campaigns targeting Latino males.

Adding to the irony of the American G.I. Forum's perpetuation of the lethal warrior hero archetype, numerous narratives and historiographies by and about Latina/os in the WWII era feature racialized, gendered, and eroticized spectacles of violence as legitimating performances of cultural and US political citizenship. As stressed in the introduction, this militarization of Latina/o citizenship enacts a fundamentally hegemonic claim to inclusion within a capitalist empire. Importantly, the reification of the Latino hyperviolent masculinist warrior hero is not confined to WWII battlefields. The aforementioned Tejano US Army veteran and folklorist Américo Paredes (1958, 1995) details how the nineteenth- and early twentieth-century acoustic Mexican American epic heroic *corrido* privileges Mexican American male social bandits firing their phallic pistols as they hurl sexualized masculinist epithets at white male enemies, such as *El Corrido de Jacinto Treviño's* "come meet your father!" Similarly, Mexican American Medal of Honor recipient Roy Benavidez introduces his memoir about combat in Vietnam by recounting a youthful episode in which he was challenged to pull the testicles of a bull to prove his "bravery" and earn twenty-five cents (1999, 9). Worse, many Latino-authored war narratives are replete with horrendous male bonding scenes involving sexual violence against women. In his semiautobiographical novel *Dogs from Illusion*, for instance, Vietnam War combat veteran Charley Trujillo depicts a Chicano soldier biting off the nipple of a Vietnamese woman during a soldier group visit to a Hanoi brothel (1994, 133). The American G.I. Forum's nostalgic recuperation of the Latino soldier as a civic category—the Soldado Razo as paradigmatic US citizen—must be juxtaposed with these pathological examples of Latino soldiering in multiple wartime contexts. Indeed, the coexistence of such discrepant pathological iterations with celebrated "heroic" Latino warrior citizens suggests a much wider and more complex spectrum of Soldados Razos than is usually acknowledged in the field of Latina/o Studies.

It remains an article of faith that Mexican American male military service in the WWII era was a watershed moment in Mexican American claims to inclusion in the polis. However, the field has undertheorized how these soldiers engaged in a wide array of political and cultural negotiations extending beyond citizenship frameworks. Historian George Sánchez offers a preliminary corrective by recognizing "the possibility of multiple identities and contradictory positions" by Mexican Americans in this era (1995, 8). Chicana feminist theorists Norma Alarcón (1994) and Chela Sandoval (2000) have theorized this epistemic and ideological flexibility as interstitial and third-space agency, which involves various, and sometimes simultaneous, migrations in and out of multiple subject positions. As established in Chapter 1, these navigations extend as far to the political right—a point rarely acknowledged in the field—as they do to the far left—which also is rarely recognized as anything but anomalous. The balance of Chapter 2 assesses the WWII Soldado Razo's fluid ideological range to further challenge celebratory renderings of this archetypal figure that are predicated upon a heteropatriarchal male warrior hero mythos.

WWII Soldados Razos, like other Latina/o archetypes, are shaped by variable though inherently violent relationships to power and counterpower, which ultimately extend beyond overstated teleologies, such as the generational progress narrative, ambiguous resistance claims, and conservative inclusion and assimilation paradigms. As illustrated in mappings of LatIndia/o ideological diversity in Chapter 1, WWII Soldados Razos also are interpellated within the dominant individualist, capitalist, and imperialist episteme, even as other Latina/o soldiers and civilians in the WWII era resist this interpellation in provocatively complex and even antithetical ways. Several operative questions thus emerge. What different types of violences undergird WWII-era performances of Mexican American male citizenship and other modalities? How do they perform or critique broader Latina/o real and imaginary relationships to power? Can there be leftist—particularly anarchist and communist— Soldados Razos, and if so, what are the contours of their subjectivities and agency? Furthermore, what is the relationship between masculinist agency and hegemonic power, and when might this nexus intersect with extreme right-wing fascism, that is, the eroticized reification of beingness-as-violence? How might otherwise misogynist homosocial agency become potentially homoerotic, and can the misogynist homoerotic contestatory Soldado Razo be considered counterhegemonic? What new insights do we gain by queering and, indeed, outing the WWII Soldado Razo? And to address a major lacuna in conventional discussions about this archetype, how are women interpellated as neoimperialist Soldaderas within the masculinist martial context of WWII?

Materialist Feminist and Queer Studies scholars provide important touchstones for exploring these inquiries. Eve Kosofsky Sedgwick has uncovered the patriarchal interdependence among men—their homosocial bonding—as performed in their collective domination and exchange of women. Her explication of these bonds in eighteenth- and nineteenth-century English literature invite analysis of the similarly patriarchal context of US American militarism, particularly in the WWII era that on the surface involved rigid gender boundaries. As Sedgwick demonstrates, literary texts become the site for rehearsing (and sometimes reassessing) real-world homosocial bonds, which are consolidated through the figural and literal exchange of women in marriage as part of male-to-male property arrangements. This homosociality, she explains, depends on:

> social bonds between persons of the same sex; it is a neologism, obviously formed by analogy with "homosexual," and just as obviously meant to be distinguished from "homosexual." In fact, it is applied to such activities as "male bonding," which may, as in our society, be characterized by intense homophobia, fear and hatred of homosexuality. (1985, 1–2)

She adds that the attendant homophobic aspect of homosociality in a heteronormative context is always potentially homoerotic (1985, 2). Extending Sedgwick's discussion of the homosocial-homosexual continuum (with the latter part of the dyad expanded by the LGBTQI+ spectrum), Michael Shapiro (1997) and Susan Faludi

(1994) have uncovered the hypersexual male culture in US military academies, and male military culture in general. Their exposés are useful for explicating the ideological inflections of gender and sexuality in World War II literature, theater, and film by and about Mexican American males beyond celebratory accounts of these soldiers as oppositional subjects claiming their citizenship rights and privileges through phallocentric spectacles of violence.

As a frame of reference for this enterprise, George Mariscal (1999a), Lorena Oropeza (2005), Stella Pope Duarte (2002), and other scholars and authors have recuperated alternative antimasculinist and feminist discourses by Chicana/os during the Vietnam War era. Ariana Vigil (2014) and Belinda Rincón (2017) have recovered feminist agency and critique from the US war in Vietnam to more contemporary wars. Yet, surprisingly little has been written about Mexican American masculinity in WWII. Moreover, even though warfare has always involved, and frequently is constituted by sexualized violence, no one has fully excavated Mexican American soldier uses of serial and, indeed, ritualized sexual violence as constitutive of both their soldiering and their citizenship. Much less has been written about the intersections between hypermasculinity, homosocial bonding during war, and the transracial homoerotic aspects of Mexican American soldiering in any war, and particularly in WWII. Accordingly, this chapter examines the distinct ideologies of violence-based, racialized, gendered, and sexualized Mexican American variations of the otherwise nostalgic WWII-Soldado Razo archetype.

The wide range of WWII-Soldado Razo permutations extends through—but also beyond—Critical Race Theory's insistence that racialized abjection denies minoritarian subjects equitable access to power; it also pressures some Marxist renderings of their segmentation and circumscribed agency at the lower rungs of various classes.[2] As this chapter's case studies reveal, WWII Soldados Razos actually were involved in myriad relationships to power and counterpower, which offered them relative degrees of enfranchisement. Sandra Soto has proposed that these navigations can only be understood within a race-gender-sexuality nexus wherein each constituent in this triad cannot be disarticulated from the others (2010, 1). Following Soto, Mexican American WWII-soldier masculinity can be understood as a fusion of homosociality, or homosocial soldiering, with violence-based claims to agency that extend through and beyond political and cultural citizenship. I call this matrix *homosoldiering*. This neologistic category recognizes a wider ideological range for soldier agency than Jasbir Puar's (2007) "homonationalism," which productively decries the conflation of queer identity politics with conservative models of soldiering and citizenship, such as efforts to end the ban on openly LGBTQI+ soldiers serving in the US military. This strategy, Puar argues, fails to interrogate the US military's role in imperialism and equally violent intersecting domestic exercises of power. In contrast, homosoldiering extends our understanding of these subjects beyond simplistic reductions of them as mystified nationalist dupes, as homonationalism suggests. It also challenges all-too-common Latina/o Studies hagiographic depictions of minoritized soldiers as unambiguous heroes, or the related cultural nationalist depictions of them as embarrassing antitheses to Latina/o liberation. As already demonstrated by case studies in Chapter 1, each iteration of a violence-based Latina/o modality of being, knowing, and doing is distinct, though oftentimes interrelated to other violentologies. Ultimately, these modalities involve performances of power and counterpower, as well as relative empowerment, disempowerment, and even self-annihilation, and sometimes all simultaneously.

The ensuing explications of select memoirs, autobiographical verse, theater, and film by and about Mexican Americans in the WWII era demonstrate the expansive range of possibilities for re-reading the cultural and political economy of the WWII-Soldado Razo's homosoldiering. Mexican American WWII Marine Corps veteran Guy Gabaldon's 1990 memoir, *Saipan: Suicide Island*, for instance, is inversely in dialogue with Judith Pérez's and Sévero Pérez's Marxist rendering of a deep friendship between two WWII combat veterans from Texas, one Mexican American and the other white, in their 1982 play *Soldierboy* (published in 1990). Other renderings of WWII-era Soldados Razos reveal ideological convergences and divergences through misogynist and homoerotic homosociality that radically alter our understanding of this archetype. These include conscientious objector and socialist visual artist and poet Carlos Córtez; protoimperialist memoirists Frank Medina and Henry Cervantes; and cultural nationalist playwright Luis Valdez. Chapter 2 ultimately illustrates how Latina/o homosoldiering denotes complex agency, which can be relatively empowering for these subjects even if it is highly circumscribed and, without a doubt, frequently disempowering and profoundly traumatic for the objects of their violent agency on and off the battlefield.

Motorcycles, the Marine Corps, and Capitalism in Guy Gabaldon's Transnational Homosoldiering

Since its inception in the 1960s and 1970s, the field of Chicana/o Studies has been informed by theories of transnationalism, with Chicana/o subjects defined by their transgressions and reappropriations of various local, regional, intranational, and international sites of power and containment, particularly in the US-Mexico borderlands and the Southwestern United States in general. However, as I argued in the introduction, Latina/o Citizenship Studies and Spatial Studies emphases on the counterhegemonic potential of Latina/o claims to geographic place and social space tend toward reductive, solipsistic, and even tautological celebrations of Latinidad. They frequently fail to recognize ideological contradictions, and embedded violences, in Latina/o negotiations of power and performances of what frequently is called "cultural citizenship," an ill-defined Latina/o inflection of hyperlocal imagined communities.[3] Closer scrutiny of celebrated soldiering by Latino WWII veterans such as US Marine Guy Gabaldon reveals how male Mexican American military personnel from the "Greatest Generation" deploy transnational and transcultural subjectivities in ways that make "cultural citizenship" models woefully inadequate for assessing the troubling ideologies of their agency. A recipient of the Navy's Distinguished Service Cross and nominee for a Medal of Honor for his combat in the Pacific during WWII, Gabaldon is symptomatic of the hypermasculinist dimensions of the Soldado Razo archetype. Gabaldon was the subject of a Hollywood film, as well as documentaries and books focusing on his bicultural and trilingual heritage as an East Los Angeles Mexican American who grew up among Nisei, or second-generation Japanese Americans. He gained notoriety for killing thirty-three Japanese soldiers, and capturing over one thousand, on the Pacific island of Saipan, which he often facilitated by speaking to his "enemy" in what he calls his "East L.A. Japanese mixed with Jap Military lingo" (1990, 87).

Gabaldon could be seen as the paradigmatic transnational, translingual, and transcultural Soldado Razo. However, his 1990 self-published memoir, *Saipan: Suicide Island*—which bears the cover proclamation, "I killed 33 and captured 'over one thousand Japanese' "—highlights another dimension of his renowned "heroism": a pathologically violent hypermasculinity, accompanying transnational fetish on Asia and Asians (particularly Japanese), and transracial homosocial soldiering that involves the symbolic exchange of women, particularly his Mexican-Japanese daughter. Gabaldon also embeds Mexican American class mobility within the capitalist world system, motored by US global imperialism in WWII and the subsequent wars in which he served as a US military contractor and anticommunist mercenary into the 1980s. Gabaldon thus inadvertently unsettles celebratory readings of the WWII Soldado Razo as a warrior hero, and demonstrates the need for a fuller ideological accounting of this foundational Latina/o Studies archetype. By interrogating Gabaldon's pathological and imperialist permutation of the Soldado Razo, we open new possibilities for theorizing the intersections between Mexican American and broader Latina/o soldiering, capitalist citizenship articulated through the commodity fetish, and global US hegemony. This contrapuntal reading also opens space for alternative WWII-era supra-Latina/o violentologies that have broad implications for the future of Chicana/o and broader Latina/o Studies, particularly an immanent postidentitarian paradigm.

For instance, in stark contrast to frequent celebrations of Gabaldon's "bravery" as a paradigmatic performance of Mexican American citizenship and transculturation, the memoir reveals his main motive for killing thirty-three Japanese soldiers was the same commodity fetish animating the WWII global contest between empires over who would emerge as the world's premiere superpower. His book opens by recounting his reason for killing three Japanese soldiers he encountered during an early solo scouting expedition: a three-wheel Harley-Davidson motorcycle. "That bike is going to be mine," he recalls thinking to himself as he lurks nearby in a sugar-cane field, adding "all I've got to do is kill three 'Samurai' and I'll have a good ol' Harley" (1990, 16). Despite his celebrated acculturation into Nisei language and culture, Gabaldon reveals a racialized chauvinism in his encounter with Japanese soldiers when he adds, "He should have had a Honda, not an American motorcycle" (1990, 18). Gabaldon kills these men for their American motorcycle and claims their Harley for himself, metonymically modeling how his soldiering would add to the broader efforts to facilitate the US claim to Saipan as part of its global patrimony after WWII.

With the phallic Harley-Davidson engine roaring between his legs, Gabaldon rides back to the American garrison victorious, merging his previous barrio bad boy biker subjectivity with jungle warfare in Asia as a US Marine. He notes that "fighting in the Pacific tropical jungles and living in the East Los Angeles ghettos had a lot in common—you had to be one step ahead of the enemy or adios Mother" (1990, 19). In the performance of his transcultural persona—which involved local and global trilingual codeswitching from English to Spanish to Japanese—Gabaldon ironically intersects with borderlands, interstitial, and, at least superficially, third-space transnational subjectivities despite the imperialist projection of his hypermasculinist and martial Mexican American agency. His differential consciousness tactics, after all, enable symbolic, social, and material empowerment and class mobility through strategic shifting from subject position to subject position: barrio boy, Nisei, biker, trilingual Marine, and back and forth as the situation requires. This dexterity, along with his hero status, allow him the latitude to militate on behalf of additional subaltern subjects, such as fellow Mexican American soldiers, as well as his adopted Nisei family, which was interned in concentration camps on the US mainland. In a further irony, some of his childhood friends opted to join the US Army's renowned all-Nisei 442nd Infantry Regiment as an alternative to this incarceration, with some remaining "patriotic" and others embittered. Identity and ideology within this violent milieu, as Gabaldon and his childhood friends inevitably reveal, is fundamentally antiteleological even as these young ethnic and racial minority males are all interpellated as agents of empire.

Despite his underclass liminal roots, but also because of his flexible performance of a hybrid subjectivity, hegemonic third-space agency, and differential consciousness in multiple transnational contexts—from East L.A. to the South Pacific to post-WWII counterinsurgency operations in Latin America—Gabaldon instantiates a model of the unabashedly imperialist model of the Soldado Razo. He even celebrates Spanish *conquistadores*, who are anathema to the neoindigenous basis of Chicana/o Studies as discussed in Chapter 1. Gabaldon, who identifies as "Hispanic" throughout his memoir and in all his interviews, even proclaims that "these pioneers were men of guts and stamina," adding, "I take pride in the valor of these men with big 'huevos' [testicles]" (1990, 25). He thus links colonialist conquest in sixteenth-century Mesoamerica to conquests in Saipan, which became a US territory after WWII. He further celebrates the failed 1961 US-supported Bay of Pigs invasion in Cuba, whose Cuban American mercenaries he later recruited for US counterrevolutionary ventures in Latin America. This includes his participation in the

Anti-Sandinista Contra War in Nicaragua in the 1980s, in which Gabaldon worked as a CIA-contracted mercenary pilot delivering supplies to anti-Sandinista militias.

Predictably, the American G.I. Forum includes Guy Gabaldon among its pantheon of the Latino "Greatest Generation," even as Gabaldon's conflation of masculinity and the commodity fetish— which collapses transcultural citizenship with transnational imperialist conquest—is pathological and patriotic or, rather, pathologically patriotic and patriotically pathological. By his own account, Gabaldon even kills some Japanese soldiers for their gold teeth, watches, money, and souvenirs, including pistols, sabers, and other weapons. "I didn't know what the Geneva Convention had to say about War Booty," he reflects after complaining about having some of his goods confiscated by officers who also participated in the looting of dead enemy soldiers. He responds, "I certainly didn't give a rat's ass what they say" (1990, 19). He concludes:

> I'm not about to leave anything on their carcasses. That might sound ghoulish, but I know that the Marine behind me will strip the Nip [*sic*] I kill. (1990, 19)

Gabaldon is such a zealous Japanese killer that he is threatened with a court martial on several occasions for his unauthorized and expressly forbidden forays, which he calls "Jap hunting" (1990, 119). Luis Alvarez identifies the morbid nature of Gabaldon's militarized transcultural citizenship by quoting his self-identification as "Dracula" for his blood lust, which Alvarez explains was Gabaldon's way of "proving his manhood and patriotism to his mostly white unit" (Alvarez 2013, 86). Gabaldon thereby debunks the presumption that subaltern subjects necessarily deploy oppositional tactics toward an egalitarian emancipatory end. His record underscores how hegemonic agents and underclass figures alike can consciously deploy their hybridity in ways that support, rather than challenge power. Sandra Soto's concerns about the potential limits of intersectionality models are apt in gauging Gabaldon's slippery agency: Soto notes that the brief and small moments of intersection pale in comparison to the much larger number and wider expanse of the differences that remain (2010, 3–5). Indeed, Gabaldon illustrates Soto's contention that intersectionality does not necessarily constitute solidarity among subaltern subjects or a performance of counterpower.

It must be noted, however, that Gabaldon's battlefield activities were undertaken in lethal combat zones in which killing (or threat of killing) are fundamental tactics, which shape every soldier's primal struggle to survive. The broader symbolic economy of Gabaldon's combat actions and related transracial fluidity nonetheless raise important questions that cannot be answered by celebratory transnationalism, intersectional, and cultural citizenship prisms. On the surface, Gabaldon is the quintessential marginal subject who successfully navigates his subordination by transforming it into interstitial agency pursuant to his own survival and enfranchisement. He thus shares uneasy similarities to other mestiza/o archetypes who anchor Chicana/o Studies. However, scholars in the field are not likely to include this self-identified "Hispanic" among the gallery of Mexican American and Chicana/o hybrid subjects. And for good reason. Even as Gabaldon recuperates Japanese American citizenship through his celebration of the Japanese American soldiering exploits of his childhood Nisei friends who had enabled his transculturation, he freely uses exoticist and racist stereotypes that jar against his transracial cultural citizenship. Gabaldon's trilingual flourishes even degenerate into bigoted invective. In his memoir he regularly refers to Japanese soldiers, businessmen, and postwar politicians as "Nips" and "Japs" (1990, 81, 85). In a 1985 letter to Japanese Prime Minister Yasuhiro Nakasone reprinted in his book, Gabaldon even mocks what he perceives to be Japanese-accented English (e.g., "rots of ruck" for "lots of luck," 1990, 230). Prime Minister Nakasone apparently claimed that "Hispanics were a detriment to the advancement of the U.S.," to which Gabaldon offers the retort: "he stuck his hoof right between his buck-teeth" (1990, 228), evoking another prevalent anti-Japanese stereotype. Gabaldon ironically notes that "I, too, cringe at the word 'Jap,'" adding "after all, the person I love most, my wife, has her roots in Japan" (1990, 10). Gabaldon's second wife is of Japanese and Mexican heritage born and raised in Mexico. Paradoxically, as a Mexican American/Nisei mestizo Gabaldon alternately recognizes, rejects, and kills Japanese as the Other, then recognizes them anew as allies, enemies, family members, and part of himself. His Soldado Razo violentology thus might be understood as an ambivalent HispaNisei who nonetheless is a consummately American capitalist imperialist.

Gabaldon's reunion and lifelong friendship with the commander of the Japanese sniper who shot him during combat also illustrates how the soldiering-as-citizenship paradigm is informed by a transracial and transnational masculinity that segues with patriarchy—*machismo* in Spanish—which is fundamentally violent at the rhetorical, social, and interpersonal levels. This reunion of *macho* men, which takes place on the same island forty years after the two groups of men tried to pierce each other with bullets and bayonets, climaxes in a homosocial symbolic exchange of women in a peculiar scene in Gabaldon's combat memoir. It occurs amid a collage of photos. The first photo features Gabaldon hugging the former Japanese soldier, Saburo Arakaki, who fought against him in the Saipan battle. Other photos feature dead Japanese soldiers, with captions such as "Jap burned to a crisp in a bunker," "Dead Japs by the Dozen," and "A Good Jap Soldier," as well as the contorted bodies of US Marines killed in combat. Yet another photo features the rising sun flag of the Imperial Japanese Army that troops carried into battle and which subsequently adorned Gabaldon's postwar home in Saipan. Amid this grotesque and perverse gallery Gabaldon ironically notes that Arakaki was firm in his belief "that the Nisei were traitors to their race" (1990, 205). But he also adds that Arakaki converted to Christianity and became lifelong friends with Gabaldon and Gabaldon's Mexican Nisei/Mexican American daughter.

The awkward bond between two WWII soldiers from opposite sides of the battlefield climaxes in a chapter dedicated to the Japanese guerrillas who served under Arakaki's command. Gabaldon writes:

> We were both eighteen year old fighters for our respective countries and did our best to kill each other. If Arakaki had ever been in my rifle-sights I would have killed him as I did several of his friends. It was his friend, Corporal Horiguchi, who finally shot me. He got the drop on me and machine gunned me in the left arm and right ribs, grazing my right ear.
>
> Now when Arakaki comes to my home here on the Island where we fought each other, I feel honored by his presence. He prays with my family, and my ten year old daughter, Aiko, sings Japanese war-time songs to him, songs that I taught her when she was three years old. Arakaki's eyes get watery and I know spiritually, something I would never have thought possible—a former Japanese soldier who I had sought in the jungle, now influencing my religious philosophy. Incredible. (1990, 206)

As numerous soldier memoirs reveal, such meetings are sincere and highly personal postcombat rites of passage adumbrated by a transcendent bond among survivors of war horrors. This bond arises from a multiplicity of experiences, insights, and related emotions, including recognition of their exploitation and sacrifice by elites, in addition to the sublime empathy shared by survivors of common traumas. For some, it also involves the mutual recognition of each man's membership in a cult of masculinity. In Gabaldon's narrative, this homosocial soldiering is a martial-cult embedded with a figural exchange of women: Gabaldon offers his young daughter to honor his guest with Japanese wartime songs. The implications of this transnational encounter are placed in greater relief when one considers the dissonance that would be created by a US soldier encouraging a daughter to sing WWII-era German songs in honor of a former Nazi soldier, particularly an officer.

One of the enduring failures of Postcolonial, Decolonial, and Ethnic Studies arises from the persistent reluctance to account for the multiplicity of ways subaltern subjects such as Gabaldon function within hegemony, which in his case involves global capitalism and US imperialism. Unlike life writing genres such as *testimonio* that chronicle the ideological transformation of naifs caught in the local inflection of a global struggle that they progressively come to understand and engage as counterhegemonic actors, Gabaldon's combat memoir underscores how he remained a masculinist, misogynist, and homophobic promoter of empire throughout his life. He even based a failed Congressional campaign on a xenophobic platform decrying "illegal immigrants" and "feminists" (Gabaldon 2000, n.p.), which he added to his memoir's pantheon of villains such as "faggots" (2000, 206).

Unfortunately, Gabaldon's bigoted and imperialist views are not anomalous in the Mexican American and Chicana/o community, which additional case studies in this book demonstrate. His memoir, and subsequent 2000 interview in the University of Texas at Austin's Voces Oral History Project, accordingly, offer opportunities to nuance the simplistic intertwined discourses about Mexican American WWII "heroism" with political citizenship models. Equally as important, Gabaldon's chameleon-like capacity to navigate through and against multiple subject positions pursuant to his own survival and relative empowerment within a capitalist imperialist episteme, ultimately signals the limits of mestizaje, mimesis, transnationalism, and third-space theories of agency. These otherwise productive prisms simply cannot account for Gabaldon's ideologically rigid and hegemonic, yet pragmatically fluid, identity that is overdetermined by multiple layers of racialized, gendered, and sexualized interpersonal and international violences.

Combat, Homosoldiering, and the Marxist Soldado Razo in Judith Pérez and Sévero Pérez's *Soldierboy*

As Gabaldon's embrace of his former Japanese Imperial Army enemy illustrates, homosocial soldiering, or homosoldiering, involves an intimate masculinity that is potentially more powerful than the most fervent nationalisms. Their transracial supranational brotherhood momentarily transcends geopolitics even as Gabaldon's identifications are always subtended by a virulent post-WWII American chauvinist and imperialist ideology. In contrast, Pérez and Pérez's 1982 WWII historical drama, *Soldierboy*, offers a Marxist rendering of the WWII Soldado Razo that layers this archetype as a palimpsest with revolutionary possibility. Written during a residency at El Teatro Campesino's center in San Juan Bautista, California, where it was first produced in 1982 under Luis Valdez's direction, this play presents a portrait of homosoldiering in which intimate combat masculinities overshadow—and even overpower—heterosexual desire. Extending, but also challenging, Sedgwick's continuum of male homosociality, *Soldierboy* tropes the WWII Soldado Razo's homosocial soldiering toward a model of transracial underclass solidarity that eschews the violent hypermasculinity cultivated within patriarchy and exploited by nationalist and imperialist militaries. Written by a male Chicano and white Jewish American husband and wife team, the play features a taboo bonding between a Mexican American soldier and a white soldier during WWII. The soldiers literally are from opposite sides of the railroad tracks in segregated South Texas. Importantly, this play rejects Gabaldon's bigoted, sexist, and homophobic capitalist imperialist politics, which is by far the dominant sentiment among WWII Soldados Razos. *Soldierboy* also challenges the petite bourgeois desires of Mexican American cultural nationalist spectators conditioned to relish depictions of the WWII Soldado Razo as a warrior hero who enabled and legitimated their middle-class aspirations and gains.

As noted in Chapter 1, theorist José Esteban Muñoz's (1999) concept of "disidentification" offers a productive extension of resistant spectatorship paradigms to explicate how queer, and especially

Queer of Color, performers deploy transgressive and relatively empowering reclamations and redeployments of stereotypes that enable actors and audience members to disidentify with old stock characters pursuant to new syntheses. This practice of rejection, reclamation, renovation, and redeployment liberates, at least symbolically, heretofore forbidden abjected subjectivities. This enables various types of enfranchisement. While none of the characters in *Soldierboy* are overtly gay, the playwrights nonetheless deploy similarly transgressive disidentificatory techniques to negotiate—and strategically disidentify—with sexist, racist, and elitist stereotypes. Concurrently, women characters in the play also enable audience disidentification with patriarchal gender role expectations. Patricia Portales has productively recovered feminist agency in *Soldierboy*, which she calls "liberatory layering" (2014, 181). This layering involves Mexican American women's resistance to sexist and racist expectations regarding highly gendered domestic and seamstress factory labor, which Portales identifies as a feminist consciousness raising component of the play. These and other gendered and racialized tensions, maneuvers, and subversions enable the playwrights to restage a transgressive disidentificatory homosoldiering that extends through and beyond rigid segregationist boundaries and equally oppressive heteropatriarchal power dynamics that existed in the WWII era and afterward. Ultimately, *Soldierboy* reconstructs a transracial, protoproletarian WWII Soldado Razo, even as this immanently Marxist supra-Latina/o synthesis remains male centered and ideologically inconsistent.

The plot in *Soldierboy* revolves around the postwar life of Frank De la Cruz, a Mexican American World War II combat veteran who has returned home to San Antonio, Texas, after surviving one of the US Army's worst battlefield defeats in the war: the Rapido River crossing in central Italy. This battle cost the lives of 1,330 soldiers from the US Army's 36th Infantry Division, a unit that consisted primarily of poor Mexican Americans and whites from Texas and Oklahoma.[4] Ostensibly a chronicle about the rise of the Mexican American middle class, the play focuses on Frank's efforts to leave his father's produce stand, where he was expected to work after the war. Frank favors more lucrative employment as a radio repairman at Kelly Field, a local Air Force base. His wife, accustomed to her independence during her husband's wartime deployment overseas, seeks to continue earning extra income, and to preserve her growing autonomy, by working in a garment factory. Frank, however, sees her employment as an affront to his masculinity and authority as a husband, and her duties as a mother. Frank's younger brother, Willie, an immature father figure to Frank's young son, was crippled by an automobile in an act of drunken bravado. He subsequently lives vicariously through newspaper and newsreel accounts of his older brother's "heroic" actions in the war.

Through a montage of shifting settings, Pérez and Pérez use intersecting trajectories of warfare, gender stratification, racial segregation, and labor conflict to propose a new rendering of the Soldado Razo's potential. They begin with a metacritical demystification of the Mexican American warrior hero mythos. For instance, the play opens with Frank's belated arrival home after a parade, brass bands, and speeches about heroism that he deliberately avoided because he rejects the very idea of a war hero that such spectacles celebrate and perpetuate. For him, the war was less about bravery and manhood and more about subservience to military authority. It involved primal human struggles to survive after soldiers and civilians alike had been reduced to their barest animal essence. Frank is especially traumatized by the death of a fellow soldier, Private Ernest Watts, who was killed saving Frank's life in the battle and now reappears in his vivid nightmares. These visitations are juxtaposed with scenes illustrating Frank's strained relationship with his younger brother Willie. These montage sequences foreground a different type of brotherhood, one based on bonds in warfare rather than biology, which becomes less about masculinist models of soldiering and more about class war.

Frank's and Watts's burgeoning awareness of the link between soldiering and exploitation arises from their participation in the deaths of combatants and civilians alike. This horror extends the Soldado Razo's otherwise enlightening demystification to the level of a classical Greek tragedy, where the catastrophe is preordained and propelled through various character flaws and errors of judgment. For instance, Frank de la Cruz, newly promoted to the rank of Sergeant in charge of a platoon of battle-scarred and reluctant soldiers, forces his men forward, knowing they will be slaughtered. He even goes so far as to place his .45 pistol to the head of a frightened draftee, threatening to shoot him if he did not continue advancing toward the lethal German machine gun nests.[5] Frank's dreams revisit these leadership decisions and recall Watts's attempts to console him. Watts has an intimate knowledge of Frank's state of mind, since Watts killed a group of Italian children with a grenade as they hid in a house, which Watts mistook for German soldiers. This experience of survival—against desperate odds and through unspeakably horrible decisions that at the time seemed logical even if they later appear to have been terribly wrong—becomes the basis of their battlefield bond. Both realize they are mere pawns and that their collective agency has been co-opted to harm other pawns for someone else's benefit. Through such depictions of horror and resulting epiphanies, the playwrights introduce an expanded horizon for the Soldado Razo that extends through and beyond homosociality. Indeed, homosoldiering, for all its masculinist dimensions, becomes the basis for their Marxist and protorevolutionary synthesis of the new protoproletarian Soldado Razo.

The play presages this intimate and potentially revolutionary bond between men in battle through an exchange of symbolically significant gifts: they function as theatrically excessive devices that underscore the tragedy of the reified warrior hero archetype. During a lull in the battle, for instance, Frank gives Watts a medallion of St. Christopher, the 250 CE Christian martyr associated with dangerous river crossings and who is believed to protect travelers. Frank's fervently devout Catholic aunt initially gifted the talisman to him, which he shares with Watts. Watts returns the favor by offering a charred wooden case of toy soldiers—the only thing he could find on the battlefield—for Frank's son, which gains a metonymic resonance later in the play. These gifts are reminders of the lethal model of manhood that has led these two men from opposite sides of the tracks onto the same battlefield. Only one of them will escape alive, though he will never truly escape the horror. Significantly, this exposé offers an opportunity for the audience to entertain the option of disidentifying with the martial caste depictions of Mexican American military soldiers, and the male warrior hero mythos in general.

But this is only part of the play's transgressive significance, as it is predicated upon a much more incisive class analysis. As previously mentioned, the unexpected, though common, battlefield bond among soldiers of different racial backgrounds rearticulates a potentially transracial materialist model of the Soldado Razo. However, a postwar visit by Watts's mother complicates this transracial bond. She traveled with her husband to the De la Cruz home in San Antonio, from their nearby rural white-majority enclave of Floresville, Texas. She seeks to learn how her son died, especially since he remained listed by the US Army as Missing-in-Action. Frank, reluctant to tell her about the horrors they experienced as subjects and agents of warfare, says that her son died instantly, ostensibly without pain. Mrs. Watts punctuates the conversation with a matter-of-fact statement that her husband refuses to enter the De la Cruz home "because he wishes it was you that was missing, and Ernest [Watts] the one that came home." Frank retorts: "Look, I'm sorry about Ernest. But I'm not sorry about coming home" (1989, 58). Frank rejects the bigoted view of this era (and subsequent eras) that Mexican Americans, and especially Mexican American soldiers, are surplus and expendable even as he commiserates with the Watts's grief.

This scene involving Frank's refusal to identify with racist expectations does more than simply appeal to its targeted petite bourgeois Mexican American audience, which has been weaned on facile Chicana/o literary indictments of racism. The play's depiction of such a powerful bond between a Mexican American and a white male from a subtly racist family offers a protorevolutionary proposal for transracial, working-class solidarity. It begins with a subtle indictment of Mexican American cultural nationalist sentiments and desires for class mobility within the capitalist imperialist context of US militarism during and after WWII, which the five military bases in San Antonio, Texas, (dubbed by civic boosters as "Military City, U.S.A.") continue to afford. It is not a coincidence that part of Frank's strategy for upward class mobility was encouraging his father to seek a large produce supply contract with a military base that had been reserved for white suppliers. The play's underlying critique of Mexican American middle-class aspirations, all of which is propelled and simultaneously circumscribed by heteropatriarchal gender role expectations, and US militarism, reaches a crescendo in the penultimate dream sequence. In this scene, Watts saves Frank, who is wounded, only to be killed in the process. Before his death, Watts shouts:

> You're crazy! You'll get yourself killed. We got to get you some help or you'll die here like the rest of them. Our company always went first. Why? The brass didn't think any better of us meskins and redneck farmboys. We didn't mean dirt to them. We always did what we was told. And you, Sarge, you were the best of what we had. We done enough. But no more. I'm saving our butts, De la Cruz. You're my ticket out of here. Goddamn it. We're not going to die here. Let's go.   (1989, 74)

This dying antiheroic soliloquy, reminiscent of Falstaff's iconic carnivalesque indictment of war-makers in Shakespeare's tragedy, *Henry IV, Part I*, closes the drama and imbues the preceding act with a new troping of battlefield brotherhood as tragic but, significantly, antimasculinist intimacy[6] (Figure 2.1). This homosoldiering bond is no longer defined by the exchange of women, but by the figural and real exchange of blood across race. This new homosociality potentially forms the basis of the Soldado Razo's disarticulation from racist, and even simplistic antiracist teleologies, so he can be relocated within a broader historical materialist critique of the political economy of warfare.

The relationship between the two combat brothers-in-arms is so powerful it will extend beyond the grave and into Frank's home, casting a long somber shadow over his postwar life with his wife and biological family that further complicates the Soldado Razo's homosocial soldiering. The dead, and Frank's yearning for Watts's

FIGURE 2.1. *Performance scene from* Soldierboy *(1982), by Judith Pérez and Sévero Pérez. Courtesy of Teatro Campesino and the University of California at Santa Barbara Davidson Library Special Collections.*

life, even displace Frank's matrimonial intimacy. After his return from war, Frank no longer experiences sexual intercourse, romantic touches, or emotional intimacy with his wife despite her entreaties, which include a special dress bought for his exclusive gaze. In a play about Post Traumatic Stress Disorder (which was diagnosed during WWII as "Battle Fatigue"), the bonds of homosoldiering are forged amid annihilating violence. The drama allows for the possibility of a new model of the Soldado Razo who is the antithesis of the heroic male warrior. Crucially, this new synthesis also supersedes the hypermasculinist heterosexual soldier desire that leads to myriad commodifications of, and atrocities against, women. In the end, the story is less about racism or marital estrangement and more about the potential for transracial working-class solidarity.

This is where the play itself disidentifies with the cultural nationalist politics of the venues such as the Farmworker Theater in San Juan Bautista, where it was composed and first staged. Like many grants-driven Latina/o cultural arts venues, such centers frequently host programming that features archetypes of the "tragic" mestiza and mestizo, or supposedly resistant subjects who seek citizenship rights within the US capitalist imperialist system. Some such centers like the Guadalupe Cultural Arts Center in San Antonio, Texas, which hosted a performance of this play, also peddle banal solipsistic Latina/o culture spectacles—from folkloric dance to popular music—devoid of substantive political critique. *Soldierboy*, on the other hand, proposes a radical alternative vision of an egalitarian society no longer predicated upon patriarchal domination and exploitation, destructive racial teleologies, or annihilating nationalist and imperialist wars that disproportionately affect the poor for the benefit of middle and upper classes. Watts, who vocalizes a class critique of the US military's use of the poor of all races to serve as cannon fodder thus tempers Frank's impatient pursuit of upward class mobility. The play recognizes the legitimacy of Frank's desire to break out of his segregated political economic realities, but also critiques this mode of empowerment for being mired in the patriarchal oppression of women and complicity in warmongering, which renders it ideologically contradictory and fundamentally corrupt. Moreover, in this play, the symbolic death of the male warrior hero, and the Soldado Razo warrior hero in particular, is less important than the introduction of a new model of homosoldiering in which the Soldado Razo becomes an oppositional transracial archetype:

the angry proletarian coming to consciousness about how they have been exploited in war, and what needs to be done to change the subjective and material conditions pursuant to a liberation that extends across classes, races, genders, regions, and the world at large. In this way, the Soldado Razo of *Soldierboy* enacts a transracial, immanently Marxist, and protofeminist supra-Latina/o violentology.

Revolutionary Brotherhood: The Homosocial Legacy of WWII-Soldado Razo Communists

As illustrated in Gabaldon's *Saipan: Suicide Island*, as well as in Pérez and Pérez's *Soldierboy*, the Mexican American WWII Soldado Razo is an ideologically inchoate figure or, rather, many different subjects who intersect but also diverge in a multiplicity of ways that may be more significant than their similarities. Paradoxically, but predictably, the WWII Soldado Razo's violent migrations across race and geography locate this archetype within, but also potentially outside, the Althusserian notion of an all-encompassing ideology. That is, a Soldado Razo can be a reactionary capitalist imperialist, such as Gabaldon models, but also a protorevolutionary Marxist, as is the case in *Soldierboy*; and sometimes the Soldado Razo's ideology is simultaneously reactionary and protorevolutionary. *Soldierboy*'s protagonist Frank de la Cruz models this paradox as the patriarchal upwardly mobile petite bourgeois merchant who never fully understands his male privilege, or capitalism's hierarchical nature, even as he meditates on his dead white friend's lessons about the evils of imperialist warfare that renders expendable the poor of all races. Significantly, Pérez and Pérez are not military veterans, and they wrote this play four decades after WWII, which may seem anachronistic for its retrospective depiction of an era that is not generally associated with revolutionary politics. However, numerous WWII-era Mexican American soldiers and civilians espoused similar sentiments through the provocative though vexed concept of "revolutionary brotherhood," which challenged racial hierarchies while reinforcing gender ones. A violentological hermeneutic enables us to identify how "revolutionary brotherhood" is not just sexism, but a violently masculinist episteme—a patriarchal Nietzschean will-to-power—in which the idea of revolutionary violence cannot be disentangled from the violence of male gender privilege.

The late printmaker and poet Carlos Córtez illustrated a WWII-era permutation of "revolutionary brotherhood." He is the "red-diaper" son of an immigrant indigenous Mexican communist father who was a member of the Industrial Workers of the World (IWW, a US-based international labor organization with anarchist, socialist, and communist affiliations that enjoyed widespread support from the 1920s through the 1950s, also known as the "Wobblies"), and an immigrant German socialist pacifist mother.[7] Through his poetry, art, and related activities, Córtez epitomizes the radical potential of a proletarian transracial homosociality, but he also models its fundamental contradictions. Córtez was born in 1923 to parents who participated in leftist revolutionary activities in the United States, Mexico, and Europe during the 1920s and 1930s. He extended this legacy into the WWII and Cold War eras as an artist, labor organizer, and outspoken critic of capitalism, imperialism, and US militarism. Drafted into the US Army in 1944 upon graduating from high school, Córtez was among the thousands of American males from diverse backgrounds who refused induction. He was convicted and jailed after his application for conscientious objector status was denied, and served two years in prison.[8] He later became renowned for his populist woodcuts of workers, strikers, and icons of the American left, such as Mexican anarchist Ricardo Flores Magón, and communists such as Swedish immigrant Joe Hill and Afro-Latina Lucía González de Parsons (Figure 2.2). Of his political imprisonment in an era when Mexican Americans felt compelled to join the military and defense industry as a patriotic duty and strategic avenue for upward social and class mobility, Córtez famously remarked:

> I've always been an anti-militarist. My parents were both anti-militarists. I went to prison back in World War II for refusing to submit to the draft. I said: if you can guarantee me a shot at Hitler *or any other head of state* you wouldn't have to draft me. But to shoot at another draftee, forget about it.   (emphasis added, 2004)

Hardly the pacifist that Scott H. Bennett has suggested (2001, 40), Córtez's animosity toward fascist Adolf Hitler, and "any other head of state"—presumably including the US president—comes close to sedition in the United States, which is punishable by imprisonment, and in some cases, death.[9] Moreover, Córtez's solidarity with workers throughout the world included countries with which the US was

FIGURE 2.2. *"Lucía González de Parsons" (1986), linocut, by Carlos Córtez. National Museum of Mexican Art Permanent Collection, 1997. Photo by Michael Tropea. Courtesy of Despina Katsikakis and the Carlos Córtez Estate.*

at war—such as North Vietnam—further expanding the revolution-ary transracial poetics and politics imagined in proto-Marxist depic-tions of the WWII-era Soldado Razo in *Soldierboy*.

Córtez's activism as a decades-long member of the Socialist Party, and later partisan of the IWW, challenges conventional renderings of the heroic Soldado Razo, even as Córtez's homosocial aesthetics un-dermine his proposed revolutionary alternative. His three militant poetry collections consist of poems published over four decades in the IWW newspaper, *Industrial Worker*, and complement his social-ist realist graphic art. Together they feature worker direct action and outright revolutionary insurrection, though the work also traffics in male warrior hero archetypes and related sexist stereotypes. For in-stance, in "Requiem for a Swede," originally published in the *Industrial Worker* and included in his 1990 poetry collection, *Crystal-Gazing the Amber Fluid, & Other Wobbly Poems*, the alternately bombastic and meditative omniscient poetic persona reflects on the

1915 execution of communist Joe Hill.[10] As a member of the IWW, Hill was renowned for his militant music. He became a *cause célèbre* after being accused of a double murder in Salt Lake City, Utah. Hill subsequently was convicted and executed by a Mormon firing squad at the age of thirty-six. Like Córtez, Hill had deployed his art as part of radical labor organizing. Córtez's elegy to him introduces a martial revolutionary poetic that all but advocates armed insurrection. The last two stanzas read:

> Somewhere
> Lodged in a decaying log
> A small pinecone sheds forth
> A green shoot.
>
> Somewhere
> In a Rebel Valhalla
> Playing an accordion
> Singing a song
> A spirit waits
> For a class conscious
> Armageddon.   (1990, 15)

The penultimate stanza illustrates the meditative pantheist quality that emerged from Córtez's imprisonment in rural Sandstone, Minnesota, where he renewed his commitment to his indigenous heritage. (This was later reflected in his moniker "Koyokuikatl," or "singing coyote," that a Nahuatl elder bestowed.) The final stanza of the poem expands the supraracial proletarian politics that animate Pérez and Pérez's play *Soldierboy*: he tropes the salience of armed insurrection through the Judeo-Christian legend of "Armageddon," which proposes violent destruction as a prelude to regeneration and humanity's salvation from evil. Córtez further embeds this martial discourse with Hill's Swedish heritage by invoking the mythic "Valhalla," which is Norse for "hall of the slain," the Viking paradise for warriors killed in combat.

Córtez's hagiography makes no allusion, however, to the circumstances surrounding Hill's arrest and conviction. Hill initially became a suspect after seeking medical attention for a gunshot wound he received in a fight with a fellow communist over a woman with whom the two men had been having a sexual relationship. Taking considerable license in recounting Hill's execution, Córtez endows class-consciousness and political martyrdom with the ritual beauty of a song, all within a hypermasculinist logic that involves strategic silences about a love triangle that may have involved feminist agency, as well as male commodification of women. A similarly masculinist martial poetic is operative in Córtez's transracial revolutionary paeans to other male warrior heroes, such as "Requiem for 'Two Dago Reds,'" "Ballad of a Draftee," and "Requiem Chant for a Half-Breed Warrior." Like most of his poetry, these minimalist socialist realist compositions lend themselves to the sort of musical performance ideal for organizing initiatives and protest rallies, but still rely upon male warrior heroes. Likewise, in his graphic art Córtez both uses and transforms the martial caste stereotype propagated by the US government and reified by Latina/os through the Soldado Razo archetype. He proposes a revolutionary analogue in the form of an insurgent army of workers. This poetic informs his famous 1964 print that glosses Karl Marx's *Communist Manifesto* slogan: "Workers of the world, unite. You have nothing to lose but your chains!" Córtez recasts this slogan as a call to action to conscripts of all the world's military forces: "Draftees of the World Unite! You Have Nothing to Lose But Your Generals!" (Figure 2.3).

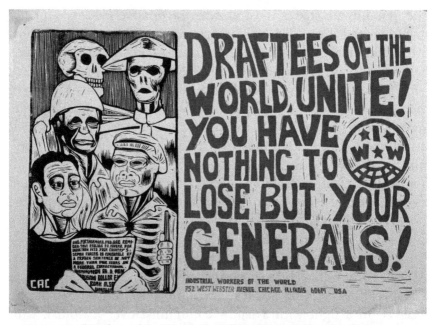

FIGURE 2.3.   *"Draftees of the World, Unite!" (1968), by Carlos Cortéz, linocut, National Museum of Mexican Art Permanent Collection. Photo by Michael Tropea. Courtesy of Despina Katsikakis and the Carlos Córtez Estate.*

Córtez's antimilitarist, but still masculinist martial *ars poetica*, did not merely pay homage to revolutionary martyrs; it also militated against the reification of art. As a Marxist he eschewed the idea of private property. As such, he refused to allow his art, or his notoriety, to be reduced as an abstract artifact for collectors. He explains:

> I made a provision in my estate, for whoever will take care of my blocks, that if any of my graphic works are selling for high prices immediate copies should be made to keep the price down.   (2004, n.p.)

Córtez's Marxist politics, socialist realist didacticism, and overt partisanship with worker and revolutionary movements, generally are *verboten* in the banal poetic practice that distinguishes much of twentieth-century American poetry. But this approach distinguishes his contrapuntal poetics. Córtez's poem, "A Difference," for instance, demonstrates his unabashed socialist realist trajectory and biting critique of pedestrian liberal sentiments:

> The scissor-bill who spits
> At my placard,
> Hurls obscenities
> And yells,
> "Go back to
> Russia!"
> Him I do not feel
> Too angry at;
> He only has a long
> Way to go.
> But the person who glances
> Around furtively
> Before confidentially whispering
> To me,
> "I agree with you;
> What you're doing is great!"
> That one I cannot
> Stand
> That one, he is going
> Nowhere!   (1990, 23)

Córtez's art deliberately sought to polarize the subjective conditions, that is, people's political maturity and determination to fight their exploitation, pursuant to a kinetic revolutionary synthesis of these material contradictions. His Marxist XicanIndio subjectivity thereby intersects with other XicanIndia/o communists, such as 1930s labor organizer Emma Tenayuca, and later, Raúl Salinas, discussed in Chapter 1. They all similarly merge their indigenous heritage with seemingly antithetical Marxist theories of praxis, particularly the insistence upon direct action and militant organized confrontation of the nation state and monopoly capital, with arms if necessary. Accordingly, Córtez is quoted as saying, "Because of my background...I'm red in more ways than one" (qtd. Bennett 2001, 30). He even wrote under the pseudonym C. C. Redcloud, invoking the nineteenth-century Sioux Chief who fought Euro-American settler colonists who, backed by the US Army, buttressed the nineteenth-century intrusion of capital into Indian Country.

Córtez's wife Marianna Drogitis Córtez provides a sobering counterpoint to her husband's XicanIndio, Marxist, and supraracial permutation of the Soldado Razo. Throughout their marriage, she was the sole worker and wage earner in the family, especially during a four-year period of Córtez's unemployment because of a debilitating illness. In one three-year period, she recalls working seven days per week from 4 a.m. to 7 p.m. without a day off! In the published account of a 2001 interview, Lydia M. Huante notes that Marianna Drogitis Córtez "was paying the mortgage, taxes, utilities, and barely had any money left over for food and transportation." Huante adds, "But she knew how to manage money and cook rice, beans and chicken wings at home" (qtd. in Huante 2001, 104). These dimensions of the traditional heteropatriarchal marriage structure, which involve double duty for a wife, do not necessarily belie her insistence that Carlos was not merely her husband, but her *compañero*, or her revolutionary comrade and lifelong partner. However, Marianna Drogitis Córtez makes several dissonant comments in the same interview that suggest her compañero's pursuit of a model of "revolutionary brotherhood" appears to be nothing other than homosociality. As she states, "I never believed any man who says I only have eyes for you; this is phony baloney" (qtd. in Huantes 2001, 106). Huantes summarizes the ensuing conversation about philandry:

> Carlos has had many female fans and admirers, and sometimes he's been too generous with his time. However, if Carlos ever stepped out with another woman, Marianna would hold him responsible. She would not seek revenge against another woman. She says "This I

cannot stand about women, that women attack women." So she tells him to be careful not to let them become infatuated with him.

(qtd. in Huantes 2001, 106)

Revealingly, in the introduction to the exhibit catalogue for Córtez's retrospective at the Mexican Museum in Chicago, Bennett reports: "sexual politics marked his *Industrial Worker* editorship" because of "Córtéz's portrayal of sexually provocative women in his cartoons" (2001, 30). He adds that Córtéz was rebuked for a 1970 May Day issue of the IWW newspaper because:

the front page cartoon featured an attractive, mini-skirted, buxom woman holding the IWW flag as an IWW male worker gazed at her, and the back page contained a photograph of a woman clad in a superimposed bikini inscribed with "IWW" and "ONE BIG UNION."

(2001, 31)

Even as Córtez elsewhere made important efforts to confront sexism, such as advocating women's pay equity and featuring feminist revolutionaries such as Lucía González de Parsons and Emma Goldman, his performance of the objectifying male gaze within his model of "revolutionary brotherhood" taints his interventions.

Córtez reveals that antimilitarist Latino leftist militants are not immune from the patriarchal politics that characterize capitalist and imperialist heterosexual male soldiering. This homosociality, which is embedded with both symbolic and kinetic violences, extends to the era's leftist political organizations that were predicated upon a similar model of "revolutionary brotherhood." Humberto "Bert" Corona, the child of Mexican anarchist revolutionist exiles, was a founder and member of transborder mutual aid organizations whose praxis invites further contrapuntal assessment of "revolutionary brotherhood" vis-à-vis hegemonic iterations of the WWII Soldado Razo. These organizations included *La Hermandad Mexicana Nacional* ("Mexican National Brotherhood"), and *La Hermandad General de Trabajadores* ("General Brotherhood of Workers"), both of which organized undocumented workers, yet operated in a hierarchical patriarchal leadership model. Corona also was a founding member of the Marxist vanguardist organization, *Centro de Acción Social Autónoma*, or "Center for Autonomous Social Action," better known by its Spanish acronym CASA, which translates as "house," a trope that ultimately proved to be inconsistent with the organization's revolutionary ends.

Ironically, or perhaps prophetically, Bert Corona's protorevolutionary activities were preceded by his attempt to become a more traditional Soldado Razo. He was a twenty-three-year-old union organizer when the Japanese Navy attacked Pearl Harbor on December 7, 1941. Despite being born into an anarchist Mexican immigrant family, Corona promptly volunteered for the US Army, with hopes of becoming a pilot in the Army Air Corps. He claims, however, that because of his leftist politics, he was subjected to numerous political interrogations and unit reassignments that truncated his promotions and opportunities, ultimately keeping him out of the combat he sought. In his biography of Corona, Mario Garcia quotes him as saying:

> I entered the service as a buck private, and I left as one. I paid the price of having been involved in progressive causes and was one of those stigmatized and red-baited because of my involvement.
>
> (qtd. in Mario Garcia 1995, 151)

Vicki L. Ruiz places Corona's claims of persecution in greater relief when she notes that CASA, the organization with which he is most associated, was in the vanguard of class struggle and simultaneously retrograde in its treatment of female members:

> Women in CASA were both inspired and frustrated.... Considering themselves the revolutionary vanguard, CASA leaders required an all-encompassing commitment on the part of its members. People left school; people left jobs; their lives totally revolved around the organization. In some instances, even choice of dating partners was not an individual decision. Women did assume very visible public roles in CASA—as examples, Kathy Ledesma Ochoa and Isabel Rodríguez Chávez served as editors of Sin Fronteras [the CASA newspaper]. Chicanas in CASA, however, were expected to bear the brunt of "women's work" in planning fundraisers, selling tickets, and preparing food. The double standard prevailed.   (2008, 118)

This transnational organization also reinforced rigid racial stratifications as a matter of organizational principle. Ruiz adds: "the whole issue of interracial dating and marriage became hotly debated" (2008, 119). She quotes a female CASA member as saying, "intermarriage results in a weakening of ties and declining sense of responsibility and commitment to La Raza" (2008, 119), though one of Bert Corona's wives was a white Jewish American woman. Despite Córtez's and Corona's provocative and visionary transformations of the WWII Soldado Razo into a communist vanguard warrior hero, their lingering gender contradictions inevitably render their "revolutionary brotherhood" praxis as highly flawed because of its coercive and counterrevolutionary rehousing of women within heteropatriarchal norms.

The WWII-Soldado Razo *Sous Rature*: Communists, Spies, and Latin Lovers

Alongside the above models of "revolutionary brotherhood," other Mexican American and Latino males further globalize and simultaneously parochialize WWII-Soldado Razo violentologies. This legacy includes figures not normally associated with radical politics, such as renowned educator, scholar, and diplomat Ernesto Galarza, who was also associated with the Friends of the Abraham Lincoln Brigade. This was the solidarity and fundraising arm of the largely communist internationalist volunteer unit, founded in the United States, that fought Spanish fascists and their Nazi and Italian fascist allies in the Spanish Civil War from 1936 to 1939. This war, in effect, was the prelude to WWII, and was the training ground for Nazi weapons and tactics. The 3,200 members of the Abraham Lincoln Brigade (in actuality a battalion) were among 60,000 internationalist volunteers from fifty-two countries who buttressed Republican forces. This unit was fully integrated with women, African Americans, Asian Americans, Irish, Latin American, and US whites of various ethnicities. It also included approximately 200 Latino combatants from a multiplicity of ethnic and racial backgrounds, though they were all male. At least ten members of the Abraham Lincoln Brigade were Mexican Americans. Also, at a time when de jure and de facto segregation in all branches of the US military circumscribed racial minority mobility into the officer corps, the Abraham Lincoln Brigade contained Latino officers. It even incorporated the 125-soldier Centuria Antonio Guiteras International Brigade (in actuality a company), which formed in New York City and primarily consisted of black and white Cuban Americans, Puerto Ricans, Mexican Americans, African Americans, as well as immigrants and their descendants from several Latin American countries (Figure 2.4). Significantly, the Abraham Lincoln Brigade's "Latino" members included numerous volunteers from Tampa, Ybor City, and surrounding areas of South Florida who were of Spanish (mostly from Galicia) and Italian (primarily Sicilian) heritage but identified as "Latin." This term referred to the pan-racial identity formed by the descendants of immigrants from throughout the world. As Gary Mormino (2014) has noted, these "Latins" were partisans of anarchist and communist causes throughout the world from the mid-nineteenth to the late-twentieth centuries.[11]

Despite these and other attempts to synthesize a revolutionary Soldado Razo, however, the ideological pendulum repeatedly swings back to the capitalist and imperialist right. One of the most glaring examples is the secular deification of United Farm Worker (UFW) labor organizer Cesar Chavez, who enlisted in the Navy in 1946 a few months after the end of WWII. Even though Chavez describes his military experience as "the worst two years of my life" (qtd. in León 2010, 73), the US Navy christened a dry cargo and ammunition ship as "U.S. Naval Ship (U.S.N.S.) Cesar Chavez" on the symbolically

FIGURE 2.4. *The Centuria Antonio Guiteras International Brigade, Circa 1937. Photographer Agustí Centelles. Courtesy of Octavi Centelles and the Agustí Centelles Estate, and El Ministerio de Cultura y Deporte, Centro Documental de la Memoria Histórica (Archivo Centelles, Foto 1520), Salamanca, Spain.*

significant day of May 5, 2012. Perhaps not ironically, the "pack mule" transport and supply vessel functions as a naval beast of burden, as it were, while inadvertently alluding to the reformist assimilationist agenda that Chavez's farmworker union pursued. Indeed, despite his aversion to the US Navy, Chavez pursued coterminous capitalist imperialist ends: he incessantly purged communists from the UFW.

Worse, Chavez's founding of an "intentional community," which some critics label a cult, supplant the warrior hero with the prophet. This was the culmination of the UFW's, and Chavez's, overt marginalization of cofounder Dolores Huerta, a longtime member of the Socialist Party U.S.A., and other women members. Matthew Garcia (2012) notes that in the later part of his UFW leadership, Chavez adopted a ritual known as "The Game," which evolved from a group therapy technique used by the drug addiction rehabilitation organization Synanon. The original practice involved participants sitting in a circle and critiquing targeted group members to stimulate candid introspection and self-assessments that presumably would enable their reform and recovery.[12] Chavez imported this practice into the UFW, with the charge of "disloyalty" replacing the ill of drug addiction that the practice originally was designed to eliminate. This iteration of a group *autocrítica* frequently degenerated into vicious humiliating diatribes and violently sexist vitriol that Chavez failed to arrest. He even enjoined and encouraged this conduct. The ritual became an incisive, personally invasive, and psychologically destructive practice that frequently targeted women. Garcia reports that Chavez's son Paul (also known as "Babo") replicated his father's frequent insults to Huerta by attacking her daughter Lori. In one episode of "The Game," for instance, Babo calls Lori "a fucking hypocrite," "a fucking bitch," and "a goddamn cunt," with similar attacks addressed to her mother, all in the presence of Chavez (rpt. in Matt Garcia 2012, 163–4). Chavez's notorious collusion with US immigration officials to arrest Mexican immigrant workers for their "scab" labor, which Chavez deemed a disruption to UFW strike negotiations, compounds his degeneration from a successful union organizer into a vicious misogynist messianic cult leader and US nationalist capitalist. Significantly, Cesar Chavez's renown as a pacifist leader also is predicated upon his famous self-flagellating fasts: they may have been "passive" responses to the violence of his antiunion foes, but his fasts also were a form of embodied self-sacrifice that had a specific political goal that parallels battlefield commander calculations.[13] A devout

Catholic, Chavez also became the symbolic Christlike sacrificial victim-savior upon his death, with rumors of canonization and possibly even sainthood in his postmortem future.

Yet other WWII-era Soldados Razos more overtly intertwine highly sexualized patriarchal privilege in the global extension of US imperialism. Robert Huddleston's 2007 biography, *Edmundo: From Chiapas, Mexico to Park Avenue*, which bears the front cover tagline, "The true story of a Mexican-American who became a World War II spy and married a German Princes," chronicles an exemplary Latin Lover and spy permutation of the Soldado Razo archetype. Lassalle's militarized path toward citizenship and upward mobility as a uniformed member of the WWII US Office of Strategic Services (OSS), the precursor to the Central Intelligence Agency, involves multiple strategic marriages, as well as politically significant jobs and OSS assignments. The back cover reveals how Lassalle anticipates the romantic image of the dandy spy made famous by Ian Fleming's James Bond character:

> Biography of Edmundo Lassalle, a Mexican who came to the U.S. in 1935 to attend Columbia University, married the daughter of a college dean, became a student/teacher at the University of California earning a Phi Beta Kappa key. He became a U.S. citizen and an assistant to Nelson Rockefeller, then a member of the Roosevelt Administration before becoming an American espionage agent in Spain while employed as the European Representative of the Walt Disney Company. At the end of the war, he divorced his first wife in order to marry a German princess whose father was an early supporter of Adolf Hitler. Later, he divorced the princess to marry the first of two wealthy American heiresses. Financially secure, he took up residence on the upper east side of Manhattan to devote his time and talents to the preservation of ancient monuments. In 1974, divorced from his fourth wife and failing in health, he took his own life in London.
>
> (Huddleston 2007, n.p.)

Lassalle's upward mobility as a WWII-Soldado Razo spy, replete with an expansive gallery of wives—one of whom brought him into relative proximity to Adolf Hitler—extends the masculinist cultural nationalist politics of the American G.I. Forum through a bizarre variation of the warrior caste archetype that interweaves feudal nobility and European antiquity. Working under the cover of a job provided by the Disney Corporation, the paragon of American capitalist imperialist fantasy, Lassalle embodied this US imperialist ideal and Mexican American interpellation within it. As illustrated in Chapter 5, Lassalle is one of many Latino CIA spies whose mestizo subjectivity, interstitial gnosis, and attendant upward class mobility are intertwined with imperialist extensions of US military power.

Similar to Lassalle's persona as the dandy lover and spy, other Mexican American WWII-soldier memoirs, verse, and unpublished archival writings reveal heteropatriarchal gazes on women from other races and nationalities that again place the transnational trope under erasure. Although most of these writers' sexual allusions are much less overt and graphic than in subsequent generations of male war writing, Américo Paredes's WWII-era poetry and related unpublished writings may be the most graphic of the Mexican American members of the "Greatest Generation." For instance, his overtly racialized discussion of Japanese women's body parts and musings on the price of prostitutes in postwar Japan, alongside his love-hate relationship with white women, betray a sexist transnational and transracial fetish. This includes meditations on Japanese women's breasts size, shape, and color, which he describes as upturned porcelain tea cups topped with strawberries.[14] Paredes's various gazes upon and identifications with Japanese culture, and especially women, intersect with Gabaldon's transracial allusions, and are intertwined with his problematic "LatinAsian" violentology discussed further in Chapter 3.

In another instance of the Soldado Razo's actualization as a warrior hero through the symbolic homosocial exchange of exoticized "foreign" women, Francis X. Medina, a tail gunner on a B-24 bomber shot down over Italy, offers a neopicaresque memoir about his evasion of Nazi and Italian fascist troops for eight months. His harrowing experience is replete with accounts of youthful encounters with the attractive Italian sisters of antifascist partisan guerrillas who sheltered him. To help Medina pass as their family, members of two Italian households taught him functional Italian. They also obtained an identity card in which his brown skin and mestizo phenotype fit seamlessly into their own dark Italian complexion. In an episode out of a juvenile coming-of-age story, but far more frightening for its lethal setting behind enemy lines, Medina recounts the jumble of emotions as he slept under an Italian widow's bed, with her on top. Throughout this dramatic and at times titillating ordeal, he must constantly evade the family's fascist uncle!

The anachronistic though ever-present lethality of the enduring neofeudal homosocial exchange of women in the WWII era becomes even more explicit when Medina recounts the aftermath of an errant US bomb that injured Antinesca, the sister of his Italian partisan host:

> "Francesco," Oreste said in a strained voice as we set out across the field, "if Antinesca had been killed, I would have had to kill you."
>
> I stopped dead in my tracks. A chill ran down my spine and I shuddered. For a few seconds, my legs refused to move, then I again fell into stride with Oreste. I didn't answer. What was there to say?
>
> "Because it was an Allied plane," he explained. "And you are an American."
>
> "But..." I protested weakly.
>
> "You are my soul brother, my Partisan brother and you are the adopted son of our family. But Antinesca, she is blood. She is my blood sister and if her blood had been spilled, I would have been obliged to avenge her." (1995, 132–3)

Despite Medina's ability to pass as an Italian among the historically marginalized, subjugated, and exploited rural Italians, particularly in the South, he still is an American. Moreover, his provisional assimilation into Italian partisan life remains contingent on the exchange-of-women logic whereby family honor, like family fortune, are tabulated by men in terms of the material and symbolic value of women's bodies and lives.

This neofeudal WWII-Soldado Razo violentology extends to cliché Horatio Alger progress narratives that are interwoven with a homosocial romance subtext involving English women and the ever-present threat of blood vengeance by their cuckolded British soldier husbands. Unwittingly paralleling Mary Louise Roberts's (2013) investigation of US servicemen's exploitation, abuse, and rape of French women during WWII, Henry Cervantes's 2002 memoir, *Piloto: Migrant Worker to Jet Pilot*, chronicles how G.I. salaries and access to rationed food products and scarce goods fueled an underground sexual economy in WWII England. English women exchanged sex and engaged in long-term relationships with multiple soldiers as a means of sustenance and survival. Illustrating his American male and economic privilege, Cervantes represents one of his affairs as a consensual romance where he satisfies the needs of a frustrated housewife whose husband is away at war:

> Over tea, she spoke about her husband for the first time. He was a squadron leader stationed nearby, they had been married seven years, were devoted to each other, and before the war, he had held a position in the office of the Lord Mayor. She sounded convincing but her eyes told me that she wanted more than he had left after a hard day in the air. We began an affair.   (2002, 67)

Similar to other male Mexican American military memoirs, Cervantes interweaves his account of trailblazing integration into the officer corps and elite pilot ranks with repeated discussions of fleeting relationships and sexual encounters with foreign women. With the nonchalant descriptive tone of a dispassionate technician, yet with sexually suggestive imagery, he recalls the mechanics of his affair with the wife of the English pilot:

> Our dates were keyed to their mailbox. Slot open meant safe. Slot closed, he's home.   (2002, 67)

Further illuminating the quasi-incestuous homosocial exchange of women among Allied soldiers in the WWII era, Cervantes's narrative includes a photo of him and his brother Gus, a US Army soldier, with a woman in between. It bears the caption:

> August 1945, Los Angeles, California. Hank and Gus met Esther Soto. They asked her to decide between them; she chose Gus.   (2002, 110)

The homosociality governing this iteration of the Mexican American WWII-Soldado Razo archetype inevitably suggests other possibilities, as illustrated in another photograph in which Cervantes hugs a fellow pilot. The caption reads: "Hank and an unidentified friend couldn't find any girls willing to have their pictures taken with them so they did the next best thing." A lifelong bachelor, Cervantes's memoir also includes photos of him with the Nazi suicide pilot who rammed the tail of Cervantes's B-17 bomber, offering yet another postwar homosocial male bonding between former enemies. His memoir closes with an account of Cervantes's role in the development of a camera for surveillance aircraft used in the Cuban Missile

Crisis, further layering the protoimperialist resonance to his global homosocial gaze as a Soldado Razo Latin Lover and quasi spy.

Despite their political divergences, the Mexican American WWII memoirs, theater, verse, autobiographies, and biographies discussed above frequently converge as they narrativize "manly conquests" of women amid harrowing and oftentimes tragic tales of war and insurrection. In his memoir Henry Cervantes also presents profound and potentially productive slippages in his depiction of homosoldiering, particularly in regards to the legendary tensions between US military personnel and the equally hypermasculinist Pachuco Zoot Suiter. This lumpenproletarian figure is infamous in the WWII era for his defiance of authority, which was signified by the flamboyant excesses of the oversized suit (sometimes called "drapes"), long watch chain, bulbous shined shoes, vernacular patois, and general counterculture aura. Early in his memoir, Cervantes recounts a fight he and his brother Gus, a US Army enlisted man, had with two Mexican American Pachuco Zoot Suiters they encountered in a bar during a leave:

> Gus and I were there, telling each other war stories when he nudged me and nodded toward two zootsuiters with slicked-back hair, long sideburns, and droopy mustaches. One of them eyed me and said to the other, "*Carnal, estoy watchando ese vato* (Pa, I'm watching that jerk) with the wings and fancy ribbons." "*Chale mano*" (Yeah, dude), replied the other, "I'll bet they're not his." Gus handed me his beer, grabbed the nearest one by the lapels and shook hard. Only the outsized drapes swished back and forth while the fellow remained stationary. Frustrated, Gus said, "I know you're in there somewhere you sonavabitch, take that back or I'll wipe the floor with you." (translation in original, 2002, 107)[15]

Cervantes claims his brother Gus beat both Pachuco Zoot Suiters, who eventually fled. This episode conjures the 1943 Zoot Suit Riots in Los Angeles, in which off-duty sailors, soldiers, and Marines beat and stripped male Zoot Suiters, and raped female Zoot Suiters. The infamous Hearst Corporation's "yellow" journalism inflamed these incidents, depicting them as tantamount to a domestic race war, with the mostly dark-skinned Mexican American Zoot Suiters as the enemy. Ironically, in Cervantes's memoir, it is a Mexican American soldier who beats Mexican American Zoot Suiters. Cervantes and his brother further denigrate and ridicule their Zoot Suiter adversaries for their vernacular dress, unaware that the oversized dimensions of their lapels are part of their *rasquache* (improvised vernacular Chicana/o) aesthetic and counterculture uniform. Like other conflicts between Cervantes and childhood farmworker friends who no longer see him as one of their own after he dons a US military uniform, this scene introduces an ideologically laden palimpsest: Cervantes associates Zoot Suiters with the underclass Mexican American farm worker past that his Air Force commission enabled him to flee. They are simultaneously like him and dissimilar. This distance is underscored by Cervantes's incorrect translation of the Zoot Suiter's Pachuco patois. His iteration of the Soldado Razo thus ultimately enforces the ideologically conservative soldiering-as-citizenship paradigm that Zoot Suiters disrupt through their undisciplined and allegedly unpatriotic dress and demeanor. Other case studies of Soldado Razo and Pachuco encounters, however, reveal that both archetypes ultimately intersect in a multiplicity of unexpected ways.

The Zoot Suit as Drag: World War II Mexican American Hypermasculinity as Homoerotic Spectacle

Closer scrutiny of the homosocial tensions between Zoot Suiters and US military personnel also reveals the homoerotic dimensions of Mexican American masculinity in the WWII era. The 1981 cinematic version of Luis Valdez's 1978 play, *Zoot Suit*, eroticizes this violence as constitutive of a homosocial—and homoerotic—hybrid Pachuco-Soldado Razo synthesis. After decades of cultural nationalist overdetermination of Pachuco Zoot Suiters as pathological villains, urban warrior heroes, tragic mestiza/o antiheroes, and irredeemable sexist exploiters by authors and scholars such as Mario Suarez (1947), Tomás Rivera ([1970] 1992), and Mauricio Mazón (1988), the Zoot Suit was reclaimed as a site of countermasculinist agency by Luis Alvarez (2009), Elizabeth Escobedo (2013), Catherine S. Ramírez (2008), and Patricia Portales (2014). Ramírez also queers the Zoot Suit, contrapuntally citing a neoeugenicist psychological "diagnosis" published in a 1944 criminal justice magazine that notes how men's use of Zoot Suits "completely hid...the genital characteristics" (2008, 75). She adds:

> pachucas and pachuos represented an unsettling gender paradox: the former were simultaneously regarded as excessively and inadequately feminine, while the later were masculinized, emasculated, or homo-eroticized by their critics, Anglo-American, Mexican, and Mexican American alike. Together, pachucas and pachucos queered not only dominant American culture but respectable (that is, middle-class and heteronormative) Mexican American culture as well.   (2008, 80)

Key scenes in Valdez's 1981 cinematic version of *Zoot Suit*, which features the *Über*-Pachuco played by Edward James Olmos, invite further queering. Indeed, Valdez's play, which initially had a brief 1979 Broadway run, is loosely structured on a real event in 1942 involving a brawl between rival groups of Zoot Suiters who had gathered for a late-night party at a Los Angeles swimming hole known as the Sleepy Lagoon, which left one person dead. The play's focus on the racially loaded—and overtly racist—mass criminal trial and imprisonment of teenaged male and female Zoot Suiters revolves around Henry "Hank" Reyna, the protagonist who takes the fall for his younger brother who was responsible for the killing. The film illustrates the confluence of hypermasculinist performances of violence on the home front, homosocial soldiering on domestic battlefields, and spectacles of homoerotic desire among male Zoot Suiters, and also between male Zoot Suiters and male soldiers and sailors.

The play's patriarchal homosocial aspects are obvious and center around a father's overprotectiveness of his daughter, in addition to male Zoot Suiter fights with sailors over women. However, the film also introduces a provocative Narcissus trope that invites a queer reading beyond these binaries. It begins with the play's form. A limited budget hampered the film version of *Zoot Suit*, but this also led to dynamic innovations. It became a staging of a staging that self-consciously involves the viewer's spectatorship of the play's spectators. In some shots, audience members played by Chicana/o actors also gaze back at the spectators. The layers and multiplicities of performances, gazes, and countergazes segue with the gender bending of masculinist warrior archetypes. In this play, everything and everyone is under scrutiny. This provocative metacritical intervention arises from the play's campy adaptation of rasquachismo, which takes the principle of cinematic redundancy to new levels of absurdity. The intersections between queer camp and Chicana/o rasquachismo were established in Tomás Ybarra-Frausto's essay, "Rasquachismo: A Chicano Sensibility," in which he recalls a flamboyant barrio resident who made a fashion statement out of kitschy pairings and layering of a ragged tuxedo stitched together and improvised that might be said to be a figural form of drag (1991, 157). The queer roots of rasquachismo enable new interpretations of beauty and style, and especially the homosocial pleasure of gazing upon it all, which are the signature features of the cinematic version of *Zoot Suit*. The film's frequent self-reflective gazes upon its own theatrical construction of male archetypes renders Zoot Suiter and Soldado Razo alike into hypermasculine palimpsests of each other.

This piling of signifier upon signifier—a rhetorical dog pile if you will—is depicted in highly stylized fight scenes involving Zoot Suiters upon Zoot Suiters and even Zoot Suiters upon soldiers and sailors, and vice versa. They were not just fighting against each other but may even be symbolically modeling the violent interpenetration of Zoot Suiter and Soldado Razo archetypes. Most celebratory appraisals of Zoot Suiters suggest that they adumbrate a nascent Mexican American oppositional consciousness, with the Pachuco emerging as a social bandit who is the antithesis of the uniformed US soldier. But Pachuquismo and soldiering are less antithetical than such claims suggest. The *Über*-Pachuco poet and US Navy veteran José Montoya illustrates this confluence in his 1969 mock-epic poem, "El Louie," which profiles a wounded Korean War veteran who also was a Pachuco (Montoya 1997). Before Américo Paredes's US Army service in WWII, the celebrated author also dressed the part of a Pachuco in his youth. Even reluctant sailor Cesar Chavez is pictured in a Zoot Suit! As these examples demonstrate, the Pachuco's hypermasculinist homosociality is perfectly suited for the equally hypermasculinist homosocial culture of the military. Indeed, these figures are mirror images of each other.

The Zoot Suiter-versus-sailor binary may actually be an axis in homoerotic recognition scenes in the film. For instance, in Act I of the 1992 published version, the play's Zoot Suiter protagonist Hank Reyna receives news that he is being charged with murder in the Sleepy Lagoon brawl. The ensuing dialogue between Hank and his surreal alter ego, the slick Pachuco dressed in black and red "drapes" played by Edward James Olmos, resonates with popular cultural references that have become mainstays in queer camp poetics and performance:

> HANK: They can't do this to me!
>
> PACHUCO: Haven't I taught you to survive? Just a marijuana dream, ese [dude].
>
> HANK: And I was supposed to report to the Navy tomorrow.
>
> PACHUCO: Muy [Very] Popeye the Sailor Man.
>
> HANK: You really couldn't stand to let me go, huh, carnal [blood brother].
>
> PACHUCO: They were gonna cut off your D.A. [Duck's Ass], carnal, give you those tight busto pants, make your ass look like an apricot.
>
> HANK: What business is it of yours, it's my ass!
>
> PACHUCO: Ah, muy [very] patriotic, ah. The Japs have sewed up the Pacific. Rommel's kicking ass in Egypt, but the Meyer valley has declared an all-out war on Chicanos, and you are the jura [law].
>
> HANK: I don't want to hear that.
>
> PACHUCO: As soon as Uncle Sam finds out you are in jail again, ya estufas [that's it for you]. Unfit for military duty due to your record. Forget the war overseas, carnal [blood brother], your war is on the home front.   (Valdez 1981, n.p.)

Most readings of the play focus on the last part of this exchange, which suggests that the real war for Mexican Americans concerns formal segregation and widespread discrimination on the home front. This of course is profoundly important to a play whose troping of reportage also serves as a metacritical spectacle about racist mainstream historiography in the WWII era. But what about the apricot?! Hank literally was going to offer his "ass" up to the Navy. It is difficult to separate this scene from common queerings of the Navy in popular culture. The Navy oftentimes is referred to as the "Gay branch" of the military, with the lily-white uniform and tight bell bottom pants being a prominent icon in gay popular culture. This queering includes the sailor character in the Village People, discussed in Chapter 1. Openly queer Chicano US National Figure Skating Champion Rudy Galindo further extends this queering of the US Navy into Chicana/o popular culture through his regular routine set to the Village People medley of hit songs. In one prominent routine, he dresses as a sailor who does a mock striptease as the soundtrack transitions from "In the Navy" to the more overtly homoerotic "Macho Man."[16]

Zoot Suit's homoerotic aspects emerge more clearly through its fetish on stripping, which invites a nuanced Chicana/o cultural nationalist queer spectatorship. In the 1943 Zoot Suit riots this ritualized tearing off of a Zoot Suiter's flamboyant garb—sometimes down to the underwear—has been theorized as figural emasculation. But the actual staging of key strippings in *Zoot Suit* is so over the top and cinematically excessive that the seminude brown male body invites male spectator *homo*scopophilia. As established in Chapter 1, José Esteban Muñoz predicates his Queer of Color disidentificatory performance upon a contrapuntal spectatorship that defiantly reclaims, reconnotes, and redeploys homophobic and racist stereotypes to new ends:

> As a practice, disidentification does not dispel those ideological contradictory elements; rather, like a melancholic subject holding on to a lost object, a disidentifying subject works to hold on to this object and invest it with new life. (1992, 12)

Such a disidentificatory reading of stripping occurs in Act Three, in which the stripped Pachuco transubstantiates into a finely sculpted, virile, seminude Aztec warrior hero rising from the beaten Zoot Suiter on the ground. The transformation from stripped Zoot Suiter to Aztec warrior hero is seamless and continuous, making it impossible to identify when the Zoot Suiter ends and the Aztec Warrior begins. For instance, at the start of this musical theater-of-the absurd scene, Hank's Pachuco alter ego (played by Olmos) *voluntarily* drops his knife to be carried away by sailors to be stripped and beaten in a racist sadomasochistic encounter offstage that apparently involves a mix of pain and ecstatic sacrificial pleasure. The sailors' smiles add to this resonance. The next scene cuts to the beaten Pachuco, who transubstantiates as Hank's stripped younger brother laying on the ground naked. This young Zoot Suiter indicts his older brother Hank, who had abandoned him in the chaos of the gang fight, shouting through tears, "they stripped me!" Finally, as the crying, stripped, emasculated, and seminude Zoot Suiter on the ground rises, he is no longer Hank's defeated brother, but the Aztec warrior played by

Edward James Olmos (who also plays the Pachuco alter ego). Olmos
is bare except for a loin cloth with an extralong brown front flap, his
tightly cut abs and pectorals glistening in sweat as he fades back up-
stage into the blackness to the Aztec rhythm of *concheros* (conch
shell rattles). Valdez and the cast may not have intended a queer cultural nationalist Aztec warrior hero, but it is impossible to occlude
these receptions. This scene, in fact, may even emerge as a queering
of Aztlán that anticipates Gloria Anzaldúa's and Cherríe Moraga's
late 1980s interventions.

Other scenes extend the homoerotic spectatorship to the Zoot
Suiter's mirror image: the Soldado Razo. In a closing Jitterbug dance
sequence, for instance, two male Chicano Zoot Suiters relish in the
gazes cast upon them as they also gaze upon other Zoot Suiters
prancing down the stairs, diva-like, to join the fun fighting with each
other and with soldiers wearing competing and equally flashy uniforms. The camera signals their pleasure with close-up shots of their
smiling faces. As Zoot Suiter males gaze upon competing male Zoot
Suiters and soldiers, these immaculately dressed human peacocks
momentarily forget the female Zoot Suiters on their arms. Their own
competing and coterminous homoerotic beauty is more important.
The *coup de grace* in the evolution of this homoerotic Pachuco-
Soldado Razo fusion occurs in the closing montage, when a Pachuco-
cum-infantryman marches on stage in a US Marine Corps uniform
holding a four-foot-long switchblade like a rifle as he is flanked by
two Pachucas, a Pachuco, and a sailor, who all figurally consummate
the union of these archetypes. Another instance of cinematic excess,
this oversized phallic knife, extended at a forty-five-degree angle,
reminds us of the homosocial context that set the action on its
course, that is, various Zoot Suiter attempts to pierce each other in
phallocentric rituals of power, which got them into this gender trouble
in the first place. By the end of the play, the Zoot Suiter and the
Soldado Razo are finally coupled, or at least reveal their desire for it.

As indicated in the *Zoot Suit* film's susceptibility to disidentificatory queer spectatorship, the Mexican American WWII Soldado
Razo is a coherent yet highly diverse and ideologically varied archetype. The ideological contours of the different iterations surveyed in
this chapter are directly related to their distinct underlying forms of
racialized, gendered, and sexualized violences, which as demonstrated, extend across the full length of political and sexuality

spectrums. Coupled with the diverse range of LatIndia/o figures surveyed in Chapter 1, the Soldado Razo and Pachuco archetypes examined in this chapter cumulatively destabilize familiar and convenient teleologies that forever change our understanding of Latinidades. The three chapters comprising Part II of this book further explore distinct violentological syntheses of Latinidades in broader global contexts that further pressure for a postteleological Latina/o Studies paradigm shift.

PART II

Violence and the Global Latinidades

3

Latina/o-Asian Encounters

TRANSVERSAL SYNTHESES IN ASIA, THE "ORIENT," AND THE *UMMAH* IN LATINA/O WARTIME NARRATIVE, TRAVELOGUE, SPOKEN WORD, AND HIP HOP

US Army Special Forces Master Sergeant Raul "Roy" Perez Benavidez opens his memoir about military service in the US war in Vietnam by recounting the battlefield actions for which he was awarded the Congressional Medal of Honor.[1] After volunteering for a suicidal mission to rescue fellow Green Berets being annihilated by North Vietnamese troops, Benavidez was repeatedly wounded by rifle fire, fragmentation grenades, and a bayonet. Despite thirty-seven wounds, he rescued his fellow American soldiers, hurling them into a US Army helicopter along with three wounded North Vietnamese troops, whom he mistook for Americans in the chaos of battle, and perhaps for other reasons. As the wounded and dead were unloaded from the helicopter, Benavidez lay on the ground near death, barely able to breath and unable to speak as he choked on his own blood. To his horror, he found himself being zipped into an airtight plastic body bag by a white US Army medic. He recalls:

> I waited, eyes closed, and listened as men clambered into the chopper and began handing the wounded out the door.
>
> "Hey look," someone called. "These three ain't ours. Somebody was throwing NVAs [North Vietnamese Army Soldiers] on too."
>
> I struggled to look toward the voices. Two soldiers were standing near the dwindling cache of bodies. One pointed at three remaining corpses.

Violentologies: Violence, Identity, and Ideology in Latina/o Literature. B.V. Olguín, Oxford University Press (2021).
© B.V. Olguín.
DOI: 10.1093/oso/9780198863090.001.0004

"Must not have had time to check I.D.'s," the other said as he tugged at an arm.

I retreated to the darkness behind my eyelids. Soon, I felt arms lifting me and sensed the sunlight fall across my face as they handed me through the doorway.

"Just put him over here with the other three on the ground," said the voice belonging to the arms holding my legs.

The other three? "Oh, Christ, No!" my mind cried as realization dawned. Half of the blood I had just dumped over Southeast Asia belonged to the Yaqui Indian nation. More than once my Native American features had been mistaken for Oriental [sic]. Now, by God, they were going to get me dumped with the enemy dead.

(Benavidez 1999, 4)

In perhaps the most dramatic scene of mistaken identity in Latina/o literature, Benavidez is misrecognized as an enemy soldier because of his racial markings: specifically, his brown skin and presumed "Oriental" facial features. It is only after he spits up his own blood into the white medic's face—grotesquely signaling he is an American even though his heritage is Mexican and Yaqui Indian—that he is recognized as "The Bean Bandit," or "Tango Mike Mike" (the phonetic acronym for "The Mean Mexican"), which are epithets his fellow soldiers used with equal amounts of derision and affection.

This misrecognition scene—a topos in multiethnic literatures, and especially war literature—is antithetical to Guy Gabaldon's translingual, transcultural, and transracial WWII HispaNisei subjectivity discussed in Chapter 2. Indeed, Benavidez fundamentally rejects a ChicanAsian identity. Despite their differences, however, both Gabaldon and Benavidez illustrate the ever-widening range of Latina/o-Asian encounters through which legions of Latina/os violently construct and repeatedly reconstruct Latinidades on a global scale through and beyond the familiar US-Mexico borderlands and Caribbean venues. As noted in the introduction, Latinidades are undergirded by multiple forms of violence that traverse time, geographic place, and social space, all of which are distinctly racialized, gendered, and sexualized. These confluences extend throughout the XicanIndia/o and broader LatIndia/o violentologies explicated in Chapter 1, and the contrapuntal Latina/o homosoldiering violentologies recovered in Chapter 2. The Chicana/o-Asian and broader Latina/o-Asian encounters explored in Chapter 3 introduce distinct violentological syntheses, for which neologisms such as ChicaNisei, ChicanIndiAsian, ChiKorean, and LatinOrientalist, serve as preliminary heuristic categories. Admittedly clunky, these and other attempts to precisely name emerging formations of violence-based Latinidades—which are all chronotopal—describe the vast cultural diversity and ideological dissensus effaced by the homogenizing category of "Latina/o." Significantly, these neologisms refer less to Latina/os of various Asian heritages (though they are included), and more to suprabiological hybridities that emerge in specific Latina/o encounters with Asian peoples, cultures, and nations over time and place, during war, and also in "peacetime."

The LatinAsian syntheses explicated in this chapter thus resonate with Francoise Lionnet's and Shu-Mei Shih's "minor transnationalisms" and related "cultural transversalism," which denote "minor cultural articulations in productive relationships with the major (in all its possible shapes, forms, and kinds), as well as minor-to-minor networks that circumvent the major altogether" (2005, 8). Lionnet and Shih recognize that even as various marginalized populations use each other as frames of reference for circumventing the center, their hybridized and doubly minoritized subjectivities remain ideologically inchoate. Transversalism, therefore, is useful for explicating Latina/o-Asian encounters, which involve convoluted multidirectional gazes and transculturations in margin-to-margin encounters throughout US imperialist ventures, and even outside them. Western (including Latina/o) gazes upon, and identifications with Asia, Eastern Europe, and the Middle East invariably intersect with Edward Said's definition of *Orientalism* as "a style of thought based upon an ontological and epistemological distinction between 'the Orient' and (most of the time) 'the occident'" (1979, 3). Lisa Lowe (1996) reminds us that these gazes and frameworks are fundamentally patriarchal, and equally as important, always confronted by anti-Orientalist countergazes and agency. Within this spectrum, Lionnet and Shih productively propose that transversal exchanges can exist within and outside the nation state, global hegemonic power relations, as well as inside and outside of Orientalism and even anti-Orientalism:

> expressions of allegiance are found in unexpected and sometimes surprising places; new literacies are created in nonstandard languages, tonalities, and rhythms; and the copresence of colonial, postcolonial,

and neocolonial spaces fundamentally blurs the temporal sequence
of these moments.   (2005, 8)

Accordingly, this chapter recovers myriad LatinAsian fusions that
revolve around, and are shaped by, different violent encounters—
both symbolic and kinetic—between and among Latina/os and
Asians (broadly defined) from throughout transcontinental Eurasia,
the Levant (the eastern Mediterranean part of western Asia), northern Africa, and the Americas.

Significantly, the violences undergirding margin-to-margin alliances and hybrid formations also extend beyond cultural transversalism. The violentological prism enables us to avoid romanticized
accounts of the myriad transversal hybridities, passings, mimicries,
mestizajes, mulattajes, and other transculturations that occur within
and at the margins of these contact zones. Following Cuban sociolo-
gist Fernando Ortiz ([1940] 1995), Mary Louise Pratt (1992) reminds
us that contact zones are "social spaces where cultures meet, clash,
and grapple with each other, often in contexts of highly asymmetrical
relations of power, such as colonialism, slavery, *or their aftermaths as
they are lived out in many parts of the world today*" (Pratt 1992, 4,
emphasis added). The specific LatinAsian violentologies examined
in this chapter are shaped by these and other lingering power differ-
entials, which come from multiple sources and extend in a variety of
ideological directions. These ultimately render Latinidades—and especially LatinAsian syntheses—as variably unique, thereby requiring
historical precision, context-specific qualifiers, and a new nomenclature for the field of Latina/o Studies.

Bering Strait Borderlands: Ancient Diaspora and the Asian Antecedents of Transversal Latinidades

Roy Benavidez's ambivalent triangulation of his Mexican American
heritage and Mesoamerican indigenous genealogy with a presumed
Vietnamese "phenotype" adumbrates what might be called a
ChicanIndAsian paradigm: a radical Asian relocation of the locus of
enunciation for indigenous-based Latinidades. Rodolfo Anaya, the
renowned Chicano author of the 1972 novel, *Bless Me, Última*, and
the less-known 1986 travel diary, *Chicano in China*, further destabilizes the cultural nationalist indigenist conceit by proposing the

original ChicanIndia/os as Asian, specifically, Chinese and their nomadic "Asiatic" ancestors (1986, vi). Anaya diverges from Gabaldon's and Benavidez's ambivalent Latina/o-Asian wartime encounters and transversal syntheses by proposing a genetic basis for his immanent Asian subjectivity as a Chicano of Native American heritage. Anaya attempts to thicken ChicanIndiAsian subjectivity by rendering it as a distinct ontological formation with a corresponding epistemological signature, though this effort ultimately is burdened by his use of romanticized stereotypes. Written during the Cold War—a period of incessant Soviet Union, Chinese, and US superpower hostility that threatened nuclear war and global annihilation—Anaya's one-month sojourn in China in May of 1984 presents a variation of the nostalgic "roots" reverse migration saga common in US multiethnic literatures. In the process he reveals layers and distinct forms of violence that shape his proposed transversal synthesis.

Anaya's travelogue begins with suppressed family lore about his maternal grandfather's Chinese connection. In the first entry dated "May 12, 1984, Albuquerque," he reveals that "a family story whispers that our grandfather, when he was a young man, visited China," to which Anaya's mother responds, "Don't speak ill about the dead" (1986, 3). She corrects the young Anaya by confirming that his grandfather could speak Chinese but had never traveled to China. This anecdotal account of latently bigoted Mexican American transculturation in various contact zone encounters with Chinese Americans alludes to their common railroad and agricultural labor in early-twentieth-century New Mexico, the Southwestern United States in general, and Mexico.

However, Anaya is not interested in a historical materialist inquiry into these encounters. Of his motivations for traveling to China, he writes:

> To be truthful, I did not know exactly what I sought. I would be a traveler in search of symbols that could speak the language of my soul. I would be a wanderer in a country that was the birthplace of the Asiatic people who thousands of years ago wandered over the Bering Strait into the Americas. (1986, v–vi)

The roots quest nevertheless becomes a political endeavor, however naïve it may be. Arriving ten years after US President Richard Nixon's Cold War détente with Mao Tse Tung, Anaya notes, "I am the first

Chicano from the Southwest to journey to China" (1986, vii).
Claiming that his travelogue was inspired by a desire to communi-
cate insights to improve East-West relations, he adds: "as a Chicano
I also take pride in the part of me that is a native American, that is,
an indigenous person of this American continent" (1986, vii). Anaya's
reverse migration to retrace the Asian origins of his Chicano genealogy inevitably articulates his ChicanIndiAsian identity with the Cold
War, in which ambassadorial visits are always intertwined with geopolitics. That is, his trip is a pacifist gesture but also an unabashed
pro-American initiative.

Anaya's naïve Cold War sojourn in China is nonetheless significant for proposing an even more radical shift in the locus of enunciation for theories of Chicanidad than Benavidez performs, even as
Anaya's intervention remains similarly mired in his identity and
privileged subject position as an American. Anaya foregrounds his
relatively new formation upon his return to the United States. In a
passage recounting his first night after returning to Albuquerque,
he writes:

> I sleep, or try to sleep. I am awake long into the night, wondering if I
> am a Chicano in China, dreaming I am a Chinese visitor to New
> Mexico, or if I am a Chinese visitor to New Mexico dreaming I am a
> Chicano in China. I keep refusing to look at straight lines, so the rest
> I am accustomed to eludes me. I keep listening to the sound of wind-
> bells on the terrace.   (1986, 192)

Anaya's phenomenological meditation in this liminal space between
sleeping and waking, East and West, Chicano and Chinese, capitalist
and communist, mimics a Zen Buddhist *Kōan*, or paradoxical riddle
with no answer. He underscores the difficulty, and perhaps impossibility, of his quest to fix the point where one strand of his genealogy
ends and another begins. Anaya's psychoaffective yearning and theorizing about his origins as a ChicanIndiAsian inevitably is embedded with layers of warfare, particularly Native American genocide,
but also Cold War proxy conflicts such as in Vietnam and Korea, as
well as the threat of direct superpower thermonuclear war. His haphazard foray into this lethal geopolitical chess game, which threatens
a nuclear winter more dramatic than the Ice Age that enabled his
ancestors' epic migrations, nonetheless productively decenters the
US-Mexico borderlands, and even Christianity, as essential to
Chicanidad.

Unfortunately, Anaya performs this epistemic shift by trafficking in nostalgic essentialisms and exoticist clichés. Toward the end of his narrative, for instance, Anaya broadens his Chicana/o-Asian recognition scene beyond China to include "small, brown people from the jungles of Thailand or from the villages of Vietnam" he sees in the San Francisco airport upon his return to the United States (1986, 191). His expansive and somewhat paternalistic LatinAsian archaeology also includes facile overstated transmutations that pass as transversalism. In one scene he presumes to be the masculine embodiment of China, writing: "a dragon sleeps in me...the penis of the dragon fits into my penis, and at night when I awaken to urinate, I pee the water of Chinese ponds and lakes and the Yangtze River" (1986, 194). Accordingly, Jayson Gonzales Sae-Saue indicts Anaya's nostalgic claim to Asia as an unmitigated performance of first world privilege:

> China is a means for the narrator to project onto his political self an Indigenous identity without having to claim contemporary social, economic, or political Asian life as matters of his own.   (1986, 105)

While this is true, and also segues with the nostalgic rendering of mestizaje in *Bless Me, Última*, Anaya makes an important contribution to the recovery of LatinAsian transversalisms: he locates this formation before the more frequently studied Latina/o-Asian wartime contact zones in Japan, Pacific Islands, Korea, and Vietnam. This, of course, is exactly what concerns Gonzales Sae-Saue. Yet, by transcribing his Cold War journey, Anaya provocatively imagines that Latina/o-Asian encounters, and syncretic transversalisms, are more ancient than even the Mesoamerican indigeneity that many Chicana/os claim as the basis of Chicanidad. However nostalgic and appropriative Anaya's indigenous-Asian transversal rhetoric may be, it introduces a range of new archaeologies that have the potential to alter the epistemic basis of Chicana/o and Latina/o Studies by suggesting Latina/os are only recently Amerindian. That is, Latina/os are not entirely native to the Americas and, moreover, their mestizaje may be as Asian as it is indigenous and European! Only a mulattaje paradigm extends further back in time and place—to the origin of the human species in Africa—though this is only recently, and still very reluctantly, acknowledged in Chicana/o Studies.

Subsequent explications of the historical violences inscribed within Mexican American and Chinese encounters, however, temper Anaya's provocatively nostalgic ChicanIndiAsian claims that Chicana/os are always already Asian, and particularly Chinese. Rosaura Sánchez, for instance, provides a contrapuntal touchstone for theorizing Latina/o-Asian transversalisms in her examination of Mexican American antipathies toward Chinese immigrants and Chinese Americans in nineteenth-century California. She documents how Salvador Vallejo, one of many elite Mexican-descent Californians, or *Californios*, dispossessed after the US invasion and annexation of half of Mexico following the US-Mexico War in 1848, turned his resentment not just to the invading white Americans, whom Californios viewed as morally and culturally inferior, but also toward Chinese residents of the region. Vallejo associates the Chinese population with "prostitution and the introduction of syphilis" (Sánchez 1995, 301–2). Sánchez adds that other Californios represented Chinese immigration as catastrophic for the well-being and ethnic integrity of the Californio population (1995, 302).

Gabaldon, Benavidez, Anaya, and nineteenth-century Californios such as Vallejo thereby introduce intersecting yet radically diverging Latina/o-Asian encounters and trajectories that are further complicated by expanded archaeologies of LatinAsian mestizajes in which violence is simultaneously a distant trace, contemporary rhetorical practice, and enduring ontological foundation. Jayasri Majumdar Hart's 2000 documentary film, *Roots in the Sand*, for instance, chronicles the Punjabi Mexican American community that coalesced in Southern California's Imperial Valley in the early 1920s and 1930s as single Hindu, Muslim, and Sikh male Indian immigrants from the Punjab area of the South Asian Subcontinent married Mexican immigrant and Mexican American women farmworkers. These mixed marriages navigated a lethal web of nativist and segregationist laws. Their white neighbors and US authorities alike identified people from the South Asian subcontinent as "Aryan," but still not culturally "Caucasian" or white enough to violate miscegenation laws if they married dark-brown-skinned mestiza Mexican American women (Leonard 1994, 33). Within this segregationist milieu, in which the threat of lynching remained an ever-present threat for the crime of interracial copulation, the subsequent religious, cultural, political, and linguistic transversal fusions of multiple generations of Punjabi Mexican Americans—a transliteral troping of ChicanIndiAsian subjectivity—propelled new reverse migrations to India and Mexico. *Roots in the Sand* even references one Punjabi Mexican American who apparently became a general in the Mexican Army, bringing the trope of violence to another level of transversal, transnational, and ideological signification.

Charles Mann records that the broader legacy of South Asian-based Latina/o mestizajes extends to the fifteenth-century European colonization of the Americas. In his 2012 study, *1493: Uncovering the New World Columbus Created*, Mann notes that less than a decade after Cortez's invasion, a sizable population of South Asian sailors of various religious backgrounds were living in Tenochtitlán, which became Mexico City.[2] Some were combatants, or *conquistadores*, infamous for mass killings and rapes. Many also were subaltern laborers and tradesmen. They inevitably fathered children and intermarried with indigenous and mestiza women throughout subsequent eras, adding more layers of militarized LatinAsian transculturations and transversalisms to the foundational Latina/o Studies tropes of mestizaje and mulattaje. These excavations add to other transversal LatinAsian genealogies, such as Rudy P. Guevara's (2012) and Anthony O. Campo's (2011, 2016) recoveries of MexiPino (Mexican American and Filipino) mestizajes, Jerry García's (2014) cultural anthropology of Japanese Mexicans, Julia Maria Shiavone Camacho's recovery of Chinese descent Mexicans, Mary-Alice Waters's (2017) profile of Chinese descent generals in the Cuban Revolution, and Jayson Gonzales Sae-Saue's (2016) aforementioned survey of tropes of Asia in Chicana/o literature. Together, they add to the expansive range of LatinAsian violentologies that gets increasingly more convoluted and complex.

The Forgotten ChiKorean: Contrapuntal Reassemblages of Korean War Soldados Razos

As illustrated above, the network of proliferating supra-Latina/o violentologies is predicated upon multifarious violences and transversal variables, and thus can be understood as a series of assemblages, which Manuel DeLanda (2006) proposes as the interrelated yet semiautonomous array of components that make up the whole. The assemblage enables multiple entrées for explicating the constitutive parts of transversal formations arising from Latina/o-Asian encounters throughout diverse regions in Eurasia and the Eurasian diaspora. The assemblage is particularly useful for understanding the violent disarticulations and rearticulations—or reassemblages—of Chicana/o bodies and beings in the Korean War vis-à-vis the Soldado Razo paradigms examined in Chapter 2. The intertwined psychic and physical dimensions of Chicana/o-Korean encounters and ensuing transversal mestizajes coalesce in a multivalent ChiKorean arche-type, whose variations can be explored from multiple vantages, or entrées. These offer new understandings of the radical and never-ending renovation of Latinidades, which are plural and fundamen-tally constituted through different latent and overt forms of violence.

The Korean War began in 1950 after the communist Democratic People's Republic of Korea (DPRK) attempted to unify a country devastated by the Japanese occupation during WWII, and subse-quent US occupation of the southern half of the Korean Peninsula. US forces and their South Korean Army allies were quickly overrun by DPRK forces. After the United States deployed additional troops for a successful counterattack, China intervened in defense of the DPRK, pushing American and South Korean forces back to the orig-inal demarcation line—the Thirty-eighth Parallel circumventing the globe—rendering the war a stalemate. An armistice was signed in 1953, but no peace treaty was ratified; the Korean War thus never formally ended.[3] For its survivors and their families, the war is a dis-tant memory but ever-present reality. The ensuing reference to the Korean War as the "forgotten war" decries the lack of knowledge about this conflict. However, this trope also inadvertently references the ideological practice of ambivalent remembering, which enables one to forget multiple aspects of a war that continues to destabilize American triumphalism.

Beatriz De La Garza's 1997 young adult novel, *Pillars of Gold and Silver*, rehearses this imperialist amnesia in her celebratory render-ing of the Korean War Soldado Razo as a warrior hero and martyr. The narrative opens with the pathos-laden scene of a young mother, Lilia, crying over the photo of her husband, who was killed in the war. Her daughter, Blanca Estela, is still too young to understand her father will never return, and she is helpless in the face of multiple forms of indoctrination that normalize her loss. These include a school viewing of a film "about knights going off to war that they called the Crusades" (1997, 32), which of course were the Catholic-instigated religious wars from the eleventh to the fifteenth centuries in the "Middle East" that sought to wrest control of Jerusalem and the proximal "holy land" from Muslim rulers. The novel subsequently focuses on the young girl's efforts to reacculturate after she and her mother move to Mexico to live with Blanca Estela's maternal grandmother. Unfortunately, this matriarch ventriloquizes the male warrior hero archetype by stressing that it was her son-in-law's "duty" to go to war because "he was born in the United States, and that country was at war" (1997, 24). When Lilia, the dead soldier's widow, complains, "but he volunteered for the most dangerous things," Lilia's mother emphasizes, "he was a brave man" (1997, 25), oblivious to the coloniality of this Soldado Razo paradigm. This character's ambiguous rendering of US militarism and Chicano hypermasculinist soldiering demonstrates the ideological vicissitudes of this particular ChiKorean formation: she remembers her soldier-citizen son-in-law by forgetting about the Korean War's link to the long legacy of US imperialism that predetermined his necro-citizenship and rendered Mexico foreign to her daughter and granddaughter.

Half a century after the Korean War armistice suspending combat, De La Garza's Soldado Razo martyred warrior hero inadvertently invites a contrapuntal entrée into the "forgotten war" trope. In rehearsing remembrance as historical amnesia, for instance, the grandmother calls attention to what her dead son-in-law represents: this three-year-long conflict claimed four million lives, including 36,000 Americans, and became the first modern war the United States did not conclusively win. Moreover, it involved huge battlefield losses for US forces, as well as broader tactical and strategic victories by North Korean and Chinese communists. This inaugural battle in the Cold War between the United States and its communist adversaries, primarily the Soviet Union and China, became an open wound and unfathomable cipher for Americans. They find it easier to strategically forget the war than honestly assess the causes and outcomes. De La Garza's novel is symptomatic: it engages in the politically expedient practice of remembering, and deifying, the dead Korean War Soldado Razo warrior hero martyr to forget US imperialism, its provisional defeat, and enduring vulnerability.

Part of this ambivalent remembrance involves an obvious but obfuscated contradiction: the link between Chicana/o and Latina/o patriotism with lethal battlefield acts that place their citizenship under erasure. The ChiKorean Soldado Razo is a variation of the masculinist imperialist Latina/o warrior hero archetype whose combat death, dismemberment, and disappearance are constitutive of their absent "presence" as American citizens. De La Garza's Korean War Soldado Razo thus intersects with morbid hagiographic biographies such as Raúl Morin's *Among the Valiant: Mexican Americans in WWII and Korea*, originally published in 1963 during the US war in Vietnam. In a rehearsal of Morin's transtemporal linkage of past and present wars, Morin's son reissued the book in 2013 at the crest of the US War on Terror, which has been centered in western Asian countries such as Afghanistan and the "Middle Eastern" nation of Iraq. *Among the Valiant* participates in the construction of a Latina/o warrior caste through its lionizing of Medal of Honor recipients, who paradoxically rise to the status of Mexican American patriots by their physical erasure on the battlefield. This irony is underscored in award citations that celebrate Soldado Razo Medal of Honor Award recipients for "gallantry and intrepidity on a seemingly suicidal mission" (1963, 167), "complete disregard for his personal safety" (1963, 144), "willing self-sacrifice" (1963, 198), and "gallantly gave his life for his country" (1963, 261).

Other ChiKorean syntheses critique these problematic renderings of the Korean War Soldado Razo's expected self-sacrifice as the consummation of their US citizenship by explicating this logic as a feature of the racialized class warfare that is integral to the geopolitics of domestic, hemispheric, and global underdevelopment. Postcolonial and Decolonial Studies as well as various world system theories propose that underdevelopment and attendant dependency emerge from the deliberately enforced political and economic truncation, military subordination, and financial control of third world economies to serve first world nations. In another entrée into the ChiKorean Soldado Razo archetype, José Montoya's 1969 long poem, "El Louie," features the eponymous Korean War veteran and Pachuco who becomes a *tecato*, or heroin addict, and eventually dies of a drug overdose. This poem proposes a violentological allegory of Chicana/o underdevelopment that intersects with, but also diverges from prominent interpretations of the Pachuco archetype discussed in Chapter 2. For instance, "El Louie" frequently is described as an elegy to a tragic hero (Landiera 2010), prime example of Chicana/o linguistic hybridity (Trujillo, Sommers, and Ybarra-Frausto 1979), performance of Freudian generational angst (Limón 1994), and exemplar of flawed but defiant Chicano warrior hero resistance (Rosaldo 1993; Guillermo Hernández 1991; José David Saldívar 1986). The poem also is part of historical materialist depictions of barrio under-development in contemporaneous verse, such as Abelardo "Lalo" Delgado's short engagé diatribe about the effects of racism, "Stupid America" (1969); Rodolfo "Corky" Gonzales's mock epic dystopian exposé of Mexican American life as colonized subjects, "I Am Joaquin" (1969); and Raúl Salinas's Pachuco picaresque portrait of poverty, internecine warfare, and dystopian visions of the United States as a carceral space, "Un Trip Through the Mind Jail" (1970).

In a microcosmic hyperlocal rehearsal of the geopolitics of under-development, Montoya's protagonist, "Louie Rodriguez," is denied access to educational, nutritional, economic, and political resources that would enable his dealienation, self-actualization, and full en-franchisement in the US polis. After all, capitalism requires marginal subjects such as this deliberately undereducated, unskilled, unem-ployable, and predatory figure whose own efforts to survive fre-quently disrupt working-class efforts to organize. Ironically, Louie Rodriguez emerges as a Chicana/o critique of the very underdevel-opment he embodies. He is defined by the multiple forms of violence that constitute this underdevelopment: colonial warfare and subor-dination, police and military violence against Pachucos, Pachuco in-ternecine violence, and soldier combat in an imperialist war that renders him as a deeply wounded tragic antihero who succumbs to a narcotics dependency that inevitably kills him.

In contrast to frequent deifications of the Chicano Korean Soldado Razo, Montoya, a Korean War–era US Navy veteran, articulates his immanent theory of Chicana/o underdevelopment through a class-specific, racialized troping of the violences that layer El Louie's alien-ation and erasure. For instance, the twenty-fifth stanza reads:

> His death was an insult porque no murió en acción – no lo mataron
>   los vatos, ni los gooks [sic] en Korea.
> He died alone in a rented room – perhaps like in a
> Bogart movie.   (lines 43–5)[4]

The implication is that Louie Rodriguez's demise was caused by a country that would never accede to his incorporation as anything other than an abject member of the underclass caught in cycles of internecine warfare that make them the ideal expendable soldiers in imperialist wars. The narrator underscores the antithetical nature of the Soldado Razo's soldiering and citizenship by adding: "Y en Korea fue soldado de levita / con huevos and all the paradoxes del soldado raso / —heroism and the stockade!" (lines 29–31).[5] In a challenge to Morin's contradictory heroic-death-as-citizenship paradigm, Montoya's ChiKorean Soldado Razo picaresque antihero is defined by his masculinist "bravery," ascribed deviance, and repeated incarceration, which is a different synthesis of the Korean War Pachuco Soldado Razo's necro-politics. That is, his US citizenship—emblematized by his US military uniform—overdetermines his tragic life and death.

Montoya's seminal archetype of the flawed Pachuco Soldado Razo—a PachuKorean, if you will—introduces a unique rendering of disembodiment that underscores the immanent yet necessarily incomplete negative dialectical syntheses of his alienated self. This is the essence of Montoya's PachuKorean violentology. His Latina/o pessimist model revolves around the PachuKorean pose, the staging of a presence, which in this case revolves around dismemberment and, ultimately, absence. Montoya was an accomplished visual artist, and his pencil and colored ink drawings feature Pachucos in stylized poses, usually with one leg cocked outward to feature their Zoot Suit pants and flamboyant *calcos*, or shoes (Figures 3.1 and 3.2). This pose dramatizes one of the most distinguishing features of their *Pachuquismo*: a defiant testosterone-laden posture. As detailed in the discussion of Luis Valdez's play and film *Zoot Suit* in Chapter 2, the Pachuco's phallic overcompensation for economic and political disempowerment comes in the form of oversized Zoot Suit "drapes" (replete with long watch chain), hypermasculinist violence, counterculture spectacles of dance (wildly gyrational Boogie Woogie), and their signature vernacular argot (Caló).[6] Similar to Luis Valdez's archetypal Pachuco, Montoya's poem "El Louie" intertwines the lumpenproletarian Pachuco with the subordinate Soldado Razo in a neobaroque piling of visual images, in which the phallic, bulbous-tipped airborne (paratrooper) jump boots become Pachuco *calcos*, and vice versa (e.g., "And on leave, jump boots shainadas and ribbons, cocky from the war, strutting to early mass on Sunday morning," line 32). In a subversive series of reversals, the Korean War accoutrements US soldiers used in combat against North Korean and Chinese soldiers, are symbolically transformed into Pachuco fashion such as "calcos" that these Chicano lumpenproletarian warrior (anti)heroes used to defend themselves against US soldiers in the Los Angeles Zoot Suit Riots in 1943! As such, the Korean War Pachuco Soldado Razo is caught in a symbolically suicidal cycle of self-flagellation as his

FIGURE 3.1. *"Pachucos" (Untitled) (n.d.), by José Montoya. Courtesy of the José Montoya Estate and Davidson Library Special Collections, University of California, Santa Barbara.*

raison d'être, a point Mauricio Mazón proposed in his study of the symbology of the proverbial Zoot Suit Riots. Each aspect of the PachuKorean's embodiment—shoes, cocked-leg pose, uniforms, calcos, defiant attitude—all become synecdoches of underdevelopment and attendant alienations.

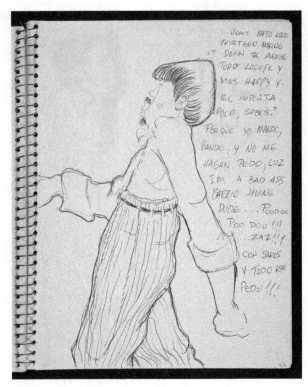

FIGURE 3.2. *"Bato Loco 13" (n.d.), by José Montoya. Courtesy of the José Montoya Estate and Davidson Library Special Collections, University of California, Santa Barbara.*

The Chicana/o "oldies" musical group, Grupo Serpentino, rehearses the PachuKorean Soldado Razo's absent presence in their 1999 lowrider paean, "Cruzin." Underscoring how a Chicana/o ontology can be constituted by violent dismemberment and resultant absences, as well as by the manifest presence of the assemblage's constituent parts, the singer returns to the defiant pose made famous in Montoya's drawing and poetry:

> y mi tío con sus Raybans,
> cool drapes, su pompador,
> fabuloso '56 outside my 'buelita's house,
> had his guiza take a picture of him
> striking a firme pose in front of his chingón ride.
> Remember those big wayside baggy pants of his?
> You couldn't even tell that he left one of his legs in Korea.
> That he sacrificed it for the American way.[7]

The indecipherability of the absent leg lost in Korea—which we see as an absent presence that literally supports a foundational Chicano archetype—becomes a legacy that endows the stiff-legged Pachuco with a simultaneous physical aperture, biopolitical aporia, and new ontological possibilities despite, and because of, the overarching tragedy.

Subsequent Chicana/o authors and filmmakers trope this absent presence—and present absence—in ever more complex negative dialectical syntheses of the ChiKorean chronotope. For instance, Mexican American novelist and poet Rolando Hinojosa Smith, a former US Army officer and Korean War veteran, complicates Benavidez's LatinAsian misrecognition scene, De La Garza's and Morin's celebratory tropes of remembering and forgetting, and Montoya's and Grupo Serpentino's PachuKorean allegory of tragic underdevelopment. Hinojosa similarly reiterates the primacy of violence, specifically combat killing, mass murder of civilians, and both real and figural suicide. However, in contrast to these other models, Hinojosa Smith proposes an expanded range of transversalisms and reassemblages of ChiKorean and broader LatinAsian formations that open ever more expansive horizons for reimagining the theoretical subjects of Latina/o Studies. He offered the first sustained literary rendering of Mexican Americans in the Korean War in his 1978 collection of narrative free verse, *Korean Love Songs*, which he followed with a prose rendition in 1993, *The Useless Servants*. Hinojosa Smith frequently reelaborates multiple linguistic versions (rather than translations) of the same stories that are part of his Klail City Death Trip Series set in a South Texas Mexican American community. These multiple versions, in English and Spanish, add nuances that carry a Bakhtinian dialogic resonance, especially in both his Korean War texts. Hinojosa Smith's thinly veiled autobiographical poetic persona, Rafe Buenrostro (Spanish for "nice face," or "handsome"), is a South Texas Mexican American soldier attached to a US Army artillery unit deployed to Korea at the start of the war. In these additions to his multivolume, multigenre, multilanguage series, Hinojosa Smith's narrativized theory of Mexican American spatial ontology is, fundamentally, a negative dialectical enterprise predicated upon dystopic scenes of primal violence and corresponding existential crises by multiple characters in different parts of the world that can only be resolved through profoundly discrepant transversal violentologies.

Both verse and narrative renditions of Rafe Buenrostro's rehearsal of his Mexican American (and specifically Tejano) abjection as the antithetical Soldado Razo revolve around multiple battlefield misrecognition scenes among Mexican American G.I.s, various ethnicities of white American soldiers, North and South Korean troops, Chinese communist combatants, as well as Korean and Japanese civilians. Hinojosa Smith reminds us that battlefield conditions are so intense, and confusion about allies and enemies so pervasive, that US soldiers are instructed to assume all Korean civilian refugees are embedded with North Korean soldiers in disguise. This leads to frequent US soldier massacres of civilians. In this dystopian context, US Army commanders are forced to deploy armed "battle police" to capture routed, mutinous, or lost American soldiers so they can be returned to battle, sometimes at gun point (1993, 33–4; 1978, 11).

These battle police are successful at forcing soldiers to keep killing and dying, but they fail to prevent transversal survivances from the detritus of this Cold War conflict. As I have previously argued (Olguín, 2002), Hinojosa Smith introduces radical racial and ideological slippages of Mexican American identity. His poetic persona Rafe recalls, for instance, how a white US Army general tries to reassure battle-weary and defeated US troops that they should not be alarmed at the presence of Chinese soldiers on the battlefield:

We should not expect the Chinese Communist to be committed in force. After all, a lot of Mexicans live in Texas.   (1993, 87)

Adding to Rafe's growing alienation, a Jewish American soldier in the same unit commits suicide in defiance of orders to engage in mass killings of soldiers and civilians so soon after the Holocaust.

Equally as dramatic, and transgressive of teleological models of Latina/o cultural citizenship that remain moored in the Western Hemisphere, Rafe's hometown friend and fellow Mexican American artilleryman, Corporal David Ruiz, flees the battlefield "AWOL" (Absent Without Official Leave), eventually settling in Japan. He acculturates and marries a Japanese woman, eventually assuming the identity of a hybrid first-generation and second-generation Mexican American Japanese male, or a ChicanIssei/ChicaNisei. Perceived phenotypical similarities between Mexican Americans and some Asians facilitate this new wartime transversal synthesis, and recalls Roy Benavidez's infamous misrecognition scene, albeit with different filial and ideological resonances. Even though Rafe is unable to resolve his own existential crisis, he gives testimony before a military review board investigating the circumstances of Corporal Ruiz's disappearance. He thus facilitates his friend's transversal violentology. By testifying that his friend was killed in combat and his remains obliterated and absorbed into the Korean battlefield, Rafe, in effect, converts a Mexican American G.I. into a hero and simultaneous defector-cum-Asian. This renders Ruiz a de facto enemy, since he can return home only upon death, which is the maximum US military penalty for wartime desertion. Adding to the ironies, within this expansive range of reassemblages, if Ruiz is any of these identities, he is all of them.

After his wartime experiences, Rafe also is caught in this kaleidoscope of possibilities, especially after realizing his commanding general conflated his identity as a Mexican American US soldier with the North Korean and Chinese enemy. He will never be the same. The intimacy of the title, "Korean Love Songs," thus frames one pole in the diptych binary, with "Useless Servants" forming the other, in a never-ending synthesis of the dystopian, existentialist, inchoately antiimperialist, necro-political, Latina/o-Pessimist, and fundamentally transversal ChiKorean archetype.

Gregory Nava's televised serial, *American Family*, further tropes the ChiKorean as a metonym for the broader concept of supra-Latina/o violentologies. This show premiered in 2002 after production was temporarily disrupted by the 9/11 attacks, with the War on Terror subsequently incorporated into the script. Set in East Los Angeles in the early 2000s, it uses a Korean War veteran named Jesús Gonzalez, or Jess (played by Edward James Olmos) to interweave multigenerational Mexican and Mexican American experiences with warfare and related violences from the Mexican Revolution to the US War on Terror. Warfare and underclass violence are the unifying threads. In fact, warfare continually imprints Jess's entire life and subsequent understanding of his raison d'être: his beloved grandmother was a *soldadera* in the Mexican Revolution; his WWII-era childhood was spent conducting juvenile beach patrol on the lookout for a feared Japanese invasion following the Pearl Harbor attack; he was an infantry soldier in the Korean War who survived combat while losing a close friend; his brother is a homeless veteran of the US war in Vietnam who gets murdered by Los Angeles Police officers; his attorney daughter provides legal aid to immigrants displaced by the US-supported dirty wars in Latin America, with her law firm partner venturing to southern Mexico as a supporter of Zapatista rebels; and his eldest son Conrado, named after the friend who died in combat in Korea, is killed in Iraq after joining the Army to serve as a doctor. In this web of warfare, there is no part of Jess's extended family's Mexicanidad and Chicanidad that exists outside war and myriad other violences.

Episode 10 of the first season of *American Family*, subtitled "The Forgotten War," is based on the life of a real Chicano Korean War veteran, and embeds the ChiKorean archetype with a violently embodied resonance that serves as a crescendo to the troping of this figure. It opens with the nonstop television coverage of the 9/11 attacks, which sends Jess into a series of flashbacks to a Korean battlefield. The ensuing montage literally inscribes the Korean War—and Koreans—onto Chicana/os, while also locating Chicana/os within the broader imperialist construct of the "Orient" through War on Terror battlefields in Iraq and Afghanistan. "This is worse than Pearl Harbor," Olmos's character says as he gazes on the wreckage of the 9/11 attacks on television. The episode reveals that Jess, the grizzled combat veteran, bears a traumatic reminder of the war: a scar frozen onto his chest of a dead Korean baby he tried to save with his own body heat while fleeing Chinese soldiers in the battle in which his best friend was killed. The episode progresses with Jess's son Conrado—the epitome of the upwardly mobile Mexican American— announcing he has joined the Army as a doctor to "save lives." In Season Two, Conrado becomes yet another permutation of the Soldado Razo—the warrior hero saint—after he disobeys orders and provides medical treatment for wounded Iraqi enemy soldiers, which ultimately gets him killed in a Scud missile attack. The series ends with no resolution beyond underscoring the supra-Chicana/o dimensions of history, culture, and identity for which Jess's ChiKorean subjectivity serves as an overarching, yet still incomplete, violentological signifier.

Transracial Syntheses: Chicana/o *Testimonios* and Fiction from the US War in Vietnam

Chicano Vietnam War combat veteran Charley Trujillo extends the ambivalent transversal assemblages embodied by De La Garza's, Hinojosa Smith's, Montoya's, and Nava's Korean War–era characters, in addition to Benavidez's narrativization of his combat in the US war in Vietnam, toward a more deliberately metacritical, antinostalgic, and pacifist Chicano-*Pan*-Asian violentology. Inducted into the US Army as a teenaged farmworker, Trujillo was deployed to Vietnam in 1969 (Figure 3.3). He spent all but five days of his nine-month deployment in the jungle before he was wounded in combat by his own US Army-issued grenade launcher, which he prematurely discharged a few feet from his position in the chaos of a firefight with communist Viet Cong guerrillas. Trujillo credits the subsequent loss of his eye for helping him "see better," referring to his postcombat epiphanies.[8] Upon his discharge and convalescence, he graduated from the University of California at Berkeley. After multiple jobs, he founded the Chicana/o-focused Chusma House Press, which he deliberately named using the vernacular epithet, *la chusma*, shared by ancient Roman galley slaves and contemporary Chicana/o working-class people. In addition to publishing foundational works of Chicana/o literature, such as José Montoya's sole poetry collection, Trujillo is renowned for his sardonic insights about Chicana/o history, culture, and politics. For instance, in response to frequent Chicana/o nostalgic claims to being descendants of soldiers from Pancho Villa's famed División del Norte in the Mexican Revolution, Trujillo remarks: "Everyone says their grandfathers fought with Villa, but if no one fought for the federal army there wouldn't have been a revolution."[9] Turning his sardonic metacritical gaze closer to home, Trujillo states that the penitentiary built in his hometown of Corcoran, where his extended family previously labored as farmworkers, created new opportunities and ironies: "Half my family is in prison," Trujillo observes, "and the other half is guarding 'em."[10]

Trujillo's metacritical interrogation of Chicana/o interpellation within systems of oppression—as both oppressors and oppressed—adumbrates his transversal Chicano-Pan-Asian literary and cinematic exposés. Contributors to his compilation of Chicano veteran testimonials from his hometown, *Soldados: Chicanos in Việt Nam* (1990), for instance, span wide ideological positionings, ranging from an ultra-right-wing military veteran who became a prison guard, to his own leftist leanings. Trujillo's corresponding autobiographical novel, *Dogs from Illusion* (1994), also presents an unexpurgated portrait of pathological misogynist models of Chicano masculinity unleashed in wartime contexts against Vietnamese soldiers and civilians, as discussed in Chapter 2.

FIGURE 3.3.   *Charley Trujillo in Vietnam, May 1970. Courtesy of Charley Trujillo.*

But Trujillo also recasts Latina/o-Asian encounters, especially in wartime contact zones, pursuant to a counterhegemonic vision of transversal and transracial syntheses. This includes a collaboration with Korean American filmmaker Sonya Rhee, the daughter of Korean War immigrants, with whom he adapted his anthology of *testimonios* into a documentary film, *Soldados: Chicanos in Việt Nam* (2003). The film opens with Trujillo rehearsing an encounter with an Immigration and Naturalization Service officer on the cotton fields where he once labored as a farmworker. In response to the officer's skepticism about his citizenship, Trujillo removes his prosthetic eyeball and offers it to viewers, adding: "Here are my papers, hijos de la chingada [sons of bitches]!" (Figure 3.4). He thereby dramatizes the collective transversal counter gaze as a violentology by intersecting Mexican, Chicana/o, and Korean migrants, immigrants, and their descendants who have found each other, through warfare, on the margins of US imperial power.

In a further troping of the missing eye as a portal to a new metacritical vision, Trujillo predicates his pan-Asian collaborations on the view that his healing and continued survivance requires multiple levels of Latina/o-Asian rapprochement. Accordingly, Trujillo

FIGURE 3.4. *Still from* Soldados: Chicanos in Việt Nam *(2004), by Charley Trujillo and Sonya Rhee (coproducers and codirectors). Courtesy of Charley Trujillo.*

traveled to Japan in 2018 to return a blood-stained Imperial Japanese battle flag his father, a US Army infantryman in WWII, brought back from his service in New Guinea (Figure 3.5). As a gesture of mutual healing from the lingering traumas of US wars against various Asian nations and peoples, Trujillo met with descendants of the Japanese soldiers who had signed the banner, which had served as their guidon flag while fighting against US soldiers.[11] Following this more deliberately leftist pacifist variation on the Chicana/o roots migration to Asia that Rodolfo Anaya inaugurated with his 1984 trip to China, Trujillo is writing a fictionalized memoir, *The Real Life of a Dead Chicano: Patas de Perro* ("Dog Feet"). It features yet another transformation of the Soldado Razo warrior hero archetype, he notes, as "the main character Patas [feet] calls himself a Chicano Cong when he returns from Nam" (Trujillo 2020, n.p.). It thus both marks the continual rebirth, and never-ending syntheses, of Trujillo's post–Vietnam War contrapuntal, pacifist, transversal Chicano-Pan-Asian violentology.

However, the prevalence and proliferation of Soldado Razo paradigms, which in the Vietnam War era involved polarized

FIGURE 3.5. *Charley Trujillo in Japan, 2018. Courtesy of Charley Trujillo.*

extremes, inevitably eclipse Trujillo's *anti*-Soldado Razo interventions. This period, and figure, are foundational touchstones for Chicana/o Studies, and broader Latina/o Studies. Ironically, literature from this conflict informs theories of oppositional Latina/o agency, even as an overwhelming majority of Latina/o Vietnam War veterans, and contemporary Latina/os in general, espouse political positions that are far more supportive of US imperialism than opposed to it. In 1999, Chicano Vietnam War veteran and scholar George Mariscal recognized this ideological dissensus in his epochal publication, *Aztlán and Viet Nam: Chicano and Chicana Experiences of the War*. Historian Lorena Oropeza followed with an equally incisive contrapuntal historiography in 2005. Together, they recover a range of ideologies, from desperate soldiers trying to survive by whatever means available, to ultra-right-wing "patriots" espousing imperialist politics, as well as an assortment of cultural nationalists and internationalists. Adding to the complexity, sometimes the same person embodies these subject positions at different points in their life!

Similar to ChiKorean violentologies, Chicano soldier-authors from the Vietnam War era introduce recognition scenes that illuminate how Chicana/o-Vietnamese transversalisms are simultaneously first world and third world, and ideologically inchoate. Within this spectrum, Chicano US military veteran authors from this war, more so than from any other war, provocatively explore the revolutionary potential of these chaotic violent encounters. This includes Chicano US Marine Corps veteran of the US war in Vietnam Joe Rodriguez. His 1989 novella, *Oddsplayer*, for instance, explores the range of possibilities emerging from racialized class conflicts and consciousness-raising combat experiences among racial minority combat troops, or grunts, that lead to several "fraggings," that is, deliberate killings of their white noncommissioned officers.[12] The fragging perpetrators are a squad of Marines who are identified as "stupid spic," "dumb Mexican," "nigger," "two-faced yellow kike," and "half-breed Indian" by the same white soldiers who referred to their Vietnamese allies and enemies alike as "gooks, slant-eyes, yellow meat, [and] yaller niggers" (1989, 63). These ethnic and racial minority Marines defiantly reclaim their reified difference by referring to themselves as "rainbows." Significantly, their violent act of retribution is radically different from the symbolic significance of fraggings in mainstream white renderings in this war, in which the execution of an officer or noncommissioned officer usually serves as the climax for the downtrodden grunt's claim to agency, which ultimately dehistoricizes and depoliticizes the war by personalizing or allegorizing it.[13] In contrast, Joe Rodriguez deploys this violent act of insubordination to transform conventional meanings of "Mexican American," "Chicano," and even "American" into a transversal and transracial cadre of potential revolutionaries.

Rodriguez's plot, characterization, and dialogue underscore this revolutionary possibility. Acting on the challenge by a black rainbow named Johnson who decries, "Why should we rainbows fight among ourselves and do the Man's work for him?" (1989, 62), Private Perez, a Mexican American draftee from rural California, decides to participate in the planned fragging of his superiors, Sergeants Talbot and Dibbs. These white noncommissioned officers were notorious for sending these racial minority troops on an inordinate amount of dangerous night guard duty, demoralizing body recovery detail, and unnecessary "suicide" patrols, which the pathological sergeants are rumored to have ambushed! In a cliché yet significant soliloquy addressed to Maria, his Chicana activist friend from college, Private

Perez presages his battlefield epiphany that "the color of skin fixed the enemy" (1989, 63). Reflecting on the broader historical events that led him to this point, Private Perez muses:

> I quit college and found work to pay father's medical bills. You, compañera, realized I would be drafted. Both of us knew many families with sangre in uniform and there were KIAs [Killed in Action]. The odds were clear. Chicanos from the university and the barrios protested.
>
> The day for induction came. I went through the routine in dread. I felt like an Indio watching the Spaniards burn sacred books. I saw racks of skulls. The pioneers were drawing the wagons in a circle.   (1989, 71–2)

Through these invocations of the traumas of Mexican American history—specifically, Spanish colonial genocide and equally violent Euro-American settler colonialism—Rodriguez dramatizes the ironic axiom popular among Mexican American veterans, "*Sangre Mexicana/Corazón Americano*," which proclaims that though their blood be Mexican, their heart is American. This proclamation resonates as a subtle apology that speaks to the lingering suspicion of Mexican American loyalty, which extends to the mid-nineteenth-century Texas-Mexico and US-Mexico Wars, in which prominent figures such as Juan Seguin switched sides more than once as discussed in Chapter 1. For Perez, like other rainbows drafted to fight in the US war in Vietnam, their racialized claim to citizenship and inclusion in the American polis now signifies a bloody, brutal, and tragic contradiction: he ultimately realizes he is in the wrong army, fighting the wrong war, against the wrong people.

Through the dream sequence in which he both observes and inadvertently intimates participation in foundational colonial encounters ("I felt like an Indio watching the Spaniards burn sacred books," and "The pioneers were drawing the wagons in a circle"), Private Perez figuratively claims allegiance to the indigenous heritage that Roy Benavidez had framed as a liability in his narrativization of the same war. Perez's tropes of indigeneity are nonetheless equally as ambiguous: he notes "I felt like an Indio," rather than "I am an Indio"; and it is unclear if he was among the Indian attackers or among the settler colonialists circling the wagons for protection. While it is clear that Private Perez is fighting his racist enemy noncommissioned officers, this ambiguity extends to a tentative suggestion of allegiance with the Vietnamese communists against whom he was drafted to fight. Within this confusing milieu, the preceding Spanish colonial conquest and attendant mestizaje reify Private Perez's genetic code as racially "othered." This occurs simultaneously with another imperialist venture—the US war in Vietnam in which he, as a mestizo, is both agent and object of its attendant violences. This pairing of imperialist wars inevitably renders his emergent rainbow identity as a complex and contradictory chronotope of multiple violences. That is, Private Perez embodies a liminal subjectivity produced in the violent clash between the first world and third world across time and place. His Vietnam War rainbow subjectivity thus is firmly grounded in a specific point in time, yet also is transtemporal, transspatial, transnational, and even immanently internationalist, all the while being mired in layers of colonialist and imperialist violences, which he embodies, fights, and inadvertently reifies.

After the fragging, Private Perez proclaims himself to be a Chicano in opposition to the interpellated Mexican American G.I.—or Government Issue *matériel*—he once was. He now recognizes the links between US racism and imperialism that stateside Chicana/o Movement artists and intellectuals had been decrying in their art, scholarship, and related political mobilizations during the 1960s and 1970s. Just as the rainbow moniker signifies a racialized third world opponent of US capitalist imperialism—and, indeed, an enemy of it—so does the term "Chicano" in this novel. For Rodriguez's character, it suggests a more or less indigenous-identified dialectical subject born in the clash between two economic orders in the US-Mexico borderlands, and signifies a burgeoning internationalism in which difference no longer simply involves a claim to minority status and inclusion in the capitalist imperialist polis, but the complete opposite: membership among the world's poor and exploited majority, beginning with a multiracial group of rebellious US conscripts, and extending to their Vietnamese communists enemies, who are always potential allies.

In his 1995 novel, *Shifting Loyalties*, Daniel Cano extends this meditation on Chicana/o domestic resistance vis-à-vis international subaltern allegiances to its logical conclusion: he introduces a Chicano G.I.-cum-Viet Cong communist. Cano thus relocates the Chicana/o Vietnam War Soldado Razo onto a radically different ideological terrain. This novel contains several subplots involving both Mexican American and white American soldier and civilian characters. Their various associations and disassociations intersect with the battlefield experiences of several US Army infantrymen who self-identify as Chicanos. Their combat occurs in the ambiguous geopolitical space "somewhere outside Duc Pho"—the title of the 1993 short story around which the novel evolved—and signify radically different things for all involved. The storyline focuses on Chicano US Army infantryman Jesse Peña, who is listed as Missing-in-Action but who is rumored to be leading Viet Cong patrols in combat against US troops and military installations. It thus intersects with Rolando Hinojosa Smith's depictions of Mexican American G.I.s in the Korean War, and Joe Rodriguez's depiction of racial minority infantrymen in the US war in Vietnam, all of whom are allies but perceived as de facto enemies by their military commanders. But Cano's exploration of this liminality more precisely intersects with Teatro Campesino's Vietnam trilogy: *Vietnam Campesino* (1970), *Soldado Razo* (1971), and *Dark Root of a Scream* (1971).[14] These plays offer materialist linkages between Chicana/o *campesinos*, or farmworkers, and Vietnamese peasants, intimating that Chicana/os should join the fight *against* US colonialism and imperialism at home and abroad, and specifically *against* the US government and its military forces.

Cano's rendering of this ideological trajectory is more overt than any other iteration of this topos. Cano's explosive cross-racial recognition scene and ultimate transracial synthesis converts the Chicano warrior hero, renowned for self-sacrificing bravery, into a Chicano defector-cum-Asian Communist enemy/ally. George Mariscal notes that the "shifting loyalties" theme is prominent across all wars, but he adds that "the empirical evidence of GIs crossing over to fight alongside the enemy is slight" (1999, 42). Adding to the speculation, however, one contributor to Trujillo's 1990 anthology, *Soldados: Chicanos in Việt Nam*, purports to have seen "Salt and Pepper," an infamous white and black soldier duo who purportedly defected to the North Vietnamese side. Cano's novel further tropes shifting loyalties as a Mexican American saga extending to the nineteenth century, in which Mexican Americans fought on both sides of the Texas-Mexico and US-Mexico War, as well as in the Spanish-American War, in addition to twentieth-century insurgencies up to the US War on Terror.[15] However, Cano inverts the loyalty discourse: his novel blames the US for forcing Chicanos to fight an unjust war against indigenous people in Southeast Asia, who actually are allies in the fight against US racism, colonialism, and imperialism.

Cano's radical synthesis of a transversal ChicanAsian Soldado Razo communist revolves around Peña's disappearance, and ensuing sightings of him at the head of Viet Cong patrols. Peña rejected the US military's—and his own community's—expectations of his self-sacrifice as a racial minority soldier. Instead, he challenged the conventional Soldado Razo's morbid patriotism and necro-citizenship ethos. His dramatic act creates profound dissonance among his former US Army squad members, and leads to heated arguments, especially among Chicano G.I.s. No one can agree on the significance of the rumors about Peña's disappearance, much less the meaning of their roles as Chicano G.I.s in this Cold War conflict. Although some refute the sightings as "a bunch of bull-shit" by a "bunch of fuckin' racist grunts" (1995, 81), other Chicano G.I.s believe the trauma of seeing his friends' "bodies tore up into thousan' pieces" (1995, 86), led Peña to the point of no return—defection to the North Vietnamese communists. Together, they attempt to verify the rumors and understand what it may mean that their friend is a Chicano and a suspected communist, and particularly a Chicano Communist.

The climax occurs when the Chicano troops interview a white infantryman who claims Peña confronted, and spared him, while on an ambush patrol. The white G.I. derisively recalls seeing Peña "squatting, like gooks do." The Chicano G.I.s become convinced of the sighting's veracity when the soldier, who had never before seen Peña, accurately describes Peña's prominent dimples and ever-present smile (1995, 92–3). Peña's appearance and assimilation of enemy characteristics (he wears the black pajama uniform of the Viet Cong), and his continued filiation with the perennially downtrodden G.I. grunts he refuses to shoot even as he leads the "enemy" in combat against them, convinces Peña's Chicano G.I. compatriots that their friend had become the enemy and vice versa. The white soldier's reports that Peña had smiled and shook his head from side to side in a filial gesture to keep the G.I. from picking up his rifle, which would have forced Peña to shoot him, adds to their certainty.

The debates become more incisive ruminations on political economy that embed Cano's ChicanAsian paradigm with an immanently Marxist resonance. Hector, a Chicano replacement soldier who joined the unit after Peña's disappearance, is the first to distill the collective visceral dissonance into epiphanic political critique:

The dude's got balls. I don't know how, but this guy Peña understands that everything here means nothing. It's all fantasy, a joke, a big fuckin' lie, man. I ain't never met the guy, but I been thinking about him a lot. I heard the stories. I heard that Peña lived in San Antonio, in some rat hole that he couldn't afford to buy because the bank wouldn't lend him the money. I heard that in the summer when it hits a hundred, him and his neighbors fried like goddamn chickens because they couldn't afford air conditioning. So now they send him here to fight for his country, for his land! Wow, what a joke, man.   (1995, 98)

Here, Cano disarticulates the link between violent masculinity and citizenship promulgated by the US military and assimilated by legions of Soldados Razos. Indeed, he lays bare the contradiction—and lie—of the self-effacing acts of "bravery" they have been led to hold as an ideal and an aspiration. Slowly, but steadily, the Chicano G.I.s in Cano's semiautobiographical novel realize that it takes even more "balls" to refuse to fight in the US military than it takes to serve blindly in a US imperialist war. This is especially so given the degree to which Chicana/os like Peña are systematically forced to live in the same conditions that demarcate the third world countries whose people Chicana/os are enlisted to subordinate and kill.

Cano undermines the binary construction of allies and enemies to obfuscate battle lines even further. He shows how Peña's (former) Chicano G.I. compatriots are forced to rethink inherited notions of nation and nationality as well as US citizenship and identity. Like Peña, they must decide on which side to fight, and also must determine if there are such things as sides in a war fought by poor people against poor people who bear a striking resemblance to each other. Peña makes some of these Chicano G.I.s realize that in some cases enemies and allies are one and the same person. This extended transracial ChicanAsian recognition scene is embedded with historical materialist analyses of the violences that undergird global underclass "peacetime" realities as well as wartime encounters. It thus offers a LatinAsian violentology that radically departs from the aforementioned iterations set in Japan, Korea, and Vietnam. Yet, it represents only a small part of the huge gamut of supra-Latina/o violentologies synthesized throughout Eurasia and adjacent regions of the "Orient," which require their own explications and nomenclature.

LatinOrientalism: War, Romance, and Latina/o Self-Actualization in the "Orient"

Post–Vietnam War Latina/o travelogues throughout Asia—particularly the Western construct of the "Orient" consisting of North African, Mediterranean, Eastern European, and Asian regions—deploy various exoticist gazes that raise important questions about the counterhegemonic possibilities, and limits, of Latina/o-Asian transversalisms. Latina/o Orientalisms, as it were, operate within different genealogical and ideological contexts from those of the nineteenth- and twentieth-century French and English iterations that Postcolonial Studies scholars have explicated. Yet, Latina/os actualize intersecting exoticist gazes through similarly discursive and no less palpable Orientalist violences. Thus, Latina/o Orientalisms are familiar but also new: they render Asians and "Orientals" as Other, and appropriate corresponding regions, cultures, and bodies through a range of nostalgic and exoticized self-actualization discourses ranging from transversal hybridizations to reifications of binary oppositions. Paradoxically, these familiar and troubling signifying practices nonetheless productively expand the loci of enunciation for Latinidades, even as the ideological implications further threaten Latina/o Studies' counterhegemonic conceits.

The charge of Latina/o Orientalism is rarely made, presumably because Latina/os were constituted as a civic and ontological entity through nineteenth-century US imperialism that was overlain upon centuries of Spanish imperialism in the Americas. This subaltern legacy invites effacement of longstanding Latina/o complicity in US colonialist and imperialist ventures throughout the world, including in their own heritage countries. After all, imperialism has never functioned without legions of subaltern functionaries drawn from previously colonized regions, and new ones, that supply the necessary agents of empire. Throughout their entire history, Latina/os have served in this role for myriad reasons: desperation, personal self-interest, and even concurring ideologies.

The debate between José Limón and Ramón Saldívar regarding whether Américo Paredes is a paradigmatic postcolonial intellectual, or indirect agent of empire, provides opportunities to further explicate LatinAsian—and especially LatinOrientalist—discourses. Limón accuses Saldívar of overstating the antiimperialist resonance of Paredes's post-WWII sojourns in Japan, China, and Korea. He further argues that Saldívar traffics in reductive effacements of national and cultural differences under the imprecise rubric of "Asia," accusing both Paredes and Saldívar of "engaging in a kind of sympathetic, left-wing Orientalism toward Japan in mostly utter admiration of its culture under the duress of occupation" (2012, 595). In response, Saldívar reiterates that while Paredes "sympathize[d] with the postwar suffering of the Japanese people, he also understood the ruthlessness of empire" (2009, 589). Saldívar adds that Paredes did not perform "an uncritical, monolithic pan-Asianism" (2009, 590), but gained an understanding about the importance of regional nuances through his military deployment in Japan, and civilian Red Cross work in China and Korea. This experience later enabled Paredes to theorize US-Mexico borderlands contact zones and hemispheric identities in the Americas. The most resonant part of Limón's critique is that "Paredes's/Saldívar's largely positive focus on Japan is centrally articulated through their women but, again, with the relative omission of Chinese women, whose fate was truly horrific at the hands of the Japanese military" (2012, 595–6).

Yet, neither Limón nor Saldívar interrogate Paredes's exoticist and eroticized signifying about Japanese women. Paredes inevitably intertwined this nascent Japanophilia with his prescient transnational imaginary. Amid Paredes's fascinating rendering of transracial Mexican American and Japanese battlefield recognition scenes in the short story "Ichiro Kikuchi," which Saldívar has expertly explicated (1994), Paredes's archives contain unpublished diaries, field notes, and poetry that betray the juvenile signifying of a male soldier in the midst of testosterone-laden ruminations. At times, these degenerate into a crass Orientalist Mexican American G.I. fetish on Japanese young women and girls. This problematic signifying extends to his published poetry. Paredes's Spanish language dramatic dialogue "Japonesa," for instance, ends:

> mysterious Japanese:
> your foreign eyes contain
> a bitter night
> and sweet deep sea,
> you were born for love...   (1991, 85)

As noted in Chapter 2, these eroticized gazes extend beyond Paredes's juvenile soldier fantasies, which also include white women muses.[16]

In a further irony, this forerunner of Chicana/o cultural nationalism had little patience for cultural imperialists such as J. Frank Dobie, the infamously racist and self-proclaimed expert on Mexicans in South Texas, even as Paredes also skirted the fine line between fetish and fascination in his writing from and about Asia. In the March 14, 1947, entry in his "Far East Notebook #1," dated March 1947 to November 1948, Paredes, whose second wife would be of Japanese Mexican descent, even invokes Lafcadio Hearn. A Greek-Irish journalist from the late nineteenth century, Hearn assimilated into Japanese society after marrying a Japanese woman and fathering several children with her. Hearn ultimately is credited as having introduced Japanese aesthetics to the West. "He was also right about Japanese women," Paredes writes, adding "they are the most lovely in the world (n.p.)."[17]

LatinOrientalisms also include discourses that are less blatantly fetishistic but which still figure the "Orient" as the site for a Western protagonist's self-actualization. Mexican American gay Persian Gulf War (1990–1991) combat veteran José Zuñiga, for instance, grounds his 1994 military coming-out memoir, *Soldier of the Year: The Story of a Gay American Patriot*, in his wartime experiences. His service as a combat medic facilitated multiple epiphanies: he embraced the assemblage of his intertwined minoritarian identities—gay, bisexual, and Mexican American—eventually evolving from a self-proclaimed conservative to a social liberal. His steadily expanding circle of identifications even come to include the Iraqi "enemy" soldiers he occasionally treated. However, Zuñiga still locates his model of multicultural and transnational egalitarianism within a US nationalist—and thus imperialist—framework. As the title of his book proclaims, he is a "Gay *American patriot*." Ariana Vigil adds that Zuñiga's narrow emphasis on lifting the ban on gays in the military, with no substantive critique of US imperialism, reveals his "ambivalent homonationalism" (2014, 127). Vigil's invocation of Jasbir Puar's term alludes to Zuñiga's intersections with civil rights (as opposed to human rights) strategies that vacate queerness of counterhegemonic difference pursuant to the normalization and assimilation of LGTBQI+ people as typical citizens within a capitalist imperialist nation state.

This latent conservatism notwithstanding, Zuñiga's role as a US Army soldier deployed to Iraq with invading US forces, and his theorizing of multiple violences experienced and witnessed as a gay, racially marked, combat medic, nonetheless performs an important though still ideologically inchoate queering of the Soldado Razo archetype. At one level, his otherwise provocative paradigm is inextricable from the Orientalist errant abroad motif made famous by gay British archaeologist and soldier Thomas Edward Lawrence, whose exploits in the early twentieth-century Arab revolt against the Ottoman Empire led to his renown through the Orientalist moniker, "Sir Lawrence of Arabia." In a different yet intersecting and no less Western imperialist context, Zuñiga is recognized as the 1992 US Army Soldier of the Year for his previous combat service in the same region, and general proficiency as a soldier. Drawing upon his renown as a closeted enlisted man, Zuñiga consolidates a new activist persona as an out gay Latino soldier—the first to publish a memoir—who seeks to overturn the ban on openly gay men, bisexual, and lesbian soldiers in the US military. (This circumscribed goal was followed by attention to the broader LGBTQI+ community by other activists a decade later.) Zuñiga's coming out leads to his dishonorable discharge from the US Army, which motivated him to write about his fighting in Iraq and in the US, as a gay soldier citizen and agent of empire.

Significantly, Zuñiga's defiant yet problematic claim to inclusion revolves around the militarization of his gay identity, Latino heritage, and citizenship in general through his collective identity as a fifth-generation soldier with antecedents in the United States and Mexico. Moreover, Zuñiga overtly renders the homoerotic dimension of military service, especially life as a frontline grunt where mandatory homosocial bonding is intensified by combat, during which blood, sweat, tears, and other bodily fluids are discharged and exchanged. It is important to note that Zuñiga's *eros* is primarily articulated in reference to other US service personnel. He avoids the alternating Orientalist eroticization and hatred of "Oriental" Others—the central dyad of Orientalist gazes—through his expressions of empathy for Iraqi soldiers wounded by US troops. Yet, he reveals ignorance about his complicity in the overall imperialist enterprise in which approximately 400,000 Iraqi soldiers and civilians were killed during the US occupation from 1990 to 1991. Moreover, Zuñiga's memoir ultimately relies upon a US war in the Middle East as the performative venue for his self-actualization and enfranchisement as a gay Mexican American US citizen.

Civilian Chicana and Latina Feminist Orientalist travelogues extend from the Persian Gulf War in which Zuñiga fought to twenty-first-century War on Terror battlefields in the same terrain that early twentieth-century Western European empires—particularly Russia and England—sought to control in the proverbial "Great Game."[18] In her 2004 travelogue, *Around the Bloc: My Life in Moscow, Beijing, and Havana,* for instance, Stephanie Elizondo Griest intertwines Orientalist and other fetishes into her mixed-heritage Chicana feminist bildungsromanesque tale. Even as her narrative productively adds new globalized spatial settings for Chicana consciousness-raising experiences and rearticulations of identity (a topos animating her three subsequent travelogues), it nonetheless presents Elizondo Griest's post–Cold War travel as an exotic adventure. Without the least bit of irony, she notes that this neoimperialist and quasi-picaresque impulse is part of a family legacy that includes service in the US military:

> Wanderlust pumped through my veins: My great-great-uncle Jake was a hobo who saw the countryside with his legs dangling over the edge of a freight train; my dad drummed his way around the world with a US Navy band. I too wanted to be a rambler, a wanderer, a nomad—the kind whose stories began with "Once, in Abu Dhabi..." or "I'll never forget that time in Ouagadougou [Burkina Faso] when _____." Who bought her funky jewelry from its country of origin instead of a booth at the mall.
>
> (2004, xi, blank space in original)

Tragically, Elizondo Griest's exoticist intertwining of foreign travel with commodity acquisition foregrounds the dangers confronting all women in a heteropatriarchal world: her depiction of the commodification of women throughout the "Orient" intersects with her rape by a Russian boyfriend for whom she was one of his six dozen *devushki,* or "girls" (2004, 140). Elizondo Griest intertwines her traumatic rape with a range of travel episodes that shape her new survivance and subjectivity as a Chicana activist, though the balance of her narrative unfortunately remains imbued with exoticist gazes from beginning to end.

Elizondo Griest's travelogue thus navigates the complicated ideological space between the Latina Feminist Orientalism operative in Eve Raleigh and Jovita González's 1930s historical novel *Caballero,* and the more or less metacritical *testimonio* ethos Chicana and Latina feminists, and their revolutionary Latin American precursors, modeled in the 1970s and 1980s. For instance, amid Elizondo Griest's incisive critiques of patriarchy as an all-pervasive global episteme, *Around the Bloc* is riddled with Orientalist sexual geographies and stereotypes such as the "Latin Lover" (2004, 139), and sexually repressed Chinese males (2004, 265). After using a neo-socialist realist image of an idealized cherubic female Chinese communist Red Guard on the book cover, Elizondo Griest chronicles underground gay culture in Beijing while ironically claiming that Chinese are so prudish they cannot even utter the Mandarin word for sex (2004, 263–4). Her alternately feminist critiques and exoticist gazes in this narrative of self-fashioning reiterate that multiple violences are ever present—especially heteronormative repression, patriarchal sexual violence, and xenophobic stereotypes—which Elizondo Griest observes, experiences, and unwittingly extends.

In her 2009 novel *The Last War*, Cuban American journalist and author Ana Menéndez further mobilizes the Orientalist trope of the "East" as repressed and repressive, and yet enticing and enabling for a female Western traveler's self-actualization, albeit in an existentialist variation of the complex and vexed legacy of Latina/o-Asian encounters. Menéndez's novel is set primarily in Istanbul during the early years of the War on Terror, with intersecting storylines throughout Eurasia, particularly Pakistan and Afghanistan, as well as the Middle East during the US occupation of Iraq. Within this Islamicate cultural and geopolitical landscape, Menéndez suggests a critique of Western chauvinism that posits women's presumed oppression under Islam as the antithesis to women's purported liberation in the largely Christian West.[19] Her novel's main storyline, however, eclipses this trajectory as it renders the War on Terror, and warfare in general, as a mere metaphor for never-ending chaos coterminous with her Latina alter ego's failed search for a raison d'être.

The novel's cliché plot centers on Margarita Anastasia Morales, a Latina war photographer known as "Flash." The author introduces her as:

American daughter of a broken Dominican father, only child of divorce, spic, illegal, quiet loser. Flash, the remade sensualist who escaped all that old-country bullshit in exchange for the rest of the world. For whom feeling became an expression on some foreign face, a frame soon to be forgotten or replaced by another of greater joy or suffering. (2009, 21)

Within this trajectory of multiple negations and self-serving gazes, Morales-cum-Flash refashions a new supranational subjectivity as a syndicated war photographer. In the process she becomes a modern protofeminist analogue to the legions of preceding alienated Western travelers who sought to actualize new subjectivities through consumptions of the "Orient." Flash is sent to Turkey on assignment for a Western publication while her husband, also a war correspondent, pursues a similarly morbid passion amid the US occupation of Iraq: "We were the war junkies: Eros and Chaos," Flash proudly states (2009, 2). The resulting domestic anomie of this separation reaches a crisis when Flash receives an anonymous letter alleging her husband had an affair with another journalist in Iraq.

This infidelity plot twist leads Flash to question her marriage's strength and integrity, and her very identity. The narrative segues into a *roman à clef* as Menéndez recounts receiving a similar letter about her husband, who resembles Flash's wayward partner. This autobiographical intersection reveals that the novel's sympathetic rendering of a war correspondent's fetish also is an expression of the author's displaced desire for her life's old order, with the Orient-as-chaos serving as the allegorical setting. In an interview appended to the novel, the author confirms this imperialist gaze by noting that writing for her, like photography for Flash, has a therapeutic function, particularly during the dissolution of Menéndez's marriage (2009, 5–6). The exoticist "veiled woman" cover image depicting two women in full hijab thus foregrounds Menéndez's inevitable critical failure as the plot reduces the novel to an iteration of petite-bourgeois feminist and consummately Orientalist discourse.[20] At one level, the author depicts Muslim and Christian women of Hazar, Indonesian, Turkish, and European backgrounds as all similarly oppressed by myriad patriarchal constraints. Yet, the plot coerces readers to care for Flash while she agonizes over the collapse of her marriage, her old life's order, and sense of self, which is interwoven with equally unsatisfying Istanbul shopping trips for Turkish rugs and Eastern antiques. After her husband is killed by a roadside bomb in Iraq, readers further commiserate with Flash as a tragic figure when she realizes he may not have been a philanderer after all. This plot twist further displaces the novel's already circumscribed feminist dimensions through the introduction of the "good husband" trope.

The novel ends with the alienated protagonist continuing her privileged Western gaze as a photographer who travels further east in search of more wars to witness and freeze in time with her camera. "I returned to covering the wars," Flash notes, "It's steady work. And I know how to do it" (2009, 223). The title—*The Last War*—thus does not imply the final war, or a yearning for the end of binaries and the wars they cause as Gloria Anzaldúa had proposed. Rather, it refers to the latest war in a never-ending pursuit of more wars to witness and frame through a Latina gaze. Moreover, and in contradistinction to the limited but nonetheless substantive transversal LatinAsian fusions discussed above, Flash's perennial outsider status suggests that an East-West rapprochement is impossible. She inevitably recalls another stranger who underscores the lethality of Orientalist gazes. In the last two pages, for instance, Flash awaits a delayed flight to Delhi, observing other travelers she believes are seeking an escape or diversion by traveling east toward exotic discoveries, danger, or both. In the morose tone common in existentialist fiction, the last line of the novel reads: "I rose to stand in line with everyone else" (2009, 225). Flash is not quite a female version of Meursault, Albert Camus's alienated, racist, and nihilist character in *The Stranger* (1942), who joyfully walks to his execution after being convicted of violently consummating his Orientalist gaze by murdering a randomly targeted Muslim man in French occupied Algeria in the 1940s. Yet, Menéndez's alienated protagonist returns to traveling, gazing, and photographing the "Orient," which becomes worthy of her effort only if someone is being brutalized, injured, or killed. Flash thus remains the somewhat—but only somewhat—reluctant war junkie the novel ostensibly sought to depict as a tragic heroine through the foil of a wayward husband. Significantly, this Orientalist gaze is constitutive of her Latina feminist yet still Western feminist agency.

Whereas it is impossible to care about Camus's racist settler colonialist murderer, Menéndez's pathos-laden narrative makes us want to care about the alienated Latina war junkie who searches for wholeness amid the rotting corpses of mostly third world Others. The only variation in Menéndez's Feminist Orientalist narrative arises from the fact that her protagonist's pursuit of war in the East does not enable self-actualization; rather, it extends her alienation. This banal ending notwithstanding, the next flight deeper into chaos allows for a potential sequel with shades of E. M. Forster and legions of other Western authors who have populated the Western literature canon with Western characters lost in the "Orient." Menéndez ultimately articulates her alter ego's otherwise prescient epiphany—the impossibility of a woman's escape from patriarchy and the futility of seeking wholeness anywhere in the world—through Orientalist clichés.

The large and popular canon of the Western journalist self-actualization wartime travelogues that Menéndez glosses includes Puerto Rican and Cuban American J. Malcolm Garcia's 2009 *The Khaarijee: A Chronicle of Friendship and War in Kabul.* This memoir focuses on a middle-aged, social worker turned journalist on an existential quest for a meaningful life that is intertwined with his genuine desire to have an egalitarian humanist impact in the world. This quixotic quest takes Garcia on assignment for the *Kansas City Star* newspaper to Afghanistan one month after the September 11, 2001, attacks. Part of the journalist's wartime travelogue made famous by masculinist authors and former war correspondents such as Stephen Crane, Ambrose Bierce, and Ernest Hemingway, Garcia's memoir refreshingly breaks with the conventional combat reporter's fetish on destruction. Instead, he offers well-rounded descriptions of the civilians who oftentimes are effaced as nameless victims through military euphemisms such as "collateral damage." His travelogue narrativizes his attempts to ameliorate this brutal human toll from a half century of warfare and layers of shifting alliances in Afghanistan.

Significantly, Garcia's mother is Puerto Rican and his father Cuban American, and he readily admits he "passes as White" (Olguín 2014, n.p.). He used this white American privilege, in addition to his professional salary and institutional influence, to help people survive the war rather than simply reporting their deaths. Similar to the aforementioned feminist LatinOrientalist discourses, however, the ideologically contradictory journalistic and humanist interventions Garcia recounts in *The Khaarijee*—the Pashtun term for "outsider"— arise from his inability to transcend his Western privilege and attendant imperialist signifying practices. At the start of his narrative, Garcia responds to an old Afghan farmer's query about his reason for being in Afghanistan by emphasizing, "No, no...I'm not an aid worker. I'm a reporter. I'm just trying to help" (2009, 45, ellipses in original). The balance of the narrative recounts Garcia's acts of compassion for everyone he meets, including six Afghan orphans he informally adopts, along with several stray dogs he nurses back to health. In addition to the unfortunate pairing of Afghan boys and stray dogs as the dual targets of his generosity, Garcia's deliberately pacifist narrative is infused with a neo-Orientalist tone. This includes the quintessential claim to power embedded in the now clichéd renaming scene endemic to colonial travelogues: he gives his informal adoptees new Western monikers.

Garcia's attempt to transform the cliché saga of the alienated journalist abroad on a journey of self-discovery also fails as praxis. He effectively goes broke using his salary to assist Afghan victims of US military violence, which reduced him to working as a day laborer and country club grounds keeper upon his return to the United States.[21] This development can be seen as a counterpoint to the profiteering extractivist trajectory of Orientalist travel and gazes. Or it could merely signal naivety. Garcia's well-intentioned attempts to save four orphans from poverty that made them prime recruits for the Taliban and Al Qaeda, for instance, ironically aligns with US foreign policy goals. Similar to the village-based "pacification" program in the US war in Vietnam, US military counterinsurgency doctrine in Afghanistan during the War on Terror involved social assistance and development funding to villagers to pre-empt their recruitment into insurgent ranks. This unintended confluence is underscored by Garcia's role as an occasional "embedded" reporter: that is, he was vetted and chaperoned by US military personnel while in Afghanistan, which effectively circumscribed what he saw.

These limits notwithstanding, *The Khaarijee* closes with sobering anti-nostalgic reflections on the limits of transnational alliances and transversal filiations among first world subalterns and third world war refugees. Indeed, Garcia recounts how Afghan friends increased requests for money long after he returned to the United States, which he felt was exploitative even as he recognized their desperation. Garcia eventually ended financial support, but not his compassion and commitment to the poor and downtrodden. Free of military handlers and censors, Garcia turned his journalist lens toward the United States. In 2014, he published an incisive exposé on the aftermath of the War on Terror, *What Wars Leave Behind: The Faceless and the Forgotten*. He followed it with profiles of noncitizen veterans caught in the long tentacles of the war's lingering effects, *Without a Country: The Untold Story About America's Deported Veterans* (2017). In this reportage, Garcia provides complex portraits of veterans suffering Post-Traumatic Stress Disorder, whose errors in judgment and mostly petty crimes led to their life-long expulsion from the country for which they went to war.

Garcia's nuanced journalist reportage and Menéndez's *roman à clef*, together with the aforementioned LatinAsian transversalisms and outright LatinOrientalist gazes, travels, and tropes, cumulatively raise important questions. What is the relationship between imperialist war and first world "subaltern" spectatorship? Can there be genuinely egalitarian Latina/o-Asian solidarity, and transversal LatinAsian hybridities, that avoid facile equivalences and exploitative fetishes? Moreover, can LatinAsian—and especially Latin Orientalist—violentologies be counterimperialist, and if so, what are the ideologies of these proposed alternatives?

Borinquen, Aztlán, and the Ummah: (Counter)Imperialist Spiritual Activism in Latino Muslim Spoken Word and Hip Hop

Despite the recurring Latina/o fetish on Asians and the "Orient," historiographies of similar black-Asian exchanges suggest Latina/o Orientalisms, as it were, may have counterhegemonic potential, however tentative these possibilities may be. Bill Mullen identifies twentieth-century black internationalists who pursued antiimperialist revolutionary epistemologies, particularly Maoism, through trans-Pacific dialogues.[22] This involved a different type of neo-Orientalist gaze, he notes, in which Asians were seen as *inherently* oppositional to Western imperialism. "Afro-Orientalism," Mullen aptly adds about this subaltern leftist essentializing, "is a counterdiscourse that at times shares with its dominant namesake certain features" (2004, xv). This problematic yet simultaneously protorevolutionary African American turn to Asia has analogues in Latina/o gravitations toward Maoist and other revolutionary organizations from the 1960s to the 1990s.[23] This legacy extends to the late twentieth and early twenty-first centuries in transversal spiritual activism that proffers romanticized notions of the "Orient" as the source of one form of salvation or another. In addition to the growing Latina/o turn to various iterations of Buddhism, for instance, the Islamicate world—and particularly Islam—has emerged as a new supraracial yet still identitarian Latina/o locus of enunciation for a theologically based protorevolutionary theory of praxis that purportedly promises liberation from US hegemony and Western Christian imperialism.

Adding to Latina/o spiritual diversity that extends to Hindu, Sikh, and Muslim legacies in sixteenth-century Mexico City, Edward E. Curtis identifies early twentieth-century mixed marriages between Puerto Rican women and South Asian Muslim sailors, whose children and descendants were raised as Muslim.[24] He also notes that in 1988, mixed-heritage Honduran American Idris M. Diaz became the first US-born Latina/o to complete the Hajj: the pilgrimage to the holy site of Mecca in present-day Saudi Arabia that is the birthplace of the Prophet Muhammad and site of his first revelation of its holy book the *Qur'an* (2009, 81–2). Diaz had converted to Islam in 1975, at age fifteen, after being inspired by members of the US-based Islamic sect, the Nation of Islam, whose members displayed dignity and self-sufficiency (though he may have had issues with their Europhobic theology that demonized his white American mother). Significantly, the growing Latina/o turn to various Islamic sects makes Latina/os the fastest growing segment of new Muslims in the United States.[25]

Despite this complex genealogy, which underscores how Islam is neither new nor foreign to Latina/os or the Americas, contemporary Latino Muslims nonetheless must negotiate the legacy of abjection ascribed to Islam, and especially American Muslim males, in the wake of the September 11, 2001, attacks on sites that symbolize US capitalist imperialist power. This abjection was earlier embodied by Brooklyn-born Puerto Rican Muslim convert José Padilla (also known as Abdullah al-Muhajir). Dubbed the "Dirty Bomber" for his purported membership in Al Qaeda and alleged plans to detonate a uranium "dirty bomb" in the United States in 2002, Padilla/al-Muhajir was convicted and sentenced to twenty-one years in federal prison.[26] In the US War on Terror's religiously polarized context, where Islamophobia and anti-Arab hatred have led to white Christian racist terrorist attacks and outright massacres of Muslims (and people misidentified as Muslims) throughout Western nations, Latino spoken word and Hip Hop artists always already operate in a complex global political terrain despite their relative obscurity. But they have their own political agendas, too. Hisham Aidi claims that twenty-first-century transatlantic Muslim youth dialogues and musical fusions are "an attempt to build an Islamic left by revisiting the Bandung era" (2014, xiii). The epochal 1955 conference in Bandung, Indonesia, involved thirty African and Asian developing nations, which at the time represented half the world's population. It sought to provide an alternative to the Cold War contest between the United States and Soviet Union, which some third world activists viewed as competing imperialists.[27]

In contrast to Aidi's claims, however, Latino Muslim lyrical and performative transversal spiritual mestizajes ultimately reveal themselves to be ideologically inchoate: even as they partially succeed at relocating the locus of enunciation for new Latinidades outside the United States and Western Christian hegemony, their discourses range from celebratory multiculturalism to competing imperialisms that are only superficially leftist. Slam poet, performance artist, and food fusion guru Robert Farid Karimi is among the most well-known Latina/o authors and artists of Muslim heritage, and his work illustrates the uniquely complex secular and nonsecular ideologies of Latina/o Muslim poetics (Figure 3.6). Karimi was born in San Francisco to a Guatemalan mother and Iranian father, whom he calls "reluctant immigrants" since they met in the 1960s in English language night school following CIA-orchestrated coups in their home countries—1953 in Iran, and 1954 in Guatemala—that heralded totalitarian regimes (2010, n.p.). Karimi reclaims these traumatic histories and ensuing religious orthodoxies and transforms them into empowering cultural fusions he calls "remixes" (2010, n.p.).

His father's Islam and mother's Catholicism animate Karimi's best-known poem, "Get Down With Yo' Catholic Muslim Self," which he performed in his winning routine at the 1999 National Poetry Slam competition in Chicago, and also in a 2004 televised Def Poetry Jam episode in New York. Slam poetry emerged from smoky bars in Chicago in the early 1980s, with the raucous readings called "bouts" in an allusion to populist kitschy wrestling spectacles.[28]

FIGURE 3.6. *Robert Farid Karimi Poetry Reading "Get Down With Yo' Catholic Muslim Self," circa 1990s. Courtesy of Robert Farid Karimi.*

The genre's frequent explorations of identity politics and populist political critique segued with African American Hip Hop. Karimi invokes these legacies in his poem, which has multiple versions. The 2004 Def Poetry Jam version opens with his angst-ridden poetic persona in a Catholic church:

> I looked around for a sign, anything.
> And right in the front of the church
> the image of Christ transformed:
> wooden hands turned to flesh.
> His naked body clothed in the most fantastic outfit.
> And right before me Christ had become a disco diva!
> And she looked at me, said: "go on boy, do yo' thing!"

The poet initially demurs, offering a dose of transversal spiritual humor to the already transgressive gender bending reinterpretation of Christianity, noting "Sometimes I pray a few rosaries to the east on Friday during a dilemma like this" (2004, n.p.). As suggested in the poem's title (which sometimes places "Muslim" before "Catholic" to reflect the order in the poem), the content and celebratory tone revolve around a proclamation of spiritual mestizaje—and all cultural mestizajes—as empowering:

> And I keep hearing this voice: "get down with yo' Muslim Catholic self!"
> I rebelled and make a crusade to rid myself of all those trying to box
>   me into one religion,
> one god, one identity.
> Jihad incarnate, Amen.
> And disco diva Jesus comes off and says:
> get down with yo Muslim Catholic self!
> Get down with yo Jewish Daoist self!
> Get down with yo rosary and Bahai Buddhist, African religion,
>   Indigenous religion, Hip Hop, salsero, rockero, everything your
>   parents told you not to do,
> question asking, X-Men reading, revolution seeking,
> your god, your way, self!   (2004, n.p.)

Karimi's risqué disco-inspired performance and the poem's crescendo identify an ever-expanding gallery of transversal fusions. However, his troping of religious angst into a suprareligious affirmation of individual autonomy also becomes a cultural relativist, yet simultaneously anarchist, politic predicated on a refusal to conform to any orthodoxy or authority. Karimi's supra-Latina/o violentology ultimately is undergirded by his negotiation of Catholic and Muslim heritages and the symbolic violence of each religion's proselytizing ethos, in addition to the latent traumas that these personal heritages bequeath to him. Significantly, his synthesis vacillates between a negative dialectic of never-ending syntheses and an immanently existentialist antiidentity, both of which ironically offer simultaneously nonsecular and secular liberatory potential.

The poem's expansive transversalisms, however, can quickly degenerate into ahistorical levelings of profoundly different genealogies and historical material realities, though Karimi's work remains grounded in an intersectional, multicultural, antiimperialist politics precisely because of its interspiritual genesis in two US-backed coups. Karimi's fusion poetic further involves an activist commitment through his persona as the "People's Cook." He travels throughout the United States to support grassroots organizations by collaboratively cooking transversal fusion food, which serves as a consciousness-raising experience and training on collectivist methods. Karimi's eclectic politicized food spectacles are featured in short films. His website description for his 2018 film, "Lumpia Campesina," describes his *ars poetica* as follows:

> A quixotic Iranian-Guatemalan cook traces his love for a special Filipino dish by taking us back to a teenage house party from his past where he learns how to transform his alienation into a recipe for empowerment.   (2018, n.p.)

Karimi's provocative multidimensional *oeuvre* thereby rehearses Cuban American Gustavo Pérez-Firmat's (2012) "life on the hyphen" paradigm: he presents transculturation itself as empowerment. Pérez-Firmat's celebratory renderings of Cuban American fusions inadvertently reinforces the idea that the United States is an ideal venue for new hybrid Latinidades. Yet, different from Pérez-Firmat, who identifies as being from an "exile" family and avoids substantive critiques of US imperialist hostility toward the socialist Cuba his family fled, the precondition for all of Karimi's work is a critique of US colonialism, imperialism, and the related material conditions that make hybridized survivances so recognizable and necessary (Figure 3.7).

FIGURE 3.7. *Robert Farid Karimi as the People's Cook, circa 2018. Courtesy of Robert Farid Karimi.*

In contrast to Karimi's highly nuanced negotiations of Islam, and religion in general, Mexican American Muslim spoken word artist and multigenre author Mark Gonzales confronts the long legacy of US imperialism and attendant Islamophobia through a didactic Islamic-based transversal poetics. Born in Alaska to a father of Mexican and French heritage who also was a US citizen and soldier, and a mother of "Tunisia's Africa Arab Indigenous lineage" (2019, n.p.), Gonzales identifies as a "Tunexican" (2018, n.p.). His literary production includes a 2015 self-help collection of Tweet-sized affirmative aphorisms titled, *In Times of Terror: Wage Beauty*, as well as a 2017 bilingual children's picture book, *Yo Soy Muslim: A Father's Letter to His Daughter*. Gonzales promotes the latter as being "about a parent who encourages their child to find joy and pride in all aspects of their multicultural identity" (2020, n.p.). His poetry presents a broader geopolitical exploration of violence against people on the margins, particularly in the global South and the Islamicate world, with a transspatial and transversal Islamic inflection of Latinidad as the antidote.

Gonzales's pacifist, supranational, transversal pairings of hyperlocal domestic US communities—primarily indigenous, Latina/o, and black—with Southern Hemispheric populations, further expand the loci of enunciation for Latinidades far beyond the conventional scope of Latina/o Studies. The poem, "West Coast to West Bank," foregrounds his intervention:

> And what does a Mexican from Alaska
> have to do with the Middle East?
> Nothing. Pues, nada.
> Unless you consider the original Lenape of Brooklyn
> whose heartbeat echo in Beirut streets
> where history free froze
> replayed slow motion genesis.
> Mesoamerican massacres at El Mazote.
> Azapo Egyptian eye duct.
> Exodus followed trails of tears into refugee camps.
> Return to see American suburbs as settlements.   (2012, n.p.)

As noted of Karimi's poetic, such transhistorical, transgeographical, and transversal pairings can easily degenerate into facile ahistorical filiations, rather than the leftist Third Worldism that Hisham Aidi suggests. But Gonzales's transspatial rhetoric and rhythm animate a significant epistemic shift: Islam is not just something to negotiate, or merely part of a transversal trope; rather, it is fundamental to his overall identity, politics, and poetics. He introduces this epiphany with a short riff on loss and alienation:

> And we are losing land lost
> like lives lost
> like wives lost.
> We who have lost children,
> are now lost children
> wandering the back alleyways and brothels
> battling the suspension of hope
> like the legacies of Cairo—Sadat;
> or Oaxaca—Vicente Fox.   (2012, n.p.)

Fusing the narrative free verse of slam poetry with the rhythm of Hip Hop, Gonzales's meditation relocates his poetic persona both inside and outside the United States, as well as within and without conventional understandings of Latina/o mestizaje and mulattaje:

> So we invoke the spirit of Rachim and Naz,
> Marmoud Darwish, Suheir, Ahmad.
> We are AfroIndigenous with Ipods
> wandering the streets of rocks.
> Bring on the tanks!
> We the beauty behind Hip Hop!
> We don't stop!
> We won't stop!
> From the west coast to the west bank!   (2012, n.p.)

Within this transversal and transtemporal genealogy that is simultaneously ancient, modern, and postmodern, Gonzales proposes that there is no Latinidad outside Africa, the Middle East, or Native American indigeneity. Moreover, his AfroLatIndigenismo is located within transracial Islam. This new epistemic cartography is further linked to the Muslim and Arab world through his references to intellectuals and artists such as Palestinian poet Marmoud Darwish, who was both Muslim and a communist.

More an Islamic multicultural humanist than a Marxist, Gonzales's poetic reveals itself to be Muslim spiritual activist signifying as he incorporates Islamic prayer and etiquette into poems such as "Letter to the Cordoba Center" (2012, n.d.). The poem addresses the Islamophobia and anti-Arab bigotry that prevented the building of a $100 million, thirteen-story mosque complex near New York City's "ground zero," a few blocks from the site of the former World Trade Center towers. Specifically, Gonzales interweaves epistolary, archaeology, and historiography to perform a transhistorical and transgeographic recentering of Muslims in America, which ultimately facilitates his embedding of Islamic Afroindigenismo within Latinidad. "They say 30% of Africans stolen from Africa were Muslim," he notes in the poem's refrain drawn from a letter by a Muslim from New York City. He adds that "in 2002, 20,000 African slaves were discovered...in the basement of what is called the World Trade Center" (2012). Each new fact in Gonzales's archaeology nudges into the archetypal sacred space of "ground zero," which in the United States has become a metonym for anti-Muslim sentiment since 2001. Gonzales's letter writer reminds readers that wherever you dig in

America—including in the "ground zero" of twenty-first-century Western neo-Crusade discourse—you find Islam:

> They called our cemetery "ground zero,"
> de facto nicknaming us in la tierra
> negative below the absence of their value. America,
> tell us in this space, moment, century
> as you stand over our grave
> that 20,000 spirits of Muslim African slaves
> still do not have a right nor a place to pray.
> New York your building zones
> built homes upon our bones.
> Must you again deny us in death
> our rights you denied us in life?   (2012, n.p.)

The poem's demand that Muslims be allowed to pray in this contested space reaches a crescendo as he adds a phrase from the Qur'an, which is also a common Muslim greeting:

> We deserve after three centuries to finally say:
> "Bismillah ir-Rahman ir-Raheem."
> Know our prayers, and, as they always do:
> "Assalamu Alaikum Wa Rahmatullahi.
> Assalamu Alaikum Wa Rahmatullahi."
> May Allah's peace and blessings be upon all and to you.
> Sincerely signed xxxxx nineteen thousand, nine hundred, ninety-five
>   times (2012, n.p.).[29]

The cross-cultural codeswitching—a signature feature of Chicana/o and Latina/o cultural nationalist poetics that usually involves Spanish, English, and indigenous languages such as Nahuatl or Taíno—now includes classical Arabic that signals a transversal Islamic supranationalism.

In contradistinction to Gonzales's global Islamic AfroLatIndigenous paradigm, which merely advocates a space in the polis free of Islamophobia, Puerto Rican Muslim Hip Hop artist Jason Hamza Perez interweaves the concept of the *Ummah*, or global community of Muslims, with a hyperlocal Puerto Rican cultural nationalism in his proposed counterimperialist violentological discourse. Hamza Perez's band, Mujahideen Team (also known as "M-Team"), is one of approximately one hundred Muslim Hip Hop groups in the United States and Britain. A self-proclaimed former "gangster" and exconvict from Brooklyn, Perez embraced Islam in between prison stints. Jennifer Maytorena Taylor's 2009 documentary, *New Muslim Cool*, features his journey as a new Muslim. The film attempts to dispel the racist and Islamophobic stereotype of the dark-skinned Muslim male "menace to society" by noting that much of Perez's time is spent with his multiracial blended family, urban youth-outreach activities, prisoner spiritual counseling, and interfaith dialogue with Jewish and Christian friends.

After FBI officers raid and damage Perez's mosque in Pittsburgh's working-class North Side neighborhood for allegedly hosting a traveling Muslim male who later appeared on the FBI "watch list," however, Perez is forced to meditate on the antithetical nature of his identity as a Latino Muslim during the War on Terror. Immediately after the raid, he commented to Maytorena Taylor, while the cameras were still filming:

> It's hard for you to tell someone who was a gangster, who's trying to live a religious life, that when someone invades your home, you have to turn the other cheek and forgive them.
>
> (Maytorena Taylor 2009, n.p.)

In a radio show interview included in the film, the show host offers a prescient response that places Perez's vacillating pacifist and martial Latino Muslim subjectivity into greater relief:

> So now, brother Hamza, you are a married man, you're American, you're Puerto Rican, you're from the Hood, you're a Muslim, you're a rapper, you're…, you know, you have all…, you sound like America's worst nightmare! (ellipses in original)   (Maytorena Taylor 2009, n.p.)

The balance of *New Muslim Cool* seeks to historicize the contemporary challenges facing the newly sober, ambivalently pacifist, Latino family man whose transformative embrace of Islam coincided with the global War on Terror dragnet that intensified the preceding War on Crime, both of which target lumpenproletarian racial minority males like Perez.

Perez uses Hip Hop as the vehicle for disseminating his new Islamic spiritual activism, which immediately becomes a theory of counterimperialist violence, and eventually a competing imperialism. Mujahideen Team's track "FTG" (2005, n.p.), or "Flag the Government," with the "F" also alluding to *Fuck*, which Hamza dutifully censors as a practicing Muslim, is dedicated to the "soldiers." It sets the tone for their increasingly martial invective. In one performance of the song featured in Maytorena Taylor's film, Perez emerges on stage with a flaming machete (Figure 3.8). He states that the machete is "a Puerto Rican custom, you know, *Los Macheteros*," alluding to the popular name of the *Ejército Popular Boricua* (the Boricua Popular Army), a Marxist insurgent group formed in the 1970s that continues to contest the US colonization of Puerto Rico in favor of an independent socialist nation. In their song, "I'm a Suspect," Mujahideen Team even honors the seventy-two-year-old commander-in-chief, Filiberto Ojeda Ríos, who died from gunshot wounds suffered in a shootout with an FBI tactical assault unit in 2005. In Maytorena Tayor's film, Hamza's brother and fellow band member Suliman—whose adopted name translates as "man of peace" but also was shared by the sixteenth-century Ottoman sultan who fought Christian crusaders—adds that the flaming machete has a pedagogical proselytizing function: "When we have interactions and discussions with people after the shows, you know, we're able to relay that to them, and let 'em know a little of what it symbolizes" (Maytorena Taylor, 2009, n.p.).

The term "Mujahideen" forms the central dyad in the band's name and translates from the Arabic as "one who struggles for Jihad," which

FIGURE 3.8.   *Scene from* New Muslim Cool *(2009). Courtesy of Jennifer Maytorena Taylor.*

is a key discursive device in the band's utopian LatinOrientalism. The oft-misunderstood Muslim concept of "Jihad," which means "struggle," simultaneously alludes to moral ("greater Jihad") and military self-defense ("lesser Jihad"). In songs such as "MT Bismillah" ("Mujahideen Team in the Name of God," 2015, n.p.), the band appears to emphasize the latter, though with an explicitly proselytizing and expansionist agenda that includes the former:

> Islamic dominant, we taking back the continent!
> Bismillah [in the name of God] we gonna rock, rock!
> So when the war…
> this bookoo sat by the door
> say something about my prophet
> I'ma bust your jaw!
> I'm an E-F-F-E-C-T
> with an armed struggle rainstorm
> FTG [fuck the government]!
> To win the warfare
> blood sweat and tears;
> a nonstop fight for fourteen hundred years.
> I'ma kill for my ahk [Muslim brother], I die for my ahk
>   [Muslim brother]
> Bismillah we gonna rock!   (2005, n.p., ellipses in original)

The Perez brothers identify as counterimperialists "effects"—subaltern subjects who rebelliously have reclaimed their abject status—and proclaim their designs on "the continent." In the context of their *oeuvre*, this means North America and the Caribbean basin, including Puerto Rico, a US colony since 1898. The duo seeks to make it "Muslim dominant," presumably meaning a liberated space free of US imperialism and Western Christian hegemony. The reference to "a nonstop fight for fourteen hundred years" alludes to the founding of Islam in the seventh century. Ironically, their presumption that Islam is inherently hostile to non-Muslims inevitably subordinates their regional anticolonial struggle for Puerto Rican independence. This hierarchy does not silence their cultural nationalist designs for a free Borinquen, the contemporary permutation of the indigenous Taíno name for Puerto Rico ("Borikén"), but it makes the desired liberation incoherent, inconsistent, and unstable.

Mujahideen Team's promotion of Boricua nationalism alongside an expansionist vision of Islam reveals a competing imperialist politics that merely masquerades as an antiimperialist ethic. Indeed, their poetics and politics are antithetical to Peter Mandaville's (2010) claim that the transnational youth-led Muslim Hip Hop movement that begin in the mid-1990s may be an iteration of a new liberation theology, given that all mainstream branches of Islam (despite some conservative cultural elements), have always emphasized a model of justice. Harold Morales is much more critical of the Perez brothers, as well as accused operatives for Al Qaeda and the Islamic State, whose agenda he sees as intersecting with Mujahideen Team. Noting that these ideologues are in the minority, Morales argues that they harm Latina/o Muslims by inadvertently invoking Samuel Huntington's (1996) racist Christian imperialist "Clash of Civilizations" thesis (2018, 161–2). Morales is especially critical of the Perez brothers for titling one of their CDs *Clash of Civilizations*. Morales fails to realize, however, that Perez and Mujahideen Team deliberately invert Huntington's thesis to propose a quasi-socialist challenge to US imperialism in Puerto Rico that simultaneously is a competing imperialist inflection of the Ummah throughout the Americas and the world at large. This clash of civilizations—and religions—is the essence of their violence-based ontology, episte-mology, and praxis. And they are not alone.

Chicano Muslim Hip Hop artist Abu Nurah, born as David Chavez to Mexican immigrants who raised him in the working-class Latina/o barrio of Pico Rivera in southeastern Los Angeles, explicates how Islam became the basis of his purported demystification and new politico-spiritual subjectivity. As a youth he claims to have found refuge from the violence of his barrio through books, Hip Hop, and break dancing. Nurah continued these interests as an undergraduate student at Harvard University, where he apparently graduated Cum Laude with an engineering degree.[30] While at Harvard, he rejected the conservative "success story" of the underclass barrio boy-cum-university student destined to achieve the American Dream of upward mobility through assimilation, a theme that has spawned a cottage industry of Latina/o neo-Horatio Alger memoirs. Instead, Nurah credits Islam for helping him resist the capitalist, imperialist, and Christian disciplining that such schools originally were created to promote. At Harvard, which was founded in the seventeenth cen-tury to Christianize Indian (specifically Algonquian) youth, he changed his name to Daoud Ali Chavez after embracing Islam, and later adopted Abu Nurah, which is Arabic for "father of Nurah" to honor his daughter. Significantly, he challenges conventional appraisals of Hip Hop as inherently counterhegemonic by noting, "I've been involved in Hip Hop for over two decades," adding that it was only "after I became Muslim, I grew in political awareness" (2018, n.p.).

Nurah's convoluted Islamic Chicana/o cultural nationalist politics intersect with the Mujahideen Team, but with a slightly more precise political-economic program that extends LatinOrientalist discourse simultaneously to the left and right. Nurah's 2009 song "My Jihad," for instance, illustrates his syncretic blend of Islamic self-defense, Pan-Arab and Pan-Muslim solidarity, and Chicana/o cultural nationalist critiques of Manifest Destiny, the bedrock of modern US expansionist imperialism. The poem foregrounds the poetic persona's angst as a colonized subject (e.g., "Manifest Destiny got the best of me"), to then proclaim his newfound epistemological center that will enable a newly liberated subjectivity:

> Haven't you heard these days I'm operating in guerrilla mode.
> Switched off CNN, crushed the remote in my hand.
> Picked up the Qur'an to read about the martyrs' end.
> What's my path? Time to choose it!
> Life is use it, or lose it!   (2009, n.p.)

In this meditation on demystification, his new gnosis and theory of praxis is distinguished for its martial vocabulary as the lyric continues (e.g., "trigger finger") and military science (e.g., "asymmetrical warfare"). He ends the song with a description of himself as a "rebel militia mujahideen on a mission!" (2009, n.p.).

Abu Nurah's epiphany balances a network of antiracist, anticapitalist, and antiimperialist sensibilities that are intertwined with various cultural nationalisms, particularly Chicana/o and Palestinian. These are all undergirded by his supranational religious proselytizing that ultimately reveals itself to be a competing Islamic spiritual imperialism. Nurah's contradictory signifying is on display in his debut 2009 CD, *Don't Be a Citizen*, which features the image of him wearing the skull cap of a devout Muslim male as he tears up a US passport, with the Statue of Liberty in the background (Figure 3.9). In the composition "Say it Loud," which appears on this CD, he raps:

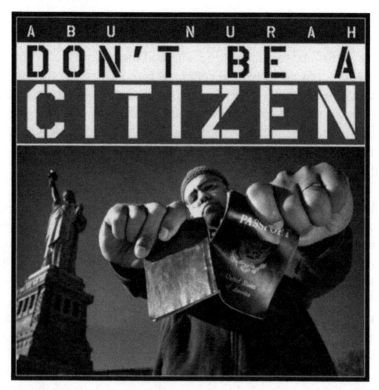

FIGURE 3.9. *Cover for Abu Nurah's CD,* Don't Be a Citizen *(2007). Image in Public Domain.*

Asking me why we fight, and the answer is imminent.
We don't target the innocent.
Youth is listening.
We act only to please the Magnificent.
Times we're living in is not easy to fight.
Why wait for governments to give us the right?
Son, it's Allah who says free the oppressed.
Martyrs among them may their souls be blessed.
[…]
Say it Loud!
Jihad and I'm Proud!   (2009, n.p.)

His fight extends beyond the nation state (e.g., "Why wait for governments to give us the right?"), with his closing zeal reminiscent of the rhetorical patterns prevalent in the cultural nationalist black and Chicana/o movements, for which "Black Pride" and "Brown Pride"

served as clarion calls for mass consciousness raising and mobilizations.

This "fight" appears to include anticapitalist politics (e.g., "free the
oppressed"), but ultimately degenerates into a strategically fluid ideology as the ultimate target is "to please the Magnificent," that is,
Allah. In an undated interview on the MuslimHipHop website that
was posted until 2018, he advocates a multifaceted political program
that includes banking and social organizations designed to build in-
frastructure for an ascendant global Muslim community:

> We need to build, build, build…institutions, scholarship programs,
> women's shelters, Islamic banking organizations, etc. We are not
> going to win militarily *at this time*, so we have to use our numbers to
> brainstorm creative solutions to our problems. We need to uplift spir-
> itually and intellectually.   (emphasis added)

Nurah reveals how the purportedly leftist Latina/o Muslim politics can
easily coexist with a proselytizing theocratic theory of counterpower
that is little more than a competing religious, cultural nationalist, and
capitalist imperialist politics. For him, the military option remains
when the subjective and objective conditions make it feasible.

Extending his odd ideological pairings, one of Abu Nurah's songs
previously used a hyperlink image from Brazilian artist Carlos
Latuff's lithograph, "Palestinian Che" (Figure 3.10). This allusion
might suggest Nurah is a revolutionary nationalist or even a communist internationalist like Ernesto "Che" Guevara. However, instead of signaling his philosophy as an analogue to the Marxist
Popular Front for the Liberation of Palestine, or other Marxist organizations in the Islamicate world such as the secular Kurdistan
Worker's Party, Abu Nurah's lyrics, interviews, and professed politics reveal him to be more aligned with any number of Palestinian
nonsecular parties that share conservative cultural politics and
agendas as the means for alleviating their people's suffering under
Israeli occupation and apartheid. But like the Perez brothers,
Nurah's philosophy quickly degenerates into a simultaneously hyperlocal and selectively global transversal cultural nationalism, which
accommodates capitalism, as well as a competing Islamic counterim-
perialism, with the Ummah providing the glue that Bandung once
proposed to subaltern peoples, subordinated regions, and developing
nations.

FIGURE 3.10. *"Palestinian Che," by Carlos Latuff (2002). Courtesy of Carlos Latuff.*

As illustrated above, Latina/o Muslim violentologies involve important nuances distinguishing them from each other. Yet, individually and cumulatively they have forever changed core concepts such as Aztlán, Borinquen, and Latinidad in general. Yet there are important qualifications to their proposed counterhegemonic and outer-national resonances. While Robert Farid Karimi's materialist reclamations of his parents' imperialist traumas embed his transversal performances with a fundamentally antiimperialist chronotopal resonance, Mark Gonzales, Mujahideen Team, and Abu Nurah intertwine their hyperlocal nationalist sovereignty claims with postnationalist global spirituality designs that can be understood within Michael Hardt and Antonio Negri's critiques of fundamentalism as a reactive gesture of "de-modernization" (2001, 147). This spiritual activism can be both anticapitalist and antiimperialist, as well as capitalist and imperialist. Indeed, such chauvinist politics are regressively naïve, nostalgic, and contradictory for yearning an illusionary episteme free of modernity's ambiguities and alienating commodity fetish.

These limits notwithstanding, the myriad LatinAsian and LatinOrientalist formations examined throughout this chapter are shaped by and variously deploy multiple forms of violence in the performance of a range of (supra)Latinidades that extend far beyond the scope of extant theories of mestizaje and mulattaje—Latina/o Studies' principal metaphors of culture and identity—and far outside the Americas, Christianity, and Mesoamerican spiritualities that have served as the fundamental loci of enunciation for the field's theoretical subjects. The next chapter further examines Latina/o literary navigations of the local and global dyad to explicate the violentological features of familiar and new regional (supra)Latinidades throughout the Americas.

4

Violence and the Transnational Question

REGIONALISM, NATIONALISM, AND INTERNATIONALISM IN LATINA/O WAR LITERATURE

Three flags fluttered in the afternoon drizzle shrouding Raúl Salinas's burial in Austin, Texas, on February 15, 2008: Mexican tricolor with golden eagle atop a cactus eating a rattlesnake from Aztec mythology; Canadian First Nations flag emblazoned with an elder holding a peace pipe superimposed over a red maple leaf; and communist red banner with gold hammer and sickle (Figure 4.1). Salinas's Zapatista comrades had earlier draped his casket with the red and black flag of the Zapatista National Liberation Army, into which they placed tobacco and other offerings for his next journey. The rotating honor guard included flag bearers from intersecting struggles. Poet and Chicano cultural nationalist Nephtalí De León bore the Mexican flag. Internationalist combat veterans of the Sandinista Revolution— Chicano Alejandro Murguía and Nicaraguan American Roberto Vargas—took turns holding the red banner. Chicano Zapatista and educator Alfred "Freddie" Porras along with the Chicano poet, muralist, and musician José Montoya of the Royal Chicano Air Force and musical trio Casindio ("Almost Indian") joined a host of people who took turns bearing the flag of the First Nations. The honor guard had formed to commemorate their revolutionary comrade, teacher, and friend by honoring all aspects of Salinas's life as an indigenous-identified Chicano who navigated different though interrelated ideological trajectories: revolutionary nationalist, Maoist, anarcho-communitarian Zapatista, and more. Adding to the ideological spectrum were the quadricolor streamers flying from the procession of vehicles that followed compañero Raúl on one last trip through his

Violentologies: Violence, Identity, and Ideology in Latina/o Literature. B.V. Olguín, Oxford University Press (2021).
© B.V. Olguín.
DOI: 10.1093/oso/9780198863090.001.0005

FIGURE 4.1. *Raúl Salinas Funeral Honor Guard with flag bearers from left: unidentified, B. V. Olguín, Nephtalí De Leon, and José Montoya, Austin, Texas, February 15, 2008. Photo by Bernadette Andrea. Courtesy of Bernadette Andrea.*

old East Austin barrio, *La Loma*, featured in his 1970 poem "Un Trip Through the Mind Jail." The red, yellow, white, and black of Pan-Indian cosmologies also signified the cycle of birth, growth, maturity, and death. A double rainbow provided the crescendo.

This brilliant display of Raúl Salinas's fluid spatial ontology and ideological mobility reflects his migrations back and forth between hyperlocal barrio boy gangster protecting his turf, Pan-Tribal XicanIndio cultural nationalist, and international communist fighting to free the world from capitalism and imperialism. As emphasized in Chapter 1, Salinas's solidarity work took him throughout the world: brutal supermax prisons in the United States; insurgent Mexico in the 1970s and again for the Zapatista insurrection in the 1990s; Sandinista Nicaragua; revolutionary Cuba; the Great Socialist People's Libyan Arab Jamahiriya under its Bedouin leader Muammar Gaddafi; Puerto Rican socialist independentista activities from the 1960s and related Vieques demilitarization campaign of the 1990s; and all throughout Indian Country. He even went to Switzerland as a delegate for the American Indian Treaty Council. Salinas's wide-ranging navigations and militancies in intersecting and diverging political movements illustrate how Chicanidades and Latinidades have always involved regional, national, and international paradigms—sometimes simultaneously.

In his 2005 study on the 1960s and 1970s Chicana/o Movement, George Mariscal provides guidance for unpacking this complex geopolitical and ideological spectrum. His explication of Chicana/o cultural nationalism departs from Benedict Anderson's (2006) definition of nationalism as an "imagined community" created by the dissemination of a presumed common history across a vast but contiguous geography. For some Chicana/os, Mariscal notes, the sense of a shared historical, cultural, racial, and ethnic background also included an expanded yet fluctuating geographical and ideological scope:

> Chicana/o cultural nationalism functioned as an organizing tool that could point either to sectarian forms of regressive "nationalism" or toward coalition building, solidarity projects, and even socialism. Chicana/o internationalism, then, existed in a complementary and at times conflictive relationship with narrow nationalisms.
>
> (2005, 91–2)[1]

In his famous 1913 thesis on the national question, Bolshevik revolutionist Vladimir Ilych Lenin formulated this ideological vacillation as inherent to nationalism:

> Combat all national oppression? Yes, of course! Fight *for* any kind of national development, *for* "national culture" in general?—Of course not. The economic development of capitalist society presents us with examples of immature national movements all over the world, examples of the formation of big nations out of a number of small ones, or to the detriment of some of the small ones, and also examples of the assimilation of nations. The development of nationality in general is the principle of bourgeois nationalism; hence the exclusiveness of bourgeois nationalism, hence the endless national bickering. The proletariat, however, far from undertaking to uphold the national development of every nation, on the contrary, warns the masses against such illusions. (1913, 64)

Lenin identified nationalist wars of liberation as part of the continuing break with feudalism, colonialism, and imperialism. But nationalism, he adds, is also dangerously bourgeois even as it is potentially allied with a broad network of revolutionary nationalists and revolutionary communists fighting to ultimately eliminate all national divisions and the capitalist episteme with which the nation-state is intertwined.

Cultural nationalist ambivalence between the local and the global, however, persists in Chicana/o and broader Latina/o discourses. At one end of the spectrum, Raúl Homero Villa recuperates the salience of hyperlocalities and micronationalisms in his revision of the 1960s cultural nationalist category "barriology," which he identifies as a "range of knowledge and practices that form the historical, geographical, and social being-in-consciousness of urban Chicano experience" (2000, 8). He posits that these localized Chicana/o vernacular sensibilities emerge as politically salient counterpoints to geopolitical containment and disenfranchisement in low income urban barrios resulting from capitalist urban renewal projects. As noted in the introduction, Latina/o Spatial Studies scholars continue to excavate new localized inflections of Chicana/o vernacular sensibilities beyond Villa's emphasis on urban barrios. The case studies in this book also reveal that increased Latina/o mobility, and ever-more-complex hybridities in regions throughout the world, incessantly transform the ideological resonance of these globalized transversal syntheses and spatial sensibilities.

Latina/o spatial ontologies throughout the United States and Caribbean productively intersect with, but also depart from Villa's hyperlocalisms and the related "radical regionalism" paradigm. Despite the predisposition of regional identities to atomize into myopic, reactionary, and xenophobic cultural nationalism, Michael Steiner (2013), Michael Denning (2008), and José Limón (2008, 2013) insist on this subfield's counterhegemonic potential. Américo Paredes's settler colonialist poetics, discussed in Chapter 1, nevertheless reminds us that cultural nationalism always involves a nostalgia about origins, which begs the question of origins and, moreover, always hides multiple violences, including genocide. Yet, barriology and radical regionalism scholars overwhelmingly ignore how localized and regionalized subjects are defined by violences enacted against them—and by them—in wildly diverging ideological variations that, despite their pretentions, do not always challenge power.

The interplay between local and global, regional and hemispheric, as well as national and international, also pressures Latina/o Studies' fixation on transnationalism as a prism for mapping Latinidades.

This includes Jennifer Harford-Vargas's (2017) otherwise productive comparative "Pan-Latina/o" and "Trans-Latina/o" examination of how totalitarian Latin American regimes have imprinted aesthetic and political traces in literature produced by Latin American-descent authors born or raised in the United States. In her study, and throughout the field, transnationalism usually refers to mobile and hybrid subjectivities, as well as cultural and multinational citizenship, across a wide range of political geographies and specific nation-states. Transnationalism accordingly has become a metaphor for virtually any place and everyplace Latina/os happen to be present, remember, or just imagine. This is why Amy Kaplan and many more American Studies scholars long ago complained that transnationalism had the virtue and limit of simultaneously referring to everywhere and nowhere.[2]

Despite the oftentimes celebratory rendering of Latina/o transnational mobility across borders, and accompanying interstitiality, scholars such as Tamara L. Mitchell (2019) remind us that multiple Latina/o cultural and civic identities across nations arise because of failed or failing nation-states, which usually involve intense instability, conflict, persecution, and trauma. Ironically, transnational paradigms remain fatally embedded with the persistent specter of the nation-state that the "transnationalism" concept seeks to transcend. In his critical reassessment of transnationalism as an operative framework for American Studies, Winfried Fluck observes that:

> the transnational project is not just innocently aiming at a cosmopolitan broadening of interpretive horizons. It also pursues the goal of reconceptualizing America—that is, the very thing from which it apparently wants to escape or distance itself.   (2011, 366–7)

Fluck is referring to American Studies. Yet, the contradictions he highlights also apply to Latina/o transnationalism paradigms, which recuperate heritage nations and regions (particularly South, Central, and North America along with the Caribbean) in new Latinidades, but always in relation to the United States.[3] This inadvertent yet inevitable recentering of the nation-state—an imperialist one no less!—truncates and even undermines the oppositional presumptions and potential ascribed to Latina/o transnational subjects.

These limits, in addition to lingering racial teleologies, discursive orthodoxies, and heteropatriarchal hierarchies, inform Ellie Hernández's contrapuntal "postnationalism" paradigm for Chicana/o

Studies, which offers alternative ways of theorizing Chicanidades and Latinidades. Hernández's (2009) framework is substantially different from Mitchell's focus on the Latin American diaspora's postnational unmooring and relative loss of agency precipitated by the political fragility and failure of various heritage countries. Hernández emphasizes subjectivities that never completely fit in cultural nationalist paradigms, much less nation-states, and especially in overbearingly heteropatriarchal Chicana/o cultural nationalist contexts from the 1960s to the 1980s. She thus opens a wide space for alternatives to the enduring cultural nationalist fetish on heteropatriarchal and masculinist models of Chicana/o and Latina/o subjectivity that are intertwined with the modern nation-state, and the imagined state of Aztlán. More importantly, Hernández's decentering of retrograde models of national consciousness also transcends transnational states of being. As illustrated in the preceding three chapters, Chicana/o and Latina/o identity formation and political subjectivity now include a range of very different multicultural, multigendered, and multisexual subjects across economic class and political sensibilities that spill far outside national and even transnational signifiers. Hernández's postnationalism recognizes these other ontological determinants, and their discrepant outcomes. Extrapolating from Hernández, we also might imagine new provisionally post-Latina/o subjects. Indeed, case studies in every chapter in this book confirm their existence, proliferation, and rising prominence.

Adding to this immanent paradigm shift in Latina/o Studies, José David Saldívar (2011) expands Hernández's postnationalism by recuperating Aníbal Quijano's and Immanuel Wallerstein's "Americanity" (1992). This historicist perspectival shift proposes that the "discovery" and creation of the Americas enabled the consolidation of a capitalist world economy, and not the other way around. This reclamation of epistemic authority for the margins, Saldívar adds, "might also help us broaden, open, and outernationalize our internally colonized horizons" (2011, xii). His expanded *Trans*-Americanity seeks to globalize the local and localize the global. Saldívar explicates narratives from the global South—Cuban, Chicana/o, African American, Colombian, and South Asian Indian—to demonstrate how "stories of global coloniality of power seek to create an epistemological ground on which coherent versions of the world may be produced" (2011, xx). This outer-national gesture performs the Archimedean task of standing outside the nation-state that has defined the modern world. Importantly, he resists facile renderings of counterepistemology and counterpower—the decolonial, if you will—as easy to perform, or already extant. Instead, glossing Adorno's negative dialectic, Saldívar emphasizes the "untotalizable totality" (2011, xvii), or the never-ending and always incomplete syntheses of outer-national alternatives to the coloniality of power.

This chapter illustrates how a diverse collection of Latina/o authors born or raised in the United States extend, and complicate, Trans-Americanity toward a post-Americanity to serve as a prism for assessing the persistent coloniality of power, proposed theories of counterpower, and new identity formations traversing through and beyond national and even transnational frameworks. Rather than prematurely signaling the demise of the nation-state yet again, however, they negotiate the national question, and equally limited transnational paradigms, through myriad inflections of regionalisms, nationalisms, and internationalisms that intersect, for instance, with Raúl Salinas's aforementioned complex navigations of ideology and spatial ontology. These negotiations are mediated through spectral, embodied, local, and global violences in so many intersecting, though distinct, ways that the category of Latinidades is rendered ever more radically insufficient a signifier of these phenomena. Equally as significant, these violence-inflected supra-Latinidades are never as ideologically coherent, or oppositional, as barriology, radical regionalism, transnationalism, or even Trans-Americanity frameworks imply. This chapter accordingly deploys the violentological herme-neutic to account for the highly contingent nature of provisionally postnational and outer-national supra-Latinidades by explicating cases from the US-Mexico borderlands, Central and South America, and expatriate barrios throughout the United States.

Tejas Versus Texas: Patriarchal Regionalism, Chicana Lesbian Insurrection, and Performative Contradictions in Emma Pérez's Counternationalist Signifying

In her 2009 historical novel, *Forgetting the Alamo, Or, Blood Memory*, Chicana lesbian historian, cultural theorist, and novelist Emma Pérez returns to Américo Paredes's nostalgic patriarchal Tejano regionalist Eden of Nuevo Santander, the mid-eighteenth-century Spanish settlement spanning from the present-day coastal Mexican state of Tamaulipas to the southern tip of South Texas. Pérez illustrates how masculinist violence defines, and inevitably undermines, Paredes's purportedly antiimperialist utopia. Similar to Eve Raleigh and Jovita González's historical romance, *Caballero*, Pérez sets her historical novel in the aftermath of the 1836 battle of the Alamo in San Antonio de Bejar (at the edge of Nuevo Santander), where pro-slavery white Texan filibusterers and their Tejano allies were annihilated by Mexican troops seeking to quell the secessionist movement. "Remember the Alamo!" subsequently became a rallying cry for pro-slavery secessionists, who eventually won the war and created the independent Republic of Texas that would eventually join the Confederate States of America. In contrast to Raleigh and González's naïve depiction of interracial heterosexual marriages and gay male pairings as liberatory alternatives to Mexican heteropatriarchy, however, Pérez's historical novel meta-critically interrogates whether women and lesbian, gay, bisexual, transgender, queer, intersex, and nonbinary people can escape the gendered, sexualized confines of competing rural Texas and Tejano regionalisms, which more accurately might be called micronationalisms. In Pérez's narrative, both these competing paradigms are driven by the exchange of women, and by imagined communities predicated upon the subordination or exclusion of anyone deemed aberrant. Pérez's framing of this transracial heteropatriarchal micronationalist milieu poses a larger ontological question and epistemological challenge: Can Chicana/os exist outside the racialized, gendered, sexualized colonial and imperial violences that give rise to them as a people, and, if so, how is this achieved? Ellie Hernández (2009, 2020) has convincingly argued in the affirmative. Yet, Emma Pérez is only partially successful in narrating an alternative in *Forgetting the Alamo* because of the lingering nationalist signifying that haunts her proposed decolonial intervention.

Pérez's novel focuses on Mexican American Micaela Campos, who at fifteen encounters her father's dead body after the Texan and Tejano secessionist massacre of Mexican and Mexico-allied Tejano troops at the Battle of San Jacinto in 1836, which marks the end of the war and secessionist victory. Earlier described by her mother as "un machito," or "tomboy" (2009, 11), Micaela dons her dead father's jacket and rides home, only to find her siblings murdered and mother traumatized after being gang raped by the killers, who are white

Texan secessionists. Having already shorn her long black braid in an act of mourning for her father, Micaela embarks on a quest for revenge with her father's rifle in her hand. This gloss of Paredes's 1958 musicology of the patriarchal race wars that linger into early twentieth-century South Texas, *With His Pistol in His Hand: A Border Ballad and Its Hero*, segues with the masculinist Western novel genre. *Forgetting the Alamo* is replete with card games, whiskey-fueled brawls, saloons doubling as brothels full of rustic cowhands and coquettish prostitutes, gunfights, horse chases, and ill-fated romances. However, rather than merely rehearse this masculinist genre, which looms large in the yeoman mythos of US settler colonialism and related regionalisms, Pérez seeks to transform the Western novel as a space to critique the heteropatriarchal and nationalist teleologies that drive it. Throughout the novel, Micaela will struggle to reclaim and refashion the idea of Texas as *Tejas*, while attempting to transcend the inherent limits of this regionally distinct, counternational construct (hence, the operative clause of the title, "*Forgetting the Alamo*").

After the novel's opening saloon card game in which Micaela holds the winning hand but lacks the confidence to play it, she progressively becomes a more extroverted "cowgirl" warrior hero who claims her presence in history, particularly in the masculinist construct of the "West," as a woman who kills men and loves women. Ironically, and provocatively, the cross-dressing lesbian Micaela occupies center stage in a genre traditionally predicated upon a binary logic that eschews her embodied interstitial subjectivity: she engages in fistfights, shoot outs, and horse chases, and kills rapists along with the men who murdered her siblings. Additionally, throughout the narrative she has a running love affair with a mixed-heritage black and Native American woman known as "La India" whose real name, ironically, is Clara, which is Spanish for "clear," "transparent," or "light." La India later joins Micaela's mother in executing a jail breakout that spared Micaela from the proverbial hanging at dawn. Micaela subsequently flees to a convent to escape death and, she hopes, the legacy of violence that has defined her life and family's history.

This novel's interrogation of whether or not Chicana/os can exist outside heteropatriarchal regional violences and settler colonial nationalist designs that birthed them as a people, instantiates Pérez's influential Chicana feminist "decolonial imaginary." In *Decolonial Imaginary: Writing Chicanas into History* (1999), she proposes this method as:

> a theoretical tool for uncovering the hidden voices of Chicanas that have been relegated to silences, to passivity, to that third space where agency is enacted through third space feminism.   (1999, xvi)

Pérez's renowned treatise recovers Chicana activist presence in, and challenges to, various nationalist, internationalist, and antinationalist (particularly anarchist) struggles in the United States and Mexico throughout the twentieth century. Significantly, she resists celebrating what other scholars might laud as transnational resistance. Instead, Pérez underscores how nationalist sentiments across borders continue to be a promising discursive space, but ultimately an unsatisfying, unsuccessful, and in some cases, lethal avenue for actualizing a liberatory paradigm for Mexican women and Chicanas. As a narratological extension of her theorizing of the local (i.e., regional and national) vis-à-vis the global (i.e., international, antinational, and postnational), Pérez's Mexican American lesbian antihero Micaela Campos, whose surname aptly signifies "fields" or "terrains," navigates the dangerous space between warring patriarchs. They are determined to transform their hard-scrabble region, originally (and still) inhabited by various indigenous peoples and nations, into a modern heteropatriarchal Western nation-state. The only thing left to resolve is whether it will be called Texas or Tejas. Micaela is caught between these two violent patriarchal poles, as it were, from which she attempts to escape.

Pérez's novel narrativizes this micronationalist quarrel between Texan and Tejano patriarchs, whose complementary projects, as noted, are genocidal and built upon the exchange of women. More importantly, Pérez recuperates women's, and particularly lesbian, vexed agency within, and provisionally without, this epistemic space. Significantly, white Texans are not the only men who are grotesquely lascivious in their reduction of women as commodities. Micaela's father Agustín is guilty of the patriarchal practice that intertwines the entire family in semi-incestuous circles of exchange. For instance, Micaela's mother Úrsula was engaged in a long-term affair with a fifty-year-old man, "El Viejo Barrera," whom her husband, Micaela's father, has inadvertently selected as the future husband for his fifteen-year-old "machito" daughter. Furthermore, Micaela expresses sexual desires for the brothel Madame Elsie ("I wanted to flee for fear someone might suspect how much I liked being buried at her chest," 2009, 5), with whom her serial philanderer father has had longstanding sexual relations. Micaela's mixed-heritage white-Mexican cousin Jedidiah "Jed" Jones is Elsie's de facto adopted son, who gazes upon his adoptive mother's buttocks and engages in sexually suggestive embraces and flirtations with one of Elsie's adopted "girls" Melina, a prostitute who essentially is his adopted sister. To further complicate matters, Jed mockingly informs his cousin Micaela that he impregnated her lover "La India." As a crescendo to this sordid network of sexual exchanges, the twins born after Jed's death are named after Micaela's murdered siblings.

Navigating between roles as a gender-bending warrior hero and picaresque antihero trying to escape the multiple violences undergirding this semi-feudal sexual economy, Micaela inadvertently, but inevitably, demonstrates the practical and ideological limits of all nationalisms, including her immanently postpatriarchal feminist and protoqueer regionalist micronationalism. The need for such an alternative is demonstrated in an important scene toward the end of the novel where Micaela is put on trial for the murder of her cousin Jed, for which she had been framed. The case immediately becomes a trial about her identity as a cross-dressing lesbian, and all it represents to the new white Texan hegemony, and, indirectly, the Tejano alternative. Karen Allison Fielder notes:

> Her masculine performance is clearly her most offensive transgression, and in the eyes of the audience at her trial, this is what transforms her into an "it" existing outside of the protection of the law. Because she successfully mimics the authentic male performance upheld as the foundation for the future state of Texas, her existence becomes far too threatening to the new Anglo hegemony. (2012, 43)

Micaela's dark skin, bequeathed by her mother's Mexican, Tonkawa, and Spanish Moor heritage, and her father's multigenerational mestizajes with Tlascaltecas, Otomí, Moor, Apache, and Comanche, further adds to her unsettling presence in the new nation-state of Texas. Ironically, she also threatens the competing Tejano alternative that is similarly sexist and homophobic, and as frequently Eurocentric, as illustrated in Chapter 1. Pérez's recuperated Tejana lesbian protagonist who previously had been written out of history thus is forced to recognize that there is no room for her, and other people like her in this time and place. Micaela's emergence onto the historical drama reveals that the battle pitting Texas-versus-Tejas is a false binary, as both regionally inflected and culturally nuanced protonationalist formations are intensely violent heteropatriarchal spaces. Pérez's novelistic ruminations on the national question thus are in dialogue with Rosemary Hennessey (1993), Silvia Federici (2012), and materialist feminist theorists and activists who propose that any feminist liberatory project must involve the eradication of all hierarchies and binaries, and corresponding modes of subordination, upon which nationalisms are predicated.

The central question arising from Pérez's proposed decolonial signifying is whether or not Micaela's reclamations of her disruptive presence, and broader resistance to warring patriarchs, involves a postnational option or merely a reformed and expanded Tejana/o pan-sexual, pan-gender, counternationalism that inadvertently, but inevitably, preserves the binary that renders her as abject. Will Micaela ever be able to escape the multiple forms of violence into which she was born, reared, defined, and that also excluded her from the polis in a nineteenth-century Texas/Tejas secular rehearsal of Giorgio Agamben's (1998) Roman "homo sacer"? Can she become one of Althusser's "bad subjects" and escape the confines of interpellation (1971, 181)? Regardless of the outcome of these inquiries and struggles, *Forgetting the Alamo, or Blood Memory* recenters the violences that made the conflicted Texas/Tejas region into a modern nation-state: the Republic of Texas. Yet, Tejanas like Micaela Campos only superficially contest the victorious proslavery heteropatriarchal nation, as their imagined alternative inadvertently, and sometimes deliberately, involves a nostalgia for a premodern past—Tejas, if not Nuevo Santander—replete with land grants and dark-brown-skinned indentured servants linked to the landed gentry by the *encomienda* system. Violence defines the milieu and is central to Micaela's navigations and proposed decolonial synthesis. Ultimately, her alternative is profoundly limited, if not altogether a counterideological failure, because it preserves the idea of the nation-state—and all that it implies—in its microcosmic regional form.

Micaela's relative successes and failures as an instantiation of Pérez's theory of third-space, interstitial, decolonial agency ironically, yet significantly, involves her father's phallic rifle, which is a recurring motif and prop throughout her picaresque travels. Pérez does not render Micaela as a nostalgic lesbian avenger warrior hero, or the stereotypical butch villain of bigoted heteronormative fears. Instead, Micaela's violence, which is neither nihilist nor solely counternationalist, enables her survivance of the rampant rapes (including her own) by white Texans that historically have been constitutive of warfare. Micaela's counterviolence also saves her from murder attempts, and the overarching genocidal war that kills members of her immediate family alongside masses of Indians and Mexicans. She engages in revenge killings, yet also allows her father's killer, Walker, to live after he admits to his crime. She rationalizes that he would suffer more by living with the realization he killed his best friend, which is a psychological inflection of Micaela's counterviolence. Tragically, even as Micaela tries to avoid replicating heteropatriarchal colonial violences, she frequently has no choice but to use them.

Ironically, by the end of the novel, as Micaela is ensconced in a convent after escaping prison and the gallows, she still harbors a less than ambivalent desire for her own nation-state. Her character thus raises important questions about Pérez's otherwise provocative novelistic rendering of third-space negotiations as an alternative to the heteropatriarchal violence subtending the modern nation-state. At one level, Micaela eschews violence, saying, "I never want to murder another sonovabitch again" (2009, 205). But she also predicts the US-Mexico War and its violent aftermath, noting "so long as men like Walker and the Colonel occupy *our land*, there will be more wars" (2009, 206, emphasis added). This yearning for "our land" adds to the ambivalence embedded within the novel's proposed decolonial resolution as Micaela affirms her presence in history:

> I'm going back for good one day and on that day our hallowed home will be ours again but not through the same kind of murdering and hate. I'm not going back like that. I can't. Not anymore.   (2009, 205)

The crescendo in this more or less pacifist—though fundamentally regionalist and counternationalist—agenda to recover her "hallowed home" rests upon the investment of extraordinary power in her violence-borne embodied knowledge:

> I'm not saying the battles ahead won't be hard on us. They will. But it's like Eagle Mother said, nobody can take away memory *in our flesh*

and nothing can take away the spirit *in our blood* 'cause that spirit is
guiding us to new days.   (2009, 205, emphasis added)

Her embodiment of regionalist nationalist violence also is a kinetic
force, however unsatisfying it may be:

Maybe the only justice we'll ever know is in surviving to tell our own
side of things. Maybe that's enough *for now*. Telling our own stories
so we won't be forgotten.   (2009, 206, emphasis added)

This narratological project—which also is an epistemological and
ontological enterprise—revolves around telling stories of one's defeat
as a prelude to continued battles and ultimate victory. The fight will
continue into subsequent generations. Ironically, Américo Paredes
long ago proposed this motif in his male-centered Tejano settler
colonialist recovery of the epic heroic corrido! The difference in
Pérez's rendering of this tragic hero, of course, is Micaela's gender-
bending, cross-dressing, and lesbian identity, which unsettles the
heteropatriarchal nation-state, even as her alternative imagined
community preserves it, and all its inherent racialized, gendered,
and sexualized violences.

Despite Micaela's contradictory yearning for a nation-state of her
own, as it were, her lesbian reclamation of Tejas nonetheless demonstrates Pérez's complex processual decolonial approach to empowerment. It begins, Pérez notes, with the recovery and reanimation of
the repressed:

The decolonial imaginary embodies the buried desires of the unconscious, living and breathing in between that which is colonialist and
that which is colonized. Within that interstitial space, desire rubs
against colonial repressions to construct resistant, oppositional,
transformative, diasporic subjectivities that erupt and move into
decolonial desires.   (1999, 110)

In Pérez's novel, the lingering, resilient, and overbearing coloniality
of power in the Americas, as Quijano and Wallerstein (1992) call it,
forces Micaela to engage in a back-and-forth navigation of power in
contradictory and incomplete acts of resistance and appropriation,
with only preliminary (or negative) syntheses possible. As frustrating
as this may be, it nonetheless challenges Althusser's concept of ideology

that posits the impossibility of moving outside this interpellating force. And it also breaks from Gramsci's model of hegemony, which relies upon its antithesis to preserve power. Pérez continues:

> Freedoms are measured by degrees; power is enacted upon the body according to regional morals and laws. The decolonial imaginary remains intangible, unseen, yet quite "real" in social and cultural relationships between the colonizer and the colonized, where the ambivalences of power come into play... To remain within the colonial imaginary is to remain the colonial object who cannot be subject until decolonized. The decolonial imaginary challenges power relations to decolonize notions of otherness to move into a liberatory terrain.   (1999, 110)

But does Pérez succeed in drafting a character who ultimately is able to transcend her violent milieu through alternative epistemologies and interventions that lead to a decolonial state of being? Or, at the very least, does Micaela adumbrate this new condition? As the preceding analysis shows, she does not. Throughout her regional-specific navigations, Micaela harbors a desire for a nation-state of her own that leaves intact the central contradictions of the national question: circumscribed essentialized inclusions, racialized gendered and sexualized exclusions, and corresponding hierarchies that lead to never-ending war. This network of contradictions in Micaela's counternationalism inevitably preserves violence as the governing telos. Indeed, even as she challenges the local manifestations of the heteropatriarchal modern nation-state—the rapes, murders, and massacres—Micaela's competing cultural nationalism inadvertently propels this dystopia forward. But she was always already within it.

The Other Side of Transnationalism: Family, Femicides, and the Border as Violence

Emma Pérez's historical novel serves as a cautionary counterpoint to celebratory Chicana/o and Latina/o Regionalism, Borderlands, and Transnationalism Studies: it simultaneously illuminates and challenges, yet replicates and inadvertently reifies the violences of the US-Mexico borderlands that Gloria Anzaldúa explicated as "una herida abierta [an open wound]" (2007, 25), a site of "intimate terrorism" (2007, 42), and a dystopian space overdetermined by binaries (2007, 102). More recently, Roberto Hernández has proposed the border as a genocidal manifestation of the nation-state, rather than merely a framing of its geopolitical parameters. He adds an urgent call for "epistemic and cartographic disobedience" (2018, 182), that is, strategic rejections of the overbearing violence of borders. However, the underlying question, as Fanon lucidly framed, is whether a people constituted through imperialist violences as the embodiment of national boundaries can ever exist outside this teleology. The fact of the deaths subsumed under the category of femicide vis-à-vis the discursive dimensions of Mexican and Chicana/o on-the-ground antifemicide activism, as well as imaginative literary, cinematic, and performative interventions, all suggest an inextricable relationship between the injury and proposed alternatives. Even as Femicide Studies and related antifemicide activism suggest an alternative beyond self-negation may be possible, they inadvertently but inevitably confirm that the violences at the border also are constitutive of the contemporary borderlands, its culture, and its subjects.

A relatively new field of academic inquiry, Femicide Studies has a contrapuntal relationship to celebratory Borderlands, Regionalism, Nationalism, and Transnationalism Studies. This subfield emerged in response to the serial murders of over 1,000 girls and women roughly beginning in 1993, primarily in Ciudad Juarez across the border from El Paso, Texas, though the terrain also encompasses other border cities. This period coincides with the rise of the border *maquiladora*, or assembly plant, industry following the 1992 ratification of the North American Free Trade Agreement (NAFTA). Factory labor was supplied by the mass migration of rural young Mexican workers, many of them women. The sexual exploitation, rapes, disappearances, and serial murders of these working-class Mexican women resonate on both sides of the porous international border that residents, workers, and visitors traverse daily. The border's fungibility signals a sobering reality: perpetrators also are interstitial transnational borderlands subjects! In a figural and literal sense, they are family. The antifemicide movement—which includes grassroots, as well as petite bourgeois artists, writers, and intellectuals—reveals how the violences of the heteropatriarchal family subtend the modern Western nation-state at is borders, and vice versa.

After a quarter century of organizing, femicide researchers and antifemicide activists pose several questions that become progressively more difficult—and frightening—to answer. In the era of neoliberal transnational flows of people and commodities—and people as commodities—is the femicide a function of the waning significance of the nation-state, or a symptom of the nation-state's enduring potency? Is the normalization of femicide a historical anomaly, or is this violence inextricable from US-Mexico borderlands historiography, and all borderlands globally? And what can we say about the ideologies of Latina/o transnational borderlands subjectivities given that femicidal killers and related drug and human trafficking cartel assassins are also border dwellers, that is, part of the extended Mexican and Mexican American families and corresponding cultural nationalist and transnational imagined communities? Perhaps more importantly, what are the ideologies of the proposed interventions? How might they reinforce traditional gender norms and hegemonic power relations even as they attempt to challenge the depredations against young women whom the neoliberal economic order has moved from oppressive heteropatriarchal homespaces into differently exploitative but not less-alienating maquiladoras as independent wage earners?

An important trajectory of Femicide Studies explicates how the historical heteropatriarchal exchange of women remains the basis of the modern nation-state that, in the transnational borderlands between states, has metastasized into an unrestrained genocidal supranational violent force. The Femicide Studies challenge to powerful political, economic, and cultural interests inevitably makes this subfield dangerous. It is also controversial and contested. Journalist Molly Molloy, for instance, challenges the claim that murders of women and girls in Ciudad Juarez constitute femicide. She argues that the murder rate for women in this border city is lower than in US cities such as Houston, Detroit, and New Orleans (Hooks 2014, n.p.). However, Molloy misses the main point about the use of "femicide" as an operative term: antifemicide activists, artists, and scholars deliberately take a holistic approach to misogyny that makes it an accurate assessment. They deliberately aggregate domestic violence with all other forms of violence against women: undercompensated domestic labor, workplace exploitation, restrictive gender norms and expectations, intimate partner violence, sexual assault, economically coerced prostitution, and human trafficking, as well as the widely documented kidnappings, tortures, and ritualized murders more commonly associated with the US-Mexico border femicide.

All these phenomena constitute a genocidal war against women, and particularly poor and working-class Mexican women.

The femicide paradigm thus enacts an important deviation from Borderlands Studies, a field that has steadily drifted away from Gloria Anzaldúa's foundational emphasis on multiple forms of violence as definitive of the borderlands, toward a more celebratory privileging of cultural hybridity. In a rejection of the abstraction and aesthetization of the borderlands, femicide-victim family members, along with activists, scholars, and artists allied with them, have innovated a powerful genre of collaborative activist scholarship reminiscent of the testimonial collaborations of the 1970s and 1980s throughout Latin America, an era punctuated by genocidal state violence, as well as violent revolutionary resistance. These projects were overtly partisan and committed to the material transformation of the root causes of violent oppression, without sacrificing their empathy for the symptomatic victims. In one of the many analogous interdisciplinary Femicide Studies anthologies published in the United States, *Making A Killing: Femicide, Free Trade, and La Frontera* (2010), coeditors Alicia Gaspar de Alba and Georgina Guzmán unite a wide range of stakeholders on both sides of the border to explore the structural and superstructural dimensions of this transnational borderlands war against women. Contributors expose the confluence of legal codes, neoliberal economic incentives, and cultural mores that render poor brown working-class women as consumable and expendable commodities. Significantly, they also emphasize these women's agency beyond victimhood.

Contributors also offer metacritical interrogations of victim commodifications, underscoring the difficulties of navigating ideology in the violent interstitial borderlands space. For instance, Julia E. Monárrez-Fragoso and Clara E. Rojas examine the ever-widening web of appropriations by politicians, celebrities, and middle-class residents of Ciudad Juarez noting that:

> legitimate pain has been transformed into the painfulness experienced by victims' families, and it has acquired a symbolic capital value that has come to be used by hegemonic groups against civil organizations that have protested against violence.   (2010, 189)

In addition to being used by political opportunists, victim family members have become caught in this web of reification by refusing to recognize the legitimacy of solidarity activists not directly affected by the femicides. This phenomenon—violence-as-identity that supersedes national consciousness and even feminist solidarity—segues with the set of inquires that subtend the violentologies paradigm. These inquiries include the status of violence in culture, violence-*as*-culture, and the difficulties of examining this violence—from within the violence—pursuant to an extrication from it.

Imaginative literature about the femicides, particularly Chicana-authored novels proposed as partisan interventions, poignantly demonstrate the difficulties in overcoming this quandary. Few, if any, femicide arts interventions succeed at avoiding a gaze that fetishes Mexican women and girls as helpless victims, or bit players in exotically violent foreign landscapes. After all, similar to literature about the Holocaust, war, rape, abuse, prisoner, and trauma in general, border femicide depictions must navigate multiple mine fields: the ethics and political economy of producing novels and other petite bourgeois art forms about the murders of these young women; susceptibility of such works to scopophilic appropriations that extend the violence they seek to expose and end; and the even broader danger of rendering the atrocities as representable and thus mundane.

Alicia Gaspar de Alba's well-intentioned literary intervention into the femicides demonstrates these limits. Her 2005 femicides novel, *Desert Blood: The Juarez Murders*, degenerates into a binary that inadvertently privileges US citizenship, and thus the nation-state, to the detriment of the proposed testimonialesque gesture of transnational solidarity. The novel begins by glossing the detective procedural: Ivon, a Chicana professor and protagonist who lives on the US side of the border, descends into the femicide morass in Juarez in search of her kidnapped younger sister, Irene, an El Paso high school senior who crossed the border for a carnival and never returned home. Gaspar de Alba juxtaposes this episode about two Chicana sisters who are US citizens with the disappearance of a young female Mexican maquiladora worker. The search for Irene results in a successful rescue that exposes the layers of masculinist bias and government corruption that fuel the femicides. Yet, the anonymous Mexican woman is killed, with the novel offering graphic descriptions of her mutilated body. Kasey Butcher aptly argues:

> Gaspar de Alba perpetuates media portrayals of the victims as subaltern and fails to trouble the relationship between class and citizenship

inscribed on the border. The novel never addresses the fact that Irene survives largely because of her class privilege and US citizenship (and luck). Instead, it resolves with Irene recovering at home while Ivon, capitalizing on her first-hand experience with the femicide, folds the experience into her dissertation.   (2015, 8)

This *dénouement*, of course, can be read as Gaspar de Alba's exposé of the multiple layers of commodification, including by would-be antifemicide allies. Indeed, she presents a salient critique about the failure of the academy and academic discourse to intervene into this atrocity. Yet, ironically, the novelist also models the commodifications of femicide victims by artists and academics, which is a nodal point in Gaspar de Alba's coedited anthology, in addition to other studies. While her book's sales never lifted it onto the *New York Times* Bestseller List, it nonetheless is part of the proliferating novels, poems, and even Hollywood films focused on the femicide.[4] Moreover, the unfortunate dichotomy of *Desert Blood*'s plot remains: US first world privileges and protections are accessible to Chicanas who, on the surface—but only on the surface—appear similar to the Mexican third world female subjects who remain vulnerable and consumable by maquiladoras and male murderers, in addition to Chicana middle-class academics and authors. Gaspar de Alba is a sophisticated intellectual and long-time activist aware of these limits and contradictions, but her relatively unsuccessful attempt to extricate her work from the inherent violence of the borderlands—for which femicide has become the most recent of its many metonyms—ultimately underscores the salience of violence in, and *as*, the Latina/o milieu.

A signature feature of antifemicide cultural production interweaves localized domestic violence, sexual abuse, sexual slavery, and mass murder with macroeconomic neoliberal phenomena such as the assembly plants that have proliferated on the Mexican side of the US-Mexico border. Gaspar de Alba's novel illustrates that the proposed contrapuntal depictions of these violences also are ideological performances. In other instances, the antifemicide intervention can become an extension of the very masculinist fetish that drives the violences. Stella Pope Duarte's 2008 novel, *If I Die in Juarez*, is indicative of this tragic discursive irony. On the surface, the novel lucidly deconstructs how the heteropatriarchal family anchoring nationalism also has become the engine of transnational capital—emblematized by the maquiladora—that consumes and kills young women workers. However, despite the novel's incisive exposé, Pope Duarte's graphic depiction of the sexual abuse of a twelve-year-old Mexican girl inevitably renders *If I Die in Juarez* even less successful than *Desert Blood* at navigating scopophilia.

The novel opens with the young girl, Evita, being kicked out of the family home by her mother, Brisa, after a well-meaning taquería waitress informed Brisa that her daughter was being inappropriately coddled by the mother's boyfriend, Ricardo. Instead of protecting Evita, Brisa accuses her of trying to seduce Ricardo, who is thirty years older than the young girl. Evita is sent to her older sister's house, but instead goes to the home of an older woman, Isidora. Evita had met this woman at the Juarez central plaza, where the young girl would go to escape the chaotic daily domestic abuse she witnessed her sister suffer at the home that was her occasional refuge. This is the worse decision Evita could have made in a life of circumscribed choices. As it turns out, Isadora is both critical of men's desires even as she serves them by providing a home for runaways who work for her as prostitutes in Juarez's bustling sex industry. The refuge Isidora offers Evita becomes the pathway to the twelve-year-old girl's eventual sexual abuse and near murder. The victimizers include older men such as her mother's boyfriend, Ricardo; male taxi drivers and police officers, who ostensibly help Evita; and women like Isidora, who acts as a surrogate mother and brothel madam.

Ironically, despite the novel's interrogation of the structural and superstructural dimensions of these lethal commodifications of girls' and women's bodies, *If I Die in Juarez* reifies the multiple forms of violence it exposes. Specifically, it presents the familial web of domestic violence and sexual exploitation through graphic depictions of various grooming techniques and sexual assaults of young girls. These allow for empathetic identifications, but prurient appropriations, too. Evita's inaugural sexual assault, for instance, is depicted in graphic gratuitous detail, ending with the proverbial "money shot" characteristic of heterosexual pornographic films: one of the police officers who fondles Evita as he masturbates concludes by ejaculating on the young girl's face. Evita's detailed recollections of the texture and taste of the semen add sensory dimensions that give the sexual assault a viscerally aestheticized resonance. None of this is necessary to convey the main point about the abuse.

Such scenes are reminiscent of Vladimir Nabokov's grooming episodes in his 1955 novel, *Lolita*, about a white American professor and
pedophile named Humbert Humbert who engages in serial abuse of
his twelve-year-old prepubescent stepdaughter. Evita's father figure
Ricardo, who has a child and newly pregnant wife, in addition to
Evita's mother as a girlfriend, emerges as a permutation of Nabokov's
protagonist. In Pope Duarte's novel, the narrator describes his rape
of Evita as follows:

> Ricardo sat with her on the bed as if she was a tiny baby and caressed
> her, rocking her back and forth. He put his face in her hair and kissed
> her and said he loved her, and would she like to take off her shoes and
> get comfortable? Ricardo was nothing like the policeman. He was
> gentle and his voice was soft, soothing, and it made Evita cry. Little by
> little, Ricardo convinced Evita to take off all her black clothes, until
> she was lying in his arms—her naked body, a tender white reed he
> gently embraced. Then Ricardo covered her with a thin sheet and laid
> her down next to him on the bed. He switched off the lamp, and in
> the dark he took off his pants and underwear and began to caress her
> passionately. He said she was the most beautiful girl in the world and
> he was so lucky to have her close to him.   (2008, 80.)

Like Nabokov's precursor, Pope Duarte's novel uses situational and
verbal irony to expose the pedophile's vile techniques. However, as is
the case with *Lolita*, scopophilic readers can easily reject the irony,
thus making the rape scene susceptible to prurient appropriation.
This danger becomes apparent as the above passage in Pope Duarte's
novel continues with a prescient explication of the power of patriarchy to shape a woman's sense of self:

> Evita thought of her mother, and new tears started. She would kill her
> if she saw her lying naked next to Ricardo. Her mother's image made
> Evita feel powerful, and something came into her mind, vague at first,
> then clearer. She wanted to be better than her mother and mean more
> to Ricardo than her mother ever had. She remembered how Ricardo
> had defended her the day her mother had thrown her out on the
> streets, and this made her embrace Ricardo as he gently kissed her
> lips.   (2008, 80)

References to Evita as a "tiny baby" underscore the abusive nature of
this situation (2008, 80), which is punctuated by the description of
her violent and painful penetration in the succeeding sentence.

Yet, the grooming scenario leading up to this rape, in addition to descriptions of their subsequent encounters, come dangerously close to rendering the serial abuse as a romance. This is especially the case in another graphic scene in which Ricardo teaches Evita to masturbate and achieve an orgasm. Perversely, it ends with Evita's reciprocation of Ricardo's purported love:

> That night, Ricardo left without paying Evita a thing. It was then that Evita began longing for him and pining over him, wishing he would take her to El Paraiso [The Paradise Hotel] over and over again.
>
> (2008, 86)

Whether or not this novel intentionally glosses Nabokov, its scopophilic dimension is almost inevitable once the author embarks on the strategy of exposing family secrets—and the secret of family— through graphic depictions of the sexual predations interwoven with the femicide. Lourdes Portillo's 2003 film, *Señorita Extraviada* ("Missing Young Woman"), one of the few antifemicide films that succeeds at circumventing exploitative appropriations, places this scopophilic feature of purportedly antifemicide art in greater relief. Portillo's film refuses to depict graphic details of sexual abuse that might be misappropriated, and instead focuses on interviewing male suspects alongside survivors and their families.

Despite the limits that inevitably emerge in privileged metropolitan attempts at solidarity with subaltern subjects in the geographical and socio-economic margins, Estella Pope Duarte's graphic rendering of the femicide exposes how transnationalism in the US-Mexico borderlands remains fatally imbricated with heteropatriarchal family structures. Ironically, her novel performatively underscores, through its contradictory poetics, the need for a nonheteropatriarchal, postnational, and even posttransnational paradigm. Indeed, the nationalism that both creates and is delineated by borders, and the transnationalism that the novel implicitly proposes as a way out, inevitably intersect to rehouse the young girl in an interracial heteropatriarchal romance: Evita is rescued from her life as a child prostitute by a white US Army soldier from a nearby base who marries her. This "happy ending," as it were, is juxtaposed to her mother Petra's capture, serial torture, and eventual death by a perpetrator of the femicide. It bears noting that Evita's romantic salvation in this otherwise horrific resolution is unlikely in the real world of Juarez prostitution, where sex workers are enslaved and highly monitored by pimps and cartel agents. Significantly, US soldiers from regional bases help drive the region's sex industry. In Pope Duarte's forced partial resolution of an already compromised scopophilic novel, the young protagonist is recontained within the heteropatriarchal family structure; instead of serving as a metonym of imprisonment and exploitation, heterosexual marriage is depicted as salvation. Moreover, Evita's purported rescue remains inscribed with lingering colonialist and imperialist overtones: Juarez's emergence as a source of cheap labor for maquiladora and sex work industries in the neoliberal era is rooted in the US economic domination and chronic underdevelopment of the region following the 1848 US military invasion, occupation, and annexation of half of Mexican territory. The border, and attempted real and aesthetic transnational crossings, perpetuate rather than erase this reality.

Traveling Torture: The Fatherland, Fascism, and Latina/o Civil Wars

As noted above, the borderlands femicide and prominent Chicana and Latina contestatory novelistic exposés inadvertently converge to reiterate how transnational spaces violently reinforce the heteropatriarchal nation-state rather than transcend it. In these spaces, a state of terror permeates everything, and this becomes a form of state terror itself given the layers of governmental neglect in preventing it, and overt state actor complicity in perpetrating it. The literature of state terror from US counterinsurgency interventions in Central America further complicates Spatial Studies prisms, particularly transnationalism, in even more productively troubling ways. This corpus illustrates the enduring salience, mobility, and power of violence to define Latina/o subjects across multiple sites as they seek to escape the horror. While state-sponsored torture, like executions, enact and thus verify the state's power, Latina/o narratives about torture survivances—and coterminous torturer migrations—across national borders reveal the suprastatutory and supraterritorial function of violence in defining Latinidades separate and apart from the nation-state. Place is central to all spatial ontologies, including the transnational trope, but in Latina/o history—and particularly these state-terror histories—place is far less significant than the harm occurring in particular sites. As demonstrated throughout this book, this is the defining feature of a violence-based ontology, that is, a violentology: the principal sites are Latinidades, per se.

Harford-Vargas has examined a relatively new archive of novels written by US-born, -raised, and -immigrant Latina/os that intersect with the broader Latin American literature about dictatorships to propose a "Latina/o counter-dictatorial imaginary," which ultimately segues with the celebratory resistance paradigm (2017, 6). Significantly, a large body of related literature left unexamined in Harford-Vargas's transnational comparative project reveals that the genocidal counter-insurgency campaigns and corresponding civil resistance and outright revolutionary movements from the 1970s to the 1990s provide an entirely different subtext beyond authoritarianism that shape unique and ever-more-complex supra-Latina/o subjectivities. Indeed, traumatic manifestations of the nation-state do not lead to coherent visions of a "truly 'post' dictatorship future that will no longer be haunted by the traumas of the past and mired in the persistent inequalities and oppressions of our present" (2017, 33), as Harford-Vargas proposes. Rather, the underlying violences subtending the Latina/o literature of state terror segues with the literature of the heteropatriarchal nation-state more broadly. More importantly, this body of writing offers important contrapuntal insights into ongoing Latina/o navigations of the national (and transnational) question at the site of traumatized, tortured, mutilated, dismembered, and dead human bodies. As such, these texts inevitably gesture toward a radical rejection of ontological certainty, and the very category of "Latina/o" as we have come to know it in the field of Latina/o Studies.

A significant and underexamined trajectory of the Latina/o literature of state terror explores how state-sanctioned physical and psychological torture undermines phenomenological certainty, which survivors narrate through existentialist and, in some cases, fatalist nihilist gestures. Olga Talamante is one of the first documented Chicana political torture victims in Latin America. A former farmworker from Gilroy, California, Talamante gravitated to the United Farmworker's Union organizing activities while she was attending the University of California at Santa Cruz in the 1970s. On a field research trip to Chiapas, Mexico, in her junior year, her growing political consciousness was catalyzed into an internationalist sensibility. Of this transformative period she writes:

Mexico also introduced me to the Latin American reality and I became aware of the young Cuban Revolution, of Che Guevara's example of internationalism, and the various struggles going on in the continent. The rise of revolutionary organizations in Uruguay, Peru, and the resistance against the Somoza dictatorship in Nicaragua, provided a new context within which to understand our own struggle as Chicanos in the U.S. We were part of a larger political movement throughout the American continent, which had as its epicenter the impact of the policies of the U.S. government on the working classes and the poor of all those countries, as well as oppressed communities and communities of color here in the U.S.

While I was in Mexico, I met Hugo and Norma, two Argentines who had been traveling throughout Latin America and were on their way back home. They were enthusiastic about the changing political climate there, which promised a return to democracy. Inspired by their vision of a continental movement, which, very importantly, included the Chicano and other progressive movements in the U.S., I decided to travel to Argentina.   (qtd. in Dodd 2006, 110)

Talamante traveled to Argentina in 1974, where she joined the Argentine Marxist organization Juventud Peronista, and eventually was captured by the fascist Junta. She survived sixteen months of political imprisonment and torture.

The searing pain from high voltage electric shocks being applied to your body is hard to describe. There is absolutely nothing you can do; it doesn't matter what you know or don't know, or what you say or don't say. They hold complete control over your life and they make you feel like there is nothing that can protect you in that moment.
                                                    (qtd. in Berkowitz 2006, n.p.)

Here, and in other accounts, Talamante describes the radical vulnerability and loss of agency from her torture by US-supported anticommunist fascists in 1970s Argentina. Ironically, her contestatory words reiterate the authority of the two nation-states responsible for her transnational torture. Indeed, her defiant testimony exposing torture recalls her past, and in many cases her enduring subordinate status within these nation-states, which still remain unsanctioned for their crimes against her and legions of other victims and survivors of Argentina's dirty war.[5]

Talamante's unresolved contestatory revelations segue with Catholic Nun Dianna Ortiz's *testimonios* about her torture in Guatemala: both Chicanas underscore the lingering impact of these traumas through unique survivances. Ironically, their challenge to nostalgic renderings of Latina/o transnationalism simultaneously indict, yet again inadvertently reify, the nation-state. While working with her Catholic Ursuline Order's mission in a rural indigenous community in Guatemala in 1989, the twenty-eight-year-old nun was kidnapped and tortured by Guatemalan government soldiers and a shadowy blond American advisor, who suspected her of sympathies with indigenous guerrillas. She recounts this experience in her 2002 *testimonio, The Blindfold's Eye: My Journey from Torture to Truth*. Author Ana Castillo also has written a chilling 2005 two-sequence play about Ortiz, *Psst...I Have Something to Tell You, Mi Amor*. Ariana Vigil has emphasized Ortiz's countertorture agency, and the "polyvocality" of these two authors' companion literary works, to argue that the collaboration "underscores the collective nature of both oppression and healing" (2014, 78).

But healing is relative in this context. For instance, Ortiz's explications of torture in *The Blindfold's Eye* (2002) pair horrific episodes with banal ones that follow, through which her family home, parents, friends, fellow nuns, and once-familiar and safe domestic spaces in convents and in her native New Mexico are rendered as unrecognizable, foreign, and frightening. In a rehearsal of Elaine Scarry's (1987) claim that torture obliterates the real for the victim, Ortiz recalls:

> Suddenly I am in the corner of the room, watching myself curled under the stack of bodies. These people must be your family, I tell myself. Keep your mouth shut. Pretend to know them.
>
> But why don't I know them? Could they be imposters? Has this been staged by the torturers? (2002, 12)

This lack of certainty over the real has material consequences that extend through and far beyond the torture victim: it creates interpersonal and ontological schisms. Torture violences—from the electric shocks Talamante endured to Ortiz's multiple rapes and forced stabbing of a fellow prisoner—ultimately obliterate pretorture lives, necessitating new survivance strategies and subjectivities. There is a dissensus about the degree to which abuse survivors are able to articulate lives free of their past abuse, with many arguing that it is possible to do so with the appropriate counseling and support network. Ortiz, however, shows that her survivance remains inscribed with torture violences. Her description of scars such as cigarette burns across her back become part of a countertorture text that merely places her torture *sous rature* rather than concluding it. Her exceedingly graphic violentological signifying scripts an embodied posttorture identity through antiviolence utterances; yet, as important and empowering as these utterances are for Ortiz, they inevitably reiterate the violence against which they are made. This is not just a manifestation of the always already violent nature of her Latinidad, or Latinidades in general. Rather, this paradox reveals the violent essence of the nation-state—that in Guatemala at the time was figured as the fatherland—which transnational mobility neither effaces nor ameliorates. On the contrary, at the 1980s dawn of the neoliberal era in which the United States still occupied the role of hegemon in the Americas, Sister Dianna Ortiz again exposed transnationalism itself as violence.

Latina/o testimonialesque fiction about the contemporaneous Salvadoran civil war from 1980 to 1992 further links the violence of US foreign policy in Central America, and the third world in general, with the transnational trope through a contrapuntal rendering of the Latina/o subjects formed of this violence. Demetria Martinez's 1990 novel *Mother Tongue* features a traumatized Salvadoran war veteran, José Luís, who relocates to Albuquerque, New Mexico, after the US-sponsored right-wing Salvadoran government's scorched-earth counterinsurgency campaigns targeting civilians and guerrillas drove him out of the country. He subsequently subjects his nineteen-year-old Chicana girlfriend Mary to sexualized domestic violence. This violence compounds the trauma of her childhood sexual abuse, which she experienced as the television broadcast news about the US war in Vietnam. These intertwined imperialist-instigated wars and rapes lead to multiple schisms: the couple separates, and war veteran and abuser José Luís goes further into exile in Canada. Neither character is able to actualize a new subjectivity free of their statutory, domestic, and embodied violences. On the contrary, they are layered with multiple levels of harm: as survivors they are shaped by the intertwined global and hyperlocalized embodied violences of US foreign policy, which they attempt to recover without rehearsing the harms, but with only very limited success.

Guatemalan American journalist and novelist Hector Tobar maps US-sponsored traveling torture across multiple borderlands in his 2000 novel, *The Tattooed Soldier*. He extends Olga Talamante's, Sister

Dianna Ortiz's, and Demetria Martinez's rendering of Latina/o transnationalism-as-violence toward the Femicide Studies exposé of transnational torturers and murderers as part of the extended Latina/o family. The protagonist in his novel is a former Guatemalan soldier assassin who immigrates to Los Angeles. In his close-knit Central American enclave, another Guatemalan American immigrant—the husband and father of the wife and child murdered by the soldier—recognizes the killer's distinctive tattoo, and eventually confronts him. Despite a convenient and conventional resolution involving the revenge murder of the soldier, Tobar breaks an important taboo by rendering Latina/o ideological diversity through a well-rounded antagonist—an unrepentant murderer no less!—who may be less anomalous than his absence in Latina/o Studies scholarship suggests, as I discuss further in Chapter 5. Tobar thus invites, and necessitates, a new prism for accounting for this discrepant subject. His Latino fascist character does not completely, or even partially, fit within any extant Latina/o Studies analytical framework, even as some scholars have sought to fold such figures into nostalgic transnationalism and celebratory resistance paradigms, in addition to heroic or tragic Soldado Razo archetypes.

These exposés of domesticized state terror—and related articulations of suprastatutory, supraspatial subjectivities as war veterans, victims of war veteran domestic violence, abuse survivors, torture survivors, abusers, torturers, and assassins—all call our attention to another family secret: Latina/o right-wing nationalist fascists. Even more so than Tobar, Salvadoran-Mexican journalist, author, and performer Rubén Martínez nuances our understanding of Latina/o relationships to hegemony through his intimate rendering of familiar—and familial—Latina/o supporters of Salvadoran right-wing political parties whose genocidal violence extends multiple directions from the civil war's "formal" start in 1980. This ranges from the Salvadoran military's 1932 massacre of 40,000 peasants, to the 1992 armistice with rebels in a war that was punctuated by the displacement of one million Salvadorans, most of whom emigrated to the United States. Martínez's meditation on the prominence of violence in the Salvadoran diaspora ultimately questions the efficacy of barrio localism, regionalism, nationalism, borderlands, transnationalism, and general spatial ontology frameworks. He predicates his alternative rendering of a Salvadoran diasporic ontology upon multiple negations in his 1992 mixed-genre *testimonio*, *The Other*

Side: Fault Lines, Guerrilla Saints, and the True Heart of Rock 'n' Roll.
Specifically, Martínez elaborates an existentialist variation of the
transnational Latina/o borderlands figure through candid depictions
of his family schism during the Salvadoran civil war and concurrent
diaspora.[6]

José David Saldívar productively describes this first-person testimonial travelogue—which traverses back and forth between Los
Angeles, San Salvador, Tijuana, Mexico City, and Havana—as an
"autoethnography-crónica" (1997, 140). He adds:

> Such a deconstruction of "home" allows the authoethnographer from
> Los Angeles to undo the traditional home/abroad oppositions so
> common in travel writing.   (1997, 141)

Yet, Saldívar is only partially correct in adding that "Martínez's
autoethnography writes into existence an alternative geography by
mapping an emergent transnational, US Latino/a identity" (1997,
145). Closer attention to Martínez's rendering of fluid Mexican and
Salvadoran migrations throughout the Americas reveals the author's
profound ambivalence to, and frustrations with, the transnational,
interstitial, and diasporic resonances that are certainly part of his
milieu. *The Other Side* is part of a wave of critical immigration literature preceded by Luís Alberto Urrea's 1993 dystopian reportage of
borderlands slum dwellers, *Across the Wire: Life and Hard Times on
the Mexican Border.*[7] Martínez further debunks celebratory borderlands and transnationalism discourses with his 2001 journalistic
profile, *Crossing Over: A Mexican Family on the Migrant Trail*, about
a Mexican immigrant family that suffers the tragic deaths of three
sons in an automobile accident on their journey north along the
migrant worker trail. Accordingly, throughout his *oeuvre*, Martínez's
metaphor of "the other side" reminds readers that Latinidad is never
fixed on any side of any border, or even within the borderlands. It
never fully arrives anywhere. He rejects the type of empowering
border gnosis and agency that Anzaldúa is able to synthesize and
which José David Saldívar (1997) intimates of Martínez's narratol-
ogy. Indeed, Martínez's own poetic persona is always on the other
side, and thus never on any side.

Martínez's narrative is part of a huge but still ignored corpus of
Latina/o existentialism predicated on phenomenological doubt and
ontological negation. Moreover, his discourse deliberately recenters

violence as constitutive of myriad forms of supra-Latinidad; in this case, a Salvadoran-Mexican existentialism that bares shades of Afro-Pessimism that may even be more fatalist than Mbembe's (2019) "necro-politics." Martínez's meditations on recurring schismatic encounters with family members in El Salvador, and Salvadoran Americans in Los Angeles, reveal how the lingering daily specter of a half-century-long civil war continues to shape and circumscribe Salvadorañedad as a negative dialectic. As the aforementioned texts reveal, the waves of migrants who perform their constitutive violences all along their escape routes are perennially liminal; in many cases, they are never fully actualized as one thing or another. Always on the other side, Martínez's own subjectivity is emblematic: he is a coherent subject, yet paradoxically never completely satiated as whole. Whether he is at his grandparents' upper-middle-class hilltop house in San Salvador, a café at the National University of El Salvador, or various locales in Los Angeles, his autobiographical poetic persona is intensely uncomfortable and out of place at every location. Like Los Angeles, every stop on his journey becomes his "anti-home," as José David Saldívar aptly notes. Adding to his unfixedness, Martínez's family members both resist and reinforce his existentialist quandary by reminding him of their simultaneous filiation and schism. He notes:

> I believed every one of Grandfather's words when I was younger—even about how General Maximiliano Martinez had to get rid of the communists for the sake of the Fatherland. Grandfather's reactionary paradise, my socialist one…both impossible now. Death surrounds both our dreams: the war, the earthquake, his cancer. When I leave the house for the trip back to Los Angeles, we will embrace each other wordlessly.   (1992, 21, ellipses in original)

At this same family gathering, an aunt extends his grandfather's and an uncle's anticommunist diatribes: "What we need right now is someone who isn't afraid of using force to get us out of this mess" (1992, 37). Martínez intimates that this part of his family is allied with the ultra-right-wing party ARENA (Nationalist Republican Alliance) headed at the time by Roberto D'Aubuisson, a former military officer linked to El Salvador's notorious death squads. Martínez's grandmother punctuates the festivities by adding, "This thing about communism scares me," reiterating that her grandson's beard "looks too much like Che" (1992, 37). The fact that close friends and cousins fear being kidnapped and killed by death squads, the National Guard, and Treasury Police, further adds to the deepening family divisions. This ever-present danger thus repeatedly manifests in intersecting family member attempts to reclaim violence in their competing revolutionary and counterrevolutionary projects, none of which are completely successful.

Arturo Arias has poignantly explicated how "the historical memory of rape and violence has led Central Americans in the United States to keep themselves on the margins of social visibility and presentability," which revolves around a "strategic nonidentity" (2007, xxiii). Extending Arias's prescient reading of violence as constitutive of Central American-American "non-identity"—more a negative dialectic than nihilism—Martínez depicts the civil war as more than a historical event, cultural referent, ideological negotiation, and family schism. It is all this and more: for Salvadorans who have collectively endured a period of violence almost as long as the Colombian scholars who created *violentología* as a subfield of sociology, violence has become ontological and epistemological. It has become intertwined with the Salvadoran DNA. Martínez links his own family's awareness about their vexed relationship to the nation-state, both Salvadoran and US. It is a transhistorical function of violence that ranges from the 1932 anticommunist pogrom known as "La Matanza" (the killing spree), in which approximately 40,000 peasants and Indians were murdered, to the diasporic street gang Marasalvatrucha that mainstream media incorrectly credits with raising the militarized lethality of Latina/o internecine barrio warfare in 1980s Los Angeles, where the group emerged. This immanent proposal of Salvadorañedad-as-violence, of course, can be easily misappropriated to proffer exoticist and racist characterizations of male Latino immigrants and urban dwellers as inherently pathological. Nonetheless, Martínez's violentological hermeneutic becomes a de facto antispatial ontology that enables us to account for a vexing problem that continues to confront Latina/o Studies: how do we assess our various relationships to the violence of power, and power of violence, which involves profound ideological diversity, including fascism, domestic abuse, and proposed revolutionary redeployments of lethality?

Martínez accomplishes this antinational—and anti*trans*national— synthesis of the Salvadoran condition in the 1980s and 1990s in a set of literally explosive scenes toward the end of his multigenre testimonial. In one scene set in Los Angeles, Martínez thinks he hears a shotgun blast in the distance, which he muses could be fireworks in San Salvador. This hallucinatory unfixedness reaches a climax in the final prose installment of a recurring intermezzo section titled "L.A. Journal":

> Then the shellshocked ex-Salvadoran army footsoldier in the apartment upstairs took out an automatic and started spraying bullets at enemies visible only to himself. The mothers and children screamed and everyone hit the ground. Somebody knocked over a lamp in a desperate attempt to turn off the light, and someone else crawled towards the telephone and frantically dialed the police. We were no longer in Los Angeles, but back in the middle of the war in San Salvador.   (1992, 145)

Martínez's—and other Salvadoran Americans'—inability to distinguish their location in this instance, and in others, may be rhetorical. Yet, this geographical uncertainty is part of a deliberate trope that renders place, as well as social location, far less significant than the violence occurring in it. For Martínez, internecine violence defines everyone's being, which of course simultaneously threatens it with annihilation.

As a crescendo to his exposé on the existential threat of nationalism, and further illustration of the radical insufficiency of transnationalism as an operative term for diasporic populations such as Salvadorans, Salvadoran Americans, and Salvadoran-Mexican Americans like himself, Martínez punctuates his *testimonio* with poems such as "Manifesto" (1992, 135–7). This free verse bilingual composition offers a phenomenological rendering of his (anti)Salvadoreña/o gnosis as a simultaneous antignosis:

> Can anyone tell me what time it is?
> ¿O es que nadie lo sabe?
> Doesn't anyone know?
> [...]
> there's the FMLN in downtown San Salvador,
> (and the death squads are in L.A.)   (1992, 135, lines 1–3, 20–1)

Through postmodern reassemblage, the poem emphasizes a fluid, dystopian, and ever-expanding liminal zone that is neither liberating nor empowering as most renderings of borderlands and transnational subjectivities suggest. On the contrary, the overarching militarized international and internecine violence shaping the Salvadoran diaspora is fundamentally lethal, inhumane, and constitutive of being-as-nothingness as Jean-Paul Sartre (1993) famously proposed. The poem continues:

> All kinds of battles are yet to come
> (race and class rage bullets and blood);
> choose your weapons...
> just know that everyone is everywhere now
> so careful how you shoot.   (1992, 136–7, lines 54–8)

Expressing a series of role changes and a disorienting fusion of different locales in which everyone is everyone else and "everyone is everywhere now" (1992, 137, line 57), Martínez's rendering becomes an existentialist and possibly even a nihilist negation. Violence is the mediating factor in his ontological (ir)resolution.

Revolutionary Suicide: Antiimperialist Violence and the (Inter)National Question in Borinquen

The examples of glocalized activism, regionalist counternationalism, first world borderlands gazes, exposés of state terror's domestic reach, as well as antinational and antiidentitarian existentialism surveyed above, variously reveal that violence is a far more substantive determinant of Latinidades than any imagined or real relationships to regions, nations, or transnational spaces. Despite the many different contradictions inherent to these positionalities, and immanent yet frustratingly incomplete iterations of the contrapuntal epistemic shift José David Saldívar (2011) calls TransAmericanity, these formations nonetheless offer important interventions into Latina/o Studies' reification of tired archetypes and celebratory discourses. Ironically, Latina/o navigations of "revolutionary nationalism" and related theories of "revolutionary violence" also productively redirect attention to violence-based theories of being and praxis precisely because of their archetypal structure and celebratory tone. Mariscal's aforementioned examination of Chicana/o nationalism vis-à-vis Chicana/o internationalism reveals a dyad that sometimes is a dialectic, and other times a rigid binary barrier between the local and the global.

Michael Hardt and Antonio Negri's (2001) neo-Marxist assessment of what they call "subaltern nationalism" reminds us of the specter of the nation-state and attendant violences embedded within this vacillation. They note that the nation is "progressive insofar as it serves as a line of defense against the domination of more powerful nations and external economic, political, and ideological forces" (2001, 106). They add that this insular oppositional posture "is itself a dominating power that exerts an equal and opposite internal oppression, repressing internal difference and opposition in the name of national identity, unity, and security" (2001, 106). This, of course, has been the logic—and illogic—of revolutionary nationalism in the global South and other colonial contexts since at least the mid-twentieth century. In a related paradox, "revolutionary violence" deployed in pursuit of a "homeland" also frequently involves hyperlocalized pantheist rhetoric that mystically transcends geography. Latina/o iterations of revolutionary nationalism range from the indigenisms and proselytizing interpretations of Islam examined in Chapters 1 and 3, to Christian-liberation theologies that animated grassroots movements throughout the Americas from the 1970s to the 1990s. Many of these theologically based navigations of national, international, and supranational paradigms inevitably represent death, and particularly martyrdom, as self-actualization. For instance, similar to most wars of national liberation, foundational Puerto Rican independentista symbologies revolve around armed insurrection and the paradoxically affirming self-negation of "revolutionary suicide," that is, combat death as a (supra)nationalist transubstantiation, which is a quasi-materialist spiritual violentology.

Fifty-nine-year-old grandmother Lolita Lebrón was among the dozen Puerto Rican independentista political prisoners released from US prison in 1979. A quarter century earlier, she was a thirty-four-year-old divorcée and longtime member of the Puerto Rican Nationalist Party when she was arrested, incarcerated, and sentenced to death for leading a commando operation with three other independentistas: Rafael Cancel Miranda, Irving Flores Rodriguez, and Andrés Figueroa Cordero. Together, they executed an armed takeover of the US House of Representatives Chamber of the US Capitol building in 1954, which resulted in gunshot wounds to four congressmen, one nearly fatal. Lebrón anticipated Black Panther Huey Newton's discussion about "revolutionary suicide" adapted from Che Guevara's axiom proposing only two outcomes for the revolutionary:

death or victory (1961, 276). Newton emphasizes that "the first lesson
a revolutionary must learn is that he is a doomed man [sic]" (Newton
2009, 3), a position Lebrón also adopted. Upon her arrest, for
instance, she was found to be carrying a suicide note that read in
part: "Before God and the world, my blood claims for the independence of Puerto Rico. My life I give for the freedom of my country.
This is a cry for victory in our struggle for independence" (qtd. in
Roig Franza 2004, n.p.). Lebrón expected to die in the operation that
paradoxically was undertaken to actualize her raison d'être as a
Puerto Rican national subject via the eventual independence of her
nation-state.

A common trope in nationalist movements posits the idea that
blood sacrifice is necessary to consummate the desired nation and
actualize the (now-dead) fighter's true and unfettered subjectivity.
Lebrón's prison poetry deploys this nationalist-pantheist discourse,
especially the resonance of blood as the medium for the revolutionist's
transubstantiation into a metonym of the hallowed homeland. In a
Caribbean and Latin American permutation of nationalist-pantheist
poetics, Lebrón also glosses liberation theology's secular interpreta-
tion of the Christian Gospels. She deploys this theocratic rhetoric to
ground her nationalist and quasi-socialist independentista politics
in a language easily assimilable by the Catholic-majority Puerto
Rican population. This is a prescient discursive architecture, of
course, given the intense imperialist indoctrination directed at
Puerto Ricans through US-dominated curricula, media, and legal
apparatuses. But it is complicated, too, because of the ideological
variations of independentista politics that include capitalist and
socialist, as well as antiindependence trajectories such as the pro-
Commonwealth (status quo) and also annexation sympathizers.

In a demonstration of Lebrón's ideologically inchoate antiimperialist, nationalist, liberation theology, she claims to have received
nightly prison visits from Jesus Christ, God, and angels throughout
her twenty-five years in prison.[8] These encounters inform Lebrón's
undated manifesto, *A Message from God in the Atomic Age*, an undated
diatribe against the US nuclear arsenal and its role in the Cold War.[9]
This religious gnosis distinguishes Lebrón's nationalist pantheism
from Pablo Neruda's similarly mystical but far more Marxist 1950
nationalist-pantheist paean to South America, *Canto General* (2005),
and Cuban José Martí's 1891 precursor *Versos Sencillos* (1997).

They nonetheless share many similarities. Lebrón's layered nature-based discursive texture is infused throughout her bombastic signature poem, "Vive la nación" ("The Homeland Lives"), published in her 1975 first collection, *Sándalo en la celda* (which literally translates as *"Sandlewood in the Cell,"* but which also resonates idiomatically as *Sandals in the Cell*). The poem opens with a call to sing and praise the dawn of "Borinquen renacida," or "Puerto Rico reborn" (e.g., "Everyone sing Halleluja! / That the country is being born!).[10] The engagé oratory becomes both a nonsecular and secular proclamation replete with an abundance of capitalization cues and exclamation marks that accentuate its aural dimensions and festive tone. Amid the rhetoric of liberation theology (e.g., "Long live Holy Mary! Long live God!"), Lebrón interweaves a call to arms through her reference to "battle" and invocation of the "machete" (e.g., "Halleluja for the MACHETES!"). As noted of Hamza Perez's Boricua Muslim cultural nationalist symbolic system in Chapter 3, a machete is a long steel blade that *jíbaros*, or rural mountain peasants, use in their daily agricultural labor. It served as a weapon for generations of independence fighters and insurgents who inspired the Boricua Popular Army, also known as *Los Macheteros*, or "Machete Wielders." This insurgent group has its origins in the *Fuerzas Armados de Liberación Nacional Puertorriqueña* (Puerto Rican National Liberation Army), a Marxist-Leninist organization. Lebrón's invocation of this revolutionary organization, along with a roll call of independentistas who "all marched enraptured / to the battle," underscores her enduring militancy, all of which is grounded in her secular pantheism ("The trees shout happily! / The Prieto River lifts its swan!"). Her poem ends with a crescendo: "With passion! With passion! With passion! // Halleluja! Halleluja! Halleluja!" It thus emerges as a Christian precursor to Hamza Pérez's Boricua Islamic internationalist Ummah paradigm, though Lebrón's missionary zeal is far more overtly fixated on combat, blood, and the idea of a revolutionary transubstantiation. Lebrón's solipsistic inward gaze at the antiimperialist dead guerrilla as the embodiment of the liberated former colony, however, fails to extend outward toward an international (or internationalist) synthesis even as it reaches a nationalist and simultaneously supraterrestrial crescendo.

Lolita Lebrón's confederate Rafael Cancel Miranda similarly tropes violent death, but he more overtly extends his nationalist sentiments toward a socialist internationalist Boricua liberation theology that is more consistent with the Machetero nationalist socialist program modeled, in part, on revolutionary Cuba. His 2000 collection of poetry, *Mis dioses llevan tu nombre* (*My Gods Bear You Name*), intersects with Lebrón's liberation theology, but more deliberately grounds his localized nationalism in a Marxist sensibility. For instance, under a recurring heading titled "Pensamientos" ("Musings"), Cancel Miranda notes:

> If humanity was created in god's image, something monstrous must have occurred to make him appear so much like the devil. I'm sure not even god Himself would recognize his work nor would Adam and Eve be able to recognize themselves in men and women of today. We no longer need the apple. Capitalism was able to do more than Satan himself; or are they the same thing the dollar and the apple? (2000, 97)[11]

Cancel Miranda continues his gloss of Marx's theories of the commodity fetish, alienation of labor, and reification by rhetorically asking: "In a society in which everything is given a price, how were we to avoid humans being converted into another commodity?" (2000, 97). This secular reclamation of folk knowledge through simple epigrams offers easy-to-remember and effective slogans for marches, rallies, placards, and more recently, Tweets and other social media posts that also have become integral to populist movements and mass mobilizations. Nicaraguan priest and poet Ernesto Cardenal effectively used this minimalist populist poetic in his 1961 collection *Epigramas* (2001), which denounced the US-sponsored Somoza family dictatorship that the Sandinista National Liberation Front, in which he was a member, ultimately defeated in 1979.

Cancel Miranda's Marxist liberation theology—which increasingly appears atheist despite its nonsecular vocabulary—informs poems such as "El pecado de ser pobre" ("The Sin of Being Poor," 2000, 192), and "¿Y quién llora por ellos?" ("And Who Cries for Them?" 2000, 194). The first and third stanzas of the latter poem read:

> The hurricane of poverty,
> kills thousands of children,
> year after year the misery,
> it leaves them without roof or coat.

> [...]
> And those big businessmen,
> with their huge paychecks,
> where were they all year,
> with children dying of hunger?   (2000, 194)

Glossing the simple though incisive conversational verse of his Salvadoran communist contemporary Roque Dalton, as well as myriad twentieth-century socialist realist poets from Central American revolutionary movements, Cancel Miranda closes his bombastic indictment of a vulnerable island-based and class-based society by troping the idea of "god," which he deliberately places in lower case. Puerto Rican capitalists, he notes, enter government with the sole purpose of enriching themselves at the expense of the poor. He underscores that they steal:

> And commit atrocities,
> against their own people,
> with airs of Bonaparte,
> and of an omnipotent god.   (2000, 195)

In another "Pensamientos" segment, Cancel Miranda extends his increasingly more secular historical materialist didactic verse by explicating capitalism as a predatory stage of human society: "Between savagery and capitalism there exist no ideological nor moral differences, just technical ones" (2000, 229). For Cancel Miranda, if there are any distinctions, they revolve around the lethality of modern versus ancient weapons.

Credited with firing the near-lethal gunshots that wounded four congressmen in the 1954 Capitol Building attack, Cancel Miranda's allusion to weaponry is embedded within his (inter)nationalist model of revolutionary struggle. He asserts that violence is "not inherently good or bad; but all depends upon the circumstances" ("Pensamientos," 2000, 213). Throughout his meditations on and even yearning for death, Cancel Miranda never descends into the eroticized fetish on violence that distinguishes fascism. On the contrary, Cancel Miranda recognizes violence as a tool—like a gun—which has no inherent ethics, even as he laments the violent truncation of the species being through the commodity fetish. In this context, his martial archetype is predicated upon the nationalist's death, or the capitalist imperialist's demise. For him, there is no room for both in Puerto Rico. Having had all his front teeth kicked out by FBI agents with the help of their Puerto Rican spies, Cancel Miranda was prepared to kill and die in combat. Indeed, he attempted to do so in 1954. In the poem, "Muerte, aléjate de mi ataúd" ("Death, Get Away from My Tomb"), he presents his model of "revolutionary suicide" through a biting dramatic dialogue with the large segment of Puerto Ricans who support the Commonwealth colonial status or outright annexation through statehood:

> If you are a defender
> of your own slavery,
> you are more dead than I,
> get away from my tomb.
> Because I died free
> if I died I fell fighting,
> you died without dying,
> and without dying you are dead.
> I give life to the one that follows,
> you drive in their nails,
> I am a dead one who lives,
> you are a living slave.   (2000, 221–2)

This premortem poem illustrates the negative dialectic of nationalist (im)mortality—a fatalist optimism predicated upon a purposeful revolutionary death. Significantly, this iteration of what Agamben identifies as "necro-politics" extends far outside Afro-Pessimism's nihilist resonances. For Cancel Miranda, the dead Boricua guerrilla becomes the embodiment of the liberated nation-state *qua* immanent socialist internationalist revolution, which is part of the larger struggle to free humanity from slavery and all forms of exploitation and alienation. In a corporeal demonstration of his nationalist pantheist allusions, upon his death on March 2, 2020, in the Puerto Rican capital of San Juan, all Puerto Rican flags remained at full mast as he had requested, instead of being lowered in his honor, as would otherwise have happened for a person of such national distinction. His revolutionary nationalist death became a pathway to his, and his nation's, immortality.

Here, and throughout his multivolume corpus, Cancel Miranda thickens the concept of revolutionary nationalism: he complicates yet recognizes the problematic national question formulated by

Lenin in his advocacy of both national and international socialism. Cancel Miranda's synthesis arises from his participation in the ongoing Puerto Rican war of national liberation, which for him is liminal, and thus necessarily extends outside the confines of his own desired nation-state. That is, Rafael Cancel Miranda's Boricua identity is not solely a spatial ontology in the terrestrial dimension. After all, almost half of his life was spent in exile in Cuba or in US prisons. His cultural nationalist and internationalist subjectivity is a locally inflected global—or glocal—Boricua Marxist paradigm. Alán Eladio Gómez (2006) has traced Cancel Miranda's development and dissemination of an internationalist sensibility through interactions with other political prisoners, which included Raúl Salinas as well as revolutionary white prisoners. In Marion Federal Penitentiary, for instance, they formed Marxist and Latina/o culture study groups, as well as related multiracial cadres that engaged in prison rebellions and intersecting "freeworld" revolutionary activities. Significantly, Cancel Miranda's revolutionary nationalist persona is a fluid and constantly expanding supranational revolutionary subjectivity that progressively moves toward a global citizenship paradigm. He frees the idea of the citizen from its nation-state moorings by accruing ever more international distinctions and citizenships. Accordingly, *Mis Dioses llevan tu nombre*, includes multiple iterations of his internationalist positionings: in addition to receiving the José Martí Award, the highest citation the Republic of Cuba offers to a noncitizen, his book contains a facsimile of a Dominican government proclamation naming Cancel Miranda as a "Distinguished Guest" (Cancel Miranda 2000, 109). His book also includes a photograph of the Nicaraguan passport issued to him by the first Sandinista government, which engaged in a century-long, antiimperialist, war of national liberation against the United States and its imposed Somoza family dictatorship.

Cancel Miranda's revolutionary nationalist politics and poetics reach an internationalist crescendo as his fluid plurivocal poetic persona recovers various subaltern subjects in Puerto Rico, the Americas, and the world at large. His lyrical flourish is reminiscent of Walt Whitman's late nineteenth century nationalist-pantheist aesthetic, albeit without Whitman's racism and fervent advocacy of US imperialist annexation of all Mexican territory. For instance, Cancel Miranda locates the Puerto Rican revolutionary nationalist movement into a larger global context through his invocation of Ernesto

"Che" Guevara, the Argentinian international communist who fought in revolutionary nationalist causes in Guatemala, Cuba, Congo, and Boliva, where he eventually was killed by a US-funded counterinsurgency operation. In Cancel Miranda's mixed-genre prose and verse paean titled "Che," the Boricua internationalist writes:

> I am Puerto Rican. I begin by saying that Che is as Puerto Rican as I am...Because Che is from all our countries, he is ours! And we see his portrait on the walls of our homes as part of the family, either in a slum in Nicaragua, in El Salvador, Guatemala, Bolivia, Peru, Argentina, Cuba, Santo Domingo, Haiti, Venezuela, Colombia, Chile, Panama—in our entire continent—and in Africa and Asia, because Che is universal, because Che means struggle and hope, because in his name is written the future of us all. Che is not dead. Che simply has multiplied.   (2000, 249, ellipses in original)

Che Guevara, of course, is an archetype who has been subject to multiple appropriations and ahistorical disarticulations. However, for Cancel Miranda, Che resonates as a nationalist and antinationalist, as well as an internationalist and postnationalist revolutionary who embodied—in his shape-shifting global affiliations with multiple revolutionary nationalist causes—the ends to which a war of national liberation can and must aspire: the communist new human who emerges from, but necessarily supersedes, their local, regional, and national origins. Revolutionary violence, and particularly the armed struggle, is central to this teleology.

Brigadistas: Latina/os and Glocal Epiphanies in the Sandinista Revolution, 1979–1990

Rafael Cancel Miranda is one of many Latina/os from the nineteenth century to the present who have traversed the globe as internationalist partisans in various revolutionary struggles in Mexico, Guatemala, El Salvador, Peru, Argentina, Puerto Rico, Cuba, Spain, Vietnam, Libya, and elsewhere. The legacy of Chicana/o and Latina/o participation in international brigades extends to Nicaragua's Sandinista Revolution, which triumphed in 1979 with the solidarity of legions of internationalist volunteers. The Sandinista Revolution was the continuation of a half century of Nicaraguan popular opposition to US intervention that involved a US Marine invasion and occupation from 1912 to 1933, and subsequent installation of the Somoza family dictatorship, which ruled until the Sandinista victory. The Nicaraguan revolutionary nationalist Sandinista movement—*El Frente Sandinista para la Liberación Nacional* (Sandinista National Liberation Front)— was named after the peasant-cum-nationalist leader César Augusto Sandino, whose guerrilla forces fought the US occupation until Somoza agents assassinated him. While the Sandinistas have come under increasing scrutiny for their masculinist and corrupt practices during their reign from 1979 to 1990, as well as in their subsequent electoral victory in 2006, 2011, and 2016, their antiimperialist trajectory remains a touchstone for leftists worldwide.

Pan-Latina/o emulation of Sandino, and subsequent generations of Sandinistas, extends to Américo Paredes's 1939 poem, "A César Augusto Sandino." Paredes celebrates Sandino for confronting American imperialism, noting "all the North American might / wouldn't quit nor could it beat you" (1991, 53, lines 3–4). After lionizing Sandino's ability to do what Mexican Americans still had not done, Paredes concludes with a lament:

> and in rough combat
> you threw off the oppression. I sing to you,
> I who have cried and suffered so much
> the collective oppression of my people.   (1991, 53, lines 8–11)

Subsequent Latina/o literature about the *longue durée* of the Sandinista Revolution includes Chicano Alejandro Murguía's 1990 testimonial fiction, *Southern Front*, which provides a thinly veiled fictional account of his participation in the FSLN's 1979 final offensive as an internationalist volunteer.[12] Nicaraguan American Roberto Vargas, the leader of the Northern California cell that included Murguía along with other US-based internationalist volunteers, also narrativized his role as a Sandinista internationalist in his 1980 mixed-genre collection, *Nicaragua, yo te canto besos, balas, y sueños de libertad (Nicaragua, I Sing You Kisses, Bullets, and Visions of Liberty)*.[13] Many more workers, students, teachers, and professionals became Sandinista combatants and solidarity brigade members before, during, and after the Sandinista victory in 1979.[14]

The long list of Chicana/o Sandinistas includes Alicia Armendariz, also known as Alice Bag, lead singer of the 1980s Los Angeles punk rock band The Bags. During her subsequent career as an elementary school teacher in South Central Los Angeles, Armendariz traveled to Nicaragua in 1986 to research the Sandinista national literacy campaign. In her 2011 *testimonio* published under her pseudonym Alice Bag, *Violence Girl: East L.A. Rage to Hollywood Stage—A Chicana Punk Story*, she recalls traveling there "to see if it could be adapted for use in inner-city schools in the United States" (2011, 362) (Figure 4.2). As a cofounder and lead singer of several feminist bands, Armendariz's experiences in Sandinista Nicaragua galvanized her political sensibilities as she became aware of the intersections between capitalism, imperialism, and patriarchy. In *Violence Girl*, as well as in her prequel *Pipe Bomb for the Soul* (2015) based on her Nicaraguan diary, Bag synthesizes a punk-inflected, third-wave feminist, historical materialist, Sandinista Pan-Americanist, and international proletarian discourse that is unprecedented in Chicana testimonial writing for its nimble negotiation of the national question's complexities, contradictions, pitfalls, and possibilities.

As the title of her first *testimonio* indicates, Alice Bag is the quintessential violentological subject who nimbly navigates the tragic hyperlocal domestic, regional, national, and international spaces that a multiplicity of Latina/os have traversed in ideologically diverse ways. It all began at home. While she was a young girl, Armendariz's family life was held captive by her father's domestic violence against her mother. Through it all, and in large part because of this domestic terror, Armendariz underwent multiple transformations from an indoctrinated and domesticated Catholic school girl to a sexually explorative young adult, gender-bending feminist punk rocker, Freirean barrio schoolteacher, Sandinista partisan, and ultimately a Marxist internationalist "compa" (or comrade). In a key passage in *Violence Girl*, she recalls confronting her father's repeated denials about his abuse, reminding him:

> When you hit her, you tried to strangle her, you punched her and dragged her, and spit on her and kicked her. I'm talking about when you busted her nose and the blood flew on her dress and on your shirt and on the wall! I'm talking about when you beat her with the belt buckle and tore open her scalp, and the blood dripped down her face, when she kneeled in front of you before you kicked her in the face and then kicked her some more when she couldn't get up! (2011, 354)

Armendariz's testimonial accounts of her intervention into the legacy of domestic violence in her family is part of the punk ethos of

FIGURE 4.2. *Cover of* Violence Girl *(2011), by Alice Bag. Courtesy of Photographer Louis Jacinto and Cover Designer Gregg Einhorn.*

direct confrontation. It enacts her various bands' feminist anthems. "Survive," for instance, decries the commodification of women with a high-pitched indictment: "Don't you look at me! / I'm just a commodity!" Songs such as "No, Means No" indict rape culture through an expletive-laden diatribe; another, "Suburban Home," exposes the prison house of heteropatriarchal marriage. More incisively, the song "He's So Sorry," and accompanying music video that spoofs the domesticity of 1950s Doo Wop music, serves as a feminist consciousness-raising critique against domestic violence. It challenges the abusers' excuses and explicates the mystified denial that oftentimes grips abuse victims like her mother. The undated song is framed as a dramatic dialogue, with Bag singing both roles in different voices:

Are you really going back to him?
He said he was sorry.
He always says that!
I really believe him this time.   (*Lyric Sheet* n.d., n.p., italics in original,)

The song proceeds with a catalogue of beatings: "punch to the eye," "your head hits the wall," and "boots and your ribs collide." The song ends with the didactic crescendo that, like all punk songs, is shouted into the microphone:

Just because he's sorry doesn't mean he's gonna change!
Just because you love him doesn't mean you've gotta stay!
                                                (*Lyric Sheet* n.d., n.p.)

The Bags' companion song "Babylonian Gorgon" opens with a bombastic rejection of the ideologies of commodification that enable the domestication of women as objects and their mystification as violently subordinated subjects. With allusions to totalitarianism, Armendariz, as Alice Bag, screams her retort: "Don't need no false reasons for why I'm out of place! / I don't goose step for the masquerade!" (*Lyric Sheet* n.d., n.p.).

Alternatively, Bag/Armendariz becomes the "violence girl," which is the title of one of her hit songs. This moniker recounts the painful resilience of a young woman continually assaulted by "the violent world," and concludes with a matter-of-fact paean to a survivor who has reclaimed the feminist punk ethos of *counter*violence, rather than antiviolence, as constitutive of her identity. Michelle Habell-Pallan

provides a prescient overview of Armendariz's appropriations of violence, noting "while she detested the violence that surrounded her at
home and public school, she could not help but internalize it" (2005,
158). But Bag does more than internalize the violence. The contestatory symbolic counterviolence that punk rock affords is more than
just a coping mechanism: rather, it defines Bag's new sense of self, in
addition to her increasingly more globalized underclass sensibilities
and immanent theory of revolutionary praxis.

Throughout her three-decade musical career with The Bags,
Castration Squad, Cholita, Stay at Home Bomb, and bilingual retro
punk middle-aged Chicana trio band Las Tres, Alice Bag's lyrics
traverse back and forth from hyperlocal themes—particularly gender
relations in various domestic spaces—to analytical diatribes about
imperialism. It would be a gross oversimplification to describe
Bag's mosh pit praxis as "transnational." Specific places and socio-
temporal spaces are necessary, yet insufficient, venues for her critique
of power and deployment of a feminist internationalist counterpower. Indeed, her Spanish language song, "Inesperado Adiós"
("Unexpected Goodbye"), illustrates the limits of transnationalism
by underscoring how immigrants who succeed at crossing artificial
national borders to settle in the United States inevitably face new
cycles of exploitation despite their acculturation and assimilation
into their new homeland:

> In this place that we have called home,
> we always were shadows amid the rubble.
> With blood and sweat we gave what we had to give,
> and it rose up atop our shoulders.   (*Lyric Sheet* n.d., n.p.)

In the bombastic anthem "Class War," Bag extends this vision toward
a supranationalist punk version of Marx's theory of the alienation of
labor. She follows this with an immanently revolutionary synthesis:
the two-word title that provides half of the song's lyrics are repeatedly shouted into the microphone like a mantra, transforming the
already ritualized mosh pit swirl of alienated youth into a liminal
bootcamp-like training ground for an army of insurrectionary outer-
national lumpenproletarians with their balled fists flailing in unison.

Bag's glocal meditations on patriarchal privilege, labor exploitation,
and the imperialist politics of third world underdevelopment are
thoroughly grounded in her Chicana punk sensibility. Habell-Pallan

notes that for some East Los Angeles Chicanas, such as Bag, "punk subculture was not the end of their identity formation, but it was a path to a new way of being in the world and a way to expose the world to their reality" (2005, 165). Bag's "new way of being" also involves the transformation of her past antiestablishment and historical materialist punk persona, which she eventually realizes was always immanently internationalist. In *Violence Girl*, for instance, Bag reiterates the political and cultural economy of punk in the 1980s West Coast scene she helped define:

> Ronald Reagan defeated Jimmy Carter in the November [1980] presidential elections, ushering in an era of social conservatism and militarism that would reward the rich and punish the poor and disenfranchised at home and around the world. It was fertile ground for rebellion, and punk swelled in popularity, expanding well beyond the major cities and reaching deep into the heartland.   (2011, 346)

Reagan's union busting, free market politics, and intensification of Cold War proxy battles in the third world coincide with Bag's decades-long music career and her job as an elementary teacher in inner-city L.A.:

> I started working with the children of immigrants, children who were limited English speakers, just as I'd been when I entered school…
>
> Many of the students at Hoover Street Elementary were the children of families from Central America. By the mid-1980s, several countries, including Honduras, El Salvador and Nicaragua, were caught in brutal, horrific civil wars between communist revolutionaries and US-backed governmental forces. The Reagan administration had authorized covert CIA operations to train and fund the "counter-revolutionary forces" without seeking the approval of congress to wage what was essentially a war by proxy. Few details of these secret wars were made public at the time, but the swelling population of Central American refugees in Los Angeles was evidence of a growing humanitarian crisis.   (2011, 360)

Bag posits a historical materialist theory of punk as a response to the Cold War and related free market regimes, all of which intersect with her identification with other subordinated subjects, particularly her beloved middle-school students. They teach her that capitalist imperialist politics are experienced as simultaneously global, local, and domestic traumas for adults and children alike. This epiphany ultimately motivates her transformative trip to Escuela Nica in Estelí, Nicaragua, which she notes "billed itself as a school for internationalists" (2011, 362).

Bag was transformed by the experience of living in an all-woman household of AfroLatina Nicaraguans and working alongside multiple internationalist brigadistas from throughout the world. Sandinista Nicaragua facilitated her ongoing deconstruction of the oppressive heteropatriarchal and nationalist metaphors of "home" and "homeland" pursuant to new gender roles, beauty norms, "family" models, ideas about political economy and, ultimately, the national question. Bag devotes considerable space in her 2015 *testimonio, Pipe Bomb for the Soul*, to recounting extended discussions with her new Nicaraguan family and other brigadistas about the ideologically laden nature of some gendering rituals. For instance, many women internationalist volunteers refused to use lipstick, earrings, or shave their legs and arm pits in a rejection of scopophilic male expectations. Bag recalls, however, that her use of these accoutrements is fundamental to her iconoclastic aesthetic and antiauthoritarian politics as a punk rock intellectual, in which she made ample use of unorthodox color schemes. Bag's conversation with her Nica adoptive mother Francie, a former guerrilla and single mother of five, reminds her that the main issue is a woman's power to choose and control her own standards of beauty and being (2015, 98). Bag recounts a similar discussion about hair texture and skin color with her adoptive teenage Nica sister Paca, who had recently returned from Cuba where she experienced an epiphanic recognition of her own beauty as an AfroLatina. In response to Paca's indictment as she points to a photo of a blonde woman hanging on her bedroom wall— "Why is THAT considered perfect?"—Bag muses:

> I was momentarily sent back to my childhood, remembering adults in East L.A. cooing over a child with güerrito [light] features. Kids could be ugly as sin but if they had light skin, eyes or hair they would receive heaps of praise. I had never understood it. (2015, 24)

Bag realizes that even something as apparently benign as the way a woman sits gains a political resonance in Sandinista Nicaragua. She recalls her first conversation with her adoptive Nica mother Francie, who recounted the lingering sexism women experience even after they engaged in combat just like male guerrillas (2015, 19). Bag is especially impressed by Francie's demeanor:

> Francie sat quietly in front of me, dressed in an olive drab shirt and pants. Her legs were spread open in front of her in a pose that I had always associated with men, her body relaxed and open, completely in control of her presence and ready to act at any moment. There was a hardness to her look but a quality of gentleness in her eyes. I studied her face, noticing her earrings and a hint of lipstick. I saw a woman for whom strength and femininity were whatever she wanted them to be.   (2015, 20)

However small these epiphanies may be, Bag underscores that they are part of her larger ideological transformation into a Chicana feminist Sandinista internationalist.

True to the *testimonio* ethos of chronicling an individual's consciousness-raising experiences and their resultant demystification about one's real relationship to power, Bag repeatedly finds herself in the surprising position of recognizing the patriarchal valences of some of her expectations about gender roles when she meets guerrilla leader Luisa Amanda Espinoza, also known as Comandante Gladys Baez. A combat veteran, torture survivor, and cofounder of the influential *Asociación de Mujeres Nicaragüenses* ("Nicaraguan Women's Association"), Espinoza insists that "*sin la mujer no hay revolución*" ("without women there is no revolution"). Bag confides that Espinoza "looked more like someone getting ready to bake a batch of cookies than lead an army" (2015, 37). She is astonished that someone who "looked like so many women in East L.A., ordinary working class moms and *tías* [aunts]," could be a commander (2015, 39). After Francie asks Bag why she doubted Comandante Baez's strength, Bag shares the type of recognition scene that conventionally serves as the didactic axis in a *testimonio*'s account of a neophyte's political epiphany:

> I was too ashamed to say it was because I expected muscles and a snazzy uniform; inwardly, I had to admit that I expected a man. I had never seen a woman who looked like Gladys have any power. In my world, women who looked like Gladys took care of kids, did housework, warmed up tortillas. I glimpsed myself, just for a second, in all my sexist, racist and colorist ugliness and I quickly stepped away from the mirror.   (2015, 39)

Already aware of the violent nature of gender roles and expectations in heteropatriarchal families, this episode forms part of Bag's Sandinista reeducation about the evolving nature and revolutionary potential of reconstructed notions of family, motherhood, beauty, home, and postnational identity. Her intuitive awareness and earlier punk rock interventions gain a larger geopolitical context: in Sandinista Nicaragua she is able to situate her local domestic concerns alongside her awareness about class conflict into a global historical materialist framework. She reiterates this point in her discussion of the new model of motherhood she learns from her Nica mother Francie:

> My real mother fed me when I was hungry, nursed me when I was sick and loved me unconditionally. She gave me life and I will always love her. My Nicaraguan mother feeds my mind and nurtures my soul, and loves humanity, especially those who are oppressed. She has shown me how to live.   (2015, 89)

In the recurring postdiary section, "Upon Reflection," Bag glosses Freire's concept of *conscientização*, (*concientización* in Spanish), or transformative political epiphany, to explicate the significance of this seemingly small shift in perspective:

> I can see now that the process of concientization [*sic*] was already at work in me. These new revolutionary ideas were taking hold of me both consciously and subconsciously and initiated a change within me that aligned my actions to that ideology. I was experiencing transformative awareness, a consciousness with the power to create change.   (2015, 89)

Significantly, Bag's aforementioned songs "Inesperado Adiós" ("Unexpected Goodbye") and "Class War" were composed after her trip to Nicaragua, with the latter opening: "I wanna war between the rich and the poor / I wanna fight and know what I'm fighting for / I wanna class war, class war, class war…" (2012, n.p.).

Bag, who identified as a punk before she identified as Chicana, introduces a new nomenclature that signals the hemispheric expansion of her previously localized insurgent and contrapuntally violent punk pastiche subjectivity. Bag eventually catalyzes a new identity as a *Nica* and a *compañera*, or *compa*, which is the abbreviated Sandinista revolutionary term of endearment. Bag earned the *compa* accolade despite her frequent missteps and misunderstandings: for instance, after attempting to buy toilet paper, which was unavailable in Estelí, a store clerk advised Bag to "go back to your family and live like a Nicaraguan" (2011, 370). Bag accepted the challenge. Before the end of her month-long sojourn, she is regularly referred to as a Nica and expresses pride at being called a *compa*, which she notes "can mean partner or companion" in struggle and signifies "equality" (2015, 48). Throughout her diary she refers to Salvadoran exiles and brigadistas as "our compañeros" (2015, 46). Toward the end of her trip she even identifies as a "Nica student" (2015, 92). The counterhegemonic resonance of these subtle shifts in her nomenclature is proclaimed in a banner she helped create, which read in part: "The People of the United States join the struggle of Nicaragua" (Figure 4.3). She continues:

> I outlined the letters and we all grabbed markers and colored them in. We held up our banner proudly and I was ready to leave it at that when Francie suggested we add "*¡viva el internacionalismo proletario!*" I have to confess that I hadn't really thought of myself as an internationalist until that moment, but I realized that what I've been doing with my expressions of solidarity and my support of the revolution

FIGURE 4.3. *Alice Bag (right) with American Internationalists in Nicaragua, 1986. Courtesy of Alice Bag.*

are actions consistent with proletarian internationalism. How strange. I thought I was just supporting people who were trying to improve their way of life.   (2015, 62–3)

In her postdiary "Upon Reflection" section following this entry, she adds:

I don't think I truly understood the idea of proletarian international-ism while I was in Nicaragua. It wasn't until years later when I saw the power of multinational corporations that I came to understand that the working class must unite and work as a global entity in order to protect the rights and interests of workers around the world.

(2015, 63)

Bag's humble self-deprecating tone has an important didactic function in her *testimonio*, exemplifying that *conscientização*, as Paolo Freire identified the process, must be a lifelong activity based on critical theorizing of all experiences, especially one's own ignorance and contradictions.

In a crescendo to both her *testimonios*, Bag's historical materialist *autocrítica* invites further ideological critiques of the broader Latina/o community. She recalls, for instance, how her trip to Nicaragua included a flight that also carried a US soldier destined for Honduras to train Contra mercenaries (2011, 363). This encoun-ter later resonated in Nicaragua as she was forced to jump "face down in the dirt" during a Contra attack one block away as she walked home one evening (2011, 373). "This was no tourist vacation" (2011, 373), she notes in her recollection of attacks she heard about or experienced firsthand in a trip punctuated by the frequent sound of automatic rifle fire. Bag does not indicate the race of the US soldier she encountered. However, her description conjures Haskell Wexler's 1985 film *Latino*, which features two Mexican American US Army Special Forces soldiers who travel to Honduras to train Contras. This film ends with one East L.A. Mexican American Green Beret becoming romantically involved with a female Sandinista agronomist of Nicaraguan and Costa Rican heritage. Their dialogues lead him to question the legitimacy of the US intervention. His fellow Mexican American Green Beret, however, remains committed to his anticommunist mission of murder, sabotage, and the recolonization of Nicaragua as a capitalist export economy at the service of US consumers.

FIGURE 4.4. *Felix I. Rodriguez (left) with Ernesto Che Guevara shortly before the guerrilla's execution in Bolivia October 9, 1967. Image in public domain.*

The Mexican American US Army Special Forces soldier characters in Wexler's film are more than mere cinematic creations. On the contrary, they allude to the high percentage of US Latina/os in the US military overall.[15] They also recall Felix I. Rodriguez, the Cuban American US Army Vietnam War veteran and CIA operative referenced in Chapter 2. As he chronicles in his 1990 memoir, *Shadow Warrior: The CIA Hero of a Hundred Unknown Battles—From the Bay of Pigs to Vietnam to Nicaragua*, Rodriguez participates in numerous anticommunist counterinsurgency operations throughout Latin America. In fact, he is responsible for the hunt, capture, and execution of Ernesto Che Guevara in Bolivia in 1967 (Figure 4.4). The enduring ideological dissensus framed by Bag's and Rodriguez's supra-Latinidades, and especially their competing internationalisms, ultimately introduces ever-more-complex violentological syntheses in the War on Terror, which is the subject of Chapter 5.

5

Militarized Mestizajes

COMBAT, TRANSCULTURATION, AND IMPERIALISM IN LATINA/O LIFE WRITING FROM THE WAR ON TERROR

Mexican American US Army Major General Alfred "Freddie" Valenzuela opens his jointly authored 2008 memoir, *No Greater Love: The Lives and Times of Hispanic Soldiers*, by recalling the funeral for the first US soldier killed in the preparation phase of the 2003 US invasion of Iraq: US Army Specialist Rodrigo Gonzalez-Garza, a citizen of Mexico.[1] General Valenzuela had been ordered to escort the dead soldier's body after US civilian leaders anguished over diplomatic and public relations fallout since the first US soldier killed in the US War on Terror was a "foreigner." After a novelistic description of the "ethereal early morning moonlight" preceding the US-Mexico border crossing (2008, 7)—described as an ominous impending battle—Valenzuela foregrounds the ideological dénouement of his military command memoir:

> On our journey south, I was filled with concern that the community would not be hospitable to one of its sons who embraced American life in so many ways. My worries were surprisingly unnecessary.
>
> As we approached Sabinas Hidalgo that morning, we soon found ourselves on a road flanked by people on both sides enthusiastically waving American and Mexican flags. They were mourning the loss of one of their sons, but their mood also seemed to include feelings of national *orgullo* (pride) and reverent *agradecimiento* (gratitude).
>
> (2008, 13, translation in original)

Lingering diplomatic conflicts related to Mexico's United Nations vote against the invasion, in addition to Mexican laws prohibiting

Violentologies: Violence, Identity, and Ideology in Latina/o Literature. B.V. Olguín, Oxford University Press (2021).
© B.V. Olguín.
DOI: 10.1093/oso/9780198863090.001.0006

armed foreign troops on its soil, accentuated the dramatic tension of the border crossing. These laws were mainly directed at the United States, whose soldiers have invaded and occupied Mexico several times before and after the US annexation of one half of Mexican territory following the US-Mexico War in 1848. The situation was even more volatile because of the planned rifle salute that accompanies US military funerals, which raised the possibility of Valenzuela's arrest.[2]

Specialist Rodrigo Gonzalez-Garza's three brothers were all active-duty US Army enlisted soldiers who traveled to the burial site in Mexico with Valenzuela following their brother's Catholic funeral mass in San Antonio, Texas. They apparently insisted the transborder funeral proceed despite the dangers. Wearing the uniforms of Mexico's former enemy, the Mexican American mestizo entourage crossed the US-Mexico border without incident. The ceremony concluded, Valenzuela recalls, with a poignant US flag raising:

> After the casket was removed from the hearse, the three brothers—all proudly wearing their class A [ceremonial dress] uniforms—unfolded and raised the American flag up the flagpole, resting it at half-mast. This act triggered a round of applause and cheers from the crowd.
>
> (2008, 14)

In a crescendo to his dramatic reassertion of Mexican American borderlands subjectivity, transnational citizenship, and fluid mestizaje as third world yet imperialist, Valenzuela recalls: "I was honored to meet a number of local Mexican veterans who had also proudly served in the U.S. Army in World War II, Korea, and Vietnam" (2008, 14). They, too, wore US military uniforms.

At a time when the growing volume of Latina/o life writing signals increased upward class mobility and closer proximity to power in contradistinction to preceding autobiographical and testimonial renderings of Chicana/o borderlands mestiza/o subjects as inherently subaltern and oppositional to US imperialism, Valenzuela reframes and celebrates Latinidad as inextricable from, and central to, the performance of US global hegemony.[3] Without the least bit of irony, Valenzuela notes: "The willingness of young men and women who were born in Mexico to fight for their adopted country had long puzzled many Mexicans." He adds, "it was my duty to demonstrate, through Rodrigo's example, what it means to be an American—and a Hispanic-American" (2008, 12). Regardless of their historical circumstances, geonational location, legal status, or multiplicity of motives for joining the US military, Valenzuela insists that Latina/o soldiers are paradigmatic US Americans.[4]

Valenzuela's militarization of Latina/o citizenship in the United States perpetuates the US imperialist models of Latinidad codified in wartime legislation from the nineteenth century to the War on Terror. For instance, within a few months after the September 11, 2001, attacks, US Presidential Executive Orders and corresponding legislation facilitated postmortem citizenship for noncitizen US military personnel—the proverbial "Green Card Soldiers"—killed in the War on Terror invasions and occupations of Iraq and Afghanistan. This ultimately included Specialist Gonzalez-Garza. Executive Order 329 in 2002 also allowed for accelerated paths to citizenship for still-living noncitizens serving in the military after September 11, 2001.[5] Like Gonzalez-Garza, the great majority of these military personnel were from Mexico and other Latin American countries. Before the War on Terror's compounded militarization of Latina/o citizenship, US President Harry Truman's 1948 Executive Order 9981 formally desegregated the military. This granted more opportunities for racial minorities despite lingering discriminatory practices and policies, such as circumscribed choices for military occupational specialties, and the still informally segregated officer corps. Corresponding access to G.I. benefits for housing and education made the military an attractive option for racial minorities given the even more segregated civilian world. Minority upward class mobility thus became further entwined with the United States' new role as a global hegemon. Similarly, the 1917 Jones Act had granted limited citizenship to Puerto Ricans, which facilitated Puerto Rican military service during WWI.[6] Prior to this legislation, the Treaty of Guadalupe Hidalgo ending the US-Mexico War in 1848, and Treaty of Paris concluding the Spanish-American War in 1898, forever embedded Latina/o citizenship with imperialist violences.[7]

General Valenzuela's account of the transborder funeral for Specialist Gonzalez-Garza thus dramatizes how the War on Terror's extension of the legacy of militarized Latina/o citizenship has culminated in a broader legacy of militarized civic and cultural mestizajes, as well as new iterations of militarized necro-citizenship. Significantly, through these contradictory, yet still relatively empowering frameworks, Latina/os are no longer merely the begrudgingly incorporated subjects of US imperialism; they now claim to be the quintessential

US Americans. This is an example of violentologies: distinct but related supra-Latina/o theories of being and knowing actualized by various embodied, interpersonal, international, and epistemic violences in a given time and place. The formal civic citizenship and informal cultural citizenship enacted in Valenzuela's binational spectacle thus are merely symptomatic of a raison d'être overdetermined by one form of violence or another, and usually multiple violences simultaneously. In this context, the Soldado Razo becomes a metonym for a Latina/o analogue to the aforementioned Afro-Pessimism, and particularly Achille Mbembe's (2019) intersecting "necro-politics": with their initial US citizenship constituted as de facto conquered internal enemies of the US empire in the nineteenth century, the Soldado Razo's greatest and most enduring virtue is their willingness to die to prove they are worthy of inclusion as citizens, with even this act never being sufficient to achieve the goal. This chapter surveys Latina/o life writing from the War on Terror to explore how various types of violence animate an array of Latinidades that extend through and beyond Valenzuela's binational necro-citizenship, as well as other Latinidades examined earlier. As Valenzuela's military command memoir illustrates, Latina/o life writing from the War on Terror variously narrates familiar and new subjects-in-formation, and subjects in continual transformation. In many ways, the narratives themselves perform these subjectivities, which emerge amid epic battles between Eastern and Western peoples, nations, and ideological paradigms that are intertwined with broader global geopolitical realignments.

The expansive War on Terror Latinidades rendered through print, aural, and performative life-writing genres consequently pose profound challenges to conventional understandings of subaltern identity and agency, especially regarding the populations included under the rubric of "Latina/o." As demonstrated throughout this book, the oppositional claims animating Latina/o, Ethnic, Latin American, Postcolonial, and broader Decolonial Studies are no longer valid (if they ever were) when we take seriously the expanding, and ever more discrepant, Latina/o archive. In the War on Terror, Latin American immigrants and US Latina/os are involved in a wide range of roles that have added volumes of material and ideological complexities to this archive. Some are familiar; others are new and unique to this era. They include US allies and battlefield enemies; conscientious objectors and protofascist Special Forces operatives;

neo-Orientalist military officers and pathological CIA torturers; nostalgic apologists for empire, as well as enduring anarchist and communist opponents; in addition to legions of petite bourgeois activists and mystified aesthetes ignorant of their fetish on violence, and their own interpellation within empire. The case studies animating this chapter thus ultimately enable—and demand—metacritical attention to the ideological contours of the distinct supra-Latina/o violentologies adumbrated by Rodrigo Gonzalez-Garza's funeral spectacle. The category of "Latina/o" has come to assume drastically different meanings in the early twenty-first century, even as it has always been inscribed with, and indeed overdetermined by, violence. The War on Terror features the expansive range of potentialities and even broader dangers that this nominative signifies.

Latina/o Special Forces Combat Action Memoir and the Postracial Warrior *Übermensch*

As noted throughout this book, and further illustrated in General Alfred Valenzuela's military command memoir, mestizaje and related models of Latinidad can be far more hegemonic than oppositional. If we follow Foucauldian (1995) and Gramscian (1971) definitions of power, mestizaje may have always been ideologically ambivalent precisely because of the dialectical nature of its constitutive dyad, which balances alterity alongside the normative. This ambivalence, which Homi Bhabha (2004) has celebrated for the purported epistemic disruptions colonial subjects perform through their mimesis, or cultural mestizaje, might actually be necessary for the performance of empire: it demonstrates the need for a coercive social, police, and military apparatus. As noted in preceding chapters, Michael Hardt and Antonio Negri (2002) even argue that racial minorities are ideal agents of empire precisely because of their interstitiality! This has been true of past empires—Roman, Ottoman, Spanish, and British— whose expansiveness across linguistic and cultural geographies required legions of intermediaries and enforcers.

Even before Major General Valenzuela's stewardship of Gonzalez-Garza's binational funeral spectacle, the War on Terror made the ideological fungibility of mimesis immediately evident through the US military's deployment of Latina/o mestizaje as an imperialist counterinsurgency asset. In a 2003 *Newsweek* article, journalists

Evan Thomas and Martha Brant report that an unnamed US military Central Command official claims "Special Operations forces and the CIA played a still shadow but vital role in Operation Iraqi Freedom," the mission name for the US War on Terror invasion of Iraq in 2003. Quoting this same source, they add:

> Secret operators roamed Iraq for months before the war. Some were Arabic, many were Hispanic disguised to look like Arabs and some darkened their faces and beards with dye.
>
> (Thomas and Brant 2003, n.p.)

Despite the US military's vanguard role in the nation's desegregation a half century earlier, military commanders remain cognizant of racial difference, which they have weaponized and redeployed. Marked as racially "Other" allies, Latino soldiers, like the small but growing number of Arab American soldiers and civilian contractors in the US military, have emerged as shape-shifting quasi-native informants reminiscent of nineteenth-century and early twentieth-century intermediaries who facilitated communications with imperialist anthropologists, merchants, missionaries, political emissaries, and soldiers.[8] And these Latino native informants also are *the* imperialists!

The Latino US Army Special Forces operatives who posed—and passed—as Arabs nonetheless inevitably present the potential for a disparate range of ideological slippages. As discussed in preceding chapters, these vacillations are illustrated throughout Latina/o war literature, which variously depicts Latina/o soldier and civilian identifications with Vietnamese Communists, North Korean Communists, Sandinista Socialists, and Al Qaeda networks based on racial, gender, class, spiritual, and ideological affinities. Concomitantly, the enduring racist suspicion of Latina/o susceptibility to "betrayal," also troped as "going native," informs encounters where white US troops misrecognize Latina/o soldiers as their enemy. In War on Terror literature and film, Latino US troops frequently are associated with Muslim insurgents. Kimberly Peirce's 2008 Hollywood feature film *Stop Loss* is one of numerous *in medias res* war entertainment—or *wartainment*—productions set in US-occupied Iraq that proffer Latina/o heritage as antithetical to US citizenship and soldier allegiance. For instance, in one scene set at a checkpoint, as a white US soldier inspects the trunk of an Iraqi-driven automobile in search of "hajis" (the US soldier epithet for insurgents that is derived from the honorific title of a Muslim who completes the Hajj), another white US soldier jokingly asks from the background, "are there any Mexicans in there?" The allusion, of course, is to the fixed inspection stations located twenty miles inland, parallel to the US-Mexico border, that render Mexican Americans as antithetical to US Americanness. Within this milieu, it is not surprising that coterminous Immigration and Customs Enforcement Agency raids throughout the US include deportations of Latina/o War on Terror combat veterans and their families, some of whom are US citizens![9]

Notwithstanding the prevalence of these spectacles of militarized mimesis, related racialized abjections, and ever-present possibility of slippages involving alternative transversal recognitions, Latino US Special Forces memoirs from the War on Terror deploy mestizaje and racial ambiguity into something much more primal, empowering, and problematic. In their extension of the highly popular combat action genre, racial othering has a particularly nuanced status beyond the stealth it enabled Latino and Arab American US Special Operations soldiers in the early days of the US War on Terror invasion of Iraq. In these texts, the physical markers of race—hair texture, phenotypical facial features, and skin color—are discernible but virtually invisible as their bearers fight their way toward a new ontological category: the superhuman, protofascist, warrior caste of hyperviolent Nietzschean *Übermensches*.[10] In the War on Terror, Latina/os have claimed entry into this archetype, which occupies a prominent role in the American imaginary as evidenced by the highly popular combat action genres in literature, television, film, gaming, and popular culture. Latina/o permutations of this warrior Übermensch introduce a supra-Latina/o fascist who is fundamentally distinct from previously discussed supra-Latina/o violentologies.

Fascism is a teleological, if still eclectic and historically contingent cultural and political phenomenon with complicated psycho-social dimensions. Despite a dissensus about which elements are essential for fascism to exist, most models concur that fascism involves: 1) ultra-nationalist and expansionist politics; 2) messianic eugenicist arguments justifying persecution of groups deemed inferior or a threat to the nation; 3) alarmist propaganda about national decline arising from perceived internal and external threats; 4) masculinist eroticized fetish on violence, warfare, and combat death as purifying and regenerative endeavors; and 5) widespread dissemination of these discourses through myth and eclectic religious doctrine.[11] That is, fascism is a violence-based philosophy of praxis whose adherents stress self-actualization through continual symbolic and kinetic performances of extreme violence, particularly brutal fighting, torture, killing, and combat death. Scholars, public intellectuals, and political iconoclasts as diverse as Noam Chomsky, Susan Faludi, and Bob Avakian have made convincing arguments for the emergence of fascism in the United States during the War on Terror.

Mexican American Regulo Zapata's 2007 US Special Forces combat chronicle, *Desperate Lands: The War on Terror Through the Eyes of a Special Forces Soldier*, tropes race in unique ways that foreground the emergence of the Latina/o War on Terror fascist. It opens with this twenty-eight-year veteran of the US Army describing the characteristics of each member of his commando team and military commanders. Significantly, he presents a dispassionate, mechanical, and static discussion of phenotype that renders race as insignificant as the color of a piece of equipment even as it is marked as present. Zapata thus reveals himself to be the antithesis of Haskell Wexler's fictional angst-ridden East L.A. Chicano Green Beret Sergeant Eddie Guerrero, the protagonist of the 1985 feature film *Latino: America's Secret War in Nicaragua* referenced in Chapter 4. Sergeant Guerrero (whose surname means "warrior" in Spanish) agonizes over the fact that he is fighting against other poor brown-skinned people, specifically Sandinistas, on behalf of the US military that sees all "spics" as indistinguishable. Early in the film, for instance, Sergeant Guerrero's commanding officer, Major Metcalf, underscores his Chicano subordinate's antithetical role by complaining about his imminent transfer to a US military base in Panama, which he calls "more spic country." Sergeant Guerrero eventually sees the US military intervention in Nicaragua as a fundamentally racialized class conflict facilitated by his co-optation as a quasi-native informant. In contrast, Sergeant Zapata consistently marks—but immediately effaces—race in his teleology of soldiering to propose a postracial and protofascist supra-Latinidad. He nonchalantly notes, for example, "Captain Lee was a tall, slim Asian-looking U.S. Army Ranger" (2007, 18), and Captain Omar's "facial appearance suggested a Middle Eastern or Arabic ethnic background," emphasizing he "was a 7th Special Forces Group soldier—a combat veteran" (2007, 15). Zapata uses similarly dispassionate descriptions for white soldiers, whom he calls "Caucasian," and does the same for African American and Latino soldiers (2007, 30). Their race is less significant than the unit patch worn on the right shoulder of their US Army uniform marking them as combat veterans.

Frequently referring to himself in the third person, his own racial and ethnic identity is equally inconsequential as he claims the central role of the authoritative chronicler. Zapata's aesthetic involves the clinical, field-report tone that must, of tactical necessity, dispense with subjective discussions of racialized subjectivity so he can focus on enemy troop positions, movements, weaponry, skirmishes, and postbattle analysis. His descriptions are replete with military jargon and tactical minutiae required for military planners, analysts, and soldiers on the ground. The mission comes first, and for US Special Forces soldiers, this always involves guerrilla combat zone operations—their raison d'être. Sergeant Zapata's combat action memoir therefore renders phenotypical models of race as secondary to the violence through which a postracial US Special Forces warrior Übermensch is forged. He is one of them and proud of it!

In a performance of his conscious and willful role as an agent of US imperialism, however, Sergeant Zapata nonetheless assigns racial, cultural, and geopolitical value to religion, particularly Islam. His adumbration of the supra-Latino warrior Übermensch remains inscribed within the racialized religious neo-Crusade logic of the War on Terror.[12] For instance, through a revealing epiphany in Qatar, which served as a transition point in his deployment to Afghanistan, Zapata marks the broader Western imperialist—and neo-Orientalist—legacy of his US military service:

> Suddenly, I began to hear a loud Islamic call to prayer—Muslims chanting one of their five daily prayers. The muezzin—a crier who calls the faithful to prayer—chanted aloud from a high tower in the mosque near our firebase.
>
> I found myself listening to this eerie sound and wondering who this chanting person was and what was he saying as he chanted aloud to all of us. As I listened, I felt as if I were in some faraway evil, strange, remote, desert land in some French Foreign Legion outpost, waiting for an attack by hundreds of Muslims. (2007, 19)

Similar to other US soldiers in the War on Terror, Zapata frequently uses the US soldier epithet "hajis" (2007, 142). In the passage cited above, he also inadvertently identifies with France, whose imperialist ventures throughout the Arab world, Africa, Latin America, and

Asia, were aided by the multiracial, multinational cadre of soldiers who make up the French Foreign Legion, which primarily consists of men from these very colonies. As noted in the discussion of Mexican American French Foreign Legionnaire Jaime Salazar/Juan Sanchez in the introduction, this is the same unit defeated by Mexican forces under the command of Zapotec Mexican President Benito Juarez at the May 5, 1868, Battle of Puebla. Mexicans and Mexican Americans celebrate this victory in *Cinco de Mayo* festivals. The battle also is commemorated in the same month at every legionnaire graduation ceremony in which the troops face toward the Mexican battleground where their predecessors were "martyred." In his ironic parallel, US Army Special Forces Sergeant Zapata is a de facto member of the American internal "foreign" legion who performs his role as a palimpsestic Mexican American Other-cum-imperialist warrior Übermensch.

More importantly, rather than being mystified, Sergeant Zapata is fundamentally cognizant of his role as a *hegemonic* liminal subject! His third-space soldiering, as it were, involves strategic tactical deployments and erasures of his racialized ethnicity as an empowered (albeit still colonized) US citizen and subject of history who will receive a generous lifelong pension, free medical care, and a ceremonious military funeral, among other benefits and cultural capital associated with his identity as a US Army Special Forces combat veteran. His sense of self is not predicated on his identity as a Latino, or even a Latino soldier, per se, but as a career US Army "Green Beret" with over twenty years of military experience: he is a "lifer" in Army parlance, given that twenty years of active-duty service makes a soldier eligible for retirement with full benefits. More importantly, as a Special Forces combat veteran, he embraced the self-erasure required for superhuman transcendence. Indeed, Zapata's US Special Forces commando training involves use of foreign language and cultural immersion in liaison with indigenous forces allied with the United States. For him, enemy populations are both abject and the object of study: Green Berets mimic the culture, language, and identity of people in their targeted region to cultivate and train indigenous troops as allies to be deployed against that country's government forces, or other forces deemed to be hostile to US interests. Accordingly, Sergeant Zapata's mestizaje is fundamentally militarized and imperialist, and his new identity as the warrior Übermensch is necessarily actualized through combat killing and, if necessary, dying.

Journalist profiles and biographies of US Special Forces combat operations and operators provide corollaries to the best-selling combat action memoir genre modeled by Zapata. They usually are written about dead or wounded soldiers, adding to the mythos of the warrior Übermensch as a supraracial entity who transcends the average human being by killing, being wounded, and dying in combat. Eric Blehm's 2010 *The Only Thing Worth Dying For: How Eleven Green Berets Forged a New Afghanistan*, is exemplary. Blehm, who has made a career as a coauthor for military memoirists, profiles US Army Special Forces Operational Detachment Alpha 574, which was deployed in the early days of the US invasion of Afghanistan. This unit included a Mexican American from California, Master Sergeant Gil Magallanes, who sustained debilitating wounds by a US Air Force bombing that accidentally attacked his unit because of a soldier's misuse of targeting equipment. Blehm's account also includes a cameo appearance by a Latino CIA agent identified only as "Zepeda." After Zepeda kills several suspected Taliban soldiers, a member of the US Special Forces unit acknowledges him with a nod, a wink, and the fraternal identification: "welcome to the club…the man-killer's club" (2010, 215, ellipses in original). Zepeda, like Magallanes and other members of the combined force, is represented as the superwarrior hero by the suprahuman activity of combat killing, and for courting death. As in Zapata's combat action memoir, the US Army Special Forces troops in Blehm's profile identify the enemy by racialized religious markers. But they ultimately privilege a postracial formation of superhuman beings whose chief virtue is their proficient use of lethal violence to obliterate—and supersede—the body of a mere human enemy, or a human being in general. This frequently includes their own injury and death, which are part and parcel of their raison d'être as warrior Übermensches.

The inevitability of combat injury such as US Army Special Forces Sergeant Magallanes suffers, also gives rise to a new genre: the wounded warrior hero narrative of transcendence that is intertwined with the warrior Übermensch archetype. This includes Tony Mena's 2014 poetry collection, *The Shape of Our Faces No Longer Matters*. Mena was a Navy Corpsman (or medic) who spent six years with Special Operations, specifically units of Reconnaissance Marines, in various War on Terror deployments in Iraq. Based on his experiences treating wounded warriors, Mena's poetry takes the aforementioned protofascist signifying to the ultimate extreme in poems such as

"Ode to a Pineapple Grenade." In this poem, his occasional sardonic ambivalence about the ironies of war is eclipsed by his frequent fetishizing of weapons and combat, alongside hagiographies of dead soldiers. In poems such as "Lazy Days (Because Killing is the Easy Part)," he laments time spent on a base instead of on combat operations, noting:

> On these days we truly suffer;
> when our spear-tipped skill sets are not
> needed"   (2014, 27).

His poem, "Insurgent," is a unique dramatic dialogue with a corpse, which begins by naming what he yearns in the above poem: "I killed you this morning." He follows this provocative opening line with a faux expression of sympathy for the dead sixteen-year-old boy who he surmises had been driven to join the insurgency by Iraqi Police torture. Mena's fetish on death continues with his poetic persona noting:

> …The dull opaque color of your hip bone, visible
> through the infected hole left by the bullet, whispered
> you only had days to live…
> […]
> I didn't feel much
> of anything except burning curiosity. I wanted to unzip you and
> place pointy labeled flags into your organs. I needed to see
> if your eyes turned to bliss
> or fire.   (2014, 23)

It is unclear if Mena is speaking of actually shooting this insurgent or treating him afterward or both, or if this is merely an imagined scene. However, his medical and existentialist curiosity nonetheless devolves into a nonsecular speculation about whether or not this young boy is going to "hell" or "heaven." The poem's crescendo could be an allusion to questions about the relative merits of the US War on Terror invasions of Iraq and Afghanistan, with the uncertainty never determined as we do not know if the dead insurgent was rewarded with eternal bliss or punished in the fires of hell. But the poet's dispassionate clinical fetish on the grotesque details of his dead body overshadow this doubt. Moreover, in poems such as "Hero's Prayer," Mena catalogues the warrior Übermensche's ultimate desire:

> When it is my time, let me seep
> into the sand amidst a pile of enemies.   (2014, 17)

He adds a dose of battlefield humor that supports, rather than destabilizes, the warrior Übermensch ethos: "Do not let me die / from an incoming mortar round / as I jerk off in the porta-shitter" (2014, 17).

This desire to die in combat and become immortalized in marble, as Mena writes, also animates wounded warrior narratives by Latino soldiers in the War on Terror. These include mixed-heritage Puerto Rican and Cuban American US Army Sergeant Luis Carlos Montalván's *Until Tuesday: A Wounded Warrior and the Golden Retriever Who Saved Him* (2011), and US Army Special Forces Major and New Jersey-born Puerto Rican Iván Castro's and Jim De Felice's jointly authored *Fighting Blind: A Green Beret's Story of Extraordinary Courage* (2016). Both overtly reiterate that their wounds were suffered in combat. Castro's story as an athlete and enlisted soldier who becomes an officer and combat veteran during repeated War on Terror deployments, culminates in his debilitating battlefield injuries from enemy mortars. His subsequent physical scars and blindness ultimately confirm his warrior Übermensch transcendence-in-perpetual-progress. As a living embodiment of combat that shapes his new identity as a wounded warrior—which he defiantly and proudly displays in his postcombat activities as a marathon athlete— he is a paragon of the violentological subject.

In contrast to Castro's generally positive reception by a public weaned on a quarter century of War on Terror propaganda, Montalván's commanding officer, and soldiers from his unit, challenge his claims to entering the hallowed ranks of the combat veteran, wounded warrior, and warrior Übermensch. Montalván's representations and retorts nonetheless add necro-political texture to the wounded warrior permutation of the Soldado Razo.[13] While deployed as a US Army border guard between Syria and Iraq during the US invasion and occupation of that country, Montalván claims to have been stabbed by an insurgent. Other accounts, however, report he was poked with a pen by a truck driver who had been sleeping in his cab while waiting for a roadblock to clear when Montalván reached into the truck window to jar him awake. The driver apparently panicked and lunged at his US Army inquisitor out of fear he was being attacked. Montalván claims he fell off the truck and subsequently shot and killed his attacker, though other accounts identify another US Army soldier as the shooter. Despite these discrepancies, Montalván writes about the transcendent aspects of combat that anchor his claim to a wounded warrior subjectivity and entry into the warrior Übermensch archetype:

> A firefight is one of the most intense feelings in the world. It was only later that the weight of the encounter hit me, when the high was followed by the low, like the cold ashes after a fire burns off.
>
> And that's the contradiction of Iraq. For many of us, it was the greatest time of our lives. Iraq is the country where we found our purpose, where we did the work we are most proud of, and where we encountered people and places we can never leave behind.   (2011, 51)

Whether or not he experienced the violence he depicts and celebrates, Montalván's narrative corresponds with the combat action genre that reiterates both the obvious and the occluded: the violence of combat is always palpable, bloody, and lethal; but it also is empowering, purportedly ennobling, and mystically transcendent. For Montalván it also is symbolic. Violence becomes the horizon—and medium—to access his full potential as a human being, specifically the superhuman, and suprahuman, whose raison d'être is killing and dying in combat.

Third-Space Soldiering: Militarized Latina Feminist and Homonationalist Gay Latino Combat Memoir

The Special Forces and wounded warrior fetish on combat also animates War on Terror soldier life writing by Latina feminists and lesbian, gay, bisexual, transgender, queer (or questioning), intersexed, and nonbinary people (LGBTQI+). The small but growing number of these print and performative texts eschew the fatalism embedded in the warrior Übermensch paradigm, but they still invoke combat as a consciousness raising experience, avenue for civic empowerment, and self-actualization. It is a given that the long legacy of cis-gendered women's exclusion from the combat arms branches and specialties of the military is based on paternalist, sexist, and misogynist conceits. These discriminatory attitudes persist even after the ban on women in combat was formally lifted on January 1, 2016. This change came after large numbers of women soldiers in the US military already had been serving in combat zones—and being involved in combat—since at least the 1991 Persian Gulf War. In the introduction to their epochal 2008 coedited anthology, *Feminism and War: Confronting US Imperialism*, Robin Lee Riley, Chandra Talpade Mohanty, and Minnie Bruce Pratt pressure models of feminism that are intertwined with US warfare by asking:

> What are the implications of a US imperial state laying claim to women's liberation? What is the relation between this claim and resulting US foreign policy and military action? Did US intervention and invasion in fact result in liberation for women in Afghanistan and Iraq? What multiple meanings are embedded in the phrase "women's liberation"? (2008, 6)

These questions have their analogues regarding the concomitant exclusion of openly LGBTQI+ people from the US military, which similarly is based on static models of gender and sexuality, and outright homophobia. This ban was partially overturned by US President Bill Clinton's 1993 "Don't Ask, Don't Tell" policy, which allowed "homosexual" and "bisexual" people to serve in the military provided they not openly declare their sexuality.[14] In 2011, US President Barack Obama formally lifted the ban on openly LGBTQI+ service members, though succeeding US President Donald Trump refused to expand the inclusion to transgender soldiers. These circumscribed inclusions notwithstanding, the quarter century of challenges to these legalized segregations became entangled in the militarization of women's and LGBTQI+ people's citizenship. As discussed in Chapter 2, Jasbir Puar's neologism "homonationalism" refers to the "collusions between homosexuality and U.S. nationalism" (2007, 46), which circumscribes the value of inclusion in the nation-state, and undermines the liberatory potential of intersecting LGBTQI+ political movements. Even as integration certainly facilitates political and economic mobility, LGBTQI+ claims to empowerment and full enfranchisement as US nationalists, militarists, and imperialists are antithetical to supranational human rights paradigms, the bedrock of LGBTQI+ activism. Latina feminist and Latino gay male testimonial narratives from the War on Terror segue with these contradictory negotiations in equally complicated, and ultimately self-defeating ways through their vexed syntheses of militarized Latina feminist and homonationalist gay Latino violentologies.

Latina narratives from the War on Terror largely consist of interviews, oral histories, and combat chronicles in journals and anthologies, with no full-length memoirs, autobiographies, or *testimonios* in the first quarter century of the war. Within this circumscribed but still growing archive, Latina soldiers consistently propose contemporary military service as a pathway to full US citizenship rights, social and economic equity, and broader political empowerment. This ideological texture places them far outside the critiques of patriarchy and imperialism that distinguished some Chicana and Latina feminist writing in the last half of the twentieth century before the War on Terror. Indeed, unlike some third-wave Latina feminist cultural production, all extant Latina soldier War on Terror narratives disarticulate their critique of patriarchy from third-wave feminist critiques of US imperialism. The first published Latina soldier testimonials from the War on Terror militantly maintain women's right to participate in combat operations, which they frame as a feminist intervention into patriarchy. For instance, in the 2006 anthology, *What Was Asked of Us: An Oral History of the Iraq War by the Soldiers Who Fought It*, US Army Connecticut National Guard Military Police Sergeant Tania Quiñones, who identifies as "Hispanic," recalls:

> There were situations where because I'm female, I was told there were certain things I couldn't do. For instance, there was one time we had this big mission, and there was going to be a big raid to do. All we were going to do was security on the outside, because they were going to raid these couple of buildings looking for a key individual. They called our platoon in just to do the perimeter security. It was something we did all the time. These were Special Forces—American and from a couple of other countries—and they were dropping in from a helicopter and all that crap. When they saw us, they were pissed. There was only me and this other female, and they were complaining and said they were not going to do the mission, and they went on complaining... They said, We're not doing this mission with any girls on it. This is a high speed mission and da, da, da... We're not working with any females.
>
> We ended up doing it anyway. I just kind of laughed. I laughed it off.
>
> (2006, 69, ellipses in original)

Sergeant Quiñones's figural "laugh," of course, is embedded with deep scars from layers of discrimination codified in the military's ban on women in the combat arms branches of the military, which provides the all-important experience necessary for promotion to the upper echelons and correspondingly higher pay scales. Sergeant Quiñones's "laugh" also resonates as a satirical rebuke of patriarchy and masculinist models of soldiering. She uses the term "pissing contests," for example, to describe phallocentric soldier debates about "who does this better, who saw more bombed-out roads, who shot this person, who got in a lot of firefights" (2006, 69).

However, Sergeant Quiñones's defiant and insistent participation in the infamous house raids reveals important contradictions about the use of soldiering—and especially combat—as a Latina claim to full enfranchisement as a US Army soldier and citizen. These episodes have been internationally condemned for their frequent civilian casualties and outright massacres. So, despite Sergeant Quiñones's feminist critiques of phallocentric models of power, her defiant laugh also becomes an ominous and callous claim to a presumed counterpower that fails to acknowledge the civilian trauma through which it is actualized. It includes people ensnared within the lethal perimeter she helped form in one nighttime search for Iraqis and non-Iraqis the US military deemed to be insurgents and nonstate actor "enemy combatants" who are not protected by United Nations prisoner of war and antitorture protocols. In addition to the likely torture and possible murder of these arrested Iraqi's, and the ensuing civilian deaths, which include children, the combat action raids that Sergeant Quiñones facilitated also involve US soldier rapes of women who subsequently are murdered. One such incident is recounted in Brian De Palma's 2007 film *Redacted*, which is based on the 2006 US soldier gang rape of a fourteen-year old girl, and massacre of her family in the Iraqi village of Yusufiya, Iraq. Soldiers initially reported this incident as a battle with insurgents. A Mexican American—Sergeant Paul E. Cortez—was among the five US Army soldiers implicated in the crimes.

Ironically, Quiñones's rebellious though protofascist act, as well as her quasi-disidentificatory recollection of it, and strategically essentialist uses as a claim to feminist counterpower, segue with heteropatriarchy and US imperialism. Her circumscribed model of feminist soldiering demonstrates Cynthia Enloe's claim that the war in Iraq is a masculinist and fundamentally misogynist enterprise (2010). In stressing the war's negative impact on Iraqi and American women's lives, Enloe calls our attention to the tragic ironies of women's interpellation in warfare:

> Militaries have needed, and continue to need, some women to pro-
> vide commercialized sexual services to male soldiers, other women
> to commit themselves to marital fidelity in military families; simulta-
> neously, they need still other women to find economic security and
> maybe even pride in working for defense contractors. At times gov-
> ernments even need some civilian women to act as feminist lobbyists
> promoting women's right to serve in the state's military. (2000, xii)

Enloe ultimately proposes the militarization of women's lives from the suffrage movement to the present War on Terror as fundamentally antifeminist:

> Militarized officials need women themselves to nurture the boundar-
> ies that separate them from one another. Militaries have counted on
> military officers' wives to look down on the wives of enlisted men,
> and on all military wives to look down on women working in the
> discos around a military base. Militarized civilian officials have
> needed women raped by other regimes' soldiers to remain suspicious
> of antiwar women and, instead, to be willing to serve as nationalist
> symbols. Militaries have depended on women soldiers who imagine
> their service to be superior to that of both wives and prostitutes, and
> even of military nurses.   (2000, xiii)

The paradigm of the citizen soldier, and illusions of feminist soldiering that Sergeant Quiñones promotes, thus actually interpellate
Latinas within a heteropatriarchal and concomitantly imperialist
episteme, however provisionally empowering these avenues may be.

Moreover, Sergeant Quiñones's claim to empowerment through
military service—especially combat—participates in weaponizing
her model of feminism to the point it becomes protofascist. Sergeant
Quiñones's articulation of her Latina soldier subjectivity onto a
Special Forces combat operation, for instance, enables an intrusion
of male protofascist military subculture into her feminist signifying
and extratextual agency. But the opposite is not true; that is, her feminism does not change the operation or its broader resonance.
Sergeant Quiñones makes a point at "laughing" in the face of death,
and mocks the sexist male insistence that the morbid realm of
combat remain male territory. In the process, she approximates a

feminist variation of the warrior Übermensch delineated above. As Sergeant Quiñones narrates, her embrace of danger and the nonchalant tone of her discussion about the possibility of death in combat has an important civic aim, but also carries a mystical transcendent quality: Special Forces combat operations will facilitate her full enfranchisement as a US citizen, and a woman. Moreover, this experience will transform her into a combat veteran who faced danger and death, and presumably became a superior type of human because of it; or, at the very least, it leveled the terrain by rendering the Special Forces soldiers as equal to her, and vice versa.

Ironically, even purportedly critical Latina life writing framed as a form of third-space soldiering inevitably is intertwined with imperialist ends. For instance, in *Winter Soldiers: Iraq and Afghanistan: Eyewitness Accounts of the Occupations*, the 2008 inaugural publication by the War on Terror's analogue to the Vietnam Veterans Against the War, US Army Reserve Combat Medic Specialist Wendy Barranco critiques the masculinist culture of sexual harassment in the military for ruining her "patriotic" attempt to "do something for my country" (2008, 129). Similar to Sergeant Tania Quiñones's critique of the masculinist fetish on combat zone violence that she appropriates and intertwines with her combat feminism, Specialist Barranco performs her self-actualization and career advancement as "patriotic" service in the US military. For her, the war, and its broader global political context, are mere background to the subaltern Latina-cum-imperialist feminist.

Despite Specialist Barranco's attempt to deploy soldiering and warfighting as feminist agency, Marian Eide (2008) argues that these militarized models of women's citizenship undermine efforts to transform society along feminist principles. Instead of serving as a point of departure for actualizing alternative, pacifist, and potentially revolutionary models of feminist citizenship outside patriarchal martial models of womanhood, feminists from various racial and ethnic backgrounds—including Latinas—have been co-opted within the "just war," or *jus ad bellum* framework. This discourse has existed for millennia, and its more contemporary distillation includes seven general criteria: "just cause, right authority, right intention, the goal of peace, overall proportionality of good over evil, last resort, and reasonable hope of success" (Brahimi 2010, 22). United States President George W. Bush invoked this concept to justify the US invasion of predominantly Muslim countries after the September 11,

2001, attacks, orchestrated from Afghanistan, against US symbols of imperialist power. Like Iran during the 1979–1981 hostage crisis, Afghanistan conveniently became the quintessential space of women's subjugation in the Western imagination, as the aforementioned concept of "Feminist Orientalism" alludes. The false idea that a heteropatriarchal society such as the United States can "liberate" Muslim women from similar heteropatriarchal oppression, while also serving as a venue for US women's upward mobility, subsequently was folded into the War on Terror's "just war" rationale. Noting that "war and its aftermath still disproportionately affect women and children" (2008, 59), Eide proposes an alternative:

> A feminist just war theory can thus take its point of departure both from a strong commitment to justice after war and also a freedom from the "stigma of nation." [...] I am arguing that the idea of country requires radical reconsideration, and at a moment when women have increasing access to the privileges of country, we might employ our remaining virtues of "poverty, chastity, derision, and freedom from unreal loyalties" to disabuse ourselves of the validity of this category as anything but an abstract excuse for going to war. In the place of country, feminist just war might consider a more cosmopolitan set of allegiances among peoples free of the "stigma of nation." (2008, 59)

The renowned and provocative Cuban American performance artist Coco Fusco, whose soldier brother died in a secret US Army Special Forces mission in Latin America, reiterates Eide's lament over the nation-state's co-optation of feminism:

> The more access American women have to the exercise of political power and the use of deadly force in war, the more apparent it becomes that we aren't using it very differently from men. Furthermore, our status as minorities in public office and as relative newcomers in government and military duty, and the persistence of prejudice and sexual harassment to which we are subject, don't seem to deter us from advocating and partaking in violence against the enemy. (2008, 18)

She thus provides a sobering counterpoint to the militarized feminist agency that Sergeant Quiñones and Specialist Barranco propose, which ultimately reinforces the power of patriarchy in the guise of challenging it.

Significantly, Fusco's critique, and related Latina civilian opposition to domestic and international dimensions of the War on Terror, as well as Latina/o soldier and veteran politics across the ideological spectrum, cumulatively reflect a dissensus in Latina/o Studies regarding the material benefits and ideological significance of Latina and Latina/o LGBTQI+ service in the US military. Adding to the complexity of this matter, US Army veteran Dolores Mondragon complemented her archaeology of the first woman soldier killed in combat in the War on Terror invasion of Iraq—mixed-heritage Hopi and Mexican American US Army Specialist Lori Ann Piestewa— with an itemization of the financial benefits military service affords women. This includes increased earning power for Latinas in the military that exceeds that of civilian Latino males. This earning power, however, comes with a terrible price: according to Kirby Dick's 2012 documentary film, *The Invisible War*:

> the Department of Defense estimates there were a staggering 22,800 violent sex crimes in the military in 2011. Among all active-duty female soldiers, 20 percent are sexually assaulted. Female soldiers age 18 to 21 accounted for more than half of the victims.   (n.p.)

By some estimates, the rate of sexual assaults of women soldiers is ten percent higher than in civilian contexts.[15] Significantly, almost all perpetrators are US military personnel, that is, their fellow soldiers.

Equally as provocative, Mexican American Steven Rosales, a twenty-eight-year veteran and current officer in the US Navy Reserve, extolls Latino soldier agency and relative empowerment within the military's otherwise masculinist and homophobic culture at the 2012 National Association for Chicana and Chicano Studies (NACCS). In his 2017 book on the topic, Rosales interviewed Latino veterans from WWII, the Korean War, and the US war in Vietnam to describe their varied navigations of gender and sexuality that alternately reinforced and pressured static models of Latino masculinity. He adds that these soldiers vacillate from disillusion to satisfaction with the military's promise of civic and economic upward mobility, which for him is fulfilling and continues into the War on Terror. Significantly, as a current US military officer, Rosales's membership in a Chicana/o Studies academic association whose foundation is based on contrapuntal assessments of US institutions and society, along with the coterminous consolidation of an oppositional Chicana/o consciousness, radically alters the ideological tenor of the field of Chicana/o and Latina/o Studies. Moreover, Rosales embodies and performs the field's hegemonic turn. Indeed, despite his stated intent to avoid adding to Latino soldier hagiographies, Rosales performs a *faux* critique that adds to celebratory accounts of Latina/o soldiers: he illustrates Latino soldier resilience in racist, sexist, and homophobic contexts, but fails to present broader geopolitical contextualization and ideological analysis of how this purportedly contrapuntal soldiering inevitably is folded into US imperialism.[16]

As I have noted elsewhere (Olguín, 2002), self-identified gay Mexican American US Army First Sergeant José M. Zuñiga's narrativization of his efforts to lift the ban on LGBTQI+ soldiers similarly collapses his otherwise proactive intervention into the US imperialist project. A decorated combat medic who served in the 1991 Persian Gulf War in Iraq, Zuñiga used his combat veteran status and subsequent designation as the 1992 US Army Soldier of the Year to come out as gay in a strategic effort to end the ban on LGBTQI+ people in the military pursuant to their full enfranchisement as US citizens. Dramatizing the ideological dimensions of the Latina/o Studies dissensus discussed above, Zuñiga alternately is ignored or denigrated for being gay, lauded and critiqued for privileging LGBTQI+ civil rights over human rights, and dismissed for not extending his intervention into heteropatriarchy toward a stronger critique of US militarism and imperialism. As noted in Chapter 2, Jasbir Puar (2007) has coined "homonationalism" to challenge Zuñiga's type of strategic alignment of LGBTQI+ activism with US imperialist patriotism (Puar 2007, xxiv). A similar confluence occurs in coterminous political movements such as the struggle to legalize gay marriage. This effort sought to normalize queerness in relation to heteropatriarchal social institutions as a strategy for entering into the US mainstream. It inevitably succeeded, albeit by ceding authority to the state to determine social relations. All these efforts, Puar emphasizes, are self-defeating as they undermine the oppositional ethics of LGBTQI+ movements predicated upon universal human rights. Myopic and chauvinistic national civil rights politics ultimately coexists alongside, and even legitimates US militarism and imperialism. That Latina feminist and Latina/o LGBTQI+ agency is intertwined with hegemony ultimately demands a more critical and complex understanding of Latina/o ideologies, which are fundamentally plural.

Openly gay Mexican American US Marine Eric Fidelis Alva, the first US military service member wounded in the 2003 US War on Terror invasion of Iraq, also sought to deploy a militarized model of self-actualization and patriotic claims to mainstream sameness in his aborted memoir, *Once a Marine: Coming Out Under Fire*. In 2010, Alva canceled the contract to publish his memoir after editorial disagreements with cowriter journalist Sam Gallegos, whom Alva accused of embellishing his story to emphasize homoerotic scenes that were false, stereotypical, and gratuitously salacious (2012, n.p.) (Figure 5.1). But he nonetheless continues intertwining his gay Latino subjectivity with his identity as a US citizen and former Marine in ongoing activism. Sergeant Alva's homonationalist agency, which includes numerous public-speaking engagements and participation in LGBTQI+ community-based events, also presents a gay Latino permutation of the wounded warrior archetype discussed earlier, though his discourse is noticeably missing the protofascist warrior Übermensch dimension. After stepping on a land mine during his unit's overland invasion of Iraq from Kuwait, Alva lost part of his right leg and suffered partial paralysis to his right arm and hand. He subsequently received an honorable medical discharge from the US Marine Corps. In a common refrain among racial minority veterans,

FIGURE 5.1. Once a Marine: Coming Out Under Fire *(n.d.), by Eric Fidelis Alva with Sam Gallegos. Courtesy of Eric Fidelis Alva.*

Sergeant Alva insists that his physical losses and related trauma are sacrifices that have earned his full enfranchisement as a US citizen.

After his separation from the US military, Alva publicly identified as gay, which he maintains was already known by several fellow US Marines. Similar to Navy Specialist Keith Meinhold's and Sergeant José Zuñiga's use of their distinguished military service records to advocate lifting the ban on openly gay soldiers in the US military, Sergeant Alva remains adamant that his service—and status as a wounded combat veteran and US Marine—underscore his patriotism as a citizen soldier (Figure 5.2). In Michael Rowe's front-page article of the July 3, 2007, issue of the LGBTQI+ magazine, *The Advocate*, Alva underscores these intertwined aspects of his identity and agency:

> Silence gives consent...On the battlefield they put our fingers behind the trigger, but when we come home we don't have the same rights as the rest of America...I'm speaking for all of us now. I'm standing on two strong legs, and I will be heard.   (2007, 35)

In an August 12, 2012, interview in San Antonio, Texas, before the wave of statutory legal rulings eliminating the ban on gay marriage

FIGURES 5.2. *Cover story of the July 3, 2007, issue of* The Advocate *featuring interview with Eric Fidelis Alva. Courtesy of Eric Fidelis Alva.*

FIGURE 5.3. *United States Marine Corps Staff Sergeant Eric Fidelis Alva in the* Heroes and Heritage Award Ceremony *with US Marine Corps General Christopher Cortez, 2003. Courtesy of Eric Fidelis Alva.*

in some states, Sergeant Alva reiterated a frustrating irony: "I have a purple heart but I can't get married because I am a gay man, but people who break the law like the [Charles] Manson murderers can get married" (2012, n.p.). Yet, he insists "no new political system is necessary: democracy works" (2012, n.p.). Dismissing another set of ironies, he reiterates his claim to inclusion—and interpellation within empire—through reference to multiple exclusions that required his combat, and combat injuries, as evidence of his civic legitimacy (Figure 5.3).

Militarized Spiritual Mestizajes in Latino Conscientious Objector Memoir

The Special Forces, wounded warrior, heteropatriarchal feminist, and homonational gay combat-actualization narratives examined thus far confirm that the wide range of War on Terror Latina/o life-writing genres share a common US imperialist trajectory. Ironically, these overlapping martial discourses also intersect with their purported antithesis: the Latina/o War on Terror conscientious objector narrative. This confluence signals important ideological contradictions in this latest permutation of the four-century-old pacifist genre. Since seventeenth-century English Quaker Thomas Lurting's 1710 *The Fighting Sailor Turn'd Peaceable Christian*, the first Western conscientious objector memoir by a combat soldier-turned-pacifist, this antiwar genre has been ideologically and spiritually inchoate.[17] This ambivalence extends to conscientious objector narratives published during the War on Terror by two of the seven Latina/o conscientious objectors. Former US Army Reserve Master Sergeant and mechanic Aidan Delgado, the affluent Cuban American son of a US diplomat, authored the 2007 memoir, *The Sutras of Abu Ghraib: Notes from a Conscientious Objector in Iraq.* In the same year, former US Army National Guard Infantry Staff Sergeant Camilo Mejía, the once-affluent son of a Nicaraguan father and Costa Rican mother who were Sandinista government officials but whose divorce changed the mother's and son's fortunes, authored *The Road from Ar Ramadi: The Private Rebellion of Sergeant Camilo Mejía—An Iraq War Memoir.*

Delgado and Mejía present intersecting but diverging genealogies and formative global childhood migrations that further relocate Latinidades outside familiar geographic and conceptual landscapes: Mejía moves from Nicaragua to Costa Rica, then to Spanish Harlem in New York City, and finally to Miami; Delgado migrates from Miami to Egypt, Thailand, and Senegal, then back to Miami. While their efforts to be classified as conscientious objectors involve provisionally post-Western, postracial, supranational, and nonsecular Latinidades, their distinct conscientious objector subjectivities inadvertently degenerate into protoimperialist formations. For them, race, ethnicity, and nationality are continually placed under erasure by spirituality and religion, yet their identities remain always already imprinted— and undergirded—with layers of violence, even as they eschew it. Delgado's practice as a Buddhist, and Mejía's processual evolution from an atheist to a Catholic liberation theologian to a quasi-ecumenical pacifist inspired by Islam, ambivalently disrupt, but simultaneously reiterate, the hegemonic militarization of Latinidades—as well as their proposed pacifist antitheses—in the War on Terror.

Mejía and Delgado are part of a long, if little known, history of conscientious objectors in the United States. The relatively high number of US conscientious objectors and broader rebellions of entire military units in the War on Terror has been underreported. Between 2002 and 2006—the height of the War on Terror—425 conscientious objector applications were processed, with 224 (53 percent) approved, 188 (44 percent) denied, and the rest unresolved at the time. An unknown number of soldiers were Absent Without Official Leave (AWOL), and were classified as deserters, though throughout the US history of warfare, many of these purported "deserters" identified their rationale in ways that segue with definitions of conscientious objectors, particularly opposition to all war, killing, and violence in general. During the War on Terror, at least seven Latina/os are among the US soldiers who formally declared themselves conscientious objectors and subsequently refused to bear arms, return to the battlefield, or reboard their US Naval vessels.[18] In this war, Sergeant Delgado is the only Latina/o granted conscientious objector status. More importantly, Sergeant Delgado and Sergeant Mejía diverge from preceding Latino conscientious objectors such as Carlos Córtez, a former member of the Socialist Party and later a decades-long militant in the International Workers of the World (or "Wobblies"). As discussed in Chapter 2, Córtez refused induction into the US military during WWII not out of pacifist convictions but out of a Marxist critique of capitalism and competing imperialisms. He further distinguished his conscientious objector stance as *non*pacifist, emphasizing that he refused to shoot another draftee, but would volunteer for military service if guaranteed an opportunity to shoot Adolf Hitler "or any other head of state," which presumably included the US president (2004, n.p.). United States Army Sergeants Delgado and Mejía, on the other hand, are driven by a qualified pacifist ethic decidedly less materialist, and very far removed from leftist politics, despite their rhetoric. Sergeant Mejía, for instance, calls the war "a criminal, illegitimate war for empire" (2007, 230), particularly "money" and "oil" (2007, 240, 250). Sergeant Delgado notes that the war is infused with "racist," "anti-Arab" and "anti-Muslim" sentiments among the rank-and-file soldiers (qtd. in Rockwell 2005, n.p.). Yet, both narratives also reveal their dissent to be based on personal religious beliefs they frame as *individual* struggles for spiritual transcendence, and not necessarily collectivist or antiimperialist, much less leftist revolutionary paradigms.

Sergeant Mejía's narrative, for instance, vacillates between the collectivist antiimperialist *testimonio* and individualist neo-Orientalist self-actualization memoir discussed in Chapter 3. Following the

Sandinista electoral defeat in 1990, which resulted in the loss of his privileged status as the son of Nicaraguan government officials, replete with chauffeurs and maids, the teenaged Mejía migrated with his mother to Miami. His mother eked out a living as a grocery store cashier while he worked at fast food restaurants and attended night school. With few options following his unceremonious high school graduation, Mejía became an "economic draftee" at nineteen, enlisting in the US Army with plans to use the military to fund his college education. Several months before he was to complete his final commitment in a US Army Florida National Guard unit, infantry Sergeant Mejía was caught in one of US President George W. Bush's "Stop Loss" orders that extended all military enlistments and officer commissions.

Subsequently deployed to Iraq, Sergeant Mejía became directly involved in the abuse of Iraqi prisoners, which included sleep deprivation, beatings, and mock executions. He also claims to have engaged in combat actions that resulted in civilian deaths. These experiences added to a burgeoning unease over his role as a US soldier participating in the occupation of a foreign country, especially given his family's Sandinista roots. The growing dissonance led Sergeant Mejía to dissent and rebel. He complained to military superiors about illegal or illogical orders and operations, and engaged in subtly subversive acts to keep his unit away from harm.

Sergeant Mejía eventually encountered an Iraqi geologist, Mohammed, who had been reduced to working as a propane gas station attendant after the US invasion devastated the Iraqi economy. His new acquaintance shared Islam's message of universal justice and peace, which awakened dormant Catholic liberation theology lessons Sergeant Mejía learned from Jesuit priests in Sandinista Nicaragua. "It was there that I discovered that Muslims have a deep respect for Jesus, not as the Messiah, but certainly as a valued prophet" (2007, 130), he recalls of this transformative moment. After Mohammed provocatively asks, "how can you bring freedom to us, when you don't have freedom for yourselves?" (2007, 134), Sergeant Mejía's feeble attempts to rationalize his complicity in the War on Terror as the result of his limited choices as a nineteen-year-old Army enlistee immediately led to an epiphany:

> I know that, in the end, no one could force me to do anything I didn't want to do. I knew that I could say no to keeping prisoners on sleep deprivation, and to blocking ambulances on their way to the hospital.

> I could say no to senseless missions that put the lives of both soldiers
> and innocent civilians in unnecessary danger. I could assert my free-
> dom and say no.   (2007, 134)

Sergeant Mejía consummated his personal and spiritual transformation by participating in a mass baptism. "I came to be baptized in the
waters of the biblical Euphrates" (2007, 139), he writes, adding that a
US Army chaplain performed the ceremony. This ironic collusion of
the US Army with his newfound pacifist consciousness resonates
throughout Sergeant Mejía's memoir, and eventually undermines its
oppositional potential.

This wayward soldier delivers his religious conversion in a sincere
and self-critical narrative that approximates *autocrítica* and *concientización*, the hallmarks of *testimonio*.[19] Yet, Sergeant Mejía's narrative, which he deliberately and appropriately subtitles a "memoir"
and not a *testimonio*, degenerates into a wartime permutation of the
bildungsromanesque self-actualization narrative. In Sergeant Mejía's
life writing, his individual transcendence is paramount, even as it is
different from the protofascist combat action narratives discussed
earlier. Indeed, throughout his book, Sergeant Mejía depicts freedom as an individual rather than a collective act. For instance, he
punctuates his memoir's dénouement with a proclamation that the
moment he was handcuffed and escorted to prison after his military
court-martial trial and sentencing, "I was free, in a way I had never
been before" (2007, 300). Sergeant Mejía makes a good faith attempt
to extend his epiphany beyond individual "healing" by proposing his
book as an intervention "at the community level, where grassroots
activists battle against a system that refuses to place human interest
above profit and that feeds on poverty and disadvantage to fill the
ranks of its military" (2007, xx). Yet, he recenters his conscientious
objector narrative as a "patriotic" critique similar to other Latina/o
soldiers such as US Army Specialist Wendy Barranco (2008). For
example, Sergeant Mejía and his attorneys assert that he is a "good
soldier," "good squad leader," and the embodiment of "the core and
the fundamental values of the United States Army" (2007, 296).
These claims situate *The Road from Ar Ramadi* far outside the antiimperialist imperatives that animate *testimonio*, the genre that frequently, but incorrectly is used to describe this book.

Most troubling, Sergeant Mejía's narrative projects a neo-Orientalist
fetish, which further complicates Latina/o engagements with Islam
discussed in Chapter 3. This gaze upon an exoticized Middle Eastern

Other both undermines and propels the otherwise provocative supranational dimensions of his narrative. Having noted that "the Virgin Mary is not only esteemed" in Islam, "but also considered a good example of behavior and devotion to God for Muslim women to emulate" (2007, 130), for instance, Sergeant Mejía intersperses his account of spiritual transformation with masculinist recollections of "being captivated" by a female bank cashier in Iraq. He fixates on her "intense" and "enchanting eyes," adding "the rest had to be suggested by what few lines her green and black dress allowed my fantasy to work with" (2007, 135). Sergeant Mejía fantasizes about marrying this woman, noting that she "made me wonder what it would be like to move to Iraq and fully embrace the culture." He adds:

> Of course I would have to be a Muslim in order to have a chance with her family, but wasn't our God the same God? The God of Abraham? I was going crazy and I had to stop looking at her. I had been in Iraq too long. But those Eyes! (2007, 135)

This exoticist cross-cultural identification scene also segues with Sergeant Mejía's nascent fatalism about his predicament, which he tries to fight. He thus introduces the motif of the Western imperialist male soldier who goes native at the edge of civilization, with his wanton abandonment—usually coupled with sexual desire—birthing a new self.

Significantly, Sergeant Mejía's exoticist Western male gaze intersects with the religious conviction that enables his transformation into a conscientious objector. Soon after his identification with this Arab Muslim female Other, Sergeant Mejía writes, "I started commending my body and soul to God every day" (2007, 139). He adds that his nightly prayers became transformative and transcendent:

> Before and after every mission, and before going to sleep, I would always say a little prayer. At first it was a simple request for God to let me see my daughter, Samantha, one more time. As time went by, however, I widened my prayers to ask for the safety and well being of the soldiers in my unit, and then I started praying for all the soldiers in Iraq and their families. Before long I was praying for the families of the Iraqis we killed during our missions. And then one day I realized I was even praying for our enemies, and for an end to violence in Iraq, and then for an end to all war. (2007, 139)

Sergeant Mejía's ever-widening circle of prayer leads him to go AWOL: following a short furlough from the battlefield to travel to the US to address his legal residency status, he deliberately missed his flight back to Iraq. The US Army rejected his conscientious objector application, which involved an eclectic invocation of his dual Costa Rican and Nicaraguan citizenship, international law, and claims to being a model soldier. Despite this convoluted rhetoric, and neo-Orientalist signifying that renders his narrative a faux-*testimonio*, Sergeant Mejía succeeds at recentering spirituality—and a distinctly Latina/o fusion of Islam-influenced Catholicism—as the defining aspect of his immanently postnational and supraterrestrial Latinidad. But his distinct (anti)Soldado Razo subjectivity is nonetheless inextricable from conflicting layers of imperialist violence and ambivalently antiimperialist pacifism. His convoluted negotiations fail, and he was convicted of desertion and sentenced to one year of confinement on a military base, reduction to the rank of private, and a Bad Conduct Discharge that makes him ineligible for any veteran's benefits.

In contrast to Mejía's ecumenical Catholic- and Muslim-based spiritual transformation, and the broader Christian cultural context that predominates among Latina/os, US Army Sergeant Aidan Delgado's identification as a Buddhist introduces geocultural and transspiritual displacements that offer new opportunities for theorizing Latinidad beyond common Abrahamic religious frameworks. But similar to Sergeant Mejía's failures, Sergeant Delgado's otherwise productive transversalism is insufficient to rescue his conscientious objector memoir from its protoimperialist resonance. As noted in Chapters 2 and 3, much of the scholarship on Latina/o-Asian encounters celebrates Mexican American and broader Latina/o identifications with various Asian peoples, places, and cultural practices. This effaces the intense hostility that oftentimes shape their wartime and "peacetime" encounters. Paradoxically, Sergeant Delgado's attempt to reject the violence of these contact zones through his formal conscientious objector appeal, inevitably accentuates it.

Sergeant Delgado predicates his transversal LatinAsian fusion upon a transglobal childhood as the son of a US diplomat, which included seven years in Thailand, four years in Senegal, and seven years in Egypt, where he learned Arabic. His global migrations culminated with a return to the US in his early twenties to attend college in

Florida, which he left to join the US Army amid a period of young adult anomie. Zemblanitiously, he enlisted on September 11, 2001, before learning of the attacks. This act amplifies his sense of being an outsider:

> Now that I'm in the U.S. Army, listening to the trash talk of the 320th,
> I feel more and more like a foreigner. By the time I came to America
> I had lived for eighteen years in other countries.   (Delgado 2007, 73)

Sergeant Delgado recounts his subsequent ethical dilemma in his aesthetically accomplished 2007 memoir, *The Sutras of Abu Ghraib: Notes from a Conscientious Objector in Iraq*. The title dissonantly pairs the Buddhist term for spiritual aphorisms with the name of a notorious prison, which models his proto-Buddhist yet still neo-Orientalist poetic. Assigned to a military police unit, Sergeant Delgado alternately worked as a vehicle mechanic, a translator on reconnais-sance patrols, and a prisoner guard in various locations, including the infamous Abu Ghraib Prison. Like Sergeant Mejía, Sergeant Delgado's decision to declare himself a conscientious objector arose from the shock of recognizing his complicity in various atrocities, including being photographed next to a dead Iraqi prisoner. He also took photos of a smiling fellow US soldier who was cradling a human skull at the site of a recently uncovered mass grave (Delgado 2007, 77). Sergeant Delgado ultimately comes to understand the War on Terror atrocities in Afghanistan and Iraq in terms of the temporal nature of hell in Buddhist thought, concluding that "I have helped bring a little piece of hell to earth" (2007, 86).

Reminiscent of Sergeant Mejía's experience, Sergeant Delgado's decision to declare himself a conscientious objector also involves an encounter with Islam, which began in his childhood. He notes that soldiers in his unit considered the muezzin's echoing voice and Arabic call to prayer, or *Adhan*, to be ominous reminders of their status as hated Western Christian occupiers. For Sergeant Delgado, however, the echoing call from mosque minarets five times a day became a cross-cultural spiritual axis conjuring fond memories of his residency in Egypt. He received the *Adhan* as a reminder of the universality of human spirituality, which transcends nations, eth-nicities, and race. Unparalleled in the annals of Latina/o war litera-ture, Sergeant Delgado models an eclectic spirituality that extends the broader Latina/o community's increased diversification away from still-dominant Christian sects. In this new spiritual terrain, Buddhism and Islam are becoming important touchstones for new models of Latinidad that require new theoretical frameworks.

Sergeant Delgado's decision to file for conscientious objector status from the battlefield, and attendant framing of his pacifism as "patriotic," signals the hegemonic resonance of his conscientious objector identity: even more so than Sergeant Mejía, Sergeant Delgado claims the role of the patriotic critic who merely seeks to curb the excesses of imperialism without questioning its legitimacy. "The last thing I want to be is disloyal," he recalls telling members of his unit. "I'm not a traitor and I'm not a coward," he continues. He adds, "I want to help the unit.... I'll go on missions, I'll be a mechanic, I'll translate." Revealingly, Sergeant Delgado concludes: "I can still be an asset to the company" (2007, 102). This circumscription of his purported lifelong outsider status in which he perceived everyone as an "enemy" (2007, 49), reduces his conscientious objector identity to little more than complicit liminality: his more or less de-militarized Latina/o Buddhist identity consequently becomes another hegemonic mestizaje even as it extends farther geographically than most topographies of Latina/o spiritualities. Thus, while Sergeant Delgado's Latinidad is highly nuanced and globalized, it is no less imperialist than the War on Terror supra-Latina/o violentologies discussed above. Indeed, despite his Buddhist allegiances, Sergeant Delgado infuses his new supra-Latinidad with multiple violences, going so far as to pledge his continued support of the United States' imperialist occupation of Iraq. The US Army's eventual approval of Sergeant Delgado's application for conscientious objector status subsequently endows his new "pacifist" Buddhist Latino identity with the imprimatur of militarized imperialist legitimacy (2007, 215). This is complemented by the imprisonment of other Latina/o conscientious objectors, whose own legal and public discourse about their decisions is equally vexed, and vexing, for their variously ambivalent dislocations and reiterations of their relationship to the US polis.

Islamophobia, Neo-Crusade Logic, and Fascist Pleasure in Latino Military Command Memoir and Spy Narratives

In contradistinction to Mejía's and Delgado's attempts to humanize Muslims and Iraqis of all faiths in their otherwise imperialist conscientious objector memoirs, US War on Terror political reportage frequently depicts Muslims as ignorant, uncivilized, and pathological. These neo-Orientalist stereotypes distinguish the War on Terror from its inception, which former US President George W. Bush initially proposed as "this crusade," invoking the legacy of Western religious-based imperialism from the eleventh century.[20] War on Terror Christian eschatological proselytizing in US military academies accentuate this Manichaean binary by emphasizing the superiority, and presumed preordained victory, of Christianity over Islam.[21] This ideology occupies a prominent space in War on Terror life writing, particularly by Latina/os. Indeed, the great majority of War on Terror Latina/o soldier and paramilitary narratives is mired in imperialist neo-Crusade and neo-Orientalist poetics. This is especially true of Latino military command memoirs by officers, as well as paramilitary Latino spy narratives. Their gnosis of violence and corresponding praxis transform their otherwise pedestrian imperialist sentiments into a far more significant and troubling set of supra-Latina/o violentologies.

For instance, US Marine Corps Reserve Captain Eric Navarro's 2008 combat command memoir, *God Willing: My Wild Ride with the New Iraqi Army*, extends the overarching Orientalist and Islamophobic rhetoric shaping the US War on Terror by positing Islam as incompatible with modernity. Now a Lieutenant Colonel, then Captain Navarro's memoir focuses on his first of two combat deployments in Iraq, where he was part of an understaffed and underequipped unit sent to train what he represents as an undisciplined "ragtag" group of Iraqi recruits the US sought to forge into an allied fighting force (2008, 116). His narrative immediately degenerates into an extended neo-Orientalist explication of the Arabic term "Inshallah," a secular idiomatic expression and refrain among Muslims that translates as "God willing." The first clause of the book's title—"God Willing"—suggests that Captain Navarro is aware this expression is common among Latina/o Catholics in the form of "*Ojalá*" (an eighth-century Arabic migration to Castilian) and the analogous Spanish phrase, "*Si Dios quiere*." Yet, he claims this phrase demonstrates Muslims to be inherently passive, and incapable of self-governance. Ignorant of the Western European Renaissance's debt to Muslim philosophers, artists, and scientists, Captain Navarro reaffirms this cultural imperialist chauvinism by recounting a dispute between an Iraqi soldier and a US Marine, with the latter noting:

> I am a major in the U.S. Marine Corps. I have a master's degree in applied mathematics. You, on the other hand, wipe your ass with your own hand!   (2008, 260)

As with many preceding episodes, this dialogue is delivered in a deadpan scatological description intended to serve as humor. Characteristic of combat narratives, this battlefield humor also informs Captain Navarro's bigoted binary characterizations of Iraqi males as effeminate, sexually repressed, latently homosexual (a liability in his view), and childlike imps who possess a lethal character flaw: an Islamic faith that purportedly renders them inherently passive, thereby legitimating their subordination. Despite recounting the senior officer's claim to the scientific method, Captain Navarro is unconcerned with a scientific or historical materialist analysis of third world underdevelopment that would reveal the link to Western colonialist and imperialist military interventions, and resulting scarcities. Instead, he concludes the narrative with a Western imperialist tautology: "the major was right—Iraqis did not use toilet paper" (2008, 260).

Lieutenant General Ricardo Sánchez—the highest-ranking Latina/o officer in the history of the US military up to the War on Terror—extends this neo-Orientalist, neo-Crusades signifying in his contemporaneous 2008 military command memoir, *Wiser in Battle: A Soldier's Story*. In this book, he presents an officer's permutation of the Soldado Razo as the archetypal Christian soldier. General Sánchez is infamous for his role as the commanding officer of all US troops in Iraq during the 2004 Abu Ghraib prisoner abuse scandal, in which US soldiers, CIA officers, and civilian contractors engaged in wanton beatings, physical mutilations, sexual humiliations, and other forms of torture and outright murder of Iraqi and multiethnic and multinational Muslim detainees. In his memoir, which betrays the defensive tone of public relations spin-doctoring and legal defense strategy, General Sánchez insists that he is not responsible for these or other US abuses during the US invasion and occupation of Iraq. In an astonishing rhetorical move, he even glosses the conscientious objector narratives discussed above through biting critiques of US President Bush's "rush to war in Iraq" (2008, 155), a phrase that forms the title of one chapter. Furthermore, despite having signed documents authorizing the use of "environmental manipulation," such as the use of extreme temperatures and foul smells to "soften up" prisoners in preparation for their interrogation, General Sánchez claims he was opposed to the US president's dismissal of the Geneva Conventions protocols outlining the treatment of prisoners of war (Sánchez 2003, n.p.).[22] The US Army cleared General Sánchez of any culpability in the prisoner abuse scandal, freeing him from the prosecution levied upon lower-ranking officers, especially Appalachian working-class enlisted women soldiers who took the brunt of the blame and punishment. The scandal nonetheless effectively ended General Sánchez's career. The US Army withdrew his nomination for a promotion to Full General (signified by four stars) soon after "Abu Ghraib" became synonymous with US torture and its occupation of Iraq. In a 2011 *Atlantic Magazine* report, David Freed notes that after General Sánchez's forced retirement, fellow senior military officers further vilified him for proposing a "truth commission" about the Iraq War, and for emphasizing "if we do not find out what happened we are doomed to repeat it" (qtd. in Freed 2011, 20, 22).

In Freed's profile, which bears the subtitle, "The ex-commander of troops in Iraq thinks some of his superiors should go to hell," General Sánchez offers a religious rationale for his ironic postwar call for accountability: "as a Christian, I must do what's right regardless of what my personal consequences are" (Freed 2011, 22). He invokes his Christian faith throughout the memoir, imbuing it with a missionary zeal that distinguishes his imperialist, theologically based warrior subjectivity. General Sánchez's nonsecular Latinidad is the antithesis of the antiimperialist liberation theologies of Lolita Lebrón and Rafael Cancel Miranda discussed in Chapter 4, though it segues with the theologically based de facto imperialist conscientious objector narratives of his former subordinates Sergeants Aidan Delgado and Camilo Mejía. For instance, whenever General Sánchez recounts a trying life experience or seminal moment in his military career and combat experiences, he cites the martial passage from the biblical old testament Psalm 144:

> Praise be to the Lord, my rock,
> who trains my hands for war,
> my fingers for battle.
> He is my Loving God and my Fortress.

This militarized religious subtext reasserts the Christian vectors of his Mexican American identity, and it triangulates race, religion, and warfare as he repeatedly inserts this passage amid his accounts of the war in Iraq. General Sánchez's emphasis on Christian soldiering intersects with US President George W. Bush's and President Barack Obama's promotion of a "just war" rationale, which actually was forged as a Christian proselytizing venture during the early conquest of the Americas.[23] Furthermore, in a demonstration of his militarized mestizaje, General Sánchez frequently celebrates Mexican American US military veterans from his borderlands hometown of Rio Grande City, Texas. In an intersection with Major General Alfred Valenzuela's militarization of mestizaje discussed in the introduction to this chapter, General Sánchez recalls how his love of the Mexican American delicacy *cabrito* ("barbecued goat") enabled his cross-cultural bonding and alliances with tribal leaders in Iraq who also favored the dish. He thereby reminds us that Latina/o mestizaje and cultural practice are imperialist assets in the neo-Crusade War on Terror, and for imperialism in general.

Puerto Rican US Central Intelligence Officer Abraham Rodriguez, Jr. far exceeds Captain Navarro's and General Sánchez's imperialist discourse and praxis in his 2012 memoir, *Hard Measures: How Aggressive CIA Actions After 9/11 Saved American Lives*. Born in Puerto Rico, Rodriguez served thirty-one years in the CIA, including a quarter century of undercover activities in Latin America, a stint as the director of the CIA's Clandestine Service, and six years as the post-9/11 director of the CIA's Counterterrorism Center. In contrast to Sergeant Delgado's, Sergeant Mejía's, and General Sánchez's superficial critiques of torture as self-identified patriots, Rodriguez celebrates his patriotic role as the nation's chief torturer! He emerges as the quintessential embodiment of empire—and emerging US fascism—through an autobiographical rhetoric distinguished by the fascist logic positing violence—particularly the use of torture against perceived enemies—as pleasurable.

Appointed as the director of the CIA Counterterrorism Center immediately following the 9/11 attacks, Rodriguez designed and operationalized the controversial "enhanced interrogation techniques" for War on Terror detainees, who were all Muslim males (José Rodriguez 2012, 112). He oversaw CIA officer and private paramilitary contractor training in the application of approved measures such as "walling" (calibrated beatings against a wooden wall); stress positions; climate discomfort involving extreme temperatures, sounds, and foul smells; and strategic humiliations alternating between forced prisoner nudity and use of diapers. Rodriguez also presided over the "waterboarding" program, a series of mock executions through simulated suffocation. He proudly recounts these episodes in a memoir governed by the conventions of the spy narrative genre, particularly misdirection and dissimulation, which might be called a literary extension of "trade craft," or espionage skills. More importantly, Rodriguez's signifying practices reveal a fetish for violence unparalleled in all of Latina/o literature, even as they intersect with other War on Terror genres.

As a senior Latino CIA officer, Rodriguez may be exceptional for having risen so high in the ranks of the CIA, but as noted in Chapter 2, he is not anomalous. On the contrary, Rodriguez is part of a long and ignoble legacy of male Latino spies whose narratives and corresponding fieldwork emerge as the antithesis of Latina/o resistance discourses. The Latino spy narrative genre has occupied an unacknowledged—though ever-present—space within the Latina/o literary canon for almost a century, and it offers unsettling insights into the depths of Latina/o interpellation into, quite literally, agents of empire. For instance, Rodriguez is preceded by Antonio J. Mendez, a Mexican American CIA officer who proclaims, "I was the real James Bond" (Vonledebur 2014, n.p.). Mendez rose to become the CIA's "Chief of Disguise" in the agency's technical services division. Upon his retirement in 1990, he coauthored three memoirs, one of which was made into the 2012 Academy Award winning film *Argo*, staring white actor Ben Affleck as the Mexican American spy. The most notorious Latino spy narrative, however, is Cuban American Felix I. Rodriguez's aforementioned 1998 Cold War anticommunist memoir, *Shadow Warrior: The CIA Hero of a Hundred Battles—From the Bay of Pigs to Vietnam to Nicaragua*. As discussed in Chapter 4, Felix I. Rodriguez highlights his role in the capture and murder of the revolutionary Ernesto "Che" Guevara. Even more notorious is US Army veteran and CIA officer David Sánchez Morales, known by the code name "El Indio" for his dark skin and mestizo indigenous heritage: he is reported to have served as a CIA assassin and participant in the US-backed coups in Guatemala in 1954 and Chile in 1973, in addition to other infamous covert operations and conspiracies—including the assassination of US President John F. Kennedy in 1963![24] As previously noted in Chapter 2, Latino spies also figure prominently in the historiographies and memoirs of the Central Intelligence Agency's WWII predecessor, the Office of Strategic Services. This legacy is illustrated in Robert Huddleston's 2007 biography, *Edmundo: From Chiapas, Mexico to Park Avenue*. As previously noted, this biography bears the cover tagline: "The true story of a Mexican-American who became a World War II spy and married a German Princess." As discussed in Chapter 2, Américo Paredes's historical novel written in the 1930s and published in 1990, *George Washington Gomez: A Mexicotexan Novel*, also is part of this genealogy. This tragic mestizo bildungsroman focuses on the anomie and interpellation of a fictional Mexican American US Army soldier deployed to spy on his own community in the US-Mexico border region at the dawn of WWII. Latino spies also include the renowned literary humorist, poet, performer, and visual artist José Antonio Burciaga. In his 2008 collection of prose writings, *The Last Supper of Chicano Heroes*, Burciaga writes: "I served four and a half years of active duty with the U.S. Air Force, three years in inactive reserves, two years with the Central Intelligence Agency, and four years with the U.S. Civil Service" (2008, 113). The canonization of Paredes's text, and vaulted status Burciaga occupies in Chicana/o popular culture, ultimately raise troubling questions about the intertwined nature of Mexican American life writing and cultural politics with panoptic regimes of surveillance and subordination: despite the persistent scholarly and activist silence about these confluences, Mexican Americans, Chicana/os, and Latina/os consolidate their subjectivities through narratives about, and outright performances of tradecraft in the service of US imperialism. In their spy life writing, fictions become real, and purportedly oppositional praxis comes from the quintessential "guardians" of the US empire, with the specter of multiple violences subtending it all.

Unlike some of his Latino spy predecessors, Abraham Rodriguez's memoir (cowritten with Bill Harlow and vetted by the CIA Publication Review Board) is unlikely ever to be accepted as part of the Latina/o literature canon like Paredes's and Burciaga's writings. In addition to being poorly written boilerplate prose, this memoir overtly disrupts the field's persistent oppositional posture. Moreover, it offers a discrepant illustration of the central role of militarized mestizaje in the domestic and global exercise of US hegemony and imperialist malice, which Rodriguez embodies. In an April 29, 2012, interview with Lesley Stahl on the television news show *60 Minutes*, Rodriguez emphasizes that the logic of the CIA's torture regimen was to instill a sense of desperation and powerlessness, adding "the objective is to let him know there's a new sheriff in town" (CBS 2012, n.p.). As the director of the CIA's Counterterrorism Center, Rodriguez assumed this role. Although he was formally subordinate to the director of the CIA, Rodriguez apparently operated with wide latitude that enabled him to take unilateral initiatives, such as the expanded use of rendition, the design and implementation of "enhanced interrogation techniques" in collaboration with contracted psychologists and military advisors, and the subsequent destruction of over 900 videotapes of waterboarding and other torture sessions once the program was exposed to the public and became the object of legal scrutiny.

Rodriguez used his authority to move to the center of power, and to move the center toward him. He recounts, for example, his first meeting with former US President George W. Bush, in which the leader of the most powerful nation on earth at the time deferred to Rodriguez's new authority as the director of the CIA Counterterrorism Center by speaking to him in Spanish, even though Bush's command of the language is mediocre at best. Rodriguez adds that his Puerto Rican heritage, native Spanish proficiency, and childhood living in various Latin American countries where his father worked for "international aid agencies" (a common euphemism for the CIA), enabled his rapid rise within this quintessential spy agency (2012, 16–17). Rodriguez offers yet another demonstration that transnational mestizaje, and attendant third-space *facultades*, or "knowledges," can be deployed as imperialist assets. Moreover, these capacities may even be *inherently* imperialist as they enable successful spy tradecraft and related counterinsurgency methods precisely because this interstitiality was created by imperialism and thus remains imprinted by its mechanisms and designs.

Rodriguez's spy memoir reiterates the imperialist trajectory in Latina/o War on Terror life writing, which reaches its apex in the presentation of the Latina/o imperialist as a postracial and suprastatutory fascist who achieves his life's potential as the US torturer-in-chief. *Hard Measures*, like Latina/o combat self-actualization, military command, and other spy narratives, challenges presumptions that Latina/o literature qualifies as a contestatory "minor literature," in Gilles Deleuze and Félix Guattari's (1986) reformulation of Raymond Williams's dominant-residual-emergent trialectic. This book may have been produced by a member of a numerically minority population (Latina/os) from a colonized nation (Puerto Rico), but it chronicles its subject's seamless proficiency as an agent of US imperialism precisely because of his weaponized third-space mestizaje, that is, his ability to racially and culturally shape-shift, particularly in martial or dangerous contexts. This is the essence of spy tradecraft. Rodriguez's narrative ultimately disrupts teleological historiographies of Latina/o literature that propose the corpus, and its referents, as insurgent, radical, and even revolutionary. In fact, much of the occluded and neglected literary archive may actually reveal Latinidades to be the exact opposite!

Worse, Rodriguez's deployment and justification of multiple violences—particularly embodied and psychological torture—raises his fascist violentology to a pathological level that far exceeds the ethos of the combat action narrative's Über-warrior discourse. His discussion of waterboarding is indicative of the rhetorical strategy of begging the question in defense of the presumed legitimacy of torture:

> Since it was so widely used in training of our own military personnel, we were then (and remain now) quite confident that a carefully implemented waterboarding program, such as we envisioned, in no way could accurately be considered "torture." (2012, 69)

Rodriguez continues his dissimulating rhetoric by rebutting the US Department of Justice Office of Legal Counsel memo describing the step-by-step waterboarding technique and the underlying patho-physiology of mock drowning. Citing this document verbatim, he notes that the process deliberately "causes an increase in the carbon dioxide level in the individuals' blood," which "stimulates increased effort to breathe" and "produces the *perception* of 'suffocation and incipient panic' i.e., the *perception* of drowning" (2012, 69–70, italics in original). In his attempt to dispel the notion that this technique constitutes torture, Rodriguez stretches semantics by explaining, "some people argue that because a detainee *thinks* he might be drowning, that makes it torture," adding "Al-Qa'ida detainees also could have ended the session with a single word, a word indicating that they were ready to cooperate" (2012, 69–70, italics in original). Rodriguez emphasizes that CIA interrogators took extra "care" to ensure prisoner "health," even to the point of dispatching US physi-cians to save the lives of prisoners—so the CIA could later torture them in the presence of other medical professionals (2012, 114–15).

Insisting on the legality of these practices, Rodriguez notes that the CIA meticulously catalogued prisoners during their frequent renditions to and from various "black sites" (2012, 117), or secret prisons throughout the world. Whether he was aware of it or not, he displays how the United States' War on Terror protocol for the treatment of prisoners is reminiscent of the Nazi use of medically supervised torture and accompanying fetish for record keeping on concentration camp internees. This predilection for documentation presumably confirmed to the sadists that their activities were legitimate, and a normal part of the governing order, whether it be German antisemitic Nazism or American Islamophobic imperialism. Multiple layers of violence are embedded within Rodriguez's relationship to record keeping and the chronicle of his claims to power. The CIA's record of torture, targeted purging of select records such as Rodriguez's destruction of the torture videotapes, and vetted dissemination of laudatory CIA life writing like Rodriguez's memoir, also represent a theory and praxis for enunciating the official story. It serves as a corollary to the actual acts of torture, kidnapping, and murder. Indeed, fascist claims to the right to both chronicle and erase their own testaments to terror also are part of their performance of power. That is, their writing is part of the terror, and so is their strategic erasure of the evidence.

Astonishingly, Rodriguez complements his poetic of simultaneous revelation, dissimulation, and destruction by representing waterboarding and other "enhanced interrogation techniques" as humorous, and torture in general as pleasurable. Herein lies the essence of his fascist sensibility. Rodriguez's penchant for understatement and obfuscation through a callous gallows humor underscores his sense of satisfaction—bordering on sadistic pleasure—in his role as the nation's torturer-in-chief. For instance, after detailing the torture techniques used on Khalid Sheikh Mohammed, who was charged with "being the principal architect of the 9/11 attacks" in the 9/11 Commission Report and subsequently convicted in a US Military Commissions court in 2008, Rodriguez flippantly uses the slogan from a commercial used to promote phonographs and records from the Victor Talking Machine Company (later absorbed into RCA Victrola): "he became the gift that kept on giving" (2012, 101). Rodriguez dissimulates the brutality of the interrogations by deriding Mohammed's complaint "that a guard had allegedly taken a bite out of an apple on his food tray." He adds a dose of dismissive comic relief, saying it was "just another example of our brutal treatment, I guess" (2012, 95). For these and other reasons, *The New Yorker* Senior

Editor Amy Davidson describes Rodriguez as "a textbook example of what it means to have an unreliable narrator" (2012, n.p.). When paired with his overt advocacy of targeted assassinations of "terrorists"—along with heads of state! (Rodriguez 2012, 120–2)—Rodriguez's mestizo spy narrative becomes far more dangerous than Américo Paredes's angst-ridden hybrid subjects caught between two worlds; or Latino permutations of romantic male warrior hero "James Bond" figures, as Antonio J. Mendez has been called; or even the fanatical Cold War anticommunist zealot, for which Felix I. Rodriguez is the paragon. Instead, Abraham Rodriguez introduces a new supra-Latina/o archetype: the imperialist sadist fascist. While the Latino Special Forces warrior Übermensch privileges a suprastatutory and supracorporeal transcendence actualized through violent killing and dying, Rodriguez goes further by depicting torture as an effective tool of empire that also is humorous and pleasurable to watch and execute. Moreover, by presenting himself as the new global "sheriff in town," Rodriguez personifies and embodies US hegemony in the immanently fascist New World Order proclaimed by US President George H. W. Bush in 1991 during the Persian Gulf War, which his son, US President George W. Bush would extend into the boundless and never-ending War on Terror.

Ground Zero, Broadway, and the Reification of Violence in Latina/o War on Terror Performance Art, *Testimonio*, and Theater

Despite the troubling Latina/o soldier and paramilitary personnel move from the margins to the center in the War on Terror, Latina/o literature and culture from this era is not uniformly imperialist or protofascist. On the contrary, the steadily expanding corpus of Latina/o War on Terror literature includes Coco Fusco's 2008 pacifist, feminist, antiimperialist, mixed-media spectacle, *A Field Guide for Female Interrogators*, cited in Chapter 4. Sardonically glossing the pragmatic US Army field manuals that delineate skills designed to transform a civilian into a soldier, Fusco uses her rhetorical and performative repertoire to expose the antifeminist dimensions of the militarization of women's lives in the United States. She prefaces her mock manual by reflecting on the tensions between her ideological maturation within third-wave antiimperialist feminism, and the militarization of her own family:

> I came of age at a time when feminists were resolutely anti-military, and my choice of art as a profession guaranteed me the company of every anti-establishment type. I lost a brother who joined the Special Forces and was killed in a covert mission in the 1980s, and then I watched the military do everything possible to hide the circumstances of his death.   (2008, 9)

The War on Terror, she adds, poses complicated dilemmas for materialist feminists that require her to take a different approach to intervening against war:

> Though I've joined many protests against unjust wars in my life, I'm sure there was a part of me that believed for most of my life that women were not really responsible for the battles that destroyed so many lives because we didn't fight in them. Now I find that [sic] myself transfixed by the women who are waging war in my name, sensing that their presence compels me to scrutinize my own misgivings and misconceptions about femininity and power.   (2008, 9–10)

Even before the January 2013 formal lifting of the ban on women in military occupational specialties in the combat arms, women soldiers—including Latinas—had been rising to the top ranks of the military echelon, including general officer. For instance, USMC Brigadier General Angela Salinas, from the US-Mexico borderlands town of Alice, Texas, was the highest-ranking Latina in the US military during the War on Terror, with many Latina colonels across other military branches ascending toward general officer at the same time and afterward.

This model of women's empowerment involves the militarization of key aspects of feminism such as calls for pay equity and economic mobility, while equally important goals such as the elimination of institutionalized violence against women are left unaddressed and even exacerbated by linking feminist activism to the misogynist culture of the US military. Susan Sontag's exposé about soldier online pornographic montages of torture scenes that are paired with photographs of soldiers performing sex acts further illuminates the protofascist militarization of sex in the War on Terror. The prominent role that women soldiers played in the prisoner abuses at

Abu Ghraib Prison in Iraq and at the US Detention Camp at Guantanamo Bay in Cuba underscore how a pursuit of feminist empowerment also is intertwined with a fascist fetish on violence. In both prisons, for instance, Muslim male prisoners were stripped naked and subjected to torture regimens that included women military guards flaunting partial nudity and using other sexual and scatological gestures to transgress the prisoner's individual (misogynist) religious beliefs.

Fusco's satirical text and accompanying performances seek to disarticulate this compounding weaponization of womanhood through an adaptation of early twentieth-century German communist Bertolt Brecht's (1974) epic theater technique, *Verfremdungseffekt*, or the "estrangement effect," in addition to elements of disidentification and testimonial *concientización* discussed earlier. Brecht's method presents distasteful "heroes" and resists convenient plot closure to prevent audience comfort, pleasure, and identification with protagonists. This irresolution seeks to create spectator dissonance pursuant to their self-reflection and postperformance direct action. Accordingly, Fusco's Brechtian four-part text and accompanying spectacle focuses on women's interpellation into agents of macro- and microviolences. Her intervention opens with an epistolary meditation on the enduring resonance of Virginia Woolf's (1963, 1989) early-twentieth-century reflection on the vexed nature of women's empowerment in a patriarchal society that continually produces wars. It also includes a facsimile of an FBI memo recounting the sexualized interrogation techniques used by a US female interrogator; mock speech by Fusco's Latina soldier alter ego who lauds new military career opportunities for women in the War on Terror; and graphic instruction guide on the sexualized torture practices by women interrogators at the US prison at Guantanamo Bay.

At the January 2007 "The Feminist Future" symposium in the Modern Museum of Art in New York, Fusco performed her dialogic satire, "A Room of One's Own: Women and Power in the New America," whose text and images are reproduced as the third section of *A Field Guide for Female Interrogators* (Figure 5.4). In this performance, Fusco assumes the role of a fictional Latina soldier and interrogator who lauds an important irony of the War on Terror: battlefield opportunities for women of all races to actualize their claim to inclusion and empowerment by using their marginal status and interstitial gnosis, in addition to their bodies. In the deadpan

FIGURE 5.4. *Production photo from* A Room of One's Own *(2006), by Coco Fusco. Courtesy of Coco Fusco.*

signifying for which her characters are renowned, Fusco's Latina soldier opens:

> The War on terror offers women an unprecedented opportunity to demonstrate our strength and charm by providing us with an enemy for whom sexuality is a key weak point.
>
> We exploit the vulnerability that is common to Islamic fundamentalists in order to get them to cooperate with us. The sexual freedom women gained in the course of the twentieth century has turned out to be a highly effective means of disarming our enemies.
>
> As female interrogators we can take advantage of the fact that the male populations of traditional societies cannot conceive of us as powerful or violent, much less as highly trained military officers. Thus we use the tried and true B&B tactic, posing as "bimbos and babes" to extract actionable intelligence without them knowing what is happening to them.   (2008, 97)

This character closes by noting that if audience members follow the easy steps of the purportedly disidentificatory "B&B" routine: "Everyone will have forgotten that there was ever supposed to be a feminist future" (2008, 105). Feminism can be achieved now, her character implies, through this formula. Audience members, of course, are expected to know that this is not feminist empowerment, but the opposite of it.

In an effort to reiterate the incompatibility of weaponized women's sexuality and feminist empowerment, Fusco complements the transcript of her performance with Dan Turner's two-dimensional illustrations demonstrating the sixteen "B&B" interrogation techniques her character cited as opportunities. Fusco's collaborator bases these cartoon-like images on documented accounts of the actual "coercive techniques" used in the US military prison at Guantanamo Bay, whose inmates are exclusively Muslim males. For instance, technique Number 16, labeled "Fear Up Harsh," depicts a scowling blond female soldier in an exposed black bra with one hand in her crotch under visible pink panties as the other hand smears her menstrual blood across the face of a bound and prostrate Muslim prisoner who screams in disgust (Figure 5.5). This act exploits the

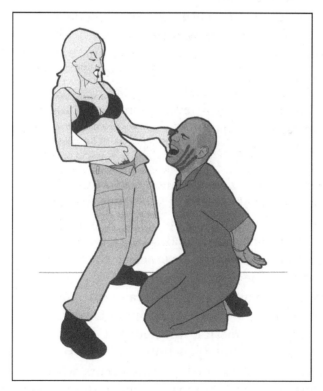

FIGURE 5.5. *"Fear Up Harsh" by Dan Turner. Image from* A Field Guide for Female Interrogators *(2008), by Coco Fusco and Dan Turner. Courtesy of Coco Fusco and Dan Turner.*

prisoner's masculinist and misogynist religious sensibilities in an effort to break his will to resist.

Within the Brechtian alienation effect, as well as the disidentifica-tory resistant spectatorship and testimonial ethos of *concientización*, dissonance is the necessary precondition for the audience's assess-ment and epiphanies about objective and subjective conditions, *autocrítica*, and transformative direct action. But this all fails in Fusco's performance. In a rare metacritical discussion by a Latina/o artist about the limits of literature and performance art to achieve palpable political ends, Fusco discusses her failure as a provocateur in the War on Terror. She notes that War on Terror programming—which might be called wartainment and torturtainment simula-cra—shapes her audience's spectatorship expectations, making it difficult for them to disarticulate pathological violence from pur-portedly pleasurable forms. Fusco inevitably fails in her goal of cre-ating a character who could demonstrate the "issues and events that had unnerved me" (2008, 27). Instead, she notes how audience members critique her for allegedly wounding them "by implicating feminism in something so terrible" (2008, 81). The corresponding discussion of her method-acting research and training in US mili-tary escape and evasion tactics, which includes being subjected to "enhanced interrogation" techniques, has even worse unintended consequences. She recalls: "even more disturbing to me are the younger women who want to ignore the issue of torture and instead consider my training experience as a foray into sadomasochism" (2008, 81).

Abraham Rodriguez's embodiment of torture as power and pleas-ure is symptomatic of the United States' steady move toward fascism in the War on Terror. And, the hostile reception of Fusco's Brechtian, disidentificatory, and testimonialesque performance is a function of Latina interpellation within this process, which is reflected in much of the Latina/o life writing from the War on Terror discussed throughout this chapter. Worse, in a later video of the 2009 perfor-mance of the skit, now titled "A Room of One's Own: Woman and Power in the New America," the audience laughs at inappropriate times that reveals the interpenetration of protofascist pleasure into Latina/o feminist spectatorship. This occurs when her character notes, while slides of interrogation and torture rooms appear on the screen:

That struggle for democracy is being waged by women applying their trade in rooms just as Woolf imagined. These are simple rooms, furnished with nothing more than a desk and a couple of chairs.

(2009, n.p.)

Fusco's satirical description of a torture cell as a Woolfian "room of her own," ultimately reveals the troubling Latina/o complicity with the rise of fascist sensibilities in the War on Terror. Indeed, Fusco's daring satirical (anti)aesthetizations of claims to feminist empowerment through torture inadvertently lead to the reification of this type of violence, rather than the rejection of it.

Fusco's performance venues, of course, directly impact audience reception—and rejection—of her proposed contrapuntal critique of the US military as a site for feminist empowerment. Her spectacle occurs primarily at universities, art museums, and art performance spaces whose patrons are accustomed to risqué and taboo spectacles that oftentimes are designed to induce spectator pleasure. These audiences rarely include the working classes that predominate in the enlisted ranks of the US military (though some of her performances have occurred in more populist spaces). Yet, Fusco's performative critiques of the US military as a vehicle for women's gender and class mobility likely would have found equally resistant audiences among the lower classes for whom the military provides economic opportunities generally not available to them in other areas of society. Her provisional failure notwithstanding, Fusco's gloss of the US Army field manual and failed Brechtian, disidentificatory, and testimonial spectacle signal more than her critique of the militarization of civilian life in the War on Terror: she demonstrates how even purportedly liberal, progressive, and even "radical" audiences are mystified and interpellated within the imperialist and protofascist milieu of the early twenty-first-century United States.

Coco Fusco's proposed intervention into the protofascist intertwining of feminism, warfare, and torture unintentionally intersect with ideologically suspect Latina/o attempts to critique War on Terror violences. Claire Joysmith's and Clara Lomas's 2005 edited anthology, *One Wound for Another/Una herida por otra*, is the first Pan-Latina/o and Latina/o-centric meditation on the epochal Al Qaeda military attacks on US financial, military, and political institutions on September 11, 2001. It pairs a wide array of emails and solicited

Internet postings from Latina/o and Latin American academics and writers. Similar to most early accounts of the attacks, these postings express disbelief and angst, particularly over the spectacular destruction of the World Trade Center towers in New York City. This anthology also critically links the September 11, 2001, attacks on the United States to the US-backed coup against the elected socialist government of Chile on September 11, 1973. Mexican author Elena Poniatowska opens the anthology by musing: "when the U.S. sent troops to Vietnam, people in the civil rights movement in the U.S. drew links between themselves—as the racially oppressed in the U.S.—and the Vietcong." She adds, "Maybe, maybe, that will happen again" (Poniatowska 2005, 25). Contributors such as Chicana writer Sandra Cisneros demonstrates this possibility by anticipating, and rejecting, the abject racialization of Muslim males in the ensuing US War on Terror invasion of Afghanistan:

> When I look in the mirror I look more like Osama Bin Laden than I do Bush. Osama looks like my *tío* [uncle] Nacho. The Afghans look like my brothers. They are my brothers.   (2005, 138)

Other contributors indict US racism and poverty as analogues to terrorism and the extended legacy of US imperialism that motivated these attacks, alongside pleas to mobilize against the impending US military response and ensuing war.

Ironically, but not unexpectedly, *One Wound for Another/Una herida por otra* also includes myopic reflections that segue with the War on Terror's legitimating rhetoric despite the anthology's framing as an antiimperialist project. In an untitled elegy, for instance, scholar and playwright Alberto Sandoval-Sánchez decries the 9/11 "loss of innocence," adding a bilingual refrain, "We will never forget" and "Nunca nos olvidaremos" (2005, 256). This phrase is uttered very soon after the attacks in a context where people across the ideological spectrum were still in a state of shock, confusion, and stress. Nonetheless, Sandoval-Sánchez's refrain seamlessly intersects with imperialist slogans in other wartime contexts such as "Remember the Alamo," "Remember the Maine," "Remember Pearl Harbor," "Remember the U.S.S. Cole," "Remember 9/11," and so on. This ideologically troubled poem may have been influenced by Sandoval-Sánchez's awareness that blue collar immigrant workers were many of the dead at the World Trade Center and surrounding buildings.

Prominent neoconservative memoirist Richard Rodriguez (not included in this anthology) makes this point in a 2008 PBS *NewsHour* video essay entitled, "Surnames Reflect Changing Face of America." Rodriguez's solipsistic paean ends with a eulogy for a Port Authority police officer—also named Richard Rodriguez—who was killed in the World Trade Center collapse with approximately 3,000 more people who passed into the status of legitimating martyrs of the American empire.

Many entries in *One Wound for Another/Una herida por otra* similarly reveal repeated identifications with the United States as "Americans" and "victims." Given these and other contradictory gestures, the anthology's back cover inexplicably includes a blurb from John Beverley, a pioneer of *Testimonio* Studies. He proclaims that the text "embodies the possibility of a different, more representative, plural, and just America" (2005, back cover). He may be alluding to Inés Hernández-Avila's painful self-reflective recognitions of Latina/o complicity in US settler colonialism and global imperialism in an attempt to complicate the reflections on this event. But the pronouns "we," "us," and "our" predominate in other contributor references to the United States, which is antithetical to the ways *testimonios* reference the United States. Indeed, *testimonios* from the 1960s to the present from revolutionaries in Latin America and the United States never represent this country as anything other than a capitalist imperialist enemy that must be defeated, rather than merely reformed to include its colonial subjects, underclass subordinates, and their descendants.

The ideological ambivalence embedded in this collection of War on Terror digital life writing arises from the double bind of the borderlands mestiza/o subject position that is embedded with layers of intertwined privileges and violences. Educator Theresa Carrillo succinctly describes—and performs—this paradoxical social and symbolic location in her entry dated October 23, 2001. She recalls a discussion with students, many of whom are immigrant Latina/os:

We have been very critical of the way our country discriminates and excludes Raza immigrants and all Latinos, but, at the same time, as Americans, we had been attacked. As my other *comadre* [fellow feminist interlocutor] put it, our link with the 6,000 [*sic*] people killed is our flag. It is a strange position to find myself in as a Chicana: pulled in by a sense of belonging to this disaster, yet marginalized as a woman of color in normalcy. (Carrillo 2005, 125)

Carrillo intertwines a metacritical awareness of her anomie as a "marginalized woman of color," with the unfortunate, though unavoidable, pairing of "Americans" and "comadre." She links the hegemonic with the Chicana/o, which is no longer fully anti–United States, if it ever was so. Carrillo's acknowledged and previously unacknowledged privileges reveal an ideologically convoluted model of Latinidad that is quite common. Its ambiguity inadvertently enjoins Carrillo's testimonialesque narrative to previously discussed War on Terror genres; in different yet unavoidable ways they raise "9/11" to the level of a multivalent chronotopal ground zero for twenty-first-century supra-Latina/o violentologies that literally, figuratively, and ideologically are all over the place.

Mixed-heritage Puerto Rican and Jewish playwright Quiara Alegría Hudes stages the War on Terror as Latina/o cultural angst and anomie, further disarticulating Latina/o life writing from its vernacular roots (or presumptions) as a tool of anticolonialist and antiimperialist insurrection. Following her 1999 musical *In the Heights*—her conventional Broadway musical about the lingering angst associated with Latina/o upward economic and political mobility that won her a Tony Award in 2008—Hudes wrote the 2007 *The Elliot Trilogy*. This play sequence focuses on a Puerto Rican US Marine Corps veteran of the Iraq War from a Philadelphia-based multigenerational Latina/o family of male and female US military veterans. The second installment of the series, *Water by the Spoonful,* won the 2012 Pulitzer Prize for Theater, with the third installment, *The Happiest Song Plays Last,* premiering in 2013. Every installment of Hudes's *The Elliot Trilogy* is a smartly constructed spectacle designed around layers of musical genres and multimedia art forms that present postmodern meditations on the wounded warrior archetype.

As required by Broadway theater audience expectations, the trilogy's subtle allusions to US racism deftly avoid crossing the Broadway market's middle-class, white-majority threshold of tolerance for ideological critique even as it introduces new voices onto the US theater world's premier stages. For instance, the signature feature in the second installment of the trilogy, *Elliot, A Soldier's Fugue* (2007), is the cacophonic exchange among a multigenerational family of Korean, Vietnam, and War on Terror veterans created by voice-overs from the son, mother, father, and grandfather characters. These characters have never been seen on Broadway. Their more or less haphazard reading of their own lines, as well as the lines of their family members, has an important symbolic significance. This polyphonic, and cacophonic, technique invokes and extends the familiar critique of the US military's overdetermination of Latina/os as a warrior caste. But it also reifies this discourse as the production degenerates into art about art.

Hudes's play is caught in the market-driven milieu of Broadway productions, and especially expectations about Latina/o-themed Broadway plays following Stephen Sondheim's and Leonard Bernstein's 1957 stereotypical urban dystopian gang musical, *West Side Story*. The informal mandate for entertaining musical scores for even the most tragic and demoralizing stories is a trap: spectacular music always overwhelms the story, and ultimately becomes *the* story, as is the case with *West Side Story*, whose songs have outlived details of the drama and the violent implications of the racist and exoticist tale. In Hudes's second installment in her trilogy, the fugue motif similarly overwhelms the multigenerational Latina/o tragedy. This classical music reference intrudes into the setting of an inner-city Puerto Rican barrio home, replete with a nostalgic pseudotropical garden, in Philadelphia during the early days of the War on Terror. At one level, this anachronistic and dissonant pairing of grimy inner-city life with neoaristocratic musical forms defiantly proclaims the matter-of-fact normalcy of the transnational, translingual, and transcultural Latina/o working middle class, which is now entrenched, growing, and fully at home enjoying a wide-range of musical tastes and traditions. However, the play's self-conscious layering of classical musical forms alongside vernacular allusions to rock, hillbilly [*sic*] music, danzón, jazz, and Hip Hop—all of which serve as script cues for characters in addition to forming the soundtrack—renders the play into a solipsistic ekphrasis, that is, art about art, and art about itself as art. In one of several didactic lines in Scene Eight, which is framed as a "Prelude" in the Western European classical mode, the Korean War veteran, Grandpop, ventriloquizes the playwright's overaestheticization of war:

> The fugue is like an argument. It starts in one voice. The voice is the melody, the single solitary melodic line. The statement. Another voice creeps up on the first one. Voice two responds to voice one. They tangle together. They argue, they become messy. They create dissonance. Two, three, four lines clashing. You think, good god, they'll never untie themselves. How did this mess get started in the

first place? Major keys, minor keys, all at once on top of each other.
It's about untying the knot.   (Hudes 2007, 22)

Yet, the trilogy's knot of self-referential staging of art about art never
gets untied. In a play ostensibly about soldier Post-Traumatic Stress
Disorder (PTSD), a grizzled retired Latino sergeant and combat veteran from the Korean War utters abstract meditations about art,
replete with the precise diction of music theory, which creates more
dissonance than likely intended.

Hudes illustrates the degeneration of mainstream US—and US
Latina/o—War on Terror theater into a solipsistic yet still dangerous
corpus of wartainment that reaches its crescendo on Broadway. The
reification of the War on Terror *as art* includes other genres, from
romance to reality television shows whose stars are real US Special
Forces operatives from War on Terror battlefields![25] In an ideological
simulacrum that perpetuates US hegemony in the guise of a critique,
the set of Hudes's third installment of the series, *The Happiest Song
Plays Last*, initially was billed in 2013 as follows:

> On a movie set in Jordan, an Iraq War veteran confronts his trauma
> while filming a war-themed blockbuster. In a humble kitchen in
> North Philadelphia, a woman feeds her hungry neighbors and falls in
> love with a local songsmith. One cousin speaks out against a com-
> munity tragedy as the other hitchhikes across the border on the eve
> of the Egyptian Revolution. A tale of two young adults who cross the
> globe in search of redemption, humility, and their place in the world,
> set to folkloric Puerto Rican songs.   (Hudes 2013, n.p.)[26]

This multicultural and transnational set and story line is wide enough
to contain all Latina/o War on Terror genres and plots examined in
this chapter, with emphasis of course on trite musicals (Figure 5.6).
The play dramatizes the overbearing shadow this global war casts
over US Latina/o renderings of their culture and themselves. But it
fails as counterhegemonic critique. Hudes's reference to art about
war inadvertently proffers the notion that war itself—the maiming and
killing, mass destruction and profiteering, and the multigenerational
consolidation of Latina/os as a warrior caste—is the quintessential
subject of Latina/o art. Significantly, these Broadway and mainstream theater stagings occur during the actual War on Terror, which
presumably has no end. It thus further blurs temporal lines, as well

FIGURE 5.6. *Playbill,* The Happiest Song Plays Last *(2013), by Quiara Alegría Hudes. Courtesy of Playbill Enterprises.*

as the lines between fact and fiction, with the centrality of violence in Latina/o life, history, culture, and identity remaining the only thing certain.

Hudes's trilogy models the quintessential simulacrum effect, Jean Baudrillard's term for describing the confusion over the real and the imaginary, both of which infiltrate each other in popular media, thereby perpetuating what some Marxists call mass mystification. As Coco Fusco has noted in her metacritical anti–War on Terror signifying, the simulacrum has become the real and principal site of struggle over Latina/o ideologies in the present, and thus Latina/o futures. This battle involves something much more dangerous than the mere mystification of Latina/o mestiza/os and Latin American immigrants, as they have become an empowered segment of the United States' threat to the world, which their life writing from the War on Terror confirms. However much the Immigration and Customs Enforcement (or ICE) raids and incessant police profiling expose Latina/o citizenship as tenuous, precarious, and illusory, the aforementioned Latina/o soldiers and spies, as well as journalists, poets, novelists, memoirists, professors, and playwrights, all claim their space as empowered subjects who are complicit and, moreover, actualized as coherent and unique beings through violence, or more precisely, violences. They articulate their War on Terror theories of being and knowing through very troubling episodes, experiences, and enactments of violence, and in some cases even emerge as transubstantiations of it.

The Latina/o migrations to the center examined in this chapter, and corollary Latina/o moves outside familiar margins examined throughout this book, inevitably threaten the survival of long-standing illusions in Latina/o Studies, particularly the field's persistent oppositional presumptions. Latina/o War on Terror life-writing genres such as *testimonio*, memoir, and autobiography, as well as semiautobiographical fiction, theater, and poetry, are central to this development. Perhaps more importantly, the replicating, multiplying, and differentiating genres and subgenres, and especially their ideological diversity, provide important new opportunities for diagnosing the broader dynamics of Latina/o actualization within US hegemony, as well as their consolidation of new formations outside it. Indeed, the growing Latina/o archive's increasing discrepancy ultimately offers apertures for candidly theorizing supra-Latina/o, as well as immanent and perhaps already fully realized *post*-Latina/o violentologies.

The Latinx Mixtape

VIOLENTOLOGIES, THE END OF LATINA/O STUDIES, AND POST-LATINA/O FUTURES

I began this study by proposing a neologism—violentologies—to signify how various types of violence are constitutive of proliferating Latina/o ontologies and epistemologies, or embodied and performative theories of being and knowing. Violentologies also is a hermeneutic, a type of Foucauldian archaeology, that enables the recovery and historical materialist assessment of the ideological underpinnings of extant and emerging Latinidades evidenced in known, as well as heretofore neglected, literary texts and culturo-political practices and performances in discrepant historical and contemporary contexts. As emphasized throughout the analysis of the more than fifty case studies anchoring this book, and over fifty additional texts that serve as frames of reference, this multivalent and multidimensional recovery of violence enables new readings of both celebrated and elided Latina/o texts, authors, archetypes, and performative spectacles. These explications render Latinidad as a radically unstable but still salient category that—when appraised as a function of violence—affords insights into the variable nature of Latina/o real and imagined relationships to power, that is, their ideologies. This violentological method also illuminates Latina/o positionalities within governing epistemes in specific times and places. My case studies demonstrate that Latinidades are inherently plural, with the wide range of modalities intersecting yet also wildly diverging in their navigations and exercises of power and proposed models of counterpower. This is no more evident than in Latina/o war literature, theater, and film, with texts extending through but also far outside extant patriotic warrior

Violentologies: Violence, Identity, and Ideology in Latina/o Literature. B.V. Olguín, Oxford University Press (2021).
© B.V. Olguín.
DOI: 10.1093/oso/9780198863090.001.0007

hero, resistance, and even strategic third-space paradigms. As I have shown, the only way to keep insisting on teleological models of Latinidad as inherently oppositional to US heteropatriarchal, racist, capitalist, imperialist hegemony is to avoid texts such as Jaime Salazar's post-Latina/o French Foreign Legionnaire memoir; settler colonialist, imperialist, militarist, and protofascist narratives by Latina/o soldiers, Marines, and spies; multiculturalist claims to inclusion in the American polis that masquerade as counterhegemonic critique; competing secular and nonsecular counternationalist and counterimperialist theories of praxis that are as nationalist and imperialist as their US antagonist; neoexistentialist and nihilist discourses that render conventional identarian politics radically inadequate; and crossover theatrical productions that claim center stage in the US American militarist and imperialist imaginary, with no space more iconic than Broadway.

Lin-Manuel Miranda's *sui generis* 2015 Broadway hit, *Hamilton: An American Musical*, follows his previous collaborations with Quiara Alegría Hudes on their award-winning 1999 Off-Broadway hit, *In the Heights*, referenced in Chapter 5 (Figure C.1). As a closing case study, Miranda's *Hamilton* conclusively demonstrates the viability of violentology as a productive prism for Latina/o Literary and Cultural Studies. This quasi Hip Hop opera, which bears the conspicuous subtitle "*An American Musical*," aestheticizes and commodifies violence in yet another mystifying text by a quasi-liberal multiculturalist and unabashedly capitalist and protoimperialist Latina/o artist. It also signifies important complexities related to warfare and Latina/o identity that invite—and require—new methodologies for explicating Latinidades. For instance, in the first year of the play's production at its Off-Broadway venue, as well as in its first two years at the venerable Richard Rogers Theater on Broadway, Lin-Manuel Miranda performed the lead role of Alexander Hamilton. A British-descent white male, Hamilton was born out of wedlock in 1755 on the Caribbean island of St. Croix, making him a multiply marginalized figure in the British colonial milieu. After being orphaned, he subsequently immigrated to the American colonies to seek his fortune. Through chance and initiative Hamilton became a central figure in the American Revolution, after which he was killed in a duel. In playing the role of Hamilton as a long-brown-haired, brown-skinned male, Miranda reclaims the country's "founding fathers" as Latino. The overall

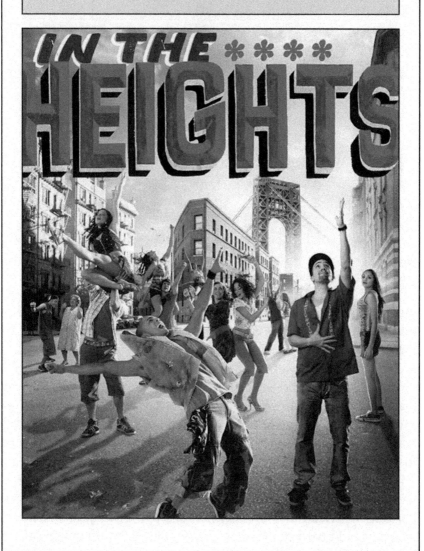

FIGURE C.1. *Playbill for* In the Heights *(2005), by Quiara Alegría Hudes and Lin-Manuel Miranda. Courtesy of Playbill Enterprises.*

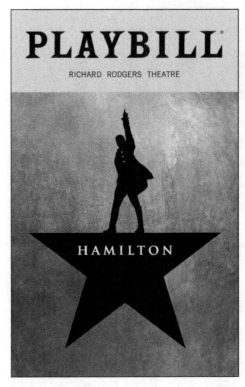

FIGURE C.2. *Playbill for* Hamilton: An American Musical *(2015), by Lin-Manuel Miranda. Courtesy of Playbill Enterprises.*

minority-majority casting, transposition of black-infused Hip Hop into the script and dance choreography, in addition to embedded Latina/o cultural allusions, further darken—or rather blacken, brown, and Latinize—the US American origin story (Figure C.2).

This unexpected hit—which in the US capitalist context is always measured by ticket and licensed product sales such as *The Hamilton Mixtape* that have made Miranda a multimillionaire—conclusively takes Latina/os into the mainstream. Moreover, it enables Latina/os to claim their culture and themselves as *the* American mainstream. It is no small feat that a playwright, composer, and actor who identifies as one-quarter Mexican and three-quarters Puerto Rican, with African American and English heritage two generations removed, has spawned broad popular interest in a figure little known outside the rarefied world of colonial Americanist historians. There certainly have been dissenting voices over the play's effacements of the racialized subtext of Alexander Hamilton's life and work, and of the American Revolution in general, particularly their concomitant Native American genocide, racial slavery, and latent capitalist imperialist designs.[1] However, the play has been universally lauded by mainstream theater critics. Furthermore, this spectacle has been celebrated in Latina/o Studies as the long-sought-after crossover hit that takes the field into the center of American culture. The overwhelmingly positive scholarly reception also adds to the many ways that *Hamilton: An American Musical* has forever changed the status of Latina/o literary and cultural production. It moves the Latina/o corpus from its reified role as a representative of the margins begrudgingly added to the US American literary canon, to its new status as a central part of American *Belles Lettres*, and the world canon in general.

Hamilton's violent subtext, and especially Miranda's racialized troping that reconfigures the meaning of Americanness (however ahistorical and nostalgic his approach may be), makes the play a perfect companion to the texts and histories examined in each of the preceding chapters. These tropes include Miranda's overemphasis on the warrior hero and martyr ethos, as well as his mystifying de emphasis of Hamilton's active complicity in racial slavery (he married into a slaveholding family and aided in the purchase of human chattel), in addition to his active complicity in the cultural genocide of Indian boarding schools (which he inspired and funded, with one even bearing Hamilton's name). The concurrent romance storyline also segues with previously discussed self-actualization triangulations of war, race, and sexuality. More, the over-the-top Hip Hop choreography and vernacular lyrics animate a disidentificatory performance of the Latina/o-as-outsider stereotype, but toward very different ends than José Esteban Muñoz (1999) imagined (Figure C.3). That is, the spectacle simultaneously enables the redeployment of hegemonic third space, as well as mestizaje and mulattaje discourses, as part of a Latina/o claim to the center in a story—the American Revolution—that will culminate in the emergence of the United States as the world's hegemon, and particularly a capitalist imperialist power.

But the play's greatest significance to this study arises from Miranda's transhistorical gaze. Miranda's storyline goes back further in US and Latina/o military history than Quiara Alegría Hudes or Gregory Nava, the two writers and directors who have offered the broadest temporal range of Latina/o violentologies. Hudes's *The Elliot Trilogy* spans wars in Korea, Vietnam, and the War on Terror invasions of Iraq and Afghanistan, as examined in Chapter 5. *In the*

FIGURE C.3. *Dance Scene in* Hamilton: An American Musical *(2015), by Lin-Manuel Miranda. Photograph courtesy of Joan Marcus.*

Heights also invokes the Spanish American War that wrested Spain's colonies for the United States in 1898, with Miranda initially playing the role of Dominican American "Usnavi de la Vega." The words *US Navy* precede the christened name of all naval ships, and this character was named after the ever-present imperialist US naval warship his immigrant mother recalled seeing. The storyline in Gregory Nava's *American Family* extends from the War on Terror to the Mexican Revolution, as discussed in Chapter 3. In attempting to equate Hamilton's story as an "immigrant" seeking "my shot" at a new beginning in a new country, Miranda's imaginative archaeology of Latinidades goes so far outside the realm of plausibility that it becomes the quintessential violentological text: it illustrates how an author has succeeded at refiguring Latinidad as quintessentially US American—a founding father no less!—by rendering violence (the American Revolution) as both the vehicle for and constitutive ontological feature of this new subject of (speculative) history—the Latino revolutionist—albeit a slave-owning, genocidal, capitalist, settler colonialist. This Latina/o subject—the Latino founding father—is borne of violence, and, moreover, his entire sense of self (and very loss of life) is actualized through a multivalent, violence-based experience and understanding of the world (Figures C.4 and C.5).

FIGURE C.4. *Lin-Manuel Miranda (center) as Alexander Hamilton in* Hamilton: An American Musical *(2015), by Lin-Manuel Miranda. Photograph courtesy of Joan Marcus.*

FIGURE C.5. *Duel Scene in* Hamilton: An American Musical *(2015), by Lin-Manuel Miranda. Photograph courtesy of Joan Marcus.*

Indeed, everything about Hamilton's life is predicated upon multiple forms of violence, from the domestic to the geopolitical: heteropatriarchal privilege that consigned him to "illegitimate" status; arrival in the British North American colony in the midst of revolutionary fervor; participation in the violent erasure of Native Americans in the Declaration of Independence he coauthored and through their incarceration in boarding schools; supporting role to George Washington in planning the rebellion against the British; and untimely death in a duel predicated upon the same hypermasculinist code of honor that had overdetermined his life's trajectory. In the overbearing context of the enduring Latina/o Studies reification of Latina/o literature, culture, and identity as inherently oppositional to US imperialism, the only way to understand *Hamilton: An American Musical* as Latina/o literature—which its authorship essentially mandates—and its central character as a Latina/o—which its author's initial performances also mandated—is to view the spectacle through a violentological lens. This Broadway musical thereby introduces yet another iteration of a supra-Latina/o violentology, with its own complexly layered ideological resonance, which adds to the increasingly more discrepant archival mix.

As odd as the idea of Miranda-as-Hamilton may be, the case studies throughout this book show that many contemporary and historical supra-Latina/o violentologies are just as discrepant—and bizarre—and equally as compelling, too. This concluding analysis of *Hamilton: An American Musical* thus confirms the main objective of this book, which proposes much more than close reading explications of Latina/o war literature, film, and popular culture texts. Rather, as the introduction and ensuing chapters underscore, this book proposes a fundamental structural intervention into Latina/o Studies. It recovers conventional war writing and related cultural production alongside a broader understanding of what constitutes warfare, to map specific forms of violence *as* performances of distinct ontological categories and epistemological projects. While some of the case studies are situated in specific wars, the totality demonstrates how warfare, however horrific and traumatic it may be, also serves as a performative venue for various modalities of being and knowing that situate the idea of Latinidad as *sous rature*—under erasure yet still operative—many times over. I emphatically insist that this reading of violence as the basis of Latina/o subject formation does not reduce warfare to a function of discourse or a mere backdrop for an academic exercise in exegesis; rather, it fully recognizes the totality and horrors of warfare and related forms of violence by placing them at the center. My main point of this book emphasizes that violences and related pathologies are not external to Latinidades, but constitutive of them, although in a multiplicity of complex ways. This is a theoretical problem and ideological dilemma that must be unpacked and confronted, and it is also an existential, collective, and deeply personal trauma that must be addressed, perhaps without end.

Finally, the recovery and recentering of violences through the neologism "violentology" ultimately enables the exploration of a unifying thread that runs through the discrepant Latina/o archive: violences. The violentological method, and recovered violentological modalities of Latinidades, militate for and demonstrate the promise of a new future for Latina/o Literary and Cultural Studies, and the field of Latina/o Studies in general, which appropriately is being reframed as "Latinx" to signal more expansive gender and sexuality, as well as racial and ethnic permutations; indeed, the emergence of the "x" affords nothing less than a comprehensive reassessment of the human and even posthuman. In the field's transformation and relocation from the margins to the center, violentologies—as an epistemological and ontological category, as well as a heuristic device and method—offers a productive perspectival shift that enables us to step outside the field's dominant paradigms: celebratory generational progress narratives, inherently conservative cultural and national citizenship models, ideologically inchoate cultural nationalist and revolutionary nationalist discourses, as well as important but overextended resistance, third-space, and interstitial frameworks. Concurrently, this book asks us to consider what happens to these operative Latina/o Studies epistemologies when we stop selectively including privileged texts while simultaneously excising entire categories of cultural production that do not fit into convenient teleologies. As I have shown throughout the case studies anchoring this book, the discoveries and possibilities can be liberating even as they are quite disorienting and even frightening. They push toward a post-Latina/o future through a metacritical understanding of a supra-Latina/o past in the Latinx present. There are, after all, some horrible realities that exist alongside the immanently revolutionary ones. The discrepant archive I have mined—which to be sure will be supplemented by even more discrepant archives that continue to be produced and recovered—provides evidence that insists upon a new synthesis of the field's theoretical subjects and practice, or at the very least a recognition of what already exists but which has been consistently effaced and ignored. The hybrid transversal supra-Latina/o—or Latinx—violentologies explicated throughout this study underscore that these syntheses are always already post-Latinidades insofar as they relate to the field as currently configured. I submit that these post-Latinidades signal the end of Latina/o Studies as we know it and herald the next necessary syntheses.

c/s

{ENDNOTES}

Notes for the Preface

1. "White" is used for European-descent ethnicities unless a specific heritage is known.
2. For a discussion of the Venceremos Brigade, see Olguín (2014).

Notes for the Introduction

1. The French Foreign Legion marching song "Eugénie" was named after Napoleon III's wife, and it commemorates the Mexican campaign from 1861 to 1866.
2. For "Chican@," see Soto; for "Latinx," see Richard T. Rodriguez (2017); for "Latine," see Merodeadora (2017); for "Nepantlerx," see Susana Ramirez (2016).
3. McKee's "Almost Latino" refers to deported Latina/os who transport their US Latina/o culture and identity to Latin American contexts. He notes how they are figured as anomalous subjects in these locations after already having been deemed too illegitimate to remain in the United States. McKee adds, "these truncated, disrupted, obstructed Latinidades call attention to the precariousness of the category" (2016, 113).
4. In this critique of the limits of "Latina/o" Harford-Vargas cites Gruesz, "Once" (2016), Beltrán (2010), Caminero-Santangelo (2007), and Sánchez and Pita (2006). For related etymological interrogations, see Richard T. Rodriguez (2017), and also Olguín, "Raza" (2017).
5. For discussions of violence as outside Latinidad, see Aldama, "Borders" (2003). In rare dissenting trajectories, Flores-Ortiz (2003) examines Latina testimonials about family violence to recenter violence as internal to the heteropatriarchal Latina/o family. Nerriccio García (2003) further discusses how select Latina reclamations of racist, sexist, and epistemically violent body and beauty standards might also be provisionally empowering.
6. See especially Chapters 6 and 7.
7. For a related discussion of capitalism's complex "creative destruction" and corresponding "violent movements of opposition," see Harvey (1991, 258).
8. For examples of Latina/o discourses on spirituality and healing from various interpersonal, systemic, and historical violences, see Medina and Gonzales (2019); Facio and Lara (2014); Calvo and Rueda Esquibel (2015); Luis J. Rodriguez (2017).
9. For an overview of Colombian violence studies, or *violentología*, see Arocha and Sánchez Gómez (1987); Sánchez Gómez (2009).
10. *Soldado Raso* (also spelled *Soldado Razo*) has several variations. All translations are mine unless otherwise indicated.
11. From 2001–2018, the United States granted citizenship to 129,587 foreign-born soldiers, and the majority were of Mexican descent. In this same period, an annual average of 7,623 noncitizens have been naturalized through military service (US Department of Homeland Security, 2020, n.p.).

12. *Raza* is literally defined as "race," which alludes to skin color, phenotype, and other physical and cultural characteristics, but it also resonates as "people." For an etymology, see Olguín, "Raza" (2017).

13. For an example of *carpa* depictions of militarized citizenship, see Haney (2014).

14. For an alternative to the celebratory progress narratives about Mexican American WWII military veterans, see George Sánchez (1995).

15. The "tragic mulatto" is an analogue to the "tragic mestizo" archetype in European colonial narratives about Latin America. These figures are part of the legacy of *castas*, or "racial castes." These Eurocentric eugenicist topologies of various racial hybridities emerged in colonial Latin America, especially Mexico, which had sixteen categories.

16. For an overview of the Soldadera archetype in Mexican and Chicana literature, see Salas (1990).

17. For discussion of the ultrapatriotic dimensions of Mexican American music from the US war in Vietnam to the Persian Gulf War, see Mariscal, *Aztlán and Viet Nam* (1999, 27).

18. For an overview of the strategic use of "whiteness" in Mexican American legal challenges to segregation, see Laura Gómez (2007), Ian Haney López (2016), and Tomás Almaguer (2008).

19. Translated by Zamora and Maya. See Zamora (2014).

20. After the war Juan Montez had a metal plate inserted in his head, which gave him a lifelong aversion to cold. He died in a military hospital in Texas several decades after serving in WWI.

21. US Army Private Victor Manuel Ledesma served in the 90th "T-O" Infantry Division, which was largely composed of conscripts from Texas and Oklahoma and informally known as the "Tough [H]ombres." Ledesma was wounded in combat in the invasion of Normandy, and he died from his injuries on June 14, 1944. In 1954, his remains were repatriated for reburial in his hometown of Austin, Texas.

22. The Islamic State in Iraq and Syria (ISIS) also is known as the Islamic State in the Levant (ISIL). Its acronym in Arabic is "Daesh" for "al-Dawlah al-Islamiyyah fi al-ʿIraq wa al-Sham."

23. For discussion of the Soldado Razo in the Latina/o speculative arts, see Olguín, "Contrapuntal" (2017).

24. For explications of Latina/o interpellation and class segmentation, see Barrera (1979).

Notes for Chapter 1

1. For models of Queer Aztlán, see Anzaldúa (2017), Moraga (1999), and Arrizón (2006); for a related Chicana/o environmentalist paradigm, see Peña; for a transnational extension of Chicana/o regionalist cultural nationalism, see José David Saldívar (1993).

2. For an anthropological assessment of Boricua *indigenismo*, see Feliciano-Santos (2001).

3. For comparative studies of the intersecting concepts of *mestizaje, mulattaje, mestiçagem,* and *mélange,* see Bost (2005); Rahier (2012).

4. *Memoria,* 1877 (original Spanish text, 16–17), translated by Earl R. Hewitt (1877, 9).

5. *ChicanIndia/o* is sometimes spelled "XicanIndia/o," with the "X" pronounced as "Ch." The capitalized "I" in *Indio* accentuates the embedded indigeneity.

6. Seguín's memoir is reprinted with a translation by De la Teja (1991).

7. See Seguin's letter to General Albert Sidney Johnston, April 10, 1837 (in De la Teja, 168).

8. For a discussion of the depredation trope in depictions of the Comanche, see Marez (2001).

9. Mexico apparently initiated these proposed collaborations and explorations of allying with Germany. The German government sought to expand this burgeoning alliance through the infamous 1917 "Zimmerman telegram" that pledged to support Mexico in reclaiming territory lost in the US-Mexico War if it formally allied with Germany.

10. For an examination of Afromestizaje in Paredes's novel, see Marco Cervantes (2010).

11. I adapt settler colonialist nostalgia from Rosaldo's (1993) related concept of "imperialist nostalgia." For settler colonialism, see Veracini (2010).

12. In the Spanish colonial *encomienda* system, a land grantee was allotted the natives living on the land, who became de facto slaves.

13. From multiple conversations with Paredes in Austin, Texas, 2001.

14. See Derrida, Part II, Chapter 2 "...That Dangerous Supplement...," (1982, 141–64).

15. For a related adaptation of Zonana's critique of "feminist orientalism" to other colonial contexts, see Andrea, *Women and Islam* (2007, especially Chapter 4).

16. Garcia's original manuscript has been lost. For a discussion of Garcia's authorship, Ben Stein's editorial role, and an itemization of embellishments, see Smith (2008).

17. The Nez Perce War of 1877 involved several bands of the Nez Perce (Niimíipuu) and allied tribes who fought against US Army troops sent to force them onto a reservation.

18. Garcia's text includes inconsistent references to In-who-lise's murder, which is alternately described as the result of a Blackfoot warrior's coup stick, a "slung shot," and US Army bullet.

19. For a discussion of Salinas's prison transformations, see Mendoza (2006), Olguín (2010), and Gómez (2006).

20. From personal conversations with Salinas, Austin, Texas, 1996–2005.

21. For a discussion of this cadre, see Cordova (2010, 2020).

22. From personal conversations with Salinas, Austin, Texas, 1996–2005.

23. Salinas possessed a personal copy of Gaddafi's *The Green Book*, which he admired for its complex blend of cultural nationalist and socialist principles. From personal conversations with Salinas, San Antonio and Austin, Texas, 1996–2005.

24. For an examination of Salinas's prison-based subjectivity as a Pinto and corresponding poetics and politics, see Olguín (2010).

25. The Spanish term *plena* roughly translates as "total," and *dignidad* as "dignity."

26. From personal interview with the author, January 21–22, 2020.

Notes for Chapter 2

1. For studies on the American eugenicist influences on Nazi eugenics and the Holocaust, see Black (2004); Kühl (1994); Stern (2016).

2. For a discussion of racialized and gendered class segmentation, see Barrera (1979).

3. For case studies of "cultural citizenship," see Flores and Benmayor (1998).

4. This play was based on the battle between US and German troops from January 20–22, 1944, at the Gari River in Central Italy.

5. This incident occurs in Act 2, Scene 6 (72).

6. Shakespeare's character Falstaff is a knight disillusioned by English King Henry IV's warmongering, and he decries the use of poor young men as cannon fodder. Falstaff feigns death to avoid fulfilling his expected battlefield sacrifice. See his soliloquy on the illusion of honor in *Henry IV, Part I*, Act V, Scene I. I am grateful to Bernadette Andrea for this reference.

7. Córtez's specific indigenous heritage is unknown. The Mexican government counts people as indigenous only if they live in specific communities that preserve their culture and language. Beyond the roughly 25 million indigenous people counted in Mexico's annual census, many indigenous and mestiza/o, or mixed-heritage, Mexicans living outside these communities still identify as indigenous, with some claiming specific tribal heritages.

8. For a discussion of this period in Córtez's life, see Bennett (2001, 16, 22–3).

9. Threats to a sitting US president are classified as a Class D Felony under US Code Title 18, Section 871, and they fall under statutes governing terrorism punishable by prison. Some classes of criminal acts deemed to be seditious are punishable by death.

10. Hill was known as Joseph Hillström, but his given name was Joel Emmanuel Hägglund.

11. For a discussion of Latina/o members of the Abraham Lincoln Brigade, see Olguín (2021).

12. For details about Chavez's development of a cult, see Bardacke (2012). For a related discussion of his adoption of Synanon's "Game," see Flanagan (2011).

13. For a discussion of Latina/o political uses of hunger strikes, see Armbruster-Sandoval (2017).

14. For further discussion of Paredes's "transnational fetish," see Olguín (2005, especially 103–7).

15. The correct translations are: "Brother, I'm watching that dude;" and "No way, dude."

16. See Galindo's 1997 coming-out memoir, *Ice Breaker*.

Notes for Chapter 3

1. Benavidez authored three memoirs that recount this episode with slight variations.

2. For a related discussion of the African Muslim sailors in Columbus's voyages, see Andrea (1997).

3. The Korean Armistice Agreement was signed by the United States, North Korea, and China on July 27, 1953. It resulted in a cessation of combat, and partition of Korea between communist North and capitalist South, but it did not end the war.

4. The translation of this excerpt is: "His death was an insult because he didn't die in action—he wasn't killed by the homeboys, nor by the gooks [*sic*] in Korea."

5. The translation of this excerpt is: "And in Korea he was a badass soldier / with balls and all the paradoxes of the Soldado Razo / —heroism and the stockade!"

6. For further discussions of Pachucos, see Catherine S. Ramírez (2008); Luis Alvarez (2009).

7. The translation of Spanish and Chicana/o vernacular Caló sections are: "*y mi tío con sus Raybans*" ("and my uncle with his Raybans"); "cool drapes, *su pompador*" ("cool clothes, his pompador"); "*fabuloso '56* outside my *'buelita's* house" ("fabulous '56 [Chevrolet sedan] outside my grandmother's house"); "his *guiza*" ("his girlfriend"); "*firme*" ("cool"); and *chingón* ("badass").

8. From personal conversations with Trujillo in San José, Stanford, and Santa Barbara California, 1990–1992, and 2020.

9. Ibid.

10. Ibid.

11. For a video interview of Trujillo's mission to Japan, see Damian Trujillo (2018).

12. For an examination of the ideological significance of fragging among US troops during the US war in Vietnam, see Moser (1996).

13. This conventional representation of "fraggings" in the US war in Vietnam is dramatized in Oliver Stone's 1987 feature film *Platoon*.

14. For an overview of Teatro Campesino's Vietnam War trilogy in relation to international protest theater about the US war in Vietnam, see Alter (1996).

15. For examples of African American Vietnam War testimonials that address defection among black soldiers, see Terry (1992); Goff, Sanders, and Smith (1982).

16. For further discussion of Paredes's "transnational fetish," see Olguín (2005).

17. Américo Paredes Papers, Box 8, Folder 12.

18. Britain and Russia sought control of Afghanistan as a protective buffer for their colonies in Eastern Europe and Western Asia.

19. For a critique of Western feminist chauvinism regarding Muslim women and women from Middle Eastern regions, see Andrea, "Passage" (2007).

20. For a discussion of feminist orientalism in contemporary contexts, see Andrea, "Passage" (2007) and *Women and Islam* (2007).

21. From personal correspondence with J. Malcolm Garcia (2014).

22. For a transtemporal study of Afro-Asian exchanges, see Prashad (2002).

23. For examples of Chicana/o associations with Asian American revolutionaries and membership in Maoist organizations, see Carlos Muñoz (2017); Pulido (2006).

24. Curtis also notes that many nineteenth- and early twentieth-century Muslims in rural and the Midwestern United States oftentimes occluded their Muslim faith, or ceased practicing it, because of the Islamophobia they encountered and the absence of Muslim communities.

25. According to Morales (2018), as of 2019, Latina/os represent eight percent of the African American Muslim population, and four percent of the overall Muslim population in the United States. Martínez-Vázquez (2010) estimates that the Latina/o Muslim population in the United States grew from approximately 40,000 in 1997 to possibly 200,000 in 2006, but recognizes other estimates for 2006 are between 50,000 and 75,000. Contemporary estimates involve a similar dissensus.

26. For further discussion of Padilla, see Olguín (2010, introduction).

27. Several of the Bandung participants joined the smaller Non-Aligned Movement founded in Belgrade, Yugoslavia in 1961. This was followed by the Organization of Solidarity with the People of Asia, Africa and Latin America (OSPAAAL) that convened in Havana in 1966, which promoted a tricontinental revolutionary movement. OSPAAAL included only a few of the original Bandung participants and Non-Aligned Movement members.

28. Poet and Poetry Slam host Gregorio Gómez recalls early slam competitions were called "bouts," and originated at the Weeds Bar in Chicago. The early unstructured events blended Hip Hop competitions, irreverent dozens duels, and free verse, ultimately evolving into formalized slam poetry competitions made famous by Marc Smith at another Chicago bar, The Green Mill. For a history of Slam Poetry, see Ortiz (2018).

29. The Arabic translations are: "In the name of God, most Gracious, most Compassionate;" and "May the peace and mercy of Allah be with you. May the peace and mercy of Allah be with you."

30. Harvard University refused to confirm or deny Nurah's attendance or graduation.

Notes for Chapter 4

1. For an example of Chicana/o cultural nationalist navigations of internationalism, see Montejano (2010).

2. See also Amy Kaplan's observation that "empire is a form of transnationalism" (2005, 10).

3. For an exception to the emphasis on the United States as the *axis mundi* for performances of Latinidades, see Habell-Pallán's (2005) research on Latina/o theater in Canada.

4. For an example of the Hollywood commodification of femicide on the US-Mexico border, see Jennifer Lopez (2006).

5. The Argentinian fascist regime was run by a military junta from 1976 until its defeat by the British in the Falklands War in 1982. During this period, a government run "dirty war" hunted, tortured, and killed leftists. This campaign of state terror was part of a US-supported regional initiative—Operation Condor—in South American countries from 1968 to 1989, which resulted in 80,000 deaths and almost half a million political prisoners.

6. The Salvadoran civil war has antecedents in peasant revolts and organized insurrections in the 1930s. Its resurgence was part of the wave of revolutionary movements in Central America from the 1960s to the 1990s.

7. For related scholarship on border dwellers, see Rosas (2012).

8. For a discussion of Lebrón's claimed visitations, see Roig-Frazia (2004).

9. Lebrón's granddaughter Irene Vilar subsequently used this title for a 1997 memoir.

10. Qtd. in Arias de la Canal (2020, 3).

11. Translated from the original Spanish.

12. For discussion of Murguía's testimonial fiction, see Olguín (2002).

13. For a discussion of the San Francisco cadre of Sandinista supporters and internationalist volunteers, see Cordoba (2010, 2020); Vargas (1980, 2011).

14. The Sandinista regime from 1979–1990 was controversial for its sexism, which extended to President Daniel Ortega, accused by his daughter of sexual abuse. The Sandinista government ultimately succumbed to the political and economic crisis created by the US-supported counter-revolutionary insurgency, the "Contras," and was voted out of office. Ortega was elected in 2006, 2011, and 2016 under the Sandinista banner. His 2011 and 2016 administrations were racked by protests from various sectors on the right, center, and left.

15. Data up to 2016 reveal "Hispanics" aged eighteen to forty-four years occupy a higher percentage of the enlisted ranks of every branch of the US military than their percentage of the civilian workforce. In the same age group, only African Americans in the US Army have a higher enlistment rate vis-à-vis their percentage of the civilian workforce. These statistics likely represent an undercount of Latina/os given that the military only uses three racial categories—black, white, and Asian—with some Latina/os likely failing to add the supplemental "Hispanic" category. No figures exist for demographics of Special Operations units. Racial minorities occupy a smaller but growing proportion of the officer corps than their representation in the enlisted ranks. Only women (of all races and ethnicities) occupy a higher percentage of officers than enlisted personnel. For general demographics of the US military, see Reynolds and Shendruk (2018); Office of the Under Secretary of Defense (2016).

Notes for Chapter 5

1. Valenzuela's memoir was cowritten with Jason Lemons, and includes chapters coauthored by Valenzuela's wife and adult children. Gonzalez-Garza and two additional US soldiers were killed on February 23, 2013, in a helicopter crash during a training mission in Kuwait before the US invasion of Iraq. The first US soldier killed in combat operations inside Iraq was Marine Lance Corporal José Gutierrez, a twenty-two-year-old Guatemalan citizen killed by "friendly fire" from other US Marines on March 21, 2003.

2. From personal interview with Valenzuela in San Antonio, Texas, 2008.

3. For examples of the mainstream and right-wing turn in Latina/o life writing, see Cantú (2018); Castro (2018); Richardson (2007); Marín (2007).

4. For a discussion of the various motives behind Latina/o military service, see Rincón (2017).

5. George W. Bush's 2002 Executive Order 329 added special wartime provisions to the 1965 Immigration and Nationality Act that accelerated approvals of citizenship applications for noncitizen legal residents, or "Green Card" holders, who served in the military after September 11, 2001. The "Naturalization at Basic Training Initiative," adopted by the US Army in 2009, and US Navy in 2010, made citizenship available after completion of military Basic Training. Approximately three percent of active military (excluding reservist and national guard soldiers) are noncitizens, and all are enlisted. See also Jarrin-Thomas (2006) for a discussion of the Department of Defense initiatives targeting Latina/o immigrant youth.

6. Despite the 1917 Jones Act, Puerto Ricans living on the island were not eligible to vote in federal elections, and neither did the island receive an allotment of federal representatives.

7. The 1898 Treaty of Paris formally granted independence to Cuba, but ceded ownership of Guam and Puerto Rico to the United States.

8. For reports on the deployment of Latina/o difference-as-Arabesque-stealth in former Navy SEAL Erik Prince's private army of Colombian mercenaries based in the United Arab Emirates, see Mazzetti and Hager (2011).

9. For accounts of deportations of Latina/o soldiers and their families, see Malcolm J. Garcia (2009).

10. Disagreements persist over Nietzsche's *übermensch*, which alternately is translated as an atheist "overman" who overcomes the mystification of religion, and "superman," an autonomous subject invested with a will and determination that also manifests as physical strength. My use references Nietzsche's (2006) emphasis on transcendence of the pedestrian, and the Nazi extrapolation of the *übermensch* that anchored their fascist eugenicist project, which fetishized physical strength, combat, and violent "heroic" death.

11. For comparative discussions of fascism, see Iordachi (2009).

12. On September 16, 2001, US President George W. Bush inaugurated the War on Terrorism by noting that "this crusade, this war on terrorism, is going to take a while" Qtd. in Ford (2001, n.p.).

13. For an exposé of Montalván's claims, see Italie (2011).

14. These are the terms used in Clinton's Executive Order.

15. For recent statistics on sexual assaults of women in the military, see Schultz (2006); Scarborough (2014); Philipps (2019).

16. For examples of these hagiographies, see Ramos (1998); Dominguez (2004); Rochín and Fernandez (2005).

17. For further contextualization of Lerting, see Andrea, *Women and Islam* (2007).

18. In the US military, conscientious objector claims must be based on religious or moral convictions against all war. Applicants can request a discharge from the military or can remain in the military in noncombat roles. Personnel who refuse to fight without first receiving conscientious objector status are subject to imprisonment. In cases involving "desertion" from the battlefield, soldiers are eligible for the death penalty. For related antiwar-activist narratives, see Iraq Veterans Against the War and Glantz (2008).

19. For a discussion of *testimonio*, see Beverley (1989, 2004); Olguín (2002).

20. Qtd. in Ford (2001, n.p.).

21. For an overview of Christian proselytizing at US military academies, see Glain (2011).

22. Smith and White first reported the existence of the memo in 2004.

23. For a discussion of the "just war" concept in the sixteenth-century Spanish conquest and colonization of the Americas, see Van Deusen (2015). For a feminist critique of Orientalist invocations of this concept to legitimate the War on Terror, see Jabbra (2006). For a Marxist critique of this concept, see Hardt and Negri (2001).

24. For references to Morales's role in various CIA activities, see Fonzi (1994).

25. The 2012 reality television series, *Stars Earn Stripes*, was produced by *Survivor* franchise creator Mark Burnett. In the show, retired US Army General Wesley Clark oversaw competing teams of military and paramilitary personnel—such as the late Navy SEAL Chris Kyle—who were paired with B-list "stars." The pairs competed in military exercises with live ammunition for prize money they donated to military charities. Latina professional wrestler Eve Torres and former US Army Special Forces "Green Beret" soldier Grady Powel won the first season. The show was canceled over protests claiming it glorified war.

26. The 2019 updated, postperformance billing reads: "In a barrio kitchen in North Philly, a professor moonlights as the local soup kitchen queen, offering rice and beans to any hungry neighbor. Halfway around the world, her cousin relives his military trauma on a Hollywood film set. With the Egyptian revolution booming in the distance, and local unrest erupting in Philly, these two cousins sing a defiant song of protest. But will Philly, or Egypt, listen?" (n.p.).

Notes for the Conclusion

1. For a critique of Miranda's effacement of slavery in the play, see Reed (2015, 2019). For the burgeoning critiques of *Hamilton* from Puerto Ricans and other Latina/os, see Pollack-Pelzner (2019).

{WORKS CITED}

Adorno, Theodor. *Negative Dialectics*. Trans. E. B. Ashton. New York: Routledge, 1990. Print.

Affleck, Ben (Dir.). *Argo*. Warner Brothers, 2012. DVD.

Agamben, Giorgio. *Homo Sacer: Sovereign Power and Bare Life*. Palo Alto, CA: Stanford University Press, 1998. Print.

Aidi, Hisham. *Rebel Music: Race, Empire, and the New Muslim Youth Culture*. New York: Vintage, 2014. Print.

Alarcón, Norma. "Conjugating Subjects: The Heteroglossia of Essence and Resistance." *An Other Tongue: National and Ethnicity in the Linguistic Borderlands*. Ed. Alfred Arteaga. Durham, NC: Duke University Press, 1994. 125–39. Print.

Aldama, Arturo J. "Borders, Violence, and the Struggle for Chicana and Chicano Subjectivity." Ed. Arturo J. Aldama. *Violence and the Body: Race, Gender, and the State*. Bloomington: University of Indiana Press, 2003. 19–38. Print.

Aldama, Arturo J. "Violence, Bodies, and the Color of Fear: An Introduction." *Violence and the Body: Race, Gender, and the State*. Bloomington: University of Indiana Press, 2003. 1–15. Print.

Alemán, Jesse. "From Union Officers to Cuban Rebels: The Story of the Brothers Cavada and Their American Civil Wars." *The Latino Nineteenth Century*. Eds. Rodrigo Lazo and Jesse Alemán. New York: NYU Press, 2016. 89–109. Print.

Almaguer, Tomás. *Racial Fault Lines: The Historical Origins of White Supremacy in California*. Berkeley: University of California Press, 2008. Print.

Alter, Nora. *Vietnam Protest Theatre: The Television War on Stage*. Bloomington: University of Indiana Press, 1996. Print.

Althusser, Louis. *Lenin and Philosophy and other Essays*. New York: Monthly Review Press, 1971. Print.

Alurista. "El Plan Espiritual de Aztlán." *Aztlán* 1: 1 (1970): n.p. Print.

Alva, Eric and Sam Gallegos. *Once a Marine: Coming Out Under Fire*. Unpublished MS.

Alva, Eric Fidelis. Personal interview. San Antonio, Texas. October 2012.

Alvarez, Luis. *The Power of the Zoot: Youth Culture and Resistance in World War II*. Berkeley: University of California Press, 2009.

Alvarez, Luis. "Transnational Latino Soldiering: Military Service and Ethnic Politics During WWII." *Latina/os and World War II: Mobility, Agency, and Ideology*. Eds. Maggie Rivas-Rodriguez and B. V. Olguín. Austin: University of Texas Press, 2013. 75–93. Print.

American G.I. Forum. "Resolution/Ken Burns Documentary, *The War*." March 13, 2007. Web. Accessed January 15, 2020. <http://laurencejarvikonline.blogspot.com/2007/04/american-gi-forum-resolution-condemns.html>.

Anderson, Benedict. *Imagined Communities: Reflections on the Origin and Spread of Nationalism*. New York: Verso, 2006. Print.

Andrea, Bernadette. "Columbus in Istanbul: Ottoman Mappings of the 'New World.'" *Genre* 30 (1997): 135–65. Print.

Andrea, Bernadette. "Passage through the Harem: Historicizing a Western Obsession in Leila Ahmed's A Border Passage." *Arab Women's Lives Retold: Exploring Identity Through Writing*. Ed. Golley Nawar al-Hassan. Syracuse, NY: Syracuse University Press, 2007. 3–15. Print.

Andrea, Bernadette. *Women and Islam in Early Modern England*. Cambridge: Cambridge University Press, 2007. Print.

Anzaldúa, Gloria. *Borderlands/La Frontera: The New Mestiza*. San Francisco: Aunt Lute, 2007. Print.

Aparicio, Frances R. *Negotiating Latinidad: IntraLatina/o Lives in Chicago*. Urbana: University of Illinois Press, 2017. Print.

Arendt, Hannah. *On Violence*. New York: Harcourt, 1970. Print.

Armbruster-Sandoval, Ralph. *Starving for Justice: Hunger Strikes, Spectacular Speech, and the Struggle for Dignity*. Tucson: University of Arizona Press, 2017. Print.

Arias, Arturo. *Taking Their Word: Literature and the Signs of Central America*. Minneapolis: University of Minnesota Press, 2007. Print.

Arias de la Canal, Fredo. *Antología de la poesía cósmica de Lolita Lebrón*. Mexico City, Mexico: Frente de afirmación hispanista, 2000. Web. Accessed January 15, 2020. <http://www.hispanista.org/poema/plibros/39/39lbp.pdf>.

Arocha, Jaime and Gonzalo Sánchez Gómez. *Colombia: Violencia y Democracia*. Bogota: Comisión de Estudios Sobre la Violencia, Centro Editorial, Universidad Nacional de Colombia, 1987. Print.

Arrizón, Alicia. *Queering Mestizaje: Transculturation and Performance*. Ann Arbor: University of Michigan Press, 2006. Print.

Bag, Alice. "Class War." 2012. Web. Accessed May 31, 2020. <https://alicebag.blogspot.com/2012/01/class-war-2012.html>.

Bag, Alice. *Lyric Sheet*, n.d. Web. Accessed May 31, 2020. <https://genius.com/artists/Alice-bag>.

Bag, Alice. *Pipe Bomb for the Soul*. Los Angeles: Alice Bag Publishing 2015. Print.

Bag, Alice. *Violence Girl: East L.A. Rage to Hollywood Stage, A Chicana Punk Story*. Port Townsend, WA: Feral House, 2011. Print.

Bakhtin, Mikhail M. *The Dialogic Imagination: Four Essays*. Trans. Michael Holquist and Caryl Emerson. Austin: University of Texas Press, 1983. Print.

Bakunin, Mikhail. *Revoliutsiinii katekhizm (Revolutionary Catechism, 1869)*. Lviv: Nakladom Pavla Volosenky (1907). Print.

Bardacke, Frank. *Trampling Out the Vintage: Cesar Chavez and the Two Souls of the United Farm Workers*. New York: Verso, 2012. Print.

Barranco, Wendy. "Wendy Barranco, Specialist, United States Army Reserve, Medic." *Winter Soldiers: Iraq and Afghanistan: Eyewitness Accounts of the Occupations*. Eds. Iraq Veterans Against the War and Aaron Glantz. Chicago: Haymarket Press, 2008. 128–9. Print.

Barrera, Mario. *Race and Class in the Southwest: A Theory of Racial Inequality*. South Bend, IN: University of Notre Dame Press, 1979. Print.

Baudrillard, Jean. *The Gulf War Did Not Take Place*. Indianapolis: Indiana University Press, 1995. Print.

Baudrillard, Jean. *Simulacra and Simulation*. Trans. Sheila Faria Glaser. Ann Arbor: University of Michigan Press, 1994. Print.

BBC News. "U.S. Memo Shows Iraq Jail Methods." BBC News. Wednesday, March 30, 2005. Web. Accessed January 15, 2020. <http://news.bbc.co.uk/2/hi/americas/4392519.stm>.

Beltrán, Cristina. *The Trouble with Unity: Latino Politics and the Creation of Identity*. New York: Oxford University Press, 2010. Print.

Benavidez, Roy P. and John R. Craig. *Medal of Honor: One Man's Journey from Poverty and Prejudice*. Washington, DC: Brassey's, 1999. Print.

Bennett, Scott H. "Workers/Draftees Of the World Unite!: Carlos A. Cortéz Redcloud Koyokuikatl: Soapbox Rebel, WWII CO, & IWW Artist/Bard." *Carlos Cortéz Koyokuikatl: Soapbox Artist and Poet*. Exhibition Catalogue. Ed. Víctor Alejandro Sorell. Chicago: Mexican Fine Arts Center Museum, 2001. 12–56. Print.

Berkowitz, Bill and Olga Talamante. "Olga Talamante: Surviving Torture." March 30, 2006. Interview with Bill Berkowitz. Web. Accessed January 15, 2020. <https://www.scoop.co.nz/stories/HL0603/S00423/bill-berkowitz-olga-talamante-surviving-torture.htm>.

Bernal, Juan. *Memoria*. Unpublished Manuscript No. D-43. Trans. Earl R. Hewitt. Bancroft Collection of Western and Latin Americana, University of California at Berkeley, 1877. Print.

Beverley, John. "Untitled." *One Wound for Another/Una Herida Por Otra: Testimonios de Latin@s in the U.S. through Cyberspace (11 de septiembre de 2001–11 de marzo de 2002)*. Eds. Claire Joysmith and Clara Lomas. Mexico City, Mexico: Centro de investigaciones sobre América del Norte, Universidad Nacional Autónoma de México, 2005. Back cover. Print.

Beverley, John. "The Margin at the Center: On *Testimonio*." *Modern Fiction Studies* 35: 1 (Spring 1989): 11–28. Print.

Beverley, John. *Testimonio: On the Politics of Truth*. Minneapolis: University of Minnesota Press, 2004. Print.

Bhabha, Homi. *The Location of Culture*. 1994. New York: Routledge, 2004. Print.

Black, Edwin. *War Against the Weak: Eugenics and America's Campaign to Create a Master Race*. New York: Thunder's Mouth Press, 2004. Print.

Blackhawk, Ned. *Violence Over the Land: Indians and Empires in the Early American West*. Boston: Harvard University Press, 2008. Print.

Blehm, Eric. *The Only Thing Worth Dying For: How Eleven Green Berets Forged a New Afghanistan*. New York: Harpers, 2010. Print.

Bost, Suzanne. *Mulattas and Mestizas: Representing Mixed Identities in the Americas, 1850–2000*. Athens: University of Georgia Press, 2005. Print.

Brady, Mary Pat. *Extinct Lands, Temporal Geographies: Chicana Literature and the Urgency of Space*. Durham, NC: Duke University Press, 2002. Print.

Brahimi, Alia. *Jihad and Just War in the War on Terror*. Oxford: Oxford University Press, 2010. Print.

Brecht, Bertolt. *On Theater*. New York: Methuen, 1974. Print.

British Broadcasting Company. "U.S. Memo Shows Iraq Jail Methods." *BBC News*. BBC. March 30, 2005. Web. Accessed May 7, 2019. <http://news.bbc.co.uk/2/hi/americas/4392519.stm>.

Brokow, Tom. *The Greatest Generation*. New York: Random House, 1998. Print.

Brooks, James F. *Captives & Cousins: Slavery, Kinship and Community in the Southwest Borderlands*. Chapel Hill: University of North Carolina Press, 2001. Print.

Broyles-González, Yolanda. *El Teatro Campesino: Theater in the Chicano Movement*. Austin: University of Texas Press, 1994. Print.

Burciaga, José Antonio. "One Who Knows Finds No Humor in Prejudice." *The Last Supper of Chicano Heroes*. Tucson: University of Arizona Press, 2008. 112–13. Print.

Burnett, Mark (Prod.). *Stars Earn Stripes*. Universal Television, 2012. Television.

Burns, Ken and Lynn Novick (Dirs.). *The War*. PBS, 2007. DVD.

Bush, George W. President of the United States Executive Order 329. 2002. Print.

Butcher, Kasey. "Constructing Girlhood, Narrating Violence: *Desert Blood, If I Die in Juárez*, and 'Women of Juárez.'" *Latino Studies* 13 (2015): 402–20. Print.

Calvo, Luz and Catriona Rueda Esquibel. *Decolonize Your Diet: Plant-Based Mexican-American Recipes for Health and Healing*. Vancouver, BC, Canada: Arsenal Pulp Press, 2015. Print.

Caminero-Santangelo, Marta. *On Latinidad: U.S. Latino Literature and the Construction of Ethnicity*. Gainesville: University Press of Florida, 2007. Print.

Cano, Daniel. *Shifting Loyalties*. Houston, TX: Arte Público Press, 1995. Print.

Cantú, Francisco. *The Line Becomes a River: Dispatches from the Border*. New York: Riverhead, 2018. Print.

Cardenal, Ernesto. *Epigramas*. Madrid: Editorial Trotta, 2001. Print.

Carrillo, Teresa. "'Untitled,' Tue, 23 Oct 2001, 15:24:52." *One Wound for Another/Una Herida Por Otra*. Eds. Claire Joysmith and Clara Lomas. Mexico City, Mexico: Centro de investigaciones sobre América del Norte, 2005. 125–6. Print.

Castañeda, Antonia. "Gender, Race, and Culture: Spanish-Mexican Women in the Historiography of Frontier California." *Chicana Leadership: The Frontiers Reader*. Eds. Susan Armitage, Patricia Hart and Karen Weathermon. Lincoln: University of Nebraska Press, 2001. 144–78. Print.

Castro, Ivan and Jim DeFelice. *Fighting Blind: A Green Beret's Story of Extraordinary Courage*. New York: St. Martin's Griffin, 2017. Print.

Castro, Julián. *An Unlikely Journey: Waking Up From My American Dream*. New York: Little, Brown, and Company, 2018. Print.

Caviglia, Franco. *Violentología: una aproximación pura a la violencia*. Buenos Aires, Argentina: Editorial Dunken, 2012. Print.

CBS (Central Broadcasting Service). "Lesley Stahl Interview with José Rodriguez." *60 Minutes*. April 29, 2012. Web. Accessed January 6, 2020. <https://www.cbsnews.com/news/hard-measures-ex-cia-head-defends-post-9-11-tactics/>.

Cervantes, Henry. *Piloto: Migrant Worker to Jet Pilot*. Central Point: Hellgate Press, 2002. Print.

Cervantes, Marco. "Afromestizaje: Toward a Mapping of Chicana/o Blackness in Tejana/o Literature and Popular Music From 1920–2010." Dissertation. University of Texas at San Antonio, 2010. Print.

Chabram Dernersesian, Angie. "And Yes…The Earth Did Part: On the Splitting of Chicana Subjectivity." *Building With Our Hands: New Directions in Chicana Studies*. Eds. Adela de la Torre and Beatriz M. Pesquera. Berkeley: University of California Press, 1993. 34–56. Print.

Chomsky, Noam. "Remembering Fascism: Learning From the Past (2)." *Truthout*. April 8, 2010. Web. Accessed January 15, 2020. <http://truth-out.org/archive/component/k2/item/89117:remembering-fascism-learning-from-the-past-2>.

Cisneros, Sandra. "'Untitled,' Mon, 29 Oct 2001 01:37:47." *One Wound for Another/Una Herida Por Otra: Testimonios de Latin@s in the U.S. through Cyberspace (11 de septiembre de 2001–11 de marzo de 2002).* Eds. Claire Joysmith and Clara Lomas. Mexico City, Mexico: Centro de investigaciones sobre América del Norte, 2005. 138. Print.

Contreras, Sheila Marie. *Blood Lines: Myth, Indigenism, and Chicana/o Literature.* Austin: University of Texas Press, 2008. Print.

Cordova, Cary. *The Heart of the Mission: Latino Art and Politics in San Francisco.* Pittsburgh: University of Pennsylvania Press, 2020. Print.

Cordova, Cary. "The Mission in Nicaragua: San Francisco Poets Go to War." *Beyond El Barrio: Everyday Life in Latina/o America.* Eds. Adrian Burgos, Jr., Frank Guridy, and Gina M. Pérez, New York: NYU Press, 2010. 211–32. Print.

Córtez, Carlos (Koyokuikatl). *Crystal Gazing the Amber Fluid, and Other Wobbly Poems.* Chicago: Kerr, 1990. Print.

Córtez, Carlos (Koyokuikatl). "Interview." *Visiones: Latino Art and Culture.* Dir. Hector Galán. Galán Productions, 2004. DVD.

Cotera, Maria E. "Hombres Necios: A Critical Epilogue." *Caballero: A Historical Novel,* by Eve Raleigh and Jovita González. College Station: Texas A&M Press, 1996. 339–50. Print.

Cuevas, T. Jackie. "Troubling the Queer Latina/o Literary Archive." Lecture. University of Texas at San Antonio. February 12, 2012. Print.

Cuevas, T. Jackie. *Post-Borderlandia: Chicana Literature and Gender Variant Critique.* New Brunswick, NJ: Rutgers University Press, 2018. Print.

Curtis, Edward E., IV. *Muslims in America: A Short History.* Oxford: Oxford University Press, 2009. Print.

Davidson, Amy. "Jose Rodriguez and the Ninety-Two Tapes." Close Read Blog, April 30, 2012. *The New Yorker.* Web. Accessed January 15, 2020. <http://www.newyorker.com/online/blogs/closeread/2012/04/jose-rodriguez-60-minutes-torture.html>.

Davies, Ioan. *Writers in Prison.* Oxford: Blackwell, 1990. Print.

Davis, Mike. *City of Quartz: Excavating the Future of Los Angeles.* New York: Verso, 2006. Print.

De Landa, Manuel. *A New Philosophy of Society: Assemblage Theory and Social Complexity.* New York: Continuum, 2006. Print.

De la Teja, Jesús Frank. *A Revolution Remembered: The Memoirs and Selected Correspondence of Juan N. Seguin.* Austin, TX: State House, 1991. Print.

De Leon, Arnoldo. *They Called Them Greasers: Anglo Attitudes Toward Mexicans in Texas, 1821–1900.* Austin: University of Texas Press, 1983. Print.

De Leon, Arnoldo. *The Tejano Community, 1836–1900.* Dallas: Southern Methodist University Press, 1997. Print.

De Palma, Brian (Dir.). *Redacted.* Magnolia, 2007. DVD.

Delgado, Aiden. *The Sutras of Abu Ghraib: Notes from a Conscientious Objector in Iraq.* Boston: Beacon, 2007. Print.

Deloria, Phillip J. *Playing Indian.* New Haven, CT: Yale University Press, 1998. Print.

Deleuze, Giles, and Felix Guattari. *Kafka: Toward a Minor Literature.* Minneapolis: University of Minnesota Press, 1986. Print.

Deleuze, Gilles and Felix Guattari. *A Thousand Plateaus: Capitalism and Schizophrenia.* Minneapolis: University of Minnesota Press, 1987. Print.

Denning, Michael. *The Cultural Front: The Laboring of American Culture in the Twentieth Century.* New York: Verso, 2008. Print.

Derrida, Jacques. "Différance." *Margins of Philosophy*. Trans. Alan Bass. Chicago: University of Chicago Press, 1982. 3–27. Print.

Díaz-Cotto, Juanita. *Chicana Lives and Criminal Justice: Voices from El Barrio*. Austin: University of Texas Press, 2006. Print.

Dick, Kirby (Dir.). *The Invisible War*. Chain Camera Productions, 2012. DVD.

Dodd, Suzie and Olga Talamante. "Dirty Wars: On the Unacceptability of Torture—A Conversation with Olga Talamante." *Social Justice* 33: 1 (2006): 106–31. Print.

Dominguez, Gil. *They Answered the Call: Latinos in the Viet Nam War*. Frederick, MD: Publish America, 2004. Print.

Eide, Marian. "'The Stigma of Nation': Feminist Just War, Privilege, and Responsibility." *Hypatia* 23: 2 (2008): 48–60. Print.

Enloe, Cynthia. *Maneuvers: The International Politics of Militarizing Women's Lives*. Berkeley: University of California Press, 2000. Print.

Enloe, Cynthia. *Nimo's War, Emma's War: Feminist Making Sense of the Iraq War*. Berkeley: University of California Press, 2010. Print.

Estrada, Gabriel S. "Indian Icon, Gay Macho: Felipe Rose of the Village People." *Performing the U.S. Latina and Latino Borderlands*. Eds. Arturo J. Aldama, Chela Sandoval, and Peter J. García. Bloomington: University of Indiana Press, 2012. 344–62. Print.

Escobedo, Elizabeth R. *From Coveralls to Zoot Suits: The Lives of Mexican American Women on the World War II Home Front*. Chapel Hill: University of North Carolina Press, 2013. Print.

Facio, Elisa and Irene Lara. *Fleshing the Spirit: Spirituality and Activism in Chicana, Latina, and Indigenous Women's Lives*. Tucson: University of Arizona Press, 2014. Print.

Faludi, Susan. "The Naked Citadel." *The New Yorker*. September 5, 1994. 62–81. Print.

Fanon, Frantz. *The Wretched of the Earth* [1961]. Trans. Richard Philcox. New York: Grove Press, 2004. Print.

Federici, Silvia. *Revolution at Point Zero: Housework, Reproduction, and Feminist Struggle*. Oakland, CA: PM Press, 2012. Print.

Feliciano-Santos, Sherina. *An Inconceivable Indigeneity: The Historical, Cultural, and Interactional Dimensions of Puerto Rican Taíno Activism*. Diss. University of Michigan, 2001. Print.

Fernandez Retamar, Roberto. *Caliban and Other Essays*. Trans. Edward Baker. Minneapolis: University of Minnesota Press, 1989. Print.

Fielder, Karen Allison. "Revising How the West Was Won in Emma Pérez's *Forgetting the Alamo, or Blood Memory*." *Rocky Mountain Review* (2012): 34–47. Print.

Flanagan, Caitlin. "The Madness of Cesar Chavez: A New Biography of the Icon Shows that Saints Should Be Judged Guilty Until Proved Innocent." *The Atlantic* (July/August 2011). Web. Accessed May 15, 2020. <https://www.theatlantic.com/magazine/archive/2011/07/the-madness-of-cesar-chavez/308557/>.

Flores, Juan. *Divided Borders: Essays on Puerto Rican Identity*. Houston, TX: Arte Público Press, 1993. Print.

Flores, William and Rina Benmayor, eds. "Introduction: Constructing Cultural Citizenship." *Latino Cultural Citizenship: Claiming Identity, Space, and Rights*. Boston: Beacon, 1998. 1–23. Print.

Flores-Ortiz, Yvette. "Re/membering the Body: Latina Testimonies of Social and Family Violence." *Violence and the Body: Race, Gender, and the State*. Ed. Arturo J. Aldama. Bloomington: University of Indiana Press, 2003. 347–59. Print.

Fluck, Winfried. "A New Beginning? Transnationalisms." *New Literary History* 42: 3 (Summer 2011): 365–84. Print.

Fonzi, Gaeton. *The Last Investigation*. New York: Thunder's Mouth, 1994. Print.

Ford, Peter. "Europe Cringes at Bush 'Crusade' against Terrorists." *The Christian Science Monitor*. September 19, 2001. Web. Accessed January 15, 2020. <http://www.csmonitor.com/2001/0919/p12s2-woeu.html>.

Foucault, Michel. *Discipline and Punish: The Birth of the Prison*. Trans. Alan Sheridan. New York: Vintage, 1995. Print.

Foucault, Michel. *The Order of Things: An Archaeology of Human Sciences*. New York: Routledge, 1994. Print.

Freed, David. "The Last Stand of Ricardo Sanchez: The Ex-commander of Troops in Iraq Thinks Some of His Superiors Should Go to Hell." *The Atlantic Magazine* 307: 1 (January/February 2011): 20, 22. Print.

Fregoso, Rosa-Linda and Cynthia Bejarano, eds. *Terrorizing Women: Femicide in the Americas*. Durham, NC: Duke University Press, 2010. Print.

Fusco, Coco. *A Field Guide for Female Interrogators*. New York: Seven Stories Press, 2008. Print.

Fusco, Coco. "A Room of One's Own: Women and Power in the New America." *YouTube*. December 2, 2009. Web. Accessed May 5, 2020. <https://www.youtube.com/watch?v=-8Voh4nLWIw>.

Gabaldon, Guy. Interview with Maggie Rivas Rodriguez. Washington, DC: Voces Oral History Project, June 7, 2000. DVD.

Gabaldon, Guy. *Saipan: Suicide Island*. Self-Published by Guy Gabaldon, 1990. Print.

Galindo, Rudy. *Icebreaker: The Autobiography of Rudy Galindo*. New York: Atria, 1997. Print.

Garcia, Andrew. *Tough Trip Through Paradise, 1878–1879*. Ed. Bennett H. Stein. Boston: Houghton Mifflin, 1967. Print.

Garcia, J. Malcolm. *The Khaarijee: A Chronicle of Friendship and War in Kabul*. Boston: Beacon, 2009. Print.

Garcia, J. Malcolm. *What Wars Leave Behind: The Faceless and the Forgotten*. Columbia: University of Missouri Press, 2014. Print.

Garcia, J. Malcolm. *Without a Country: The Untold Story of America's Deported Veterans*. New York: Skyhorse, 2017. Print.

García, Jerry. *Looking Like the Enemy: Japanese Mexicans, the Mexican State, and U.S. Hegemony, 1897–1945*. Tucson: University of Arizona Press, 2014. Print.

Garcia, Mario T. *Memories of Chicano History: The Life and Narrative of Bert Corona*. Berkeley: University of California Press, 1995. Print.

Garcia, Matthew. *From the Jaws of Victory: The Triumph and Tragedy of Cesar Chavez and the Farm Worker Movement*. Berkeley: University of California Press, 2012. Print.

Gaspar de Alba, Alicia and Georgina Guzmán, eds. *Making a Killing: Femicide, Free Trade, and La Frontera*. Austin: University of Texas Press, 2010. Print.

Gilmore, Ruth Wilson. *Golden Gulag: Prisons, Surplus, Crisis, and Opposition in Globalizing California*. Berkeley: University of California Press. 2007. Print.

Glain, Stephen. "Backward, Christian Soldiers." *The Nation*. February 28, 2011. Web. Accessed January 15, 2020. <http://www.thenation.com/article/158462/backward-christian-soldiers?page=full>.

Goff, Stanely, Robert Sanders, and Clark Smith, eds. *Brothers: Black Soldiers in the Nam.* New York: Presidio, 1982. Print.

Goldberg, Eric and Mike Gabriel (Dirs.). *Pocahontas.* Disney, 2005. DVD.

Gómez, Alán Eladio. "Resisting Living Death at Marion Federal Penitentiary, 1972." *Radical History Review* 96 (2006): 58–86. Print.

Gregorio Gómez. Interview with Author. Chicago, Illinois. January 5, 2019. Interview.

Gómez, Laura. *Manifest Destinies: The Making of the Mexican American Race.* New York: NYU Press, 2007. Print.

González, José Luís. *Puerto Rico: The Four-Storied Country and Other Essays.* Trans. Gerald Guinness. Princeton, NJ: Markus Wiener Publishers, 2013. Print.

Gonzales, Mark. "As with Most Men." *Youtube.* January 28, 2007. Video. Web. Accessed January 15, 2020. <https://www.youtube.com/watch?v=hxSADv2HVZI>.

Gonzales, Mark. *Facebook* post, June 5, 2018. Web.

Gonzales, Mark. *Facebook* post, March 22, 2019. Web.

Gonzales, Mark. *Yo Soy Muslim: A Father's Letter to His Daughter.* Illustrator Mehrdokht Amini. New York: Salaam Reads/Simon and Schuster, 2017. Print.

Gonzales, Mark. "*Yo Soy Muslim*: About the Book." New York: Simon & Schuster, 2019. Web. Accessed January 15, 2020. <https://www.simonandschuster.com/books/Yo-Soy-Muslim/Mark-Gonzales/9781481489362>.

Gonzales, Mark. "Letter to the Cordoba Centre." *Ceasefire.* March 3, 2012. Video. Web. Accessed January 15, 2020. <https://ceasefiremagazine.co.uk/def-poet-mark-gonzales-interview-performances/>.

Gonzales, Mark. "West Coast to West Bank." *Ceasefire.* March 3, 2012. Video. Web. Accessed January 15, 2020. <https://ceasefiremagazine.co.uk/def-poet-mark-gonzales-interview-performances/>.

Gonzalez, Roberto J. "Bribing the Tribes: How Social Scientists are Helping to Divide and Conquer Iraq," *Z Magazine* 21: 12 (December 2008). Web. Accessed January 15, 2020. <http://www.zcommunications.org/bribing-the-tribes-by-roberto-j-gonz-lez>.

Gramsci, Antonio. *Selections from the Prison Notebooks.* Trans. Quintin Hoare and Geoffrey Nowell Smith. New York: International, 1971. Print.

Gruesz, Kirsten Silva. "The Errant Latino: Irisarri, Central Americanness, and Migration's Intention." *The Latino Nineteenth Century.* Eds. Rodrigo Lazo and Jesse Alemán. New York: New York University Press, 2016. 20–48. Print.

Gruesz, Kirsten Silva. "The Once and Future Latino: Notes toward a Literary History *todavía por llegar.*" *Contemporary Latino/a Literary Criticism.* Eds. Lyn DiIoria Sandín and Richard Pérez. New York: Palgrave Macmillan, 2007. 115–42. Print.

Guevara, Ernesto "Che." *Guerrilla Warfare.* New York: Monthly Review Press, 1961. Print.

Guevarra, Rudy P. *Becoming Mexipino: Multiethnic Identities and Communities in San Diego.* New Brunswick: Rutgers University Press, 2012. Print.

Guidotti-Hernández, Nicole. *Unspeakable Violence: Remapping U.S. and Mexican National Imaginaries.* Durham, NC: Duke University Press, 2011. Print.

Gutierrez, Ramón. *When Jesus Came, the Corn Mothers Went Away: Marriage, Sexuality, and Power in New Mexico, 1500–1846.* Palo Alto, CA: Stanford University Press, 1998. Print.

Haas, Lisbeth. *Conquests and Historical Identities in California, 1769–1936.* Berkeley: University of California Press, 1996. Print.

Habell-Pallan, Michelle. *Loca-Motion: The Travels of Chicana and Latina Popular Culture.* New York: New York University Press, 2005. Print.

Haney, Pete. "'*Capitán, ¿a qué huele la sangre?*': Mexicana/o Vaudeville and Militarized Citizenship During World War II." *U.S. Latina/os and WWII: Mobility, Agency and Ideology.* Eds. Maggie Rivas Rodriguez and B. V. Olguín. Austin: University of Texas Press, 2014. 137–56. Print.

Hames-García, Michael. "How Real is Race?" *Material Feminisms.* Eds. Stacy Alaimo and Susan J. Heckman. Bloomington: University of Indiana Press, 2008. 308–59. Print.

Haney López, Ian. *White by Law: The Legal Construction of Race.* 10th Edition. Revised and Updated. New York: New York University Press, 2016. Print.

Hardt, Michael and Antonio Negri. *Empire.* Cambridge, MA: Harvard University Press, 2001. Print.

Harford-Vargas, Jennifer. *Forms of Dictatorship: Power, Narrative, and Authoritarianism in the Latina/o Novel.* New York: Oxford University Press, 2017. Print.

Hart, Jayasri Majumdar (Dir). *Roots in the Sand.* Public Broadcasting Corporation, 2000. DVD.

Harvey, David. *The Condition of Postmodernity: An Enquiry into the Origins of Cultural Change.* Hoboken, NJ: Wiley-Blackwell, 1991. Print.

Hennessey, Rosemary. *Materialist Feminism and the Politics of Discourse.* New York: Routledge, 1993. Print.

Hernández, Ellie. "Emma Pérez." *The Oxford Encyclopedia of Latina and Latino Literature,* by Ed. Louis Mendoza. Oxford: Oxford University Press, 2020. 981–995. Print.

Hernández, Ellie. *Postnationalism in Chicana/o Literature and Culture.* Austin: University of Texas Press, 2009. Print.

Hernández, Guillermo. *Chicano Satire: A Study in Literary Culture.* Austin: University of Texas Press, 1991. Print.

Hernández, Roberto D. *Coloniality of the U.S//Mexico Border: Power, Violence and the Decolonial Imperative.* Tucson: University of Arizona Press, 2018. Print.

Hernández-Ávila, Inés. "'Untitled', Fri, 7 Dec 201 11:23:01." *One Wound for Another/Una Herida Por Otra: Testimonios de Latin@s in the U.S. through Cyberspace (11 de septiembre de 2001–11 de marzo de 2002).* Eds. Joysmith, Claire, and Clara Lomas. Mexico City, Mexico: Centro de investigaciones sobre América del Norte, 2005. 184–9. Print.

Hernández-Tovar, Inés. *Con razón corazón.* San Antonio, TX: Caracol, 1977. Print.

Hewitt, Earl R. and Juan Bernal. *Memoria.* Trans. Earl R. Hewitt. Unpublished Manuscript No. D-43. Trans. Earl R. Hewitt. Bancroft Collection of Western and Latin Americana, U of California at Berkeley, 1877. Print.

Hinojosa Smith, Rolando. Personal Interview. Austin, Texas, February 2001. Interview.

Holm, Tom. *Strong Hearts, Wounded Souls: The Native American Veterans of the Vietnam War.* Austin: University of Texas Press, 1996. Print.

Hooks, Christopher. "Q&A with Molly Molloy: The Story of the Juarez Femicides is a 'Myth.'" *Texas Observer.* January 9, 2014. Web. January 15, 2020. <http://www.texasobserver.org/qa-molly-molloy-story-juarez-femicides-myth/>.

Huante, Lydia M. "'Cold is the Night. Warm is our Bed': An Interview with Marianna Drogitis Cortéz." *Carlos Cortéz Koyokuikatl: Soapbox Artist and Poet.* Exhibition Catalogue. Ed. Víctor Alejandro Sorell. Chicago: Mexican Fine Arts Center Museum, 2001. 100–7. Print.

Hudes, Quiara Alegría. *Elliot, A Soldier's Fugue*. New York: Dramatists Play Service, 2007. Print.

Hudes, Quiara Alegría. *In The Heights*. Composer Lin-Manuel Miranda. 2005. Performance.

Hudes, Quiara Alegría. *Water by the Spoonful*. New York: Theater Communications Group, 2012. Print.

Hudes, Quiara Alegría. *The Happiest Song Plays Last*. New York: Dramatists Play Service, 2014. Print.

Hudes, Quiara Alegría. Quiara Alegría Hudes Home Page. Web. Accessed January 15, 2020. <http://www.quiara.com/quiara.com/Plays.html>.

Hudes, Quiara Alegría, Quiara Alegría Hudes Web Page on May 1, 2013. Web. Accessed May 1, 2013. <http://www.quiara.com/quiara.com/Plays.html>.

Huddleston, Robert. *Edmundo: From Chiapas, Mexico to Park Avenue*. College Station, TX: Virtual Book Work, 2007. Print.

Huerta, Jorge. *Chicano Theater: Themes and Forms*. Tempe, AZ: Bilingual Review Press, 1982. Print.

Hurtado, Albert. *Intimate Frontiers: Sex, Gender, and Culture in Old California*. Albuquerque: University of New Mexico Press, 1999. Print.

Infante, Pedro. "Soldado Razo" (1943). Composer Felipe Valdez Leal. *Tesoros Mexicanos: Pedro Infante*. MCM Mexico/Warner Music International, 2003. DVD.

Iordachi, Constantin. "Comparative Fascist Studies: An Introduction." *Comparative Fascist Studies: New Perspectives*. New York: Routledge, 2009. 1–50. Print.

Italie, Hillel. "Comrades Question Iraq Veteran's Memoir, Memories." Associated Press, July 28, 2011. n.p. Web. Accessed January 15, 2020. <https://www.sandiegouniontribune.com/sdut-comrades-question-iraq-veterans-memoir-memories-2011jul28-story.html>.

Iraq Veterans Against the War and Aaron Glantz, eds. *Winter Soldier, Iraq and Afghanistan: Eyewitness Accounts of the Occupations*. Chicago: Haymarket, 2008. Print.

Jabbra, Nancy. "Women, Words and War: Explaining 9/11 and Justifying U.S. Military Action in Afghanistan and Iraq." *Journal of International Women's Studies* 8: 1 (November 2006): 236–55. Print.

James, Joy. *Imprisoned Intellectuals: Americas Political Prisoners Write on Life, Liberation, and Rebellion*. New York: Rowman and Littlefield, 2003. Print.

Jameson, Fredric. *Postmodernism, or, The Cultural Logic of Late Capitalism*. Durham, NC: Duke University Press, 1992. Print.

Jarrin-Thomas, Sofia. "Out of School and Into the Military." *Z Magazine*, February 2006. Web. Accessed January 15, 2020. <http://www.zcommunications.org/out-of-school-and-into-the-military-by-sofia-jarrin-thomas>.

Jeffords, Susan. *The Remasculinization of America: Gender and the Vietnam War*. Bloomington: University of Indiana Press, 1989. Print.

Jiménez, Miriam and Román and Juan Flores. *The Afro-Latin@ Reader: History and Culture in the United States*. Durham, NC: Duke University Press, 2010. Print.

Joysmith, Claire, and Clara Lomas, eds. *One Wound for Another/Una Herida Por Otra: Testimonios de Latin@s in the U.S. through Cyberspace (11 de septiembre de 2001–11 de marzo de 2002)*. Mexico City, Mexico: Centro de investigaciones sobre América del Norte, 2005. Print.

Kaplan, Amy. "Violent Belongings and the Question of Empire Today Presidential Address to the American Studies Association, Hartford, Connecticut, October 17, 2003." *American Quarterly* 56: 1 (March 2004): 1–18. Print.

Karimi, Robert Farid. "Get Down With Your Muslim Catholic Self (Def Jam Remix)," Def Poetry Jam, HBO Season 4, Episode 6 (2004). Web. Accessed May 7, 2019. <https://www.youtube.com/watch?v=An6mSSEG5Rs>.

Karimi, Robert Farid. "Robert Farid Karimi's Remixed Self." Interview with Angela Carone and Maureen Cavanaugh. February 22, 2010. KPBS. Web. Accessed January 15, 2020. <https://www.kpbs.org/news/2010/feb/22/robert-farid-karimis-remixed-self/>.

Karimi, Robert Farid. "Lumpia Campesina." *The People's Cook*. Published July 3, 2018. Accessed January 15, 2020. Web. <https://thepeoplescook.com/>.

Karimi, Robert Farid. "ParentsFairytale—Self the Remix: The Work of Robert Karimi." Vimeo. Web. Accessed May 7, 2019. <https://vimeo.com/channels/kaoticgood/151322419>.

Krug, Etienne G., Linda L. Dahlberg, James A. Mercy, Anthony B. Zwi, and Rafael Lozano, eds. *World Report on Violence and Health*. Geneva, Switzerland: World Health Organization, 2002. Print.

Kühl, Stefan. *The Nazi Connection: Eugenics, American Racism, and German National Socialism*. Oxford: Oxford University Press, 1994. Print.

Lacan, Jacques. "The Mirror Stage as Formative of the Function of the I as Revealed in Psychoanalytic Experience." *Écrits: A Selection*. Trans. Alan Sheridan. New York: Norton, 1982. Print.

Landiera, Joy. "The Chicano Elegy: Urban Lament and Consolation in José Montoya's 'El Louie' and J. L. Navarro's 'To a Dead Lowrider.' " *Confluencia* 26: 1 (Fall 2010): 112–19. Print.

Lazo, Rodrigo and Jesse Alemán, eds. *The Latino Nineteenth Century*. New York: NYU Press, 2016. Print.

Lebrón, Lolita. *Sándalo en la celda*. Cataño, Puerto Rico: Editorial Betances, 1975. Print.

Lefebvre, Henry. *The Production of Space*. Trans. Donald Nicholson-Smith. New York: Wiley-Blackwell, 1992. Print.

Lenin, Vladimir Ilych. "Critical Remarks on the National Question" (1913). *Marxism and Nationalism*. Chippendale, Australia: Resistance Books, 2002. 51–77. Print.

León, Luis D. "Mapping the New Global Spiritual Line." *César Chávez*. Ed. Ilan Stavans. Santa Barbara, CA: Greenwood Press, 2010. 70–92. Print.

Leonard, Karen B. *Making Ethnic Choices: California's Punjabi Mexican Americans*. Philadelphia: Temple University Press, 1994. Print.

Letter, Amy. "The Exile and the Nomad Are Cousins: An Interview with Ana Menéndez." *The Last War, P.S. Insights, Interviews, and More*. Ana Menéndez, *The Last War: A Novel*. New York: Harper Collins, 2009. 5–10. Print.

Limón, Jose E. "Border Literary Histories, Globalization, and Critical Regionalism." *American Literary History* 20: 1–2 (2008): 160–82. Print.

Limón, José E. *Dancing with the Devil: Society and Cultural Poetics in Mexican-American South Texas*. Madison: University of Wisconsin Press, 1994. Print.

Limón, Jose E. *Mexican Ballads/Chicano Poems: History and Influence in Mexican-American Social Poetry*. Berkeley: University of California Press, 1992. Print.

Limón, Jose E. "Imagining the Imaginary: A Reply to Ramón Saldívar." *American Literary History* 21: 3 (Summer 2012): 595–603. Print.

Limón, Jose E. "Texas, the Transnational, and Regionalism: J. Frank Dobie and Américo Paredes." *Regionalists on the Left: Radical Voices from the American West*. Ed. Michael C. Steiner. Norman: University of Oklahoma Press, 2013. 184–204. Print.

Lionnet, Françoise and Shu-mei Shih. "Introduction: Thinking Through the Minor, Transnationally." *Minor Transnationalism*. Eds. Shu-mei Shih and Françoise Lionnet. Durham, NC: Duke University Press, 2005. 1–23. Print.

Little Joe y La Familia. "Soldado Razo." *Recuerdos*. TDI Records, 2010. CD.

Lopez, Jennifer (Prod.) and Gregory Nava (Dir.). *Bordertown*. Capitol Films, 2006. DVD.

Lovell Banks, Taunya. "Mestizaje and the Mexican Mestizo Self: No Hay Sangre Negra, So There Is No Blackness." *Southern California Interdisciplinary Law Journal* 199 (2006): 199–234. Print.

López, Marissa K. *Racial Immanence: Chicanx Bodies Beyond Representation*. New York: New York University Press, 2019. Print.

Lowe, Lisa. *Immigrant Acts: On Asian American Cultural Politics*. Durham, NC: Duke University Press, 1996. Print.

Lurting, Thomas. *The Fighting Sailor Turn'd Peaceable Christian: Manifested in the Convincement and Conversion of Thomas Lurting. With a Short Relation of Many Great Dangers, and Wonderful Deliverances, He Met Withal...* (1710). New York: Gale, 2010. Print.

Lyle, Erick. "The Mission and the Revolution, as Lived and Told by Roberto Vargas." *San Francisco Bay Guardian*. September 20, 2011. Web. Accessed January 15, 2020. <https://atomikaztex.wordpress.com/2011/09/20/the-mission-and-the-revolution-as-lived-and-told-by-roberto-vargas-by-erick-lyle/>.

Lyotard, Jean-Francois. *Differend: Phrases in Dispute*. Minneapolis: University of Minnesota Press, 1989. Print.

McKee Irwin, Robert. "Almost-Latino Literature: Approaching Truncated Latinidades." *The Latino Nineteenth Century*. Eds. Rodrigo Lazo and Jesse Alemán. New York: New York University Press, 2016. 110–23. Print.

McKenna, Teresa. "On Chicano Poetry and the Political Age: Corridos as Social Drama." *Criticism in the Borderlands: Studies in Chicano Literature, Culture, and Ideology*. Eds. Héctor Calderón and José David Saldívar. Durham, NC: Duke University Press, 1991. 181–202. Print.

Maldonado-Torres, Nelson. *Against War: Views from the Underside of Modernity*. Durham, NC: Duke University Press, 2008. Print.

Mandaville, Peter. "The Rise of Islamic Rap." *Yale Global Online*. August 19, 2010. Web. Accessed January 15, 2020. <https://yaleglobal.yale.edu/content/rise-islamic-rap>.

Mann, Charles. *1491: New Revelations of the Americas Before Columbus*. New York: Vintage, 2006. Print.

Manriquez, B. J. "Argument in Narrative: Tropology in Jovita González's *Caballero*." *Bilingual Review/La Revista Bilingüe* 25: 2 (2000): 172–8. Print.

Marez, Curtis. "Signifying Spain, Becoming Comanche, Making Mexican: Indian Captivity and the History of Chicana/o Performance." *American Quarterly* 53: 2 (2001): 267–306. Print.

Marín, Rosario. *Leading Between Two Worlds: Lessons from the First Mexican-Born Treasurer of the United States*. New York: Atria, 2007. Print.

Mariscal, George. *Aztlán & Viet Nam: Chicano and Chicana Experiences of the War*. Berkeley: University of California Press, 1999. Print.

Mariscal, George. *Brown Eyed Children of the Sun: Lessons from the Chicano Movement, 1965–1975*. Albuquerque: University of New Mexico Press, 2005. Print.

Mariscal, George. "Immigration and Military Enlistment: The Pentagon's Push for the DREAM Act Heats Up." *Latino Studies* 5 (2007): 358–63. Print.

Mariscal, George. "Introduction." *Aztlán and Viet Nam: Chicano and Chicana Experiences of the War*. Berkeley: University of California Press, 1999. 15–48. Print.

Mariscal, George. "Latinos on the Frontlines: Again." *Latino Studies* 1: 2 (2003): 347–51. Print.

Mariscal, George. "Yo Soy El Army: US Military Targets Latinos with Extensive Recruitment Campaign." Roundtable Discussion hosted by Amy Goodman, *Democracy Now*, National Public Radio, May 18, 2010. Print.

Marquez, Benjamin. *LULAC: The Evolution of a Mexican American Political Organization*. Austin: University of Texas Press, 1993. Print.

Martí, José. *Versos Sencillos/Simple Verses*. Houston, TX: Arte Público Press, 1997. Print.

Martinez Sutherland, Elizabeth. *The Youngest Revolution: A Personal Report on Cuba*. New York: Dial, 1969. Print.

Martínez-Vázquez, Hjamil. *Latina/o y Musulmán: The Construction of Latina/o Identity among Latina/o Muslims in the United States*. Eugene, OR: Pickwick Publications, 2010. Print.

Martínez, Rubén. *The Other Side: The Other Side: Fault Lines, Guerrilla Saints, and the True Heart of Rock 'n' Roll*. New York: Verso, 1992. Print.

Martínez, Rubén. *The Other Side: The Other Side: Notes from the New L.A., Mexico City, and Beyond*. New York: Vintage, 1993. Print.

Massey, Dorren. *Space, Place, and Gender*. Minneapolis: University of Minnesota Press, 1994. Print.

Mazón, Mauricio. *The Zoot-Suit Riots: The Psychology of Symbolic Annihilation*. Austin: University of Texas Press, 1988. Print.

Mazzetti, Mark and Emily B. Hager. "Secret Desert Force Set Up by Blackwater's Founder." *New York Times*. May 14, 2011. Web. Accessed January 15, 2020. <http://www.nytimes.com/2011/05/15/world/middleeast/15prince.html?pagewanted=all>.

Mazzetti, Mark and Emily B. Hager. "Emirates Secretly Sends Colombian Mercenaries to Yemen Fight." *New York Times*. November 25, 2015. Web. Accessed January 15, 2020. <http://www.nytimes.com/2015/11/26/world/middleeast/emirates-secretly-sends-colombian-mercenaries-to-fight-in-yemen.html>.

Mbembe, Achille. *Necro-Politics*. Durham, NC: Duke University Press, 2019. Print.

Medina, Frank X. and Dorothy B. Marra. *Ciao, Francesco*. Kansas City, MO: Medina Marra Publications, 1995. Print.

Medina, Lara and Martha R. Gonzales. *Voices from the Ancestors: Xicanx and Latinx Spiritual Expressions and Healing Practices*. Tucson: University of Arizona Press, 2019. Print.

Mejía, Camilo. *Road from ar Ramadi: The Private Rebellion of Staff Sergeant Camilo Mejía— An Iraq War Memoir*. Chicago: Haymarket, 2007. Print.

Mena, Tony. *The Shape of Our Faces No Longer Matters*. Cape Girardeau: Southeast Missouri State University Press, 2014. Print.

Mendez, Antonio. *The Master of Disguise: My Secret Life in the CIA*. New York: William Morrow, 1999. Print.

Mendez, Antonio, Jonna Mendez, and Bruce Henderson. *Spy Dust: Two Masters of Disguise Reveal the Tools and Operations That Helped Win the Cold War*. New York: Atria, 2002. Print.

Menéndez, Ana. *The Last War: A Novel*. New York: HarperCollins, 2009. Print.

Mendiola, Jim. Personal Interview. San Antonio, Texas. May 2, 2002. Interview.

Mendiola, Jim. Personal Interview Mendiola. San Antonio, Texas. February 5, 2013. Interview.

Mendoza, Louis G. *Historia: The Literary Making of Chicana and Chicano History*. Austin: University of Texas Press, 2001. Print.

Mendoza, Louis G. "Peregrinations of a Xicanindio Poet." *Indo Trails: A Xicano Odyssey Through Indian Country*. San Antonio, TX: Wings, 2006. xi–xiv. Print.

Mendoza, Louis G., ed. *Raúlrsalinas and the Jail Machine: Selected Writings by Raúl Salinas*. Austin: University of Texas Press, 2006. Print.

Merodeadora, Andrea. "Latino, Latinx, Latine: The Grammatical Gender Neutral in Spanish." *Medium*. August 7, 2017. Web. Accessed January 15, 2020. <https://medium.com/@puentera/latino-latinx-latine-a3b19e0dbc1c>.

Mignolo, Walter. *The Darker Side of Western Modernity: Global Futures, Decolonial Options*. Durham, NC: Duke University Press, 2011. Print.

Mignolo, Walter. *The Idea of Latin America*. New York: Blackwell, 2005. Print.

Mignolo, Walter. *Local Histories/Global Designs: Coloniality, Subaltern Knowledges, and Border Thinking*. Princeton, NJ: Princeton University Press, 2000. Print.

Miranda, Lin-Manuel. *Hamilton: An American Musical*. Dir. Thomas Kail. April 21, 2016, Richard Rodgers Theatre, New York. Performance.

Mitchell, Tamara L. "Neoliberalism, Post-Nationalism, and the Ghosts of Lefts Past: Reading Roberto Bolaño and Horacio Castellanos Moya on Politics and the Literary Tradition." Doctoral Dissertation. Department of Spanish and Portuguese. Indiana University at Bloomington. May 2019. Print.

Mitchell, Tamara L. "Nuestra América through a Latinx Lens: Reading (with) Héctor Tobar." Roundtable with the author. Latin American Studies Association Conference, Boston, May 25, 2019. Presentation.

Mondragon, Delores. "Maintaining Patriarchal Ideology through Erasure of the Exception: Latina and Native American Soldiers." Annual Conference, National Association for Chicana and Chicano Studies, Chicago, Illinois, March 17, 2012. Conference Presentation.

Montalván, Luis Carlos and Bret Witter. *Until Tuesday: A Wounded Warrior and the Golden Retriever Who Saved Him*. New York: Hyperion, 2011. Print.

Montejano, David. *Quijote's Soldiers: A Local History of the Chicano Movement, 1966–1981*. Austin: University of Texas Press, 2010. Print.

Montoya, José. "El Louie" (1969). *Literatura Chicana, 1965–1995: An Anthology in Spanish, English, and Caló*. Eds. Manuel de Jesús Hernández-Gutiérrez and David Foster Wallace. New York: Routledge, 1997. 224–8. Print.

Moore, Joan. *Going Down to the Barrio: Homeboys and Homegirls in Change*. Philadelphia: Temple University Press, 1991. Print.

Moraga, Cherríe. *The Last Generation: Prose and Poetry*. Boston: South End Press, 1999. Print.

Morales, Harold D. *Latino and Muslim in America: Race, Religion, and the Making of a New Minority*. Oxford: Oxford University Press, 2018. Print.

Morin, Raúl. *Among the Valiant: Mexican Americans in WWII and Korea*. Los Angeles: Borden Publishing, 1963. Print.

Morin, Raul. *Among the Valiant: Mexican Americans in WWII and Korea*. Los Angeles: Valiant Press, 2013. Print.

Mormino, Gary R. "Ybor City Goes to War: The Evolution and Transformation of a 'Latin' Community in Florida, 1886–1950." *Latina/os and World War II: Mobility, Agency, and Ideology*. Eds. Rivas-Rodriguez, Maggie and B. V. Olguín. Austin: University of Texas Press, 2014. 13–42. Print.

Moser, Richard. *The New Winter Soldiers: GI and Veteran Dissent During the Vienam Era*. New Brunswick: Rutgers University Press, 1996. Print.

Mosse, George L. "Toward a General Theory of Fascism." *Comparative Fascist Studies: New Perspectives*. Ed. Constatin Iordachi. New York: Routledge, 2009. 60–94. Print.

M-Team. "MT Bismillah." *YouTube*. <https://www.youtube.com/watch?v=nK3iJUWQc88>. Accessed January 15, 2020. Video.

Muñoz, Carlos. *Youth, Identity, Power: The Chicano Movement*. Revised and Expanded Edition. New York: Verso, 2017. Print.

Mullen, Bill. *Afro-Orientalism*. Minneapolis: University of Minnesota Press, 2004. Print.

Muñoz, José Esteban. *Disidentifications: Queers of Color and the Performance of Politics*. Minneapolis: University of Minnesota Press, 1999. Print.

Murguía, Alejandro. *Southern Front*. Tempe, AZ: Bilingual Review Press, 1990. Print.

Nava, Gregory (dir.). *American Family*. PBS, 2002.

Navarro, Eric. *God Willing: My Wilde Ride with the New Iraqi Army*. Washington, DC: Potomac, 2008. Print.

Neruda, Pablo. *Canto General*. Madrid: Ediciones Cátedra, 2005. Print.

Newton, Huey P. *Revolutionary Suicide*. New York: Penguin, 2009. Print.

Nerriccio-García, Guillermo (William Anthony Nericcio). "When Electrolysis Proxies for the Existential: A Somewhat Sordid Meditation on What Might Occur if Frantz Fanon, Rosario Castellanos, Jacques Derrida, Gayatri Chakravorty Spivak, and Sandra Cisneros Asked Rita Hayworth Her Name." *Violence and the Body: Race, Gender, and the State*. Ed. Arturo J. Aldama. Bloomington: University of Indiana Press, 2003. 263–86. Print.

Nietzsche, Friedrich. *The Will to Power*. Trans. Anthony Ludovici. New York: Barnes and Noble, 2006. Print.

Nurah, Abu. "Departure." Music Video. *Youtube*, July 17, 2015. Web. Accessed January 15, 2020. <https://www.youtube.com/watch?v=jo5HIN6TgUc&t=39s>.

Nurah, Abu. *Don't Be a Citizen*. 2009. Web. Accessed January 15, 2020. <http://www.songlyrics.com/abu-nurah/don-t-be-a-citizen/>.

Nurah, Abu. Interview with MuslimHipHop.com. Web. Accessed June 1, 2018. <http://www.muslimhiphop.com/Stories/16._Abu_Nurah_Interview>.

Nurah, Abu. "My Jihad." *Don't Be a Citizen*. 2009. Web. Accessed January 15, 2020. <http://www.songlyrics.com/abu-nurah/don-t-be-a-citizen/>.

Nurah, Abu. "Say It Loud." *Don't Be a Citizen*. 2009. Web. Accessed January 15, 2020. <http://www.songlyrics.com/abu-nurah/don-t-be-a-citizen/>.

Oboler, Suzanne. *Latinos and Citizenship: The Dilemma of Belonging*. New York: Palgrave MacMillan, 2006. Print.

Ocampo, Anthony C. *Becoming Asian or Latino? Historical Colonialisms, Racial Contexts, and the Divergent Incorporation Patterns of Second Generation Filipino Americans.* Doctoral Dissertation. Department of Sociology, UCLA, 2011. Print.

Ocampo, Anthony C. *The Latinos of Asia: How Filipino Americans Break the Rules of Race.* Stanford: Stanford University Press, 2016. Print.

Office of the Under Secretary of Defense, Personnel and Readiness. Population Representation in the Military Services: Fiscal Year 2016 Summary Report. Web Accessed January 15, 2020. <https://www.cna.org/pop-rep/2016/summary/summary.pdf>.

O'Gorman, Edmundo. *El proceso de la invención de América.* México City, Mexico: Fondo de la Cultura Económica, 1998. Print.

Olguín, B. V. "Ambivalent Mestizaje: Spain and the Idea of Europe in the Supra-Chicanx Imagination—Towards a Global Latinidades Paradigm for Chicanx and Latinx Studies." *Aztlán: A Journal of Chicano Studies* 45: 1 (Spring 2021). Print.

Olguín, B. V. "Caballeros and Indians: Mexican American Whiteness, Hegemonic Mestizaje, and Ambivalent Indigeneity in Proto-Chicana/o Autobiographical Discourse, 1858–2008." *MELUS* 38: 1 (March 2018): 30–49. Print.

Olguín, B. V. "Contrapuntal Cyborgs?: The Ideological Limits and Revolutionary Potential of Latin@ Science Fiction." *Altermundos: Latin@ Speculative Literature, Film, and Popular Culture.* Eds. Cathryn Merla-Watson and B. V. Olguín. Seattle: University of Washington Press, 2017. 128–44. Print.

Olguín, B. V. *La Pinta: Chicana/o Prisoner Literature, Culture, and Politics.* Austin: University of Texas Press, 2010. Print.

Olguín, B. V. "Of Truth, Secrets, and Ski Masks: Counterrevolutionary Appropriations and Zapatista Revisions of *Testimonio*." *Nepantla: Views from South* 3: 1 (2002): 145–78. Print.

Olguín, B. V. "Personal Correspondence with Malcolm J. Garcia." 2014. Electronic.

Olguín, B. V. "Preface: Venceremos is Plural for Victory." *At the Risk of Seeming Ridiculous: Poems from Cuba Libre.* San Antonio, TX: Aztlán Libre Press, 2014. 1–18. Print.

Olguín, B. V. "Raza." *Keywords for Latina/o Studies.* Eds. Deborah R. Vargas, Lawrence La Fountain-Stokes, Nancy Raquel Mirabal. New York: NYU Press, 2017. 188–92. Print.

Olguín, B. V. "Reassessing Pocho Poetics: Américo Paredes and the (Trans)National Question". *Aztlán* 3: 1 (Spring 2005): 87–121. Print.

Olguín, B. V. "Sangre Mexicana/Corazón Americano: Identity, Ambiguity, and Critique in Mexican American War Narratives." *American Literary History* 14: 1 (Winter 2002): 83–114. Print.

Olguín, B. V. and Omar Vasquez Barbosa. "Introduction—Reconstructing Chicana/o Literary History: Américo Paredes Manzano and the Foundations of Pocho Poetics." *Cantos de Adolescencia/Songs of Youth (1932–1937) by Américo Paredes.* Houston, TX: Arte Público, 2007. iv–lxiii. Print.

Olmos, Edward James (Dir.). *American Me.* Universal, 1992. DVD.

O'odham Solidarity Across Borders Collective. "1st Nations and Migrants Oppose SB1070: Demand Dignity, Human Rights, and End to Border Militarization." O'odham Solidarity Across Borders Collective Press Release, 21 May 2010. Web. Accessed January 15, 2020. <http://oodhamsolidarity.blogspot.com/2010/05/mainstream-coverage-of-tucson-border.html>.

Oropeza, Lorena. *¡Raza Sí! ¡Guerra No!: Chicano Protest and Patriotism during the Viet Nam War Era.* Berkeley: University of California Press, 2005. Print.

Ortiz, Benjamin. "Hiss, Gunt, Snap: Become Well-versed." April 21, 2008. *Chicago Tribune.* Web. Accessed January 15, 2020. <https://www.chicagotribune.com/news/ct-xpm-2008-04-04-0804020643-story.html>.

Ortiz, Fernando. *Cuban Counterpoint: Tobacco and Sugar* [1940]. Durham, NC: Duke University Press, 1995. Print.

Pardo, Mary S. *Mexican American Women Activists: Identity and Resistance in Two Los Angeles Communities.* Philadelphia: Temple University Press, 1998. Print.

Paredes, Américo. Américo Paredes Papers. Box 8, Folder 12. Benson Latin American Collection. University of Texas at Austin. Print.

Paredes, Américo. *Between Two Worlds.* Houston, TX: Arte Público, 1991. Print.

Paredes, Américo. *Cantos de Adolescencia/Songs of Youth* (1932–1937). Trans. B. V. Olguín and Omar Vásquez Barbosa. Houston, TX: Arte Público Press, 2007. Print.

Paredes, Américo. *George Washington Gomez: A Mexicotexan Novel.* Houston, TX: Arte Público, 1990. Print.

Paredes, Américo. *A Texas-Mexican Cancionero: Folksongs of the Lower Border.* Austin: University of Texas Press, 1995. Print.

Paredes, Américo. *With His Pistol in His Hand: A Border Ballad and Its Hero.* Austin: University of Texas Press, 1958. Print.

Paxton, Robert O. "The Five Stages of Fascism." *Comparative Fascist Studies: New Perspectives.* Ed. Constatine Iordachi. New York: Routledge, 2009. 165–86. Print.

Pedreira, Antonio Salvador. *Insularismo: An Insight into the Puerto Rican Character.* Trans. Aoife Rivera Serrano. Houston, TX: Arte Público, 2007. Print.

Peña, Devón. *Mexican Americans and the Environment: Tierra y Vida.* Tucson: University of Arizona Press, 2005. Print.

Pérez, Emma. *The Decolonial Imaginary: Writing Chicanas into History.* Bloomington: Indiana University Press, 1999. Print.

Pérez, Judith and Sévero Pérez. "Soldierboy." *Necessary Theater: Six Plays About the Chicano Experience.* Ed. Jorge Huerta. Houston, TX: Arte Público, 1989. 20–75. Print.

Pérez-Firmat, Gustavo. *Life on the Hyphen: The Cuban-American Way.* Revised Edition. Austin: University of Texas Press, 2012. Print.

Pérez, Vincent. *Remembering the Hacienda: History and Memory in the Mexican-American Southwest.* College Station: Texas A&M Press, 2006. Print.

El Plan Espiritual de Aztlán (March 1969). Web. Accessed January 15, 2020. <http://clubs.arizona.edu/~mecha/pages/PDFs/ElPlanDeAtzlan.pdf>.

Philipps, Dave. "'This is Unacceptable.' Military Reports a Surge of Sexual Assaults in the Ranks." *New York Times.* May 2, 2019. Web. Accessed January 15, 2020. <https://www.nytimes.com/2019/05/02/us/military-sexual-assault.html>.

Pollack-Pelzner, Daniel. "The Mixed Reception of the Hamilton Premier in Puerto Rico." *The Atlantic.* January 18, 2019. Web. Accessed January 15, 2020. <https://www.theatlantic.com/entertainment/archive/2019/01/hamilton-premiere-puerto-rico-stirs-controversy/580657/>.

Poniatowska, Elena. "Prólogo/Prologue." *One Wound for Another/Una Herida Por Otra: Testimonios de Latin@s in the U.S. through Cyberspace (11 de septiembre de 2001–11 de marzo de 2002).* Eds. Claire Joysmith and Clara Lomas. México City, Mexico: Centro de investigaciones sobre América del Norte, 2005. 17–25. Print.

Pope Duarte, Estela. *Let Their Spirits Dance.* New York: Harper, 2002. Print.

Portales, Patricia. "Women, Bombs, and War: Tejanas' Changing Agency in *Soldierboy, Zoot Suit* and WWII Oral History." *Latino/as and World War II: Mobility, Agency, and Ideology*. Eds. Maggie Rivas Rodriguez and B. V. Olguín. Austin: University of Texas Press, 2014. 175–96. Print.

Prashad, Vijay. *Everybody Was Kung-Fu Fighting: Afro-Asian Connections and the Myth of Cultural Purity*. Boston: Beacon Press, 2002. Print.

Pratt, Mary. *Imperial Eyes: Travel Writing and Transculturation*. New York: Routledge, 1992. Print.

Puar, Jasbir. *Terrorist Assemblages: Homonationalism in Queer Times*. Durham, NC: Duke University Press, 2007. Print.

Pulido, Laura. *Black, Brown, Yellow, and Left: Radical Activism in Los Angeles*. Berkeley: University of California Press, 2006. Print.

Quijano, Aníbal and Immanuel Wallerstein. "Americanity as a Concept, Or the Americas in the Modern-World System." *Institute for Scientific Information* 134 (1992): 549–57. Print.

Quiñones, Tania. "Our Mission Was at Odds With Itself." *What Was Asked of Us: An Oral History of the Iraq War by the Soldiers Who Fought It*. Ed. Trish Wood. New York: Back Bay, 2006. 66–9. Print.

Rahier, Jean Muteba, ed. *Black Social Movements in Latin America: From Monocultural Mestizaje to Multiculturalism*. New York: MacMillan, 2012. Print.

Raleigh, Eve and Jovita González. *Caballero: A Historical Novel*. College Station: Texas A&M Press, 1996. Print.

Ramírez, Catherine Sue. *The Woman in the Zoot Suit: Gender, Nationalism, and the Cultural Politics of Memory*. Durham, NC: Duke University Press, 2008. Print.

Ramirez, Juan. *A Patriot After All: The Story of a Chicano Vietnam Vet*. Albuquerque, NM: University of New Mexico Press, 1999. Print.

Ramírez, Susana N. "NepantlerX Cosmologies: Spiritual Activism and New Queer Feminist Paradigms." Doctoral Dissertation, English Department, University of Texas at San Antonio, 2016. Print.

Ramos, Henry A. J. *The American G.I. Forum: In Pursuit of the Dream, 1948–1983*. Houston, TX: Arte Público, 1998. Print.

Reed, Ishmael. "CounterPunch on Stage: *The Haunting of Lin-Manuel Miranda*." *CounterPunch*. April 12, 2019. Web. Accessed January 15, 2020. <https://www.counter-punch.org/2019/04/12/counterpunch-on-stage-the-haunting-of-lin-manuel-miranda/>.

Reed, Ishmael. "Hamilton: the Musical:" Black Actors Dress Up like Slave Traders...and It's Not Halloween." *CounterPunch*. August 15, 2015. Web. Accessed January 15, 2020. <https://www.counterpunch.org/2015/08/21/hamilton-the-musical-black-actors-dress-up-like-slave-tradersand-its-not-halloween/>.

Reed, Ishmael. *The Haunting of Lin-Manuel Miranda*. Staged Reading, Nuyorican Poet's Café, January 4–7, 2019. New York, NY. Performance.

Retamar, Roberto Fernández. *Caliban and Other Essays*. Trans. Edward Baker. Minneapolis: University of Minnesota Press, 1989. Print.

Reynolds, George M. and Amanda Shendruk. "Demographics of the U.S. Military." ForeignAffairs.com. April 24, 2018. Web. Accessed January 15, 2020. <https://www.cfr.org/article/demographics-us-military>.

Richardson, Bill. *Between Worlds: The Making of An American Life*. New York: Plume, 2007. Print.

Riley, Robin Lee, Chandra Talpade Mohanty, and Minnie Bruce Pratt, eds. "Introduction: Feminism and US Wars—Mapping the Ground." *Feminism and War: Confronting US Imperialism*. London: Zed Books, 2008. 1–16. Print.

Rincón, Belinda Linn. *Bodies at War: Genealogies of Militarism in Chicana Literature and Culture*. Tucson, University of Arizona Press, 2017. Print.

Rivas-Rodriguez, Maggie and B. V. Olguín, eds. *Latina/os and World War II: Mobility, Agency, and Ideology*. (Voces Oral History Project, Volume 3). Austin: University of Texas Press, 2014. Print.

Rivera, Tomás. "El Pete Fonseca" (1970). *Tomás Rivera: The Complete Works*. Ed. Julián Olivares. Houston, TX: Arte Público, 1992. 130–7. Print.

Roberts, Mary Louise. *What Soldiers Do: Sex and the American GI in WWII France*. Chicago: University of Chicago Press, 2013. Print.

Rochín, Refugio and Lionel Fernandez, eds. *U.S. Latino Patriots: From the American Revolution to Afghanistan, An Overview*. East Lansing: Julian Zamora Research Institute, Michigan State University, 2005. Print.

Rockwell, Paul. "Army Reservist Witnesses War Crimes: New Revelations about Racism in the Military." *In Motion Magazine*. April 2, 2005. Web. Accessed January 15, 2020. <https://inmotionmagazine.com/global/pr_adelgado.html>.

Rodó, José Enrique. *Ariel*. Trans. Margaret Sayers Peden. First Edition. Austin: University of Texas Press, 1988. Print.

Rodríguez, Dylan. *Forced Passages: Imprisoned Radical Intellectuals and the U.S. Prison Regime*. Minneapolis: University of Minnesota Press, 2006. Print.

Rodriguez, Joe. "The East Side/West Side: Class of 2012. *The Mercury News*. Web. Accessed January 15, 2020. <https://www.mercurynews.com/2013/01/14/the-east-sidewest-side-class-of-2012-where-are-they-now/>.

Rodriguez, José Abraham, Jr. and Bill Harlow. *Hard Measures: How Aggressive CIA Actions After 9/11 Saved American Lives*. New York: Threshold, 2012. Print.

Rodriguez, Felix and John Weisman. *Shadow Warrior: The CIA Hero of a Hundred Battles—From the Bay of Pigs to Vietnam to Nicaragua*. New York: Simon and Schuster, 1989. Print.

Rodriguez, Luis J. *It Calls You Back: An Odyssey through Love, Addictions, Revolutions, and Healing*. New York: Atria, 2012. Print.

Rodriguez, Richard T. "X Marks the Spot." *Cultural Dynamics* 29: 3 (2017): 202–13. Print.

Rodriguez, Richard. "Surnames Reflect Changing Face of America." *PBS NewsHour*. Originally aired January 25, 2008. Web. Accessed May 15, 2020. <https://www.pbs.org/newshour/show/surnames-reflect-changing-face-of-america>.

Roig-Franzia, Manuel. "A Terrorist in the White House." *The Washington Post Magazine*. February 22, 2004. Web. Accessed January 15, 2020. <https://www.washingtonpost.com/archive/lifestyle/magazine/2004/02/22/a-terrorist-in-the-house/293c52cd-8794-47bd-9960-9c7a871e009c/>.

Rosaldo, Renato. *Culture and Truth: The Remaking of Social Analysis*. Boston: Beacon, 1993. Print.

Rosales, Steven. "Macho Nation? Chicano Soldiering, Sexuality, and Manhood during the Vietnam War Era." *The Oral History Review* 40: 2 (2013): 299–324. Print.

Rosales, Steven. "Macho Nation?: Chicano Soldiering and Masculinity During the Viet Nam War Era." Annual Conference, National Association for Chicana and Chicano Studies, Chicago, Illinois, 17 March 2012. Conference Presentation.

Rosales, Steven. *Soldados Razos at War: Chicano Politics, Identity and Masculinity in the U.S. Military from WWII to Vietnam*. Tucson: University of Arizona Press, 2017. Print.

Rosas, Gilberto. *Barrio Libre: Criminalizing States and Delinquent Refusals of the New Frontier*. Durham, NC: Duke University Press, 2012. Print.

Rose, Felipe (Swift Arrow). Felipe Rose Website. Web. Accessed January 1, 2016. <http://www.feliperose.com>.

Rose, Felipe (Swift Arrow). Felipe Rose Website. Web. Accessed May 7, 2019. <http://www.feliperose.com>.

Rose, Felipe (Swift Arrow). "Trail of Tears." YouTube. September 7, 2002. Accessed May 5, 2020. <https://www.youtube.com/watch?v=dTkIygRMreg>. Video.

Rose, Felipe (Swift Arrow). "Trail of Tears." *We're Still Hear*. Tomahawk, 2010. CD.

Rose, Felipe (Swift Arrow). "Trail of Tears." Performance, Fifth Annual Native American Music Awards, Milwaukee, Wisconsin, 2012. Web. Accessed January 15, 2020. <http://www.youtube.com/watch?v=dTkIygRMreg>.

Rubin, Steven Jay (Dir.). *East L.A. Marine: The Untold True Story of Guy Gabaldon*. Fast Carrier, 2006. DVD.

Ruiz, Vicki L. *From Out of the Shadows: Mexican Women in Twentieth-Century America*, 10th Edition. Oxford: Oxford University Press, 2008. Print.

Ruiz de Burton, María Amparo. *The Squatter and the Don* [1885]. Houston, TX: Arte Público, 1992. Print.

Saenz, José Luz. *Los méxico-americanos en la Gran Guerra y su contingente en pro de la democracia, la humanidad, y la justicia*. San Antonio, TX: Artes Gráficas, 1933. Print.

Sae-Saue, Jayson Gonzales. *Southwest Asia: The Transpacific Geographies of Chicana/o Literature*. New Brunswick: Rutgers University Press, 2016. Print.

Said, Edward. *Orientalism*. New York: Vintage, 1979. Print.

Salas, Elizabeth. *Soldaderas in the Mexican Military*. Austin: University of Texas Press, 1990. Print.

Salazar, Jaime. *Legion of the Lost: The True Experience of an American in the French Foreign Legion*. New York: Berkley Caliber, 2005. Print.

Salazar, Jaime. Personal Interview. Electronic Correspondence. November 16, 2012. Interview.

Saldaña-Portillo, María Josefina. *Indian Given: Racial Geographies Across Mexico and the United States*. Durham, NC: Duke University Press, 2016. Print.

Saldaña-Portillo, María Josefina. "Who's the Indian in Aztlán: Re-Writing Mestizaje, Indianism, and Chicanismo from the Lacandón." *The Latin American Subaltern Studies Reader*. Ed. Ileana Rodríguez. Durham, NC: Duke University Press, 2001. 402–23. Print.

Saldívar, José David. *Border Matters: Remapping American Cultural Studies*. Berkeley: University of California Press, 1997. Print.

Saldívar, José David. "The Borderlands of Culture: Américo Paredes's *George Washington Gomez* and Chicano Literature at the End of the Twentieth Century." *American Literary History* 5: 2 (1993): 272–93. Print.

Saldívar, José David. "Chicano Border Narratives as Cultural Critique." *Criticism in the Borderlands: Studies in Chicano Literature, Culture, and Ideology*. Eds. Héctor Calderón and Ramón Saldívar. Durham, NC: Duke University Press, 1991. 167–80. Print.

Saldívar, José David. *The Dialectics of Our America: Genealogy, Cultural Critique, and Literary History*. Durham, NC: Duke University Press, 1991. Print.

Saldívar, José David. "Towards a Chicano Poetics: The Making of the Chicano Subject, 1969-1982." *Confluencia: Revista Hispanica de Cultura y Literatura* 1: 2 (1986 Spring): 10–17. Print.

Saldívar, José David. *Trans-Americanity: Subaltern Modernities, Global Coloniality, and the Cultures of Greater Mexico.* Durham, NC: Duke University Press, 2011. Print.

Saldívar, José David, ed. *The Rolando Hinojosa Reader: Essays Historical and Critical.* Houston, TX: Arte Público, 1985. Print.

Saldívar, Ramón. "Asian Américo: Paredes in Asia and the Borderlands: A Response to José E. Limón." *American Literary History* 21: 3 (Fall 2009): 584–94. Print.

Saldívar, Ramón. *The Borderlands of Culture: Américo Paredes and the Transnational Imaginary.* Durham, NC: Duke University Press, 2006. Print.

Saldívar, Ramón. *Chicano Narrative: The Dialectics of Difference.* Madison: University of Wisconsin Press, 1990. Print.

Saldívar, Ramón. "Introduction." *The Hammon and the Beans and Other Stories*, by Américo Paredes. Houston, TX: Arte Público, 1994. vii-xlvi. Print.

Salinas, Raúl R. (raúlrsalinas). *East of the Freeway.* Austin, TX: Red Salmon, 1995. Print.

Salinas, Raúl R. (raúlrsalinas). *Indio Trails: A Xicano Odyssey Through Indian Country.* San Antonio, TX: Wings, 2006. Print.

Salinas, Raúl R. Personal Conversations. Austin, Texas. 1995–2005. Interview.

Salinas, Raúl R. "Un Trip Through the Mind Jail." *Aztlán de Leavenworth* 1: 1 (1970): n.p. Print.

Salinas, Raúl R. *Un Trip Through the Mind Jail y Otras Excursions.* Houston, TX: Arte Público Press, 1999. Print.

Salinas, Raúl R. and Louis Mendoza, eds. *Raul Salinas and the Jail Machine: My Weapon Is My Pen—Selected Writings by Raúl Salinas.* Austin: University of Texas Press, 2006. Print.

Sánchez, George J. *Becoming Mexican American: Ethnicity, Culture and Identity in Chicano Los Angeles, 1900–1945.* Oxford: Oxford University Press, 1995. Print.

Sánchez Gómez, Gonzalo, ed. *Colombia: Violencia y Democracia.* Bogotá: Comisión de Estudios Sobre la Violencia, Centro Editorial, Universidad Nacional de Colombia, 2009. Print.

Sánchez, Ricardo S. "Memorandum for Commander, U.S. Central Command-CJTF-7 Interrogation and Counter-Resistance Policy." September 14, 2003. Web. Accessed May 7, 2019. <https://www.thetorturedatabase.org/document/memo-re-cjtf-7-interrogation-and-counter-resistance-policy?search_url=search/apachesolr_search&search_args=filters=sm_cck_field_doc_from_agency:32%26solrsort=tds_cck_field_doc_release_date%20desc>.

Sánchez, Ricardo S. and Donald T. Phillips. *Wiser in Battle: A Soldier's Story.* New York: Harper Collins, 2008. Print.

Sánchez, Rosaura. *Telling Identities: The Californio Testimonios.* Minneapolis: University of Minnesota Press, 1995. Print.

Sánchez, Rosaura and Beatrice Pita. "Theses on the Latino Bloc: A Critical Perspective." *Aztlán* 31: 2 (2006): 25–53. Print.

Sánchez-Jankowski, Martin. *Islands in the Street: Gangs and American Urban Society.* Berkeley: University of California Press, 1991. Print.

Sands, Phillippe. *Torture Team: Rumsfeld's Memo and the Betrayal of American Values.* New York: Palgrave McMillan, 2008. Print.

Sandoval, Chela. *Methodology of the Oppressed*. Minneapolis: University of Minnesota Press, 2000. Print.

Sandoval-Sánchez, Alberto. "'September 11, 2001' (3 November 2001 1:11 p.m.)." *One Wound for Another/Una Herida Por Otra*. Eds. Claire Joysmith and Clara Lomas. Mexico City, Mexico: Centro de investigaciones sobre América del Norte, 2005. 253–7. Print.

Santisteban, Ray (Dir.). *Voices from Texas*. Cinema Guild, 2003. DVD.

Sartre, Jean-Paul. *Being and Nothingness*. New York: Washington Square Press, 1993.

Scarborough, Rowan. "Doubts on Military Sex Assault Stats as Numbers Far Exceed Those for the U.S." *The Washington Times*. April 6, 2014. Web. Accessed January 15, 2020. <https://www.washingtontimes.com/news/2014/apr/6/doubts-on-militarys-sex-assault-stats-as-numbers-f/>.

Scarry, Elaine. *The Body in Pain: The Making and Unmaking of the World*. Oxford: Oxford University Press, 1987. Print.

Schiavone Camacho and Julia María. *Chinese Mexicans: Transpacific Migrations and the Search for a Homeland, 1910–1960*. Chapel Hill: University of North Carolina Press, 2012. Print.

Schultz, Jessica, Kathryn M. Bell, Amy E. Naugle, and Melissa A. Polusny. "Child Sexual Abuse and Adulthood Sexual Assault among Military Veteran and Civilian Women." *Military Medicine* 171 (August 2006): 723–8. Print.

Schwartz, Rosalie. *Across the Rio to Freedom: Negroes in Mexico*. El Paso: Texas Western Press, 1974. Print.

Sedgwick, Eve Kosofsky. *Between Men: English Literature and Male Homosocial Desire*. New York: Columbia University Press, 1985. Print.

Seguin, Juan Nepomuceno. *Memorias* [1858]. *A Revolution Remembered: The Memoirs and Selected Correspondence of Juan N. Seguin*. Ed. and Trans. Jesús Frank De la Teja. Austin, TX: State House, 1991. Print.

Shapiro, Michael J. *Violent Cartographies: Mapping Cultures of War*. Minneapolis, MN: University of Minneapolis Press, 1997. Print.

Silliman, Stephen W. "Words of War in Indian Country: From Geronimo to Osama Bin Laden." Native American and Indigenous Studies Association Conference, June 4, 2012. Conference Presentation.

Silliman, Stephen W. "The 'Old West' in the Middle East: U.S. Military Metaphors in Real and Imagined Indian Country." *American Anthropologist* 110: 2 (2008): 237–47. Print.

Simon, David, Ed Burns, Nina K. Noble, George Faber, and Charles Pattinson, Prods. *Generation Kill*. Warner, 2008. DVD.

Smith, Diane. "*Tough Trip Through Paradise* and the Beautiful Wives of Andrew Garcia." *Montana: The Magazine of Western History* 58: 4 (Winter 2008): 3–21, 92–3. Print.

Smith, Jeffrey and Josh White. "General Granted Latitude at Prison: Abu Ghraib Used Aggressive Tactics." *Washington Post*. June 12, 2004. Web. Accessed January 15, 2020. <http://www.washingtonpost.com/wp-dyn/articles/A35612-2004Jun11.html>.

Soja, Edward. *Postmodern Geographies: The Reassertion of Space in Critical Social Theory*. New York: Verso, 2011. Print.

Sondheim, Steven and Leonard Bernstein. *West Side Story*. Dirs. Robert Wise and Jerome Robbins. United Artists, 1961. Video.

Sontag, Susan. "Regarding the Torture of Others." *New York Times Magazine*. May 23, 2004. n.p. Web. Accessed January 15, 2020. <http://www.nytimes.com/2004/05/23/magazine/regarding-the-torture-of-others.html?pagewanted=all&src=pm>.

Soto, Sandra K. *Reading Chican@ Like a Queer: The De-Mastery of Desire*. Austin: University of Texas Press, 2010. Print.

Stahl, Lesley. "Hard Measures." Interview with José Rodriguez. *60 Minutes*. CBS News. April 29, 2012. Web. Accessed January 15, 2020. <https://www.youtube.com/watch?v=MC9PP94f4OQ>.

Stanley, Goff, Robert Sanders, and Clark Smith, eds. *Brothers: Black Soldiers in the Nam*. New York: Presidio, 1982. Print.

Steiner, Michael C., ed. *Regionalists on the Left: Radical Voices from the American West*. Norman: University of Oklahoma Press, 2013. Print.

Stern, Alexandra Minna. *Eugenic Nation: Faults and Frontiers of Better Breeding in Modern America*. Berkeley: University of California Press, 2016. Print.

Suarez, Mario. "Kid Zopilote." *Arizona Quarterly* 3 (1947): 130–7. Print.

Taylor, Jennifer Maytorena (Dir.). *New Muslim Cool*. POV. Public Broadcasting Service, 2009. DVD.

Terry, Wallace, ed. *Bloods: An Oral History of the Vietnam War by Black Veterans*. New York: Ballantine, 1992. Print.

Thomas, Evan and Martha Brant. "The Secret War." *Newsweek* 141: 16 (April 21, 2003): 25–32.

Thompson, Jerry Don. *Vaqueros in Blue and Gray*. Austin, TX: Presidial, 2000. Print.

Trujillo, Charley. *Dogs from Illusion*. San Jose, CA: Chusma House, 1994. Print.

Trujillo, Charley. *Soldados: Chicanos in Viet Nam*. San Jose, CA: Chusma House, 1990. Print.

Trujillo, Charley. Personal Conversations. San Jose, Stanford, and Santa Barbara, CA. 1990–2020. Interview.

Trujillo, Charley and Sonya Rhee (Dirs.). *Soldados: Chicanos in Viet Nam*. San Jose, CA: Chusma House, 2003. DVD.

Trujillo, Damian. "Local Veteran to Return Japanese Flag His Father Took From Dead Soldier." *Comunidad del Valle*. February 9, 2018. Corcoran California NBC Affiliate. Web. Accessed January 15, 2020. <https://www.youtube.com/watch?v=OTZhEhzDppw>.

Trujillo, Orlando, Joseph Sommers, and Tomás Ybarra-Frausto. "Linguistic Structures in José Montoya's 'El Louie'." *Modern Chicano Writers: A Collection of Critical Essays*, Ed. Joseph Sommers. Englewood Cliffs, NJ: Prentice-Hall, 1979. 150–9. Print.

U S Constitution. Amendment Two. December 15, 1791. Print.

US Department of Defense. Don't Ask, Don't Tell Repeal Act of 2010 (Public Law 111–321). December 22, 2010. Web. Accessed January 15, 2020. <https://www.congress.gov/111/plaws/publ321/PLAW-111publ321.pdf>.

US Department of Defense. *Hispanics in Americas Defense*. Washington, DC: U.S. Department of Defense, 1989. Print.

US Department of Defense.Qualification Standards for Enlistment, Appointment, and Induction (DODD 1304.26). December 21, 1993. Web. Accessed January 15, 2020. <https://biotech.law.lsu.edu/blaw/dodd/corres/html2/d130426x.htm>.

US Department of Homeland Security. "Military Naturalization Statistics." Web. Accessed January 15, 2020. <https://www.uscis.gov/military/military-naturalization-statistics>.

Valdez, Luis. *Luis Valdez: Early Works: Actos, Bernabe, and Pensamiento Serpentino*. Houston, TX: Arte Público, 1990. Print.

Valdez, Luis. *Zoot Suit and Other Plays*. Houston, TX: Arte Público, 1992. Print.

Valdez, Luis (Dir.). *Zoot Suit*. Universal, 1981. DVD.

Valenzuela, Freddie and Jason Lemons. *No Greater Love: The Lives and Times of Hispanic Soldiers*. Austin, TX: Ovation, 2008. Print.

Valenzuela, Freddie. Personal Interview. San Antonio, Texas. 26 February 2008.

Van Deusen, Nancy. *Global Indios: The Indigenous Struggle for Justice in Sixteenth-Century Spain*. Durham, NC: Duke University Press, 2015. Print.

Vargas, Roberto. "My World Incomplete: To Complete My World." *Ten Years That Shook the City: San Francisco 1968–1978*. Eds. Chris Carlsson and Lisa Ruth Elliott. San Francisco: City Lights, 2011. 92–4. Print.

Vargas, Roberto. *Nicaragua: Nicaragua, yo te canto besos, balas, y suenos de libertad: Poems*. San Francisco: Editorial Pocho-Che, 1980. Print.

Vélez-Ibañez, Carlos. *Border Visions: Mexican Cultures of the Southwest United States*. Tempe: University of Arizona Press, 1996. Print.

Veracini, Lorenzo. *Settler Colonialism: A Theoretical Overview*. New York: Palgrave, 2010.

Vigil, Ariana Elizabeth. *War Echoes: Gender and Militarization in U.S. Latina/o Cultural Production*. New Brunswick, NJ: Rutgers University Press, 2014. Print.

Villa, Raúl Homero. *Barrio-Logos: Space and Place in Urban Chicano Literature and Culture*. Austin: University of Texas Press, 2000. Print.

Vizenor, Gerald. *Survivance: Narratives of Native Presence*. Lincoln: University of Nebraska Press, 1998. Print.

Vonledebur, Catherine. "Former CIA Officer Talks About Being a Real-Life James Bond." May 16, 2014. *Birmingham Post*. Web. Accessed January 15, 2020. <http://www.birminghampost.co.uk/whats-on/film-news/retired-cia-officer-tony-mendez-7124307>.

Waters, Mary Alice, ed. *Our History is Still Being Written: The Story of Three Chinese-Cuban Generals in the Cuban Revolution*. by Armando Choy, Gustavo Chui, and Moisés Sío Wong. New York: Pathfinder Press, 2017. Print.

Weber, David J. *Bárbaros: Spaniards and Their Savages in the Age of Enlightenment*. New Haven, CT: Yale University Press, 2006. Print.

Wexler, Haskell (Dir.). *Latino: America's Secret War in Nicaragua*. Lucasfilm, 1985. DVD.

White, Hayden. *Metahistory: The Historical Imagination in Nineteenth-Century Europe*. Baltimore, MD: Johns Hopkins University Press, 1975. Print.

White, Hayden. *The Content of the Form: Narrative Discourse and Historical Representation*. Baltimore, MD: Johns Hopkins University Press, 1990. Print.

White, Susana and Simon Cellan Jones (Dirs.). *Generation Kill*. HBO, 2008. DVD.

Wilderson, Frank. *Incognegro: A Memoir and Exile and Apartheid*. Boston: South End Press, 2008. Print.

Wilderson, Frank. *Afro-Pessimism*. New York: Liveright, 2020. Print.

Woolf, Virginia. *A Room of One's Own*. New York: Mariner Books, 1989. Print.

Woolf, Virginia. *Three Guineas*. New York: Harvest, 1963. Print.

Wright, Evan. *Generation Kill: Devil Dogs, Iceman, Captain America, and the New Face of American War*. New York: Berkley Caliber, 2004. Print.

Ybarra-Frausto, Tomás. "Rasquachismo: A Chicano Sensibility." *Chicano Art: Resistance and Affirmation, 1965–1985*. Eds. Richard Griswold del Castillo, Teresa McKenna, and Yvonne Yarbro-Bejarano. Los Angeles: UCLA Wight Gallery, 1991. 155–62. Print.

Zamora, Emilio, ed. *Mexican Americans and the Great War*. Trans. Emilio Zamora and Ben Maya. College Station: Texas A&M University Press, 2014. Print.

Zapata, Regulo, Jr. *Desperate Lands: The War on Terror Through the Eyes of a Special Forces Soldier*. Gilroy, CA: Nadores, 2007. Print.

Žižek, Slavoj. *Violence: Six Sideways Reflections*. New York: Picador, 2008. Print.

Zonana, Joyce. "The Sultan and the Slave: Feminist Orientalism and the Structure of *Jane Eyre*." *Signs* 18: 3 (1993): 592–617. Print.

Zuñiga, José. *Soldier of the Year*. New York: Pocket, 1995. Print.

{ INDEX }

Note: Figures are indicated by an italic '*f*' following the page number. Footnotes are indicated by the letter 'n' after the page number.

For the benefit of digital users, indexed terms that span two pages (e.g., 52–53) may, on occasion, appear on only one of those pages.